THE CAMBRIDGE COMPANION TO
CRITICAL THEORY

Critical Theory constitutes one of the major intellectual traditions of the twentieth century and is centrally important
for philosophy, political theory, aesthetics and the theory of
art, the study of modern European literatures and music, the
history of ideas, sociology, psychology, and cultural studies. In this volume an international team of distinguished
contributors examines the major figures in Critical Theory, including Horkheimer, Adorno, Marcuse, Benjamin, and
Habermas, as well as lesser known but important thinkers
such as Pollock and Neumann. The volume surveys the
shared philosophical concerns that have given impetus to
Critical Theory throughout its history, while at the same
time showing the diversity among its proponents that contributes so much to its richness as a philosophical school.
The result is an illuminating overview of the entire history
of Critical Theory in the twentieth century, an examination
of its central conceptual concerns, and an in-depth discussion of its future prospects.

The Cambridge Companion to

CRITICAL THEORY

Edited by

Fred Rush

University of Notre Dame

CAMBRIDGE
UNIVERSITY PRESS

PUBLISHED BY THE PRESS SYNDICATE OF THE UNIVERSITY OF CAMBRIDGE
The Pitt Building, Trumpington Street, Cambridge, United Kingdom

CAMBRIDGE UNIVERSITY PRESS
The Edinburgh Building, Cambridge, CB2 2RU, UK
40 West 20th Street, New York, NY 10011–4211, USA
477 Williamstown Road, Port Melbourne, VIC 3207, Australia
Ruiz de Alarcón 13, 28014 Madrid, Spain
Dock House, The Waterfront, Cape Town 8001, South Africa

http://www.cambridge.org

First published 2004

Printed in the United Kingdom at the University Press, Cambridge

Typeface Trump Medieval 10/13 pt.   *System* LATEX 2$_\varepsilon$ [TB]

A catalogue record for this book is available from the British Library

ISBN 0 521 81660 2 hardback
ISBN 0 521 01689 4 paperback

CONTENTS

vii

viii   Contents

CONTRIBUTORS

KENNETH BAYNES is Professor of Philosophy and Political Science at Syracuse University. He is the author of *The Normative Grounds of Social Criticism: Kant, Rawls, Habermas* (SUNY Press, 1992) and the coeditor of *After Philosophy* (MIT Press, 1986) and *Discourse and Democracy: Essays on Habermas's "Between Facts and Norms"* (SUNY Press, 2002).

J. M. BERNSTEIN is University Distinguished Professor of Philosophy at the New School for Social Research. Among his books are *The Fate of Art: Aesthetic Alienation from Kant to Derrida and Adorno* (Pennsylvania State University Press, 1992), *Recovering Ethical Life: Jürgen Habermas and the Future of Critical Theory* (Routledge, 1995), and *Adorno: Disenchantment and Ethics* (Cambridge University Press, 2001).

HAUKE BRUNKHORST is Professor of Sociology at the University of Flensburg. His recent writings include *Hannah Arendt* (Beck, 1999), *Einführung in die Geschichte politischer Ideen* (Fink/UTB, 2001), and *Solidarität* (Suhrkamp, 2002). His books in English are *Adorno and Critical Theory* (University of Wales Press, 1999) and *Solidarity: From Civic Friendship Towards a Global Legal Community* (MIT Press, forthcoming).

SIMONE CHAMBERS is Associate Professor of Political Science at the University of Toronto. She is the author of *Reasonable Democracy: Jürgen Habermas and the Politics of Discourse* (Cornell University Press, 1996) and has edited *Deliberation, Democracy, and the Media* (Rowman & Littlefield, 2000) and *Alternative Conceptions of Civil Society* (Princeton University Press, 2001).

RAYMOND GEUSS is Reader in Philosophy at the University of Cambridge. He is the author of *The Idea of a Critical Theory: Habermas and the Frankfurt School* (Cambridge University Press, 1981), *Morality, Culture, and History* (Cambridge University Press, 1999), *History and Illusion in Politics* (Cambridge University Press, 2001), and *Public Goods, Private Goods* (Princeton University Press, 2001).

BEATRICE HANSSEN is Professor of German at the University of Georgia, Athens. She is the author of *Walter Benjamin's Other History: Of Stones, Animals, Human Beings, and Angels* (University of California Press, 1998), *Critique of Violence: Between Poststructuralism and Critical Theory* (Routledge, 2000), and coeditor of *The Turn to Ethics* (Routledge, 2000). She is also coeditor of the series Walter Benjamin Studies, which includes the volumes *Walter Benjamin and Romanticism* (Continuum, 2002) and *Walter Benjamin and the Arcades Project* (Continuum, forthcoming).

AXEL HONNETH is Professor of Philosophy at the University of Frankfurt and the Director of the Institute for Social Research. His books in English translation include *Critique of Power* (MIT Press, 1993), *The Fragmented World of the Social* (SUNY Press, 1995), and *The Struggle for Recognition* (MIT Press, 1996).

MOISHE POSTONE is Associate Professor of Modern History and a member of the Committee for Jewish Studies at the University of Chicago. He is the author of *Time, Labor, and Social Domination: A Reinterpretation of Marx's Critical Theory* (Cambridge University Press, 1993) and coeditor of *Catastrophe and Meaning: The Holocaust and the Twentieth Century* (University of Chicago Press, 2003) as well as of *Bourdieu: Critical Perspectives* (University of Chicago Press, 1993).

JULIAN ROBERTS is Professor of Philosophy at the University of Munich. His books include *Walter Benjamin* (Macmillan, 1982) and *The Logic of Reflection: German Philosophy in the Twentieth Century* (Yale University Press, 1992).

MICHAEL ROSEN is a Fellow at Lincoln College, Oxford. He is the author of *Hegel's Dialectic and its Criticism* (Cambridge University Press, 1982) and *On Voluntary Servitude: False Consciousness and the Theory of Ideology* (Harvard University Press, 1996).

FRED RUSH is Assistant Professor of Philosophy at the University of Notre Dame. He has written several articles on Kant, Hegel, critical theory, and aesthetics. He is completing a book on the philosophical significance of early German Romanticism and its relation to Kant and Kierkegaard.

STEPHEN WHITE is Professor of Politics at the University of Virginia. Among his books are *The Recent Work of Jürgen Habermas* (Cambridge University Press, 1988), *Political Theory and Postmodernism* (Cambridge University Press, 1991), and *Sustaining Affirmation* (Princeton University Press, 2000). He is editor of the journal *Political Theory* and of *The Cambridge Companion to Habermas.*

JOEL WHITEBOOK is on the faculty of the Center for Psychoanalytic Training and Research, Columbia University and is a practicing psychoanalyst. He has written *Perversion and Utopia: A Study in Psychoanalysis and Critical Theory* (MIT Press, 1995) as well as numerous articles on critical theory and its relation to Freud and Marx.

ACKNOWLEDGMENTS

I would like to thank, first of all, the contributors to this volume for their willingness to take time away from their own research to write what are essentially expository pieces and for making editing the chapters a pleasure. Special thanks are due to Karl Ameriks and Gary Gutting for allowing me to impose upon their wisdom as editors of previous volumes in the Cambridge Companions to Philosophy series. I am also indebted to Hilary Gaskin, who went far beyond her role of press editor to provide incisive advice and much encouragement at crucial points. James Hebbeler translated two of the chapters and provided editorial support, and he would like to thank Susanne Zorn for her assistance. Angela Smith provided help with the index. Translation of chapters originally written in German was funded by grants from the Institute for Scholarship in the Liberal Arts, University of Notre Dame.

CHRONOLOGY

1918   First World War ends. German Socialist Revolution.
        Ernst Bloch (1885–1977), *Spirit of Utopia*

1919   Treaty of Versailles. Founding of the Weimar Republic.
        Walter Benjamin (1892–1940), *The Concept of Art Criticism
        in German Romanticism*

1923   Institute of Social Research founded in Frankfurt, funded by
        a private donation of Hermann Weil, a multimillionaire
        importer and grain merchant. Carl Grünberg, the "Father of
        Austrian Socialism," is installed as its first director, with
        Friedrich Pollock (1894–1970) as his assistant. The *Archive
        of the History of Socialism and the Labor Movement*, which
        Grünberg founded in 1910, relocates to Frankfurt and
        becomes the house organ of the Institute.
        Karl Korsch (1886–1961), *Marxism and Philosophy*
        György Lukács (1885–1971), *History and Class
        Consciousness*

1926   Leo Löwenthal (1900–93) joins the Institute.

1928   Theodor Adorno (1903–69) begins his association with
        the Institute.
        Benjamin, *The Origin of German Tragic Drama*

1930   Max Horkheimer (1895–1973) joins the Institute as its
        director. Grünberg's *Archive* ceases publication. Erich
        Fromm (1900–80) joins the Institute.

1932   *Journal for Social Research* begins publication. Herbert
        Marcuse (1898–1979) joins the Institute.

1933   End of the Weimar Republic. Hitler becomes chancellor.
        Institute buildings are searched by the Gestapo and

converted to use for the Nazi Student League. Institute moves provisionally to Geneva.

1934   The Institute relocates to Morningside Heights in New York City, loosely affiliated with Columbia University. Horkheimer, Fromm, Löwenthal, Marcuse, and Pollock emigrate to the United States. Adorno registers as an "advanced student" at Oxford. Institute's empirical research severely curtailed.

1936   Franz Neumann (1900–54) joins the Institute. Publication of the collaborative *Studies on Authority and the Family*

1937   Horkheimer "Traditional and Critical Theory"

1938   Adorno becomes a formal member of the Institute and moves to New York.

1939   Second World War begins in Europe. Fromm leaves the Institute. *Studies in Philosophy and Social Sciences* replaces the *Journal* as the periodical publication of the Institute.

1940   Fleeing the Nazis, Benjamin commits suicide in Port-Bou on the French–Spanish border. Hannah Arendt, who crosses the border at the same point a few months later, passes on to Adorno a manuscript copy of Benjamin's *Theses on the Philosophy of History*. The Institute publishes them in 1942.

1941   Bombing of Pearl Harbor and expansion of the war to the Pacific. Horkheimer, Adorno, and Marcuse resettle in Santa Monica, outside Los Angeles, forming part of a southern California German émigré colony including *inter alia* the novelist Thomas Mann, the composer Arnold Schönberg, and the poet and playwright Bertolt Brecht. Pollock and Neumann remain on the east coast. Last issue of *Studies in Philosophy and Social Sciences* appears, ending the Institute's ongoing serial publication of its work. Fromm, *Escape from Freedom* Marcuse, *Reason and Revolution*

1942   Marcuse and Neumann have joined the OSS (Office of Strategic Services), the war era precursor to the CIA, in Washington, DC. Pollock works for the US Department of Justice's anti-trust division. Löwenthal consults for the

Office of War Information. This leaves only Horkheimer and
Adorno to pursue purely theoretical work.

Neumann, *Behemoth*

1945   World War Two ends.

1947   Adorno and Horkheimer, *Dialectic of Enlightenment*

1949   Horkheimer and Adorno return to Frankfurt to reestablish
the Institute there. Löwenthal leaves the Institute and
remains in America, as do Marcuse and Neumann.

1951   Adorno, *Minima Moralia*

1955   Adorno appointed codirector of the Institute with
Horkheimer. Horkheimer retires in 1958. Jürgen Habermas
(1929–) becomes Adorno's assistant and a member of the
Institute in 1956.

Marcuse, *Eros and Civilization*

1964   Marcuse publishes the best-selling *One-Dimensional Man*
and becomes a philosophical mentor to the American New
Left and Student movements.

1966   Adorno, *Negative Dialectics*

1968   Habermas, *Knowledge and Human Interests* and
Technology and Science as "Ideology"

1969   SDS protests in Frankfurt. Adorno summons the police to
arrest students who have "occupied" his offices. Rupture
between the German student movement and the Institute.
Adorno dies on holiday in Switzerland.

1970   Posthumous publication of Adorno's unfinished *Aesthetic
Theory*. Habermas turns down offer to direct the Institute
and instead takes a position at the Max Plank Institute in
Starnberg, outside of Munich. Beginning of a two
decade-long period during which the Institute ceases to be
the focus for Critical Theory. Various themes in
post-Adornian critical theory taken up in the writings of
Karl-Otto Apel (1922–), Claus Offe (1940–), and Albrecht
Wellmer (1939–), among others.

1981   Habermas, *Theory of Communicative Action*

1992   Axel Honneth (1949–), *Struggle for Recognition*

1997   Honneth joins the Institute.

ABBREVIATIONS

COLLECTIONS

CTS   *Critical Theory and Society* (ed.) S. Bronner and
D. Kellner. London and New York: Routledge, 1989.

EFS   *The Essential Frankfurt School Reader* (ed.) A. Arato and
E. Gebhardt. New York: Continuum, 1978.

FRANKFURT SCHOOL JOURNALS

SPSS   *Studies in Philosophy and Social Science*

ZfS   *Zeitschrift für Sozialforschung*

ADORNO

AA   *Can One Live After Auschwitz?* (ed.) R. Tiedemann,
(trans.) R. Livingstone *et al.* Stanford: Stanford University
Press, 2003.

AE   *Against Epistemology: A Metacritique* (trans.)
W. Domingo. Cambridge, Mass.: MIT Press, 1983.

AGS   *Gesammelte Schriften* (ed.) R. Tiedemann. Frankfurt am
Main: Suhrkamp, 1970–97.

AT   *Aesthetic Theory* (trans.) R. Hullot-Kentor. Minneapolis:
University of Minnesota Press, 1998.

CM   *Critical Models* (trans.) H. Pickford. New York: Columbia
University Press, 1999.

H   *Hegel: Three Studies* (trans.) S. W. Nicholson. Cambridge,
Mass.: MIT Press, 1994.

JA   *The Jargon of Authenticity* (trans.) K. Tarnowski
        and F. Will. Chicago: Northwestern University Press,
        1973.
K   *Kierkegaard: Construction of the Aesthetic* (trans.) R.
        Hullot-Kentor. Minneapolis: University of Minnesota
        Press, 1989.
MM   *Minima Moralia* (trans.) E. F. N. Jephcott. New York and
        London: Verso, 1978.
ND   *Negative Dialectics* (trans.) E. B. Ashton. London:
        Routledge, 1973.
NL I   *Notes to Literature*, vol. I (trans.) S. W. Nicholson.
        New York: Columbia University Press, 1991.
NL II   *Notes to Literature*, vol. II (trans.) S. W. Nicholson.
        New York: Columbia University Press, 1992.
NS   *Nachgelassene Schriften*. Frankfurt am Main: Suhrkamp,
        1993–.
P   *Prisms* (trans.) S. Weber and S. Weber. Cambridge, Mass.:
        MIT Press, 1983.
PDGS   *The Positivist Dispute in German Sociology* (ed.) T.
        Adorno. New York: Harper & Row, 1976.
PMM   *The Philosophy of Modern Music* (trans.) A. Mitchell and
        W. Blomster. New York: Seabury, 1973.
Q   *Quasi una Fantasia* (trans.) R. Livingstone. New York:
        Continuum, 1992.
SF   *Sound Figures* (trans.) R. Livingstone. Stanford: Stanford
        University Press, 1999.

BENJAMIN

A   *The Arcades Project* (trans.) H. Eiland and K. McLaughlin.
        Cambridge, Mass.: Harvard Belknap Press, 1999.
BGS   *Gesammelte Schriften* (ed.) R. Tiedemann and H.
        Schweppenhäuser. Frankfurt am Main: Suhrkamp,
        1972–89.
I   *Illuminations* (ed.) H. Arendt, (trans.) H. Zohn. New York:
        Schocken, 1968.
OT   *The Origin of German Tragic Drama* (trans.) J. Osborne.
        New York and London: Verso, 1998.

SW1   *Selected Writings 1913–1926* (trans. and ed.) M. W.
         Jennings, M. Jenning, and M. P. Bullock. Cambridge,
         Mass.: Harvard Belknap Press, 1996.
SW2   *Selected Writings 1927–1934* (trans. and ed.) M. W.
         Jennings, H. Eiland, M. P. Bullock, *et al.* Cambridge,
         Mass.: Harvard Belknap Press, 1999.

FROMM

EF   *Escape from Freedom.* New York: Farrar & Rinehart,
         1941.
MCM   *Marx's Concept of Man.* New York: Continuum, 1961.

HABERMAS

CES   *Communication and the Evolution of Society* (trans.)
         T. McCarthy. Boston: Beacon Press, 1979.
FN   *Between Facts and Norms* (trans.) W. Rehg. Cambridge,
         Mass.: MIT Press, 1998.
KHI   *Knowledge and Human Interests* (trans.) J. Shapiro.
         Boston: Beacon Press, 1971.
IO   *The Inclusion of the Other: Studies in Political Theory.*
         Cambridge, Mass.: MIT Press, 1998.
LC   *Legitimization Crisis* (trans.) T. McCarthy. Boston:
         Beacon Press, 1975.
LSS   *On the Logic of the Social Sciences* (trans.) S. W.
         Nicholson. Cambridge, Mass.: MIT Press, 1988.
MC   *Moral Consciousness and Communicative Action* (trans.)
         C. Lenhardt and S. W. Nicholson. Cambridge, Mass.: MIT
         Press, 1991.
MUP   "Modernity: An Unfinished Project," in *Habermas and
         the Unfinished Project of Modernity: Critical Essays on
         the Philosophical Discourse of Modernity* (ed.) M.
         Passerin d'Entrèves and S. Benhabib. Cambridge, Mass.:
         MIT Press, 1997.
PD   *The Philosophical Discourse of Modernity* (trans.)
         F. Lawrence. Cambridge, Mass.: MIT Press, 1990.
PT   *Postmetaphysical Thinking* (trans.) W. M. Hohengarten.
         Cambridge, Mass.: MIT Press, 1992.

STP   *The Structural Transformation of the Public Sphere*
(trans.) T. Burger and F. Lawrence. Cambridge, Mass.: MIT
Press, 1991.

TCA I   *Theory of Communicative Action*, vol. I (trans.)
T. McCarthy. Boston: Beacon Press, 1984.

TCA II *Theory of Communicative Action*, vol. II (trans.)
T. McCarthy. Boston: Beacon Press, 1987.

TJ   *Truth and Justification* (trans.) B. Fultner. Cambridge,
Mass.: MIT Press, 2003.

TP   *Theory and Praxis* (trans.) J. Viertal. Boston: Beacon Press,
1973.

TRS   *Towards a Rational Society* (trans.) J. Shapiro. Boston:
Beacon Press, 1971.

TW   *Technik und Wissenschaft als "Ideologie."* Frankfurt am
Main: Suhrkamp, 1968.

HORKHEIMER

BPSS   *Between Philosophy and Social Science* (trans.) G. F.
Hunter, M. Kramer, and J. Torpey. Cambridge, Mass.:
MIT Press, 1995.

CIR   *The Critique of Instrumental Reason: Lectures and
Essays since the End of World War II* (trans.)
M. O'Connell. New York: Continuum, 1974.

CT   *Critical Theory* (trans.) M. O'Connell. New York:
Continuum, 1975.

DE   *Dialectic of Enlightenment* (with Adorno) (trans.)
E. Jephcott. Stanford: Stanford University Press, 2002.

ER   *Eclipse of Reason.* New York: Continuum, 1974.

HGS   *Gesammelte Schriften* (ed.) G. Schmid-Noerr and
A. Schmidt. Frankfurt am Main: Fischer, 1987–.

KT   *Kritische Theorie.* Frankfurt am Main: Fischer, 1968.

MARCUSE

AD   *The Aesthetic Dimension: Toward a Critique of Marxist
Aesthetics.* Boston: Beacon Press, 1978.

CR   *Counterrevolution and Revolt.* Boston: Beacon Press,
1972.

EC   *Eros and Civilization: A Philosophical Inquiry into Freud*. Boston: Beacon Press, 1955.

FL   *Five Lectures*. Trans. J. Schapiro. Boston: Beacon Press, 1970.

L   *An Essay on Liberation*. Boston: Beacon Press, 1969.

MS   *Schriften*. Frankfurt am Main: Suhrkamp, 1978–89.

N   *Negations* (trans.) J. Shapiro. Boston: Beacon Press, 1968.

O   *One-Dimensional Man*. Boston: Beacon Press, 1964.

RR   *Reason and Revolution: Hegel and the Rise of Social Theory*. Oxford: Oxford University Press, 1941.

NEUMANN

B   *Behemoth: The Structure and Practice of National Socialism, 1933–44*. New York: Harper & Row, 1963.

Introduction

Critical Theory was born in the trauma of the Weimar Republic, grew to maturity in expatriation, and achieved cultural currency on its return from exile. Passed on from its founding first generation – among others Max Horkheimer, Friedrich Pollock, Herbert Marcuse, and Theodor Adorno – to the leader of its second, Jürgen Habermas, Critical Theory remained central to European philosophical, social, and political thought throughout the Cold War period. It is still a vital philosophical and political perspective, and a third generation of critical theorists, among whom Axel Honneth is most prominent, continue to press its concerns largely in terms of the tradition that began in the Weimar years. Along with phenomenology in its various forms and the philosophy and social theory gathered loosely under the headings of structuralism and poststructuralism, Critical Theory is a preeminent voice in twentieth-century continental thought.

The Cambridge Companion to Critical Theory tracks major themes in the development of Critical Theory from its inception to the present day. While it is characterized by certain shared core philosophical concerns, Critical Theory exhibits a diversity among its proponents that both contributes to its richness and poses substantial barriers to understanding its significance. When pursuing the elements that unify it, it is important not to lose sight of the pluralistic nature of the enterprise, where individual thinkers can differ (sometimes substantially) on various matters. In fact, it is impossible to represent the tradition of Critical Theory accurately without preserving the complications introduced by the relations of the views of its individual thinkers to one another. The complexity that results from the requirement that this plurality not be swept aside is

I

especially daunting to one seeking to orient oneself for the first time. This effect is further deepened by the extremely diverse intellectual influences on Critical Theory, influences that figure in express ways in the development of philosophical positions among the thinkers associated with Critical Theory, as well as in the technical vocabulary that often figures in the statement of those positions. What is needed is a treatment of Critical Theory as a whole that respects its richness without losing its conceptual main points.

To that end, this volume emphasizes both the conceptual and the historical components to Critical Theory. Chapters 1 through 8 are roughly chronological and more historical than the others in the volume, beginning with the conceptual foundations of the early Frankfurt School, proceeding through the major statements and issues of its middle period, and ending with the Kantian turn in Habermas's thought. Although there are some chapters devoted to a single thinker or to aspects of his thought, most of even the more historical chapters are problem-oriented and involve showing how multiple perspectives from within Critical Theory bear on a select topic. This reflects the general desideratum of the volume that showing significant differences among critical theorists is as important as showing what they have in common. This aim is also present in chapters 9 through 11, which take less historically synoptic views of Critical Theory's account of contemporary mass culture, politics and its relation to its main competitor on the European philosophical scene: French poststructuralism. Chapters 12 and 13 have special places in the volume. They emphasize the relation of Critical Theory to ongoing philosophical concerns. Critical Theory is still a vital force, especially in social and political philosophy and in aesthetics. Stephen White's chapter poses and answers the question of whether there is still anything distinctive about Critical Theory. Axel Honneth's concluding chapter does the same with the question of the legacy of Critical Theory, discussing its past importance, contemporary relevance, and prospects for future development.

In the opening chapter I discuss several fundamental and distinctive features of the conceptual apparatus of early Critical Theory as it is set out in seminal articles by Horkheimer and Marcuse. Key to this is considering the contrast of Critical Theory with two competitor models of social scientific explanation: what Horkheimer calls "traditional" theory, a model that views such explanation as a special case of methodological considerations that guide the natural sciences, and "vulgar Marxism," a model of reductive dialectical materialism that analyzes superstructure elements of social formation wholly in terms of their causal relations to economic substructure elements. Michael Rosen's chapter concentrates on the complex and formative interaction between Benjamin and Adorno, showing that there are important continuities between Benjamin's early and later thought and that there was significant intellectual disagreement between Benjamin and Adorno, the nature of which the latter was not fully aware of either during Benjamin's lifetime or later. The most important strand in Benjamin's thought as a whole is his distinctive form of Kantianism that is itself critical of Kant's narrow conception of experience. This heterodox Kantianism is also the key to Benjamin's Marxism, for it is the means by which he confronts the question of what connects different areas of a culture, allowing us to see identity in their apparent diversity. Rosen shows how Benjamin answers this question by deploying the notion of "mimetic experience." The Frankfurt School was the first group of philosophers not only to embrace Freud, but also to attempt to wed his thinking to Marx's. Joel Whitebook brings out the intricacies for Critical Theory of the problem of how a Marxist political theory can incorporate Freudian insights by tracing the history of that attempted marriage in the early writings of Horkheimer and Adorno, in the seminal account offered in Marcuse, and in the problematic status of psychoanalysis in Habermas.

Consideration of the middle period of Critical Theory begins with Julian Roberts's critical assessment of the main arguments of *Dialectic of Enlightenment* and, in particular, the book's central thesis that enlightenment is, or can be, a form of myth. Roberts pays special attention to the claim that the underlying dynamic of enlightenment lies in a pathological insistence on regularity and identity, with the result that science is made to cast a "magic spell" against the terrors of disorder. Also addressed is the claimed sole remedy for this situation, a rediscovery of the particular, of the *hic et nunc*. Raymond Geuss's chapter deepens the consideration of Adorno, and along with him Marcuse, by turning with great clarity to the question of the relation between the "revolutionary impulse" and dialectic. Geuss traces conceptions of revolution through Marx and Lenin and then joins that analysis with an extended treatment of issues relevant to the possibility of revolution – for example, objectified belief and the concept of a "false need." He then canvasses the resources available in Marcuse and Adorno for responding dialectically to the substantial obstacles to revolution. J. M. Bernstein offers a detailed reconstruction of Adorno's aesthetic theory, in which he presses beyond its manifest concern with criticizing the culture industry to indicate Adorno's attempt to establish that the practices of modernist art implicitly contain or foster conceptions of knowing, reasoning, and acting that systematically diverge from the rationalized versions of the same that have become hegemonic in the world outside art. Moishe Postone addresses an aspect of Critical Theory that is often neglected in philosophical treatments of it: the analysis of economics, law, and state capitalism in the important work of Friedrich Pollock and Franz Neumann. Postone traces the arc of Critical Theory's involvement with the question of state capitalism and related issues by situating that involvement in terms of general historical movements in Critical Theory and against the background of the reception of Marx's concept of labor.

Kenneth Baynes focuses on the all-important Kantian turn in Habermas's thought that inaugurates later Critical Theory. He shows that Habermas's rejection of certain cardinal antifoundationalist and nonsystematic features of prior Frankfurt School thought is incremental and so is his adoption of the Kantianism that replaces them, arguing that there are three stages in Habermas's emerging Kantianism. In the first, Habermas's criticism of earlier Frankfurt theorists results in the measured methodological return to Kant that occupies *Knowledge and Human Interests*. The second stage involves the increasing importance of the "linguistic turn" to Habermas's thought and the development of his "universal pragmatics," culminating in *Theory of Communicative Action*. A third period reveals Habermas's increasing political liberalism to be motivated in terms of an even more specifically Kantian concept of justice.

Simone Chambers provides an incisive overview of the political theory and engagement of Critical Theory. She highlights how the experience of Fascism formed the deep skepticism of Enlightenment ideals typical of early Frankfurt School political theory and then turns to consider Habermas's embrace of those very ideals. She argues that Critical Theory's political engagement has always been a troubled issue for it, a problem for which it has yet to find

a satisfactory solution. Hauke Brunkhorst discusses Frankfurt interpretations of contemporary mass culture, tracing a central ambiva-
lence on the topic in Critical Theory back to Marx. For the early
Frankfurt School and Benjamin, the thesis of "enlightenment as
mass deception" dominates the reception of mass culture, yet the
question of the revolutionary tendencies of such culture remains in
the background all along. With Habermas the analysis moves back
closer to its Marxist point of departure – that is, it returns to the
theory of political democracy and democratic public sphere that
Marx developed in his essay on the Eighteenth Brumaire. Beatrice
Hanssen tackles the difficult task of making sense of the relationship of Critical Theory to poststructuralism by looking closely at
the case of Habermas and Foucault. She properly resists easy assimilation but sees, as did Foucault himself, a possible rapprochement
between early Critical Theory and poststructuralism for which the
concept of eristic is crucial.

In the final two chapters of the book, Stephen White and Axel
Honneth examine the question of the continuing relevance of Critical Theory. White evaluates Critical Theory as a distinctive research
program both in terms of its history and its present state. He argues
that the first issue confronting Critical Theory is whether there is
any way of thinking of critical normativity as universal that does not
err on the side of overgeneralizing some particular historical perspective. He then considers whether what once counted as "traditional"
social theory by critical lights has so changed that it is no longer
subject to charges typically brought against it. In the final chapter of
the volume, Honneth offers his view of the legacy of Critical Theory
for the future, expanding upon his well-known work on this theme
and stressing in new ways the importance of the concept of recognition and of making a proper theoretical place within social theory
for "the Other of reason."

1 Conceptual foundations of early Critical Theory

Critical Theory first develops during a period of extraordinarily complex intellectual activity in Germany. If one were to take the year 1930 as a benchmark – when Max Horkheimer becomes the director of the Institute of Social Research in Frankfurt – and were to look back upon the decade preceding that date, one would encounter in their most vibrant forms many of the most important philosophical movements of the twentieth century: the hermeneutic phenomenology of Heidegger; the logical empiricism of the Vienna Circle and the early Wittgenstein; various strands of neo-Kantianism; and the humanistic Marxism of Lukács. In political and social theory, psychology, historiography, and economics the situation is hardly less multifarious. Each of these views or schools, sometimes in combination with elements of others, vies for predominance in the Weimar period. Moreover, each of the contenders takes care to incorporate within it involved criticisms of the others.

Self-definition *ex negativo* can take many forms, but one is nearly universal in the period and is very important for early Critical Theory. All the main philosophical and social-theoretical parties to the disputes of the 1920s and 1930s place great stake in interpreting, appropriating, or otherwise assessing the significance of the history of German philosophy from the time of Kant to the late nineteenth century. This is true even for those philosophical viewpoints that do not accord history a primary internal theoretical importance, for instance, logical empiricism. For a self-avowedly historical set of views such as Critical Theory, the connection between philosophical historiography and the criticism of its contemporary competitors as products of the history of German philosophy is especially explicit, complicated, and formative. In fact, any account of the conceptual foundations of "early Critical Theory," roughly the writings of the core members of the Institute from 1930 to 1940, would be greatly impoverished were it not to view the development of Critical Theory in this phase as inherently concerned with defining itself in opposition to other social and philosophical theories. This chapter concentrates on the seminal essays of Horkheimer, Marcuse, and Adorno written in the mid to late 1930s that bring out in an especially vivid way how early Critical Theory was formed by distinguishing itself from rival approaches.

Critical Theory has always been rather fluid, even by design, and it would be a mistake to attempt to treat even its early history univocally. Nevertheless, these essays address a core set of concerns that preoccupy Critical Theory throughout its prewar period and which continue to exert an influence to somewhat lesser degrees in its later, more Adorno- and Habermas-dominated forms. It is possible to distinguish two main approaches to Critical Theory in this period. The first of these is associated primarily with Horkheimer, whose work commentators often view as the dominant force in the formation of Critical Theory. The ascription of preeminence to Horkheimer's conception of Critical Theory has a well-founded provenance – at one time or another most of the principals of Critical Theory acknowledged Horkheimer's writings of this period as establishing the blueprint for Critical Theory to come. Even so, one must be careful not to overemphasize the intellectual effect of Horkheimer at this time. His seminal essays present a number of ideas whose rhetorical and programmatic effect was extremely important for the other members of the Institute, but the ideas themselves are not developed very systematically. In some instances the lack of unity is due simply to mutually incompatible elements in his conception of Critical Theory, in others the problem is lack of theoretical detail. Another cause is perhaps that Horkheimer's stewardship of the Institute as a place in which a number of different perspectives on shared issues was possible causes him to leave open intellectual space in which potentially contrary views might be developed and even encouraged. A blueprint is, after all, not a building. Thus do Marcuse's writings from the 1930s emphasize in different ways common ground with Horkheimer, sometimes raising questions in reaction as well.

The second strand in the formation of early Critical Theory remains incipient but is highly suggestive for later trends in the Institute. This is the position of the young Adorno, who, under the influence of Walter Benjamin, begins to articulate a more "aestheticized" and guarded view of Critical Theory's systematic potential. In a much more developed form, this view of Critical Theory will come to dominate the Frankfurt School from the mid 1940s until Adorno's death in the late 1960s. Horkheimer will migrate over from the first to this second strand, coauthoring with Adorno what many scholars view as the principal text of Critical Theory, *Dialectic of Enlightenment* (1944/7).

HORKHEIMER

Horkheimer's inaugural lecture of 1930, published a year later as "The Current Condition of Social Philosophy and the Tasks of an Institute of Social Research," signals an important shift in the Institute's emphasis and scope. For the seven years from its founding in 1923 to the date of Horkheimer's address, the Institute was concerned almost exclusively with politically engaged empirical social science. Although the broadly Austro-Marxist cast of the Institute facilitated incorporation of elements of non-Marxist methodologies, its members had little interest in philosophical questions and even less in the project of providing a philosophical framework for the work of the Institute. Hence Horkheimer is covering new ground when he states:

If social-philosophical thought concerning the relationship of individual and society, the meaning of culture, the foundation of the development of community, the overall structure of social life – in short, concerning the great and fundamental questions – is left behind as (so to speak) the dregs that remain in the reservoir of social-scientific problems after taking out those questions that can be advanced in concrete investigations, social philosophy may well perform social functions . . . but its intellectual fruitfulness would have been forfeited. The relation between philosophical and corresponding specialized scientific disciplines cannot be conceived as though philosophy deals with the really decisive problems – the process constructing theories beyond the reach of the empirical sciences, its own concepts of reality, and systems comprehending the totality – while on the other side empirical research carries out its long, boring, individual studies that split up into a thousand partial questions, culminating in a chaos of countless enclaves of specialists. This conception – according to which the individual researcher must view philosophy as a perhaps pleasant but scientifically fruitless enterprise . . . while philosophers, by contrast, are emancipated from the individual researcher because they think they cannot wait for the latter before announcing their wide-ranging conclusion – is currently being supplanted by the idea of a continuous, dialectical penetration and development of philosophical theory and specialized scientific praxis. (*BPSS* 8–9; *HGS* iii, 28–9)

Horkheimer hopes to create a new, philosophically informed, interdisciplinary social science to displace both social philosophy and sociology as they were then represented in Europe. In his view the benefits of including social philosophy in the social scientific paradigm developing at the Institute go beyond clarifying general research orientation, important though that may be. Philosophy also enables social scientists to identify and explore questions that might not otherwise be raised. Without philosophically informed social theory of the right sort whole ranges of phenomena might be sealed off from investigation and the potential political impact of the research diminished to that extent.

But, what *is* social philosophy "of the right sort"? The answer to this question is superficially simple: the right sort of social theory is "critical." But given the myriad uses of the term *critical* since Kant, the simple answer is no answer at all. The question then becomes: what does it mean for a social theory to be "critical" according to Horkheimer? What is "Critical Theory"?

Prima facie one might be tempted to think that Critical Theory is "critical" just because it "criticizes" existing political life. Horkheimer takes the term *critical theory* from Marx and early Critical Theory of course is broadly Marxist. It is an account of the social forces of domination that takes its theoretical activity to be practically connected to the object of its study. In other words, Critical Theory is not merely descriptive, it is a way to instigate social change by providing knowledge of the forces of social inequality that can, in turn, inform political action aimed at emancipation (or at least at diminishing domination and inequality). Following this thought one might think that Critical Theory is "critical" just to the extent that it makes social inequality apparent, specifies some plausible candidates for the causes of the inequality, and enables society in general (or at least its oppressed segment) to react in appropriate ways. Critical Theory is "critical" because it answers the charge laid by the last of Marx's *Theses on Feuerbach*: "The philosophers have only *interpreted* the world in different ways; the point is to *change* it."[1]

But this is still not an adequate characterization of what makes Critical Theory "critical," for the relevant use of the term *critical* must be understood against an even broader historical background that begins with Kant's idea of a "critical philosophy."[2] Kant's understanding of critique is important to early Critical Theory for a number of reasons. First, it specifies the *object* of critique, that is, what critical activity operates upon. Kant's critical philosophy directs itself upon "reason." One of Kant's leading themes is that reason has an inherent tendency to seek application regardless of cognitive context, and it is the job of critique to circumscribe reason's epistemic application to what Kant considers to be the bounds of knowledge. Kant calls both the propensity of reason to seek unconditioned epistemic deployment and the insoluble metaphysical problems that result from it "dialectic."[3] Second, Kant's conception of critique also supplies Critical Theory with its understanding of the *subject* of critique, that is, with a specification of the agent that carries out criticism. According to Kant reason is also what performs critique. Kant thinks that any justification for placing limits on reason's demand for global scope that did not have a source in that very reason would be incompatible with rational autonomy. Critique is for Kant, then, necessarily *self-critique* and freedom from dialectical illusion possible only upon rational self-regulation. Critical Theory is also concerned to explicate conditions upon rationality and regards this task as implicating its assessment of its own rational limitations. Critical Theory's reflexive structure is thus a third inheritance from Kant.

Critical Theory dissents from some specific core elements of this Kantian picture, but it remains allied to the self-reflective critical model according to which there is never equivalence between thought and its object – that is, the concept of experience still plays a central philosophical role in Critical Theory. In keeping with this complex relation to Kant's thought, early Critical Theory's reaction to Kant does not involve a point by point refutation of elements of Kant's theory based upon criteria internal to Kant's own thought as much as it questions whether the idealist paradigm that Kant establishes, and within which he works, is not itself ultimately a limitation to critique. This sort of charge is of course not unique to Critical Theory; most of Kant's idealist successors made similar claims. But all of those reactions to Kant are, more or less, voiced from within the idealist paradigm and thus will share features with Kant's philosophy that make them insufficiently critical as well. Accordingly, an elaborate project of a philosophical reconstruction of idealism stands at the center of early Critical Theory. Because all of Critical Theory's philosophical competitors also viewed themselves in strong reaction to German idealism, each offering its own account of the advantages and disadvantages of it, Critical Theory's particular understanding of idealism was also an important way for it to criticize rival contemporary positions.

Horkheimer first uses the term *critical theory* in his seminal 1937 essay "Traditional and Critical Theory." Although the core members of the early Institute viewed this essay as the classic statement of the structure and aims of Critical Theory, focusing on it alone provides a simplified and overly neat answer to the question of what is supposed to make Critical Theory critical. This is because the traditional–critical dichotomy is only one way in which Horkheimer characterizes the nature of the social theory of the Institute. Two other contrasts are prominent in Horkheimer's early essays: between (1) "idealism" and "materialism" and (2) "rationalism" and "irrationalism." A complete picture of Horkheimer's views requires coordinating these classifications with the traditional–critical distinction.

Idealism and materialism

The earliest contrast Horkheimer deploys is between idealism and materialism. He distinguishes two basic forms of materialism. The first of these one might call "simple" or "reductive" materialism. Its main historical representative is the materialism of Enlightenment French philosophy that reduces real features of the world to a physical base. Its primary instantiation contemporary with Horkheimer is the logical empiricism of the Vienna Circle. The second sort of materialism is "dialectical" or "critical," and Critical Theory will turn out to be "materialist" in this sense. Up to the seminal 1937 essay, Horkheimer refers to the developing Frankfurt social theory simply as "materialist" and not as "critical."

Materialism of both sorts is distinguished from idealism. As Horkheimer uses the term, *idealism* has a very broad extension. There is a subdivision of idealism into "rationalist" and "irrationalist" sorts. Rationalist idealism comprises not only philosophical theories that are ordinarily grouped under the label *idealist* – for example, the German idealism from Kant to Hegel that has already been discussed – but also the rationalism of Descartes and Leibniz and the empiricism of Locke and Berkeley. Irrationalist idealism includes eighteenth- and early nineteenth-century German counter-Enlightenment thought (including romanticism), Hume, Nietzsche, the *Lebensphilosophie* of Dilthey, the vitalism of Bergson and Klages, and the hermeneutic phenomenology of Heidegger.

Following Lukács, Horkheimer's basic strategy is to reclaim aspects of rationalist idealism, and especially German idealism from Kant to Hegel, in order to free materialism from its reductive tendencies. Horkheimer analyzes idealism as an inherently bourgeois philosophy that depends upon impoverished conceptions of self, nature, and freedom. It has a progressive phase, culminating in Hegel, where there are truly revolutionary notions of autonomy that have critical potential. But these are inevitably straitjacketed by the limitations of the general conceptual framework of rationalist idealism. After its apex in Hegel, idealism degenerates into progressively fainter shadows of itself, intuitionalist and conservative aspects of it becoming much more prominent. This ends up in what Horkheimer calls "irrationalism" and, to the extent that idealist doctrine bleeds over into more recent forms of materialism, "positivism."

THE LEGACY OF IDEALISM.   Although Horkheimer will take much of the content of Critical Theory from salvageable parts of rationalist idealism, there is much about that idealism that must be set aside. One main problem with idealistic theories taken as a whole is that they promote what Horkheimer calls "transfiguration" (*Verklärung*).[4] Some value V is transfigured if: (a) V is (correctly) thought to be valuable but not present in the world as a general matter, (b) V's not being present in the world is attributed to features of the world thought (falsely) to be immutable, entailing (c) that the abiding presence of V in the world is thought to be impossible, with the result that (d) V is posited as attainable in a supernatural sphere. Of course, (d) only follows if one discounts that V's general presence not be possible at all. But acceptance of contingency of this sort in the case, say, of happiness or worthiness to be happy was beyond the pale in a philosophical climate in which standards meant to assure the rational goodness of the world and the promise of redemption of the value in question were so prevalent. Put another way, one of the chief organizing themes of idealism is giving a theodicy, even if in a rather secularized version. The idea that the world is structured in a way that ensures human well-being or happiness, and the understanding that part of that happiness involves the world being able to be discovered to be that way, issues in the sort of foundationalist epistemology and moral philosophy typical of idealism. Platonic Ideas, *res cogitans*, Spinoza's *Deus sive Natura*, Kant's *summum bonum*, and Hegel's *Geist* are all due to transfiguration (and are transfiguring concepts in their own right). In Horkheimer's view such eternal standards are not sensitive to the ineliminable, indeed defining, contingency of being human. Moreover, transfiguration severely compromises the potential for social justice, since transfiguring theories allow that the ultimate relief from suffering is achieved only outside contexts in which human action can be effective. False optimism in a "world beyond," in which reward and rectification is possible, promotes tolerance of suffering and quietism concerning human redress for injustice and deprivation.

Nevertheless, there are several positive features of idealism that Horkheimer wants to preserve in order to combat allegedly reductive and instrumental tendencies of early twentieth-century European philosophy and social science. In some of its forms, idealism is complicit in this reductive and instrumental form of thought, but the idealist tradition has within it resources for resisting this complicity, although only finally through a materialist reinterpretation of those resources. This is just to say that one of the things Horkheimer desires is a nontransfiguring form of rationalist idealism, if that is possible at all.

Horkheimer argues that much philosophy and social theory of the early twentieth century rests on fundamentally mistaken views concerning: (1) the nature of the theory–object relation, (2) the relationship between belief and desire, (3) the systematic requirements of theory, and (4) the relevance of history to knowledge. This set of claims falls neatly into the commonplace view among certain neo-Kantians (e.g. Windelband, Rickert) and others (e.g. Dilthey) that there is a principled distinction that must be drawn between the epistemology of the natural sciences (*Naturwissenschaften*) and social or "cultural" sciences (*Geistes-/Kulturwissenschaften*). In the first instance, that distinction is a response to claims that the physical sciences provide a general model of acceptable scientific methodology applicable across the board, that is, to philosophy and the social sciences as well. The strategy underlying making the distinction is to purchase the freedom of the social sciences from the constraints of principles governing the natural sciences by arguing for essential dissimilarities between the two. In itself, establishing this point leaves untouched the traditional way of conceiving the relationship of theory to object *within* the natural sciences. And, in a sense, Horkheimer is willing to allow for the propriety of traditional theory within that limited scope. Undertaking even high-level empirical research may not require more. But, like Rickert and Dilthey, he goes on to claim that the theory–object relation considered in the way appropriate to the social sciences is epistemologically fundamental and that traditional conceptions of the same are simplifying abstractions from this more basic and adequate critical approach.

Traditional theory by and large conceives of its objects as self-standing entities that have properties that do not depend upon the attentions of theory. Theories "picture" the world; they do not contribute to it. Horkheimer's basic contention concerning (1) above is that, contrary to the accepted view within the physical sciences generally, they are characterized by a property usually only attributed to the social sciences, and one that, in the estimation of the physical sciences, marks the social sciences as being not fully "scientific" – the theory-dependency of their objects. Any theoretical activity unaware of the constitutive contributions of conceptual frameworks and theories to the objects of their study is fundamentally flawed and, in effect, self-deceptive.

Horkheimer presses these themes by drawing upon a line of thought that originates in Kant. For Kant the invariant and universal features of subjectivity structure reality even in terms of its perception.[5] This structuring is not frictionless – sensate matter is required in order to have experiences – but any experience will be "constituted" in part by subjective discursive activity. This Kantian outlook is apparent in Horkheimer's statements of one of the most distinctive features of Critical Theory: its insistence upon the inherently theoretical nature of objects of social science and philosophy (see e.g. *CT* 19, 171, 200; *KT* I, 40, II, 121, 149–50). Horkheimer advances this thesis of "theory-laden" data in many forms, in varying strengths, and not always consistently.[6] The strongest form of the thesis that he endorses is that *any* cognitive contact with an object will involve the contribution of antecedently held beliefs to it. Put another way, according to Horkheimer there is no coherent formulation available for a notion of an object that is not already constituted *as that object* by the interpretative activity of taking it as an object of study.[7]

But acknowledging that observation is theory-laden does not suffice to fully characterize the constitutive nature of thought, for it focuses solely upon the *conceptual* penetration into the level of facts (*CT* 158; *KT* II, 108–9). Horkheimer extends to nondiscursive states or dispositions a constitutive role in thought, claiming that concepts themselves are prediscursively guided by more basic orientations in the world, that is, desires and the interests they implicate ([2] above). When one deploys a concept one singles out some particular feature of an object as being significant in terms of the possibility of grouping that object together with other objects on the basis of the shared feature. Picking out which among the many qualities of a thing to treat as salient is purposive and involves interests that one has in understanding the world to be a certain way. This understanding of the world is broadly what Horkheimer calls "instrumental"; one deploys concepts in order to achieve predictive and manipulative control over things. Seeking such control is not optional, at least not for humans at most points in their history. Because subjects largely confront a nature from which they are alienated, reconnection to nature will take the form of a distanced exercise of control over it. This both reinforces the essential division between instrumental thought and its object and alleviates the threat of a nature that is uncontrolled. Because conceptual mediation is present implicitly and indeterminately in even the perception of objects, those encounters with the world will be anticipations of instrumental thoughts. Traditional theory either ignores the instrumental connection of desire and cognition altogether, or it domesticates it by limiting its application to scientific research that is explicitly impinged upon by politics. On the other hand, Critical Theory asks the question of whether instrumental thought can ever achieve its goal of overcoming the fear of a distanced nature, what effects such distancing has both cognitively and politically, and whether and how it is possible to eliminate the base alienation that is claimed to produce the perceived need for instrumental thought.[8]

One can find strands of this connection of concept use to instrumental thought in Kant (the contrast of his epistemology with his aesthetic theory is very important in this connection), but the pragmatic aspect of concepts is much more pronounced in later German idealism, particularly in Schopenhauer and Hegel.[9] Of most direct importance to the issue of the relation of theory to praxis, or of concept to interest, is Hegel's view that agency and belief can only be adequately understood holistically and historically. Concepts, their systematic organization, and the interests they express have their content relative to particular historical, whole forms of life in which they develop and whose development and persistence they ensure. Even science is "conditional" in this sense (CT 35–6; KT I, 56–7). Horkheimer accepts Hegel's extreme holism on the issue of the content of concepts within conceptual systems, holding that the only relatively stable unit of meaning is the whole of a conceptual scheme at a given historical time (BPSS 236, 308–9; KT I, 141, II, 256–7).[10] This is here equivalent to saying that any object is conceivable in any number of ways, all of which rely upon the semantic resources of entire theories (BPSS 204; KT I, 261–2). Although more recent forms of traditional theory have embraced epistemic versions of holism (Quine, even Carnap) and certain minority trends in philosophy of science contemporaneous with Horkheimer also did so (Neurath), Horkheimer's charge is that the preponderance of traditional theory disclaims it.

Moreover, even those representatives of traditional theory that embrace holism tend to do so ahistorically and, to that extent as well, remain traditional. This is to say that issues of theoretical holism and the unity of theory and praxis are inextricably connected to those of historicism in Horkheimer's version of early Critical Theory. This is also a Hegelian legacy and one that is, in turn, directly connected to Hegel's reconception of the nature of the agent of thought. Just as Kant's conception of the transcendental subject displaced empirical and rationalist accounts of the self, so Hegel argues that historically situated forms of social rationality determine the content of the concepts and the nature of the objects that the content is about. His *Phenomenology of Spirit* (1807) is a demonstration of and guidebook to attaining this truth. It begins with allegedly simple forms of a conception of thought or reason as essentially separate from reality, and argues that when pressed far enough that conception will break down internally through contradiction. In its place, following directly from the contradiction, will be a new, slightly more sophisticated way of trying to maintain this separation in the teeth of the countervailing requirements of an adequate account of reality. But it too, and in fact all dualistic understandings of the relation of thought to object, will end up in irresolvable internal conflict. But Hegel thinks that this is a *progression* of less to more adequate ways to think of the thought–world relation, one way succeeding upon the other seamlessly and with dialectical necessity. The linchpin to the progression is what Hegel calls "determinate negation," the immanent realization on the part of a particular form of consciousness that the particular form of the thought–object separation it held central to its conception of the world keeps it from a true account of its relation to the world – that is, is "alienating" or "negating" (this why Hegel sometimes calls determinate negation "negation of negation"). Determinate negation is then *negation* because the scheme in question has been shown inadequate through immanent critique and *determinate* because the scheme in question is shown to be limited in its "truth" to certain background assumptions relative to the scheme. When one reaches what Hegel calls the "absolute standpoint," one sees that there is no ultimate distinction between thought and world, only distinctions relative to schemes that are partially true.

Hegel's account of truth and knowledge is historicist *and* essentialist, and Horkheimer wants to preserve the former and jettison the latter. The historicist element involves two components important to Horkheimer. The first of these is epistemic. Because it is itself a historical artifact and constituted by historically conditioned beliefs, desires, and so on, the conceptual framework Critical Theory brings to bear on the objects of its study will be relative to historical circumstance. Further, because Horkheimer accepts the Kantian idea that data is imbued with framework content, Critical Theory cannot lay claim to strictly universalizable principles (*BPSS* 258–9; *KT*1, 168). Critical Theory is an explicitly interpretative venture aware of its own place in the inventory of "things to be studied." The second aspect of Hegel's views that is inviting to Horkheimer has to do with the semantic possibilities for Critical Theory. According to Hegel no form of consciousness prior to the absolute standpoint, not even the most remote and basic one, is false (*BPSS* 309; *KT* II, 254–5); they are all partially true. Hegel can say this because he is committed to a teleological stepwise progression of forms of consciousness that ends in one all-encompassing final form. The truth which all other forms of consciousness are approximations of is that of this "absolute standpoint." Hegel does not think that forms of consciousness short of the absolute standpoint are partially true *just* because seen to be so retroactively from the final vantage point. Rather (and this is a feature of Hegel's account that is often downplayed in contemporary "nonmetaphysical" interpretations of it) the endpoint is indeterminately and implicitly present in every stage of the progression and it is this presence, and the degree of its explicitness present in any one form of life determines how partially true that nonfinal form is. Progression towards the final end is measured in terms of a succession of increasingly adequate expressions of an underlying, ever-present truth.[11]

Horkheimer is very drawn to this idea that conceptions of social phenomena are all partially true (*BPSS* 184ff., 308–9; *KT* I, 236ff.; II, 256–7), but is left with an obvious problem in appropriating this doctrine straightaway from Hegel. Horkheimer rejects Hegel's essentialism as a remnant of outdated metaphysics, and with it the idea that there is an end to dialectic (*BPSS* 115, 239–40; *KT* I, 13, 145).[12] This means that Horkheimer must, in a Kantian vein, reject Hegel's claim that subject and object can be known to be identical (cf. *CT* 27–8; *KT* II, 48–9). Only if this "identity thesis" is denied can Horkheimer hope to motivate the idea of everlasting dialectic, since what makes dialectical transition possible is the failed attempt of a form of consciousness to achieve a stable understanding of the thought–object relation.[13] The problem for Horkheimer is, therefore, that freeing Hegel's account from its teleology seems to leave no measure for partial truth. This raises questions of relativism. Because there is no one "total" truth, there can be no partial approximations of *it*. All truth then becomes "partial" and there are significant questions whether this is a coherent conception of truth (in essence, the concept of a part without the concept of a whole of which it is a part). The standard Kantian move here – to interpret the whole as a regulative idea or ideal – is problematic for Horkheimer because of the tinge of transfiguration it carries with it, although Horkheimer sometimes seems to embrace it (CT 27; KT 1, 48). As it turns out, Horkheimer never had an adequate response to the charge of relativism, though he was well aware of the issue. I shall return to this problem in a bit more detail at the conclusion of this section.

Horkheimer claims that traditional theory is characterized by a complete disregard for the allegedly constitutive role of social life in knowledge and by a rigid antihistorical bias. Again, the model of the physical sciences as they were developed in the modern era dictates (a) the dualistic character of traditional theory, in which human agency is either alienated from nature or reduced blindly to it, (b) its vocation of strict universalism of methodology and result, and (c) its nonhistorical character. While Kant is a somewhat heroic motivating figure for much of Horkheimer's negative critique of traditional theory, it is obvious that Kantian critical philosophy is in many ways traditional. Of course, because Kant is the "limit case" of traditional theory, his thought throws into greatest dialectical relief the inherent inadequacies of traditional theory. That is, he adheres to the three desiderata just mentioned in very revealing ways. Hegel is likewise a watershed figure because he stands at another border: one that separates idealism and socially and historically informed materialism. Hegel's thought is still universalistic and this compromises the dialectical historicism it introduces. This pull of traditionalism is also felt in Hegel's "solution" for dualism. It ultimately rests on his historical essentialism. While Horkheimer certainly agrees that traditional theory rests on an improper, alienating form of dualism, he does not believe that the distinction between thought and object can never be entirely collapsed.

THE MATERIALIST TURN.   Materialism "contradicts" idealism "essentially" because "According to materialism neither pure thought, nor abstraction in the sense of the philosophy of consciousness, nor intuition in the sense of irrationalism, is capable of creating a connection between the individual and the permanent structure of being" (BPSS 223; KT 1, 125). In replacing justification with explanation, materialism decisively moves away from the latent theodical tendencies of idealism (CT 23; KT 1, 44). But some forms of materialism still retain the instrumental aspect of rationalist idealism and are not, therefore, critical. The materialist turn from idealism must include within it a critique of universalist conceptions of instrumental reason and a place for historicism (*CT* 36ff.; *KT* I, 56ff.).

As was mentioned at the outset of this chapter, early Critical Theory is a brand of Marxism, and the historical figure central to Horkheimer's account of the right sort of materialism to reform idealism is Marx. Marx furthers the dialectical potential in Hegel by inverting his idealism into a dialectical materialism, according to which the sensible activity of humanity determines and transforms reality in light of historically conditioned desires, needs, and impulses that are grounded in physical existence (*CT* 42; *KT* I, 62–3). The marriage of the emphasis on material or natural base with historically available means for its transformation permits a variety of interpretations, and Marxists of various stripes have taken different positions on the dominance of one factor over the other. Horkheimer's critique of instrumental reason causes him to favor emphasis on the historical element, but replacing Hegelian *Geist* with cooperative human labor as the primary category of agency does not require skepticism concerning instrumental thought (as is evidenced by Marx's own views). "Orthodox" Marxism typically views overcoming alienation and class dominance as involving the development of just these capacities for manipulating nature. So, while constructive human activity has as its primary category "social labor" for Horkheimer, and while he emphasizes material human activity, he wants to avoid a reductive and overly naturalistic understanding of the role of "sensuous existence." To do otherwise, in Horkheimer's estimation, would replicate in Marxism many of the objectionable features he finds in traditional theory. The sort of Marxism found in Engels or Plekhanov, which is also indicative of the Second International's peculiar form of the "back to Kant" movement, must be avoided.[14]

Horkheimer is interested in mining Marx's early social theory, which other "humanistic" Marxists had emphasized as important, for example György Lukács and Karl Korsch, but which orthodox Marxism treated as an idealist remnant of Marx's youth well outgrown.[15] In this way Horkheimer preserves a central role for the dynamic relationship of subjectivity and objectivity in his account of alienation. While it is true that knowledge and even perception is based in material, natural sensation, the *experience* of sensation varies with historical conditions, which are not themselves reducible to a material base (*CT* 42–3; *KT* I, 62–4).

Two contemporary adversaries

POSITIVISM.   Overreaching, reductive materialism takes two forms that Horkheimer is particularly concerned to blunt: the sociological positivism of Comte and the logical empiricism of the Vienna Circle, whose members include Moritz Schlick, Rudolf Carnap, and Otto Neurath. (Horkheimer also considers Ernst Mach and the Berlin group gathered around Hans Reichenbach in this light as well.) His account of Comte and his followers is perfunctory and of less importance to understanding the development of early Critical Theory than the critique of the Vienna Circle.[16]

Horkheimer's analysis of logical empiricism is complex. Fundamentally he objects to the doctrine central to most forms of logical empiricism: that a statement is meaningful if and only if it can be proven true or false by means of experience – the so-called "verifiability principle." As I have discussed in passing, Vienna Circle positivism also embraces the view that there is a given and, in principle, incontrovertible set of facts that can be considered wholly apart from the theoretical framework from which they are identified (this is presupposed by the verifiability principle). Horkheimer also questions logical empiricism's claim that it is purified of metaphysical elements and holds that it is still related in ways that it does not fully appreciate to rationalist idealism. Logical empiricism, no matter how empiricist, has residual Kantian features, which, while rejecting the notion of the transcendental subject, retains a surreptitious a priori in the form of "formal invariance" (*CT* 148; *KT* II, 98–9). Additionally, the view that only scientific knowledge counts as knowledge is a metaphysical "romanticization" of facts and therefore a form of "irrationalism" (*CT* 181n, 183; *KT* II, 131n, 132).

Horkheimer's understanding of the complexity of the Vienna Circle is superior to that of the later critique of positivism in the writings of Adorno, but it may still seem somewhat unsatisfactory.[17] One problem involves the degree to which Horkheimer recognizes that some logical empiricists share features of "critical" epistemology and politics. Neurath is interesting in this connection. Horkheimer does recognize that Neurath dissents from a simple theory–fact dichotomy that Horkheimer otherwise ascribes generally to the Circle.[18] And Neurath's committed socialism, more committed than Horkheimer's own if willingness to engage in active political life at great personal risk is any indication, cannot have escaped him. The reason why Horkheimer believes he can treat Neurath as unexceptional hinges on Horkheimer's views concerning the relation of epistemology to politics that positivism requires. His claim is that consistent positivism commits one to reactionary conservatism, no matter what one's politics turns out to be, and, therefore, that there must be a very firm distinction in place between the views that individual members of the Vienna Circle happen to hold and what political views a *consistent* positivist would hold. It is not difficult to trace the source of this claim. One consequence of the verifiability principle is that ethical and political statements are meaningless – that is, they are neither true nor false – and this might seem to doom any project according to which political life is to be criticized on a rational basis. In Horkheimer's view the fact that some members of the Vienna Circle were overtly Left and, in some instances, engaged Marxists does not insulate positivism from criticism on the political front. It is not that positivism entails political conservatism in any specific form (or any positive political affiliation). Horkheimer seems to think, rather, that positivism's political disengagement and ethical neutrality abets the status quo, whatever that might be, and that *that* is conservatism by another name. No philosophical theory can be truly politically neutral. For Horkheimer, politically Left logical empiricists are, therefore, merely "accidental" radicals. That positivists so close to one another on questions in the philosophy of science could so diverge on political matters is a liability, not a strength, of the theory (*CT* 184; *KT* II, 134). Moreover, Horkheimer writes that any philosophical position that identifies itself so readily with the methodology and content of the special sciences under conditions of capitalism is bound to fall prey to the demands of the status quo, given economic control over scientific research programs (*CT* 179; *KT* II, 129). As background, it is worth mentioning that the more radical amongst the logical empiricists were Austro-Marxists, for whom an analogy between theoretical science and scientific Marxism was a given. As we have seen, Horkheimer denies that Marxism can be "scientific" in the sense upon which the analogy turns. With this in view, the dispute between the Vienna Circle and the Frankfurt Critical Theorists can be recast as one having to do with the proper form of Marxism – Hegelian versus scientific. The fact that the pre-Horkheimer Institute was Austro-Marxist in origin and temperament only makes this more pointed.

IRRATIONALISM. A second philosophical tradition that Horkheimer is concerned to challenge is what he terms "irrationalism" or "irrationalist idealism." It comprises the life-philosophy of Dilthey, neo-Kantianism of the so-called "Southwest" school of Windelband and Rickert, the vitalism of Bergson and Klages, and particularly the hermeneutic phenomenology of Heidegger. Horkheimer also discusses the historical roots of early twentieth-century irrationalism in the German counter-Enlightenment, early German romanticism, and Nietzsche.

Horkheimer analyzes irrationalism as an idealist overreaction to some of rationalist idealism's deficiencies, especially its tendency to discredit the significance of nondiscursive forms of thought and its strongly rational conception of systematicity and foundationalism. Because irrationalist idealism stands in a dialectical relationship to its rationalist counterpart, Horkheimer acknowledges the importance of some of its criticisms of rationalism but avoids its overreaction. Irrationalism at best contains the beginnings of an interesting critique of both rationalist idealism and reductive materialism in its historicism and perspectivism (CT 11; KT 1, 31–2).

Irrationalism's critique of rationalist idealism is one-sided and "negative" (BPSS 244; KT 1, 150–1) and, because of this, irrationalism is not sensitive to its own continued involvement in idealism. The irrationalist overreaction to rational idealism consists in a critique of instrumental reason and nonhistoricism, which advocates a return to an atavistic, authoritarian, prerational conception of human life. In such a conception the individual has no essential role and the perceived disintegration of modern culture is replaced with a mythical unity of being that discursive life cannot capture. In turning towards the unity of "life" or of "the preconscious," irrationalism has replicated the supernatural ground of existence that is the hallmark of idealism; irrationalism merely provides another gloss on the project of transfiguration (BPSS 252–4; KT 1, 160–2). Put another way, irrationalism shares with rationalism a gulf between concept and reality typical of bourgeois philosophizing (*CT* 12–13; *KT* 1, 33–4). The way over this gulf for the irrationalist is a leap to faith, one which trails behind itself a critique of discursive thought as falsifying reality. Politically, irrationalism is tantamount to fascism.

As we have seen, Horkheimer is sympathetic to a critical analysis of discursive thought as the exclusive and basic form of knowledge, remote from the interferences of interests and nondiscursive orientations in the world, but his objection is *not* that concepts necessarily distort reality by distancing one from one's immediate experience of the sheer individuality of things (*BPSS* 232–3; *KT* 1, 136–7). Although he is often not very clear on the point, it seems that Horkheimer holds the weaker, and more plausible, view that discursivity can tend towards fixity of thought – that is, towards not being open to other possible ways of seeing things. Horkheimer does not accept the critique of technology that often goes hand in hand with irrationalism's attack on discursivity. From the fact that capitalism harnesses instrumental reasoning to bourgeois ideology it does not follow that there is not an important place for this sort of thought, if it is dialectically situated in the appropriate way. Although Horkheimer ends up closer to the more radical thesis he here disputes in virtue of his allegiance with Adorno in the 1940s, his view during this period is much closer to Habermas's early writings on technology.

Horkheimer is also critical of the radical skepticism that informs much irrationalist theory. In Horkheimer's view skepticism has had two great liberating and cosmopolitan periods, Hellenistic (e.g. the later Academy, Pyrrho) and sixteenth-century French (e.g. Montaigne, Bayle), where a new-found plurality of alternative ways to live and express life philosophically undercut dogmatic acceptance of mores inherited through single cultures. Skepticism has since become intolerant and conformist, in essence a vehicle for relativism and irony. The modern skeptic is not truly open and tolerant of other forms of life and thought, for modern skepticism is allied to a theory of high individualism that is conceived to be universal and which fosters and is fostered by a highly specific economic order based upon that conception of individuality. Modern skepticism is a form of nondialectical false consciousness, no matter how disdainfully high-minded: "The skeptics, who stand up against racial and other misguided doctrines without theory and purely in the name of doubt, are Sancho Panzas who dress themselves up as Don Quixotes" (*BPSS* 296; *KT*, II, 241).

Traditional versus critical theory

With the taxonomy worked out in the various essays leading up to "Traditional and Critical Theory" in hand, it is now possible to schematically represent the relationship of traditional to critical theory as follows. Traditional theory includes rationalist idealism and reductive materialism, wed as they are to universalistic nonhistoricism and to an instrumental conception of reason. The scientific model that it believes to have universal application across theoretical and historical boundaries, is, in fact, related to a very specific historical form of human organization – the economic form of capitalism constitutive of and expressed in bourgeois self-understanding. Certain kinds of socialism are scientistic enough to be included under this classification as well. Although irrationalism shares with rationalist idealism an appeal to transfiguration and with reductive materialism a passive, intuitionist account of experience, it is unique. Horkheimer neither counts it as "traditional" nor as "critical." Irrationalism tends towards noncapitalistic forms of economic organization, but ones that sacrifice critical individuality to unthinking and mythic absorption in the *Volk*. Critical Theory attempts to rescue from idealism a conception of reason as unified in its practical and theoretical employment, coupled with a dialectical and materialist account of human flourishing. The point upon which the rehabilitation turns is clearly Hegel, though Hegel tempered in a Kantian way. Marx is also pivotal, but not the Marx that can be made to slide into a form of materialism that joins hands with instrumental thought, but rather the "humanistic" Marx of the 1844 *Manuscripts*.

In the course of surveying the development of Horkheimer's early thought certain general methodological constraints upon Critical Theory emerge, having to do with reflexivity of social theory, its open-ended nature, and its views on the prospects for systematicity. There are of course many questions, both philosophical and social-scientific, about the internal workings of such a program. To conclude this section on Horkheimer, I turn briefly to one of these: the degree to which Horkheimer's formulation of Critical Theory is open to charges of relativism.

If it is the case that both theory and its objects are always mutually related in the way Horkheimer takes them to be, and are defeasible upon change in historical circumstance, what sort of critical purchase can they have and what account can they provide of the objectivity of their objects? We saw that Horkheimer cannot draw his account of truth directly from Hegel, since the relativity of truth to historical circumstance for Hegel is mitigated teleologically. Without some sort of end or ends towards which historically constituted self-understanding can be said to progress, critique seems to come unmoored from any fixed standard and it is hard to see how there might be any progress at all towards the sort of social freedom Horkheimer so values. It seems that early Horkheimer is satisfied to deny any absolute conception of truth and to affirm that truth is relative to historical and conceptual circumstance. And if Horkheimer rejects any idealizing of absolute truth (as covert transfiguration) as well, it would seem that he rules out even an ideal asymptotic convergence on truth. Does this require giving up on the objectivity of criticism and on any idea of truth? Horkheimer does not think so; to think that one must choose between accepting the idea of a final, eternal truth and accepting the idea that everything has merely "subjective validity" is to embrace a false dilemma (CT 183–4; KT I, 236–7). Critical standards that are relative to historical contexts can be nonetheless objective – in fact, for Horkheimer, this "internal objectivity" is the only sort of objectivity there is.

There have been subtle attempts to defend versions of relativism against claims of nonobjectivity in recent ethical and political philosophy, but Horkheimer never really undertakes this necessary task. Later, when he breaks bread with Nietzsche and comes under the influence of Adorno's expressly negative version of immanent critique, the problem of relativism is even more pressing. In the essays of the 1930s purely immanent critique stands in tension with Horkheimer's hopes for social progress. Indeed, to say that there is "tension" between his theory of truth and his practical theory is a vast understatement. Horkheimer is apt to speak of truth in entirely practical terms as that which promotes the overall rationality of society or as what is politically progressive. But of course determining what is "more rational" or "progressive" requires criteria. How one is to go about grounding such claims without an appeal to truth is not obvious and requires additional argument that Horkheimer never provides.

MARCUSE

Marcuse joined the Institute three years into Horkheimer's directorship in 1933, after having studied with Husserl and Heidegger in Freiburg, where he would have submitted his *Hegel's Ontology and the Foundation of a Theory of Historicity* as a habilitation thesis under Heidegger had not his political better judgment intervened. The Hegel book strongly shows the influence of Heidegger's analysis of historicity and the social concept of *Mitsein*, but even at this early point Marcuse argues that there is an insurmountable limitation to the social conception of *Existenzphilosophie* having to do with the basis for transformation of the leveled-down world of inauthenticity into a world in which human beings are free. Marcuse turns to Marx to complete the analysis, becoming perhaps the earliest instance of a philosophical type of the twentieth century – a thinker rooted in existentialism who attempts to accommodate Marx within it.

Although the influence of Heidegger is never entirely absent in the early Marcuse, after joining the Institute he moves much closer to Horkheimer. As is Horkheimer, Marcuse is committed to the idea of a continuing dialectic (*N* 86, 137; *MS* III, 84, 229), to a reciprocal relationship of theory and praxis (*N* 77; *MS* III, 76), and to the formation of an interdisciplinary hybrid of social science and philosophy (*N* 134–5; *MS* III, 227–9). In view of his attraction to Heidegger, it is interesting to note that the overwhelming emphasis that Marcuse places on labor in his essays of the 1930s makes him a more steadfast Marxist than Horkheimer. He also comes to take a more orthodox view of Hegel, one that is tolerant of the thesis of identity of subject with object. This means that Marcuse finds dialectical potential in preserving aspects of idealism that Horkheimer treats as transfiguring or utopian.

The three principal components of Marcuse's early conception of Critical Theory are (1) a distinction he makes between essence and appearance, (2) his account of "reason" and "imagination" as central critical capacities, and (3) his close connection of unalienated labor with happiness and pleasure.

Following Hegel, Marcuse holds that any particular form of human organization can be thought of in terms of its appearance as opposed to its essence. "Essence" is "formally" the "totality of the social process as it is organized in a historical particular epoch" (*N* 70; *MS* III, 69). Individual elements considered in isolation of the totality are "appearances" of it because treating them in a less than holistic or "total" way abstracts from their full meaningfulness. Only when considered in the light of an entire system of thought can discrete events and actions be understood correctly. The interconnection of the diverse elements of their lives (and thus what is driving and in some sense "determining" those lives) for the most part will not be reflectively available to agents immersed in a form of life. This is due to inadequate and underdeveloped representations of the structures involved from within the form of life itself, which representations distort and limit one's understanding of what is truly actual (i.e. the appearance) and what is possible (i.e. the essential, seen as supporting other possible and perhaps superior ways of life). The controlling idea is that Critical Theory pushes through what is inessential in any given social formation and reveals the potential in it for change. Obviously, this way of putting things has close ties to the Marxist distinction between superstructure and base, but Marcuse also thinks it charts the distinction between existentiell and existential understanding in Heidegger. Marcuse claims that "essence" is a historical concept, that is, that there is not one, unchanging essence that underpins all social life, but he does seem to court the idea that the formal structure of appearance/essence is invariable (*N* 74–5; *MS* III, 73–4).

Seeing potentiality in spite of actuality requires imagination or "fantasy." By this Marcuse does not mean the ability to think up extravagant counterfactual situations that are only marginally connected to dealing with the actual world. Marcuse's sense of a "possible world" is much closer to Heidegger's, where *possibility* is an existential and not a logical concept. Imagination allows the critical theorist to juxtapose a given "bad facticity" with what is better and possible, given the essence of the social form in question. This is very closely connected to the importance Marcuse gives to reason (*N* 135–6; *MS* III, 228–9) or to the ability to immanently criticize a given social order in terms of how adequately it measures up to the standards of rationality it presupposes. Imagination requires reason because criticism and cognitive distance is a precondition for and a spur to imagining things in a way that remains connected to present concerns.

The social status of happiness and pleasure is a recurring theme in Marcuse's work. His early approach to it distinguishes him from Horkheimer's treatment of the issue. The concept of alienated labor lies at the core of Marcuse's analysis of happiness, whereas Horkheimer holds that overemphasizing labor tends to valorize "instrumental" rationality expressed in consuming or mastering nature. Instrumental reason is not in itself a source of social oppression and alienation, although some forms of it, that is, capitalism, are. So, while Horkheimer argues for an abiding contrast between labor and happiness, Marcuse seeks their unity. He argues that traditional forms of hedonism preserve the important idea that individual happiness (*Glück*) plays a necessary part in ethical life but are compromised by theories of subjectivity that reduce happiness to the satisfaction of atomistic, egoistic desires. Besides constraining the understanding of what can count as happiness by limiting the sorts of desires whose satisfaction could qualify towards its realization, traditional hedonism also leaves no conceptual space for distinguishing between "true" and "false" pleasures (*N* 168; *MS* iii, 257). For Marcuse, happiness is the fulfilling of all the potentialities of the individual and freedom is the ability, in principle, to be so fulfilled. The potentialities of humans are more or less well developed depending upon the relative freedom that exists. Under present conditions, labor and true happiness do not often coincide. But if society is arranged to allow for the free production and distribution of goods according to need, labor will not be laborious; happiness comes uncoupled from capitalist consumption, and the seemingly intractable opposition of labor to happiness disappears (*N* 182; *MS* iii, 270). The problem with happiness, for Marcuse, is then just the problem of alienated labor, the cure for which is economic. This more orthodox Marxist account of change of consciousness through economic change of material conditions is not unique in the Institute at this time but is, again, quite unlike Horkheimer's and Adorno's much more "humanistic" approaches.

Marcuse writes that "all materialist concepts contain an accusation and an imperative" (*N* 86; *MS* iii, 84), linking negative critique to a demand for change. Like his other Frankfurt cohorts, Marcuse does not think that Critical Theory can prescribe what precise changes should take place. Its role is limited to displaying the relevant possibilities. But what can one hope for in the way of possibility? Marcuse is not clear on this point. There is a utopian strain in Marcuse's early thought that lessens in *Reason and Revolution* (1941) and then reasserts itself in a more pronounced way in the work of the 1950s and especially the 1960s – the time during which Marcuse is sometimes charged with or celebrated for ministering to "the children of Marx and Coca-Cola."

Compared with Horkheimer and Adorno, Marcuse's early thought has a pronounced tendency to seek absolute answers to philosophical and social problems. In practice, Marcuse hews to a very Hegelian conception of the progress of philosophy, according to which Kant is superceded without remainder by Hegel, that is married to an account of Marx's Hegel critique that concentrates on the most Hegelian aspects of Marx's own work, seamlessly "materializing" what was already almost materialistic enough. The importance of fairly unalloyed Hegelianism is apparent in many aspects of Marcuse's thought: the degree to which he endorses the Hegelian thesis of the identity of thought and object, his conception of the unity of reason, and his utopianism. Marx provides the dual service of translating Hegelian idealistic absolutes into materialistic ones and freeing the dialectic from teleological presuppositions. The latter point is telling. Whereas Horkheimer might exploit Kant's conception of regulative reason in conjunction with Marx to defeat Hegelian teleology, Marcuse is apt to treat Marx alone as definitive, rendering less complex Critical Theory's relationship to its philosophical roots.

ADORNO

Adorno's publication in the *Zeitschrift* during the 1930s is limited to four essays in the philosophy of music: two in the sociology of music, a collection of *aperçus* on Wagner, and an invective on swing jazz (written under the fitting pseudonym "Hektor Rottweiler"). Music was a central concern for Adorno throughout his life (he had briefly studied composition in Vienna with the composer Alban Berg) and his later conception of philosophical systematicity is avowedly musical, even "atonal."[19] Nevertheless, these early essays do not really contribute to the conceptual formation of early Critical Theory.

Adorno's early conception of Critical Theory is best gleaned from "The Actuality of Philosophy," a lecture he presented upon taking up a teaching position at Frankfurt in 1931. Coming only a year after Horkheimer's own inaugural lecture, "The Actuality of Philosophy" affirms many of Horkheimer's pronouncements but does so in ways that are distinctive of Adorno. As with Horkheimer, Adorno is concerned with the "end of philosophy" (AGS 1, 331) and the question of what sort of discipline will replace it. His answer is fully in agreement with Horkheimer. The replacement theory will be an interdisciplinary hybrid of dialectical materialism and social science that criticizes current cultural and political conditions in light of their historicity. Critique will have done its work by showing internal contradictions in the status quo; what particular changes are to take place in order to set the contradiction to rest are a matter of political action and not a subject for theoretical declamation. Such critique is unending, at least in the sense that the theorist always operates under the assumption that further critique is possible.

Adorno shapes his account of the task of Critical Theory around the problem of the demise of idealism. After providing a survey of the various philosophical developments of neo-Kantian idealism and *Lebensphilosophie* remarkably similar to Horkheimer's, Adorno turns to consider two reactions to the "idealist crisis": phenomenology and positivism. Adorno's views on phenomenology divide into his treatments of Husserl and Heidegger. Adorno claims that, as much as Husserl's nonpsychologism and denial of a theoretical place for the concept of a thing in itself indicates a turning away from classical idealism, Husserlian phenomenology is formed around the paradox of attempting to realize an objectivity that idealism denies by use of the very Cartesian categories fundamental to idealistic thought (AGS 1, 327). Run up against the wall of the failure of idealism made manifest in its extravagant theodical claims, Husserl returns full circle to Kant, recapitulating the idea that knowledge of the necessary structure of the world requires proper limitation on thought (in Husserl's case, by means of the phenomenological reduction).

This theme of Husserlian phenomenology as the last gasp of the "philosophy of the subject" is amplified in a book-length critical study of Husserl undertaken in 1934 when Adorno was an "advanced student" at Oxford.[20] In addition to discussing the strongly foundationalist and scientifically rigorous aspects of Husserl's thought that bring it into unlikely connection with positivism, Adorno also argues that the foundational concept of intentionality is politically suspect, a retreat of praxis alienated from its proper arena of concern (*AE* 55; *AGS* v, 61–2). Similar lessons are drawn from the importance given to the category of immediacy that is the goal of the first phenomenological reduction, with the additional charge that the alienated praxis typical of Husserl's phenomenology purchases its Cartesian foundation at the price of "transcendental xenophobia" in which the ego and its home culture have unassailable primacy (*AE* 222; *AGS* v, 223; see also *AE* 163–4, 196–7; *AGS* v, 167–8, 200).

Adorno's reaction to Heidegger, whom he views as the most threatening competitor to Critical Theory, is filtered through his critique of Kierkegaard, contained in his habilitation thesis *Kierkegaard: Construction of the Aesthetic*. Adorno analyzes Kierkegaard as an idealist as well and Heidegger as a follower. Treating Heidegger as Kierkegaard *réchauffé* is, tactically, very astute. For much of Heidegger's thought at this time is involved with diagnosing idealism as a form of "metaphysics" that none but Heidegger can resist.

As with Horkheimer and Marcuse, Adorno is drawn towards a version of Marxism that emphasizes continuity with Hegel.[21] Not surprisingly then, another polemical function of the Kierkegaard book is to rehabilitate Hegel by defusing the Kierkegaardian critique that was generally accepted at the time and which was especially prominent in Heidegger and his followers. While Kierkegaard is correct to criticize the unity of thought and being in Hegel, his own replacement for that enterprise appeals to the suspect idealist category of transcendence via the irrationalist appeal to immediacy. Adorno argues that Kierkegaard's view of the interior life of the subject "in truth" is a remnant of idealistic and romantic subjectivity. This claim is provocative because Kierkegaard is a stringent critic of romanticism, assigning it to the "aesthetic" sphere of existence and arguing that it degenerates into dandyism that is incapable of a stable orientation in life. But Kierkegaard treats the aesthetic sphere nonhistorically and nondialectically and is thus open to repeating its problematic character in his account of the allegedly superior stages of ethical and religious life.[22] The renunciation of society necessary to the content of a Kierkegaardian "true" subject is itself a socialized, bourgeois action that, far from being a more "concrete" improvement upon the abstract Hegelian idea of a subject, leaves the concept of "subject" all the more abstract (K 29, 73–8; AGS II, 45, 106–12). This outcome is absolutely general according to Adorno. Any attempt to move outside of idealism by nondialectically resolving one of its two central concepts – thought and being – to the other compounds abstraction (K 106; AGS II, 151–2). Although Heidegger is intent on denying the philosophy of subjectivity, he lapses into an attenuated version of it. As with Kierkegaard, Heidegger relies on the idea of a leap in his account of a committed life – not a leap into otherworldly faith, but rather one into this-worldly immediacy (AGS I, 329–30). While Heidegger pays lip service to the constitutive importance of history, his concept of historicity is mired in covert essentialism by conceiving of the structure of temporality as eternal (AGS I, 330), also a remnant of idealism.

Adorno writes that philosophy is distinguished from science in terms of their relative attitudes towards their findings. Science treats its results as "indestructible and static," subject to passing rigorous confirmation, whereas philosophy has a more skeptical and negative cast towards its conclusions. They are always "signs" (Zeichen) that require further "deciphering" (enträtseln):

Plainly put: the idea of science is research; that of philosophy is interpretation [Deutung]. In this remains the great, perhaps the eternal paradox: philosophy, ever and always and with the claim of truth, must proceed interpretively without ever possessing a sure key to interpretation: nothing more is given to it than fleeting, disappearing traces within the ciphers [Rätselfiguren] of what is and their wondrous entwinings. The history of philosophy is nothing other than the history of such entwinings. That is why it reaches so few "results," why it must always begin anew, and why it cannot do without the slightest thread which earlier times have spun, and which perhaps completes the literature that might transform the ciphers into a text. (AGS I, 334)

The first part of the distinction that Adorno is considering here may be understood as the difference between giving an explanation of a thing and interpreting it. Boyle's Law explains why my bicycle pump works, but it does not interpret it. The bicycle pump does not *mean* anything, when the question is one of its physical properties, although as a cultural artifact it may mean quite a lot. Unless one views the world in all its constituent parts as the product of an intent and as thus meaningful in virtue of that source, explanations will not take objects whose meanings (if they have any) figure in their explanation. But Adorno also does not think that Critical Theory is a theory of interpretation in the ordinary sense. Critical Theory does not study its objects with the aim of revealing meanings that are already there, independent of the interpretive process (ibid.). The objects of interpretation, as well as any particular interpretation of them, are always subject to further interpretation. To stop interpretation is to settle on a meaning, and Adorno equates this, in ways we have seen in Horkheimer, with transfiguration – with making life meaningful *qua* status quo and to that extent justifying it.

The influence of Walter Benjamin, whom Adorno had met through his friend and tutor Siegfried Kracauer in 1923, is decisive here. Both Benjamin and Adorno had studied Kant in depth and devoted their early work to developing a new form of Kantianism around a liberalized conception of "experience." Benjamin and Adorno reacted especially strongly against the so-called Marburg school of Kant scholarship that interpreted Kant's philosophy to be overwhelmingly concerned with providing the transcendentally necessary conditions upon the possibility of scientific knowledge or experience. Benjamin's early project was to argue for a very broad understanding of experience in general, including subliminal or unconscious elements (*Erfahrung*), over and against the experience of objects of conscious instrumentality, or more broadly, knowledge (*Erlebnis*). Adorno was especially impressed by Benjamin's notion of the "micrological" analysis of detailed phenomena according to a methodology that promised to preclude systematic preconception of the object of study, allowing the phenomema to emerge collectively with much of their singularity still intact.[23]

As part of his answer to the problem of a new Kantianism, Benjamin had worked out an idiosyncratic understanding of the philosophical legacy of Kant in German romanticism and joined it with neo-Platonic elements and mystical Jewish philosophy.[24] The capstone of his early writings, before his attempt to marry this romantic-Platonic-kabalistic conglomerate even more complexly with Marx, is his *Origin of German Play of Lamentation* (1928). In this text, copiously cited in both Adorno's 1931 lecture and the

Kierkegaard book, Benjamin develops his allegorical understanding of the significance of artworks (and by extension social products) by referring metaphorically to them as "constellations" (*Konstellationen*) or fragments whose structures are only revealed upon the works' dissolution under criticism (*OT* 27–56; *BGS* I.I, 207–37; *AGS* I, 335; see also *BPSS* 11; *HGS* III, 32; *BPSS* 182; *KT* I, 234). Deploying this idea, Adorno holds that the objects of social theory (and the theory itself as such an object) are best treated methodologically as historically constituted, theoretical constructs that chart from the interpretative vantage point of a theory at a given time the interconnection of elements of a projected social whole. The relevant idea of the whole here is not that of a closed system under laws, but rather an open-ended system of things whose relation to one another may change with changes in its interpretation. In sum, Adorno's interpretive procedure in the Kierkegaard book is to graft Benjamin's allegorical method to Hegelian dialectic. This is very close in form to what Adorno will later call "negative dialectic," which places a premium on thinking of the systematicity of the objects of social and philosophical thought on the models of artworks and argues for an open-ended dialectic in which skepticism about the stability of any system is always present.

The Kierkegaard book also announces another recurring motif in Adorno's work: its emphasis on the importance of philosophical style to content. Adorno is obviously drawn to Kierkegaard by this problem – both because Kierkegaard had very interesting ideas on the subject, and a practice based upon those ideas, and because it is Kierkegaard's style that Adorno sees as the point of attack that will eventually lead to a subversion of his account of subjectivity. With these issues in mind, *Kierkegaard: Construction of the Aesthetic* is written in an intentionally obscure style that reflects the kind of mosaic Adorno thinks proper to philosophy. It prefigures many of his later works, which are self-conscious exercises in embodying the movement of ideas in negative dialectic in a style of philosophical writing.

NOTES

1. Marx, *Early Political Writings*, ed. J. O'Malley (Cambridge: Cambridge University Press, 1994), p. 118, original in *Marx-Engels-Werke* (Berlin: Dietz, 1983), III, 7.

2. Horkheimer had studied Kant intensively, writing his habilitation thesis *Über Kants Kritik der Urteilskraft als Bindeglied zwischen theoretisher und praktischer Philosophie* (1925) on the theme of the unity of reason.

3. Kant also holds that reason's dialectic has a positive role in setting ideal ends for theoretical inquiry, but I cannot discuss this here.

4. The term derives from Hegel. See *Enzyklopädie*, §158. Zusatz.

5. Kant, *Critique of Pure Reason*, B167.

6. This term is associated with approaches to the epistemology of science – for example those of Norbert Hanson, Thomas Kuhn, and Paul Feyerabend – developed largely from within "traditional" philosophy of science in the late 1950s and early 1960s.

7. "Theory-laden" might mean simply that understanding the meaning of a word requires understanding it in the context of its theoretical use. And the thesis that observation is theory-laden need not mean that perceptual awareness is conceptually articulated. One might hold that observation is more than mere perception, involving extracting information for later judgment. But epistemologists have sometimes found it difficult to draw a line between that which is and that which is not conditioned by judgmental capacities. Presumably no one would want to deny that, at some level, cognitive agents come into nonconceptual contact with the world. But one may feel a need to qualify this by saying that, to the extent that objects can potentially figure in judgments or reports, object perception is already mediated in terms of indeterminate belief. Discursivity would then penetrate *experience* to its base and all perception would involve perception "as." This is the basis for the stronger thesis that what one sees is affected by one's theoretical beliefs; that is, that people with different beliefs may see different things.

8. On instrumental reason, see Roberts, chapter 3 below.

9. See, e.g., *The World as Will and Representation*, II, §19.

10. The only fully stable unit is the whole of the teleological progression of *Geist*, see *infra*.

11. I am not suggesting an account of Hegel where the controlling idea is what one might call "extrinsic-agent teleology," that is, that the teleological structure of *Geist* rests upon a conception of *Geist* acting to enforce an ends-oriented structure. Hegel's conception of teleology is better understood as a distinctive variant of Kant's notion of "intrinsic purposiveness," according to which teleological direction of entities is understood as a systematic property without external "guidance." On this understanding, the forms of consciousness that each partly and cumulatively constitute the whole (*Geist*) are progressive because

part of an organized system. This is admittedly difficult to see in the case of Hegel, since the parts of the organized whole themselves are agent-entities.

12. Horkheimer had developed this view of Hegel quite early. See "Ein neuer Ideologiebegriff?" (1930) *HGS* II, 233–4.

13. To say that dialectic is ongoing and unending is *not* to say that social science is inherently progressive. Progress is possible and desirable according to Horkheimer, but that does not happen by necessity, it depends on highly contingent matters having to do with what historical possibilities are present at a particular time. Thus Horkheimer writes in notes from the period 1926–30, collected and later published under the title *Dämmerung*, that failure to "prove" socialism (i.e., that it is the necessary successor to capitalist breakdown) is no reason for "pessimism" (*HGS* II, 342).

14. Horkheimer treats pragmatism as a close relative of positivism and, by extension, of vitalism – all inherently capitalist. Eventually he is concerned to address its relation to Marx as well. Marxist revolutionary politics and pragmatism were conjoined in the (early) influential work of Sidney Hook. This marriage of Marx and pragmatism made it imperative to redouble the criticism of pragmatism, since Horkheimer thinks this just a watered-down American form of orthodox Marxism. See *ER* 40–57, 58–91. A good discussion is Martin Jay, *The Dialectical Imagination: A History of the Frankfurt School and the Institute of Social Research, 1923–1950* (New York: Little, Brown, 1973), pp. 83–5.

15. The primary document of the "humanistic" Marx is the *Philosophic and Economic Manuscripts* (1844). An incomplete version, which Marx composed in Paris between April and August 1844, was translated into Russian and published in Moscow in 1927. They first appeared in German in 1932. Discovery and publication of the *Manuscripts* added the weight of historical provenance to the mostly speculative emphasis on Marx's early humanism, vindicating especially Lukács's prescient *History and Class Consciousness* (1923). Lenin had proposed a reassessment of Marx in light of Hegel's conception as well, but his work was not readily available outside of Russia.

16. Comte argues that human behavior obeys laws that are just as strict as natural laws. This is unacceptable to Horkheimer because Comte treats human behavior as a brute fact that is strictly divorced from theory. As is true of logical empiricism, positivist social science will not be emancipating because it takes this fact to be "well-formed," that is, not as distorted by pressures of social servitude. Moreover, and this becomes something of a leitmotif in early and middle period Critical Theory, Horkheimer claims that Comte's positivism spills over into

an irrationalist, faith-driven ersatz religiosity. This is a real feature of Comte's later thought, showing its intellectual roots in the English Romanticism of Coleridge and Carlyle, and allows Horkheimer to intimate a connection of reduction to faith. Horkheimer also connects the strict limitation of science under positivism to the development of vitalism as a supplement to it (*CT* 39–40, 60–1; *KT* I, 60, 290–2; *BPSS* 196; *KT* I, 251–2).

17. See Hans-Joachim Dahms, *Positivismusstreit: Die Auseinandersetzung der Frankfurter Schule mit dem logischen Positivismus, dem amerikanishen Pragmatismus und dem kritischen Rationalismus* (Frankfurt am Main: Suhrkamp, 1994).

18. Cf. Marcuse's comments at *N* 76; *MS* III, 75. He agrees with Horkheimer that logical empiricism does not give an adequate account of even natural science. As to its lack of a tangible connection of interest to cognition, Marcuse thinks Neurath's views only lead him to a mild recognition of theoretical underdetermination, which (1) still treats all fact as "the same" or "identical" and (2) limits the sort of interests that might impinge on cognitive judgment to the personal evaluations of individual scientists.

19. For instance, the title of the posthumous *Aesthetic Theory* should be understood to mean both a theory of a subject matter "aesthetics" and a theory that is itself "aesthetic."

20. The work was first published in revised form in 1956 as *Toward a Metacritique of the Theory of Knowledge*. Because it contains elements of Adorno's later critique of instrumental reason and identity thinking, one must take care in using the text as an indication of Adorno's views in the 1930s.

21. Although the category of social labor is important for him, Marx perhaps figures less directly in Adorno's thought than in any other major Frankfurt School theorist. So tangential is Marx at the end of Adorno's career that even the rather tepid socialism of Habermas was seen as a turn back to Marx.

22. This criticism is very similar to Lukács, "The Dashing of Form against Life: Søren Kierkegaard and Regine Olsen" (1909), collected in *Soul and Form*, trans. A. Bostock (Cambridge, Mass.: MIT Press, 1974).

23. Less impressive to Adorno was Benjamin's mysticism, which was an ongoing source of contention between the two. See chapter 2 below.

24. The extent of the importance of Jewish mysticism for Benjamin is debated. Benjamin at times disclaimed serious interest in kabalistic scholarship to his friend, the great Judaicist Gershom Scholem, and in fact Benjamin was not very interested in mysticism based in specifically religious texts. His primary orientation was always toward the

expression of esoteric truth by means of *art* and his historical interests were firmly rooted in German *Geistesgeschichte* and especially
the history of aesthetic theory. Nevertheless, Benjamin was keen for
reports of Scholem's own ground-breaking scholarship and apparently
insisted that no one could understand the very difficult preface to his
Trauerspiel book without knowledge of Kabala. See Gershom Scholem,
Walter Benjamin – Geschichte einer Freundschaft (Frankfurt am Main:
Suhrkamp, 1975), pp. 157–8.

2   Benjamin, Adorno, and the decline of the aura*

In 1931, three years after the publication of *The Origin of German Tragic Drama*, the obscure masterpiece that he had intended as his habilitation thesis, Walter Benjamin wrote about it to the Swiss editor, Max Rychner:

[W]hat I did not know at the time of its composition became more and more clear to me soon after: that, from my very particular position on the philosophy of language, there exists a connection – however strained and problematic – to the viewpoint of dialectical materialism.[1]

The location of that connection – whether, indeed, it can be said to exist at all – remains deeply problematic. Nor should this be in the least surprising. What could be further removed from what one would normally understand by "materialism" than Benjamin's early writings, with their predilection for mystical theories of language and unblushingly antiscientific metaphysics? To put them together with the ideas of Marx and Engels can only, it would seem, undermine the latter: the connection appears at all plausible only if Marxism, its scientific pretensions notwithstanding, rests upon a mystical view of the world.

Not the least complexity – but not the least interest – in the dispute over the nature of Benjamin's relation to Marxism is that it involves just as much the question: what is Marxism? – a scientific materialism in the spirit of nineteenth-century natural science, a quasi-Hegelian eschatology, or what? It is not, though, just Marxism's inner tensions – ambiguities, to be more blunt – which have made Benjamin's relationship to it so controversial. The intellectual issues are themselves, in turn, almost inextricably entangled with Benjamin's own personal and political circumstances.

Successful, it seems, only in sabotaging whatever alternative prospects were offered to him, Benjamin was never in a position to pursue the life of independent scholarship for which alone he regarded himself as suited. Conflicts with his family, money troubles, and political upheavals were to disrupt his plans repeatedly. One effect of this has been to create an image of Benjamin (like Kafka, whom he so much admired) as a helpless victim, a kind of frail and exotic butterfly blown on the gales of Europe between the wars. One should treat this with a considerable degree of caution, however. It is true that Benjamin was, indeed, helpless in many ways – incapable, apparently, of even preparing a cup of coffee for himself. But, at least where his work was concerned, he was self-assured, even calculating. Nor was he ever the withdrawn, otherworldly figure that his fascination with the forgotten byways of intellectual history might lead one to imagine. From his schooldays he showed a strong commitment to radical political activity. Though it was, no doubt, his love affair with Asja Lacis, the Soviet communist whom he met on Capri, which brought him to think more seriously about Marxism than before, there is no reason at all to suppose that even that forceful personality could have manipulated Benjamin's work into a direction which he himself did not want it to take.

His financial difficulties were frequently to force Benjamin to leave aside cherished projects in order to try to support himself by his pen, and – which is particularly confusing as one now comes to reconstruct his ideas – also led him to try to present his more serious work in such a light as would, he felt, appeal most to potential sponsors of it. (In this he proved naïve, however; very few such hopes bore fruit, and, throughout the 1920s and 1930s, Benjamin's finances veered between the precarious and the desperate.)

Working on his own left Benjamin heavily dependent for intellectual companionship on three friends, all major figures in their own right: Gershom Scholem, Bertolt Brecht, and Theodor Adorno, and the relationship to these three adds a further level of complication to the question of Benjamin's Marxism. Inevitably, it has been their perspectives – above all, those of Scholem and Adorno, the devoted guardians of Benjamin's literary legacy and tireless promoters of his reputation – which have dominated later interpretations. Yet, genuine and close as his relationship was with all three men, it did not prevent Benjamin from preserving a certain intellectual distance, and even, at times, playing one off against the other. What is more, Benjamin knew well that all three had reservations about his Marxism – reservations that, of course, will only have increased his innate caginess.

Brecht and Scholem – opposed to each other in every other way imaginable – were equally dismissive of the idea of Benjamin as a Marxist. Scholem spoke of Benjamin's "Janus face"; he was, Scholem said, caught in theoretical vacillation: "torn between his sympathy for a mystical theory of language and the necessity, felt equally strongly, to combat it from within the framework of a Marxist world-view."[2] Brecht, typically, was even more trenchant. His comment on Benjamin's "Marxist" essay, "The Work of Art in the Age of its Mechanical Reproducibility": "All mysticism, from an attitude against mysticism. This is how the materialist view of history is adapted! It is quite dreadful."[3]

Whereas Brecht and Scholem reject the idea of Benjamin as a Marxist out of hand, Adorno's attitude is much less simple. It is true that Adorno did not take Benjamin's early ideas to be inherently incompatible with Marxism. To the contrary, he made the idea of their reconciliation his own. Yet he was by no means convinced by Benjamin's own attempts to bring the two together. In a series of letters written in the 1930s – responses, for the most part, to work which Benjamin had submitted to the *Journal for Social Research* – Adorno expressed the fear that Benjamin, under the influence of Brecht, was sacrificing the dialectical subtlety of his early work in favor of a simplistic "vulgar Marxism." In the face of this, Adorno took his own task to be "to hold your arm steady until Brecht's sun has sunk once more into exotic waters,"[4] his aim to reinforce the theological element in Benjamin's writing; only then, he believed, would the social dimension of Benjamin's theory develop its full scope and power: "A restoration of theology, or, better yet, a radicalization of the dialectic into the glowing heart of theology" would at the same time, Adorno argued "have to mean the utmost intensification of the social-dialectical, indeed economic, theme."[5]

Adorno's passionate engagement with Benjamin's work was, notoriously, to become the source of much bitterness. As the German New Left rediscovered Benjamin in the 1960s, suspicions were raised that Adorno had used Benjamin's financial dependence on the Institute for Social Research and his subsequent control over access to

Benjamin's unpublished writings to promote that side of Benjamin's work which was most congenial to his own ideas. Exaggerated though many of these accusations were, there can be no doubt that Adorno's intellectual relations with Benjamin were marked with something of the intensity (and difficulty) of those between master and disciple. To write, as Adorno once did to Benjamin, claiming to speak as "the advocate of your own intentions"[6] cannot have made his criticisms any easier to bear.

Adorno placed his chief hopes on *The Arcades Project* (*Passagenwerk*) which Benjamin worked on for the last thirteen years of his life, but whose fragments were only published in the 1980s. Taking as its starting point the "latent mythology" of Parisian urban architecture, *The Arcades Project* was to provide an *Urgeschichte*, a "fundamental history" of nineteenth-century culture. What Benjamin left behind him, however, is little more than a sketch pad: a set of observations, quotations, and reader's notes, with nothing to show how these elements would have been woven into the form of the final work. Thus we cannot now tell whether Adorno was justified in maintaining what he called his "*Passagenorthodoxie*" except in relation to their other writings. In the remainder of this chapter I shall argue, first, that there are important continuities between Benjamin's early and his later thought, and, second, that, whatever the verdict on the character of the personal relations between Benjamin and Adorno, there was, indeed, a substantial and significant intellectual disagreement between them, the nature of which Adorno was not fully aware of, either at the time or later.

I

Most important of the continuities between Benjamin's early and mature thought is his allegiance to a distinctive form of Kantian philosophy. He enunciates this first in an early essay (written as a twentieth birthday present for Scholem), "On the Programme of the Philosophy to Come." Here Benjamin argues that Kant's philosophy is to be accepted, but criticized. What is to be accepted, he thinks – and this, I believe, is a matter on which he never changed his mind – is the fundamental turn given to philosophy by Kant; what Kant himself calls his "Copernican revolution" – a turn away from purporting to investigate the nature of reality, towards an investigation of our

experience of that reality.[7] Yet, fundamental though Benjamin considers Kant's turn to the question of experience to be, he is critical
of what he takes to be the restricted conception of experience – as
if to experience were simply to catalogue sense-images under formal, general rules – which Kant himself presupposes. This critical
encounter with Kant leads to what Benjamin proclaims to be contemporary philosophy's prime task: "to undertake the foundation
of a higher conception of experience, under the auspices of Kantian
thought" (*SW1* 102; *BGS* 11.1, 160): Scholem, in his touching and
revealing memoir of Benjamin, recalls a conversation from that time
in which Benjamin explained his point more vividly:

He spoke of the breadth of the concept of experience which this meant,
and which, according to him, included the mental and psychological links
between man and the world in areas not yet reached by knowledge. When
I made the point that, in that case, the mantic disciplines would be legitimately included in this conception of experience, he replied with an extreme
formulation: A philosophy which does not include the possibility of divina-
tion from coffee-grounds cannot be true.[8]

Thus, even at his most mystical and apparently antiscientific, Benjamin's chief concern is Kantian; that is to say, he wants to articulate
the distinctiveness of certain kinds of experience – the allegorical
world of the *Trauerspiel*, for example, or the struggle against myth
in Greek tragedy – which a scientifically oriented culture dismisses
or takes to be insignificant. But this does not mean that their claims
must be treated as cognitively valid; the experiences are important
in their own right, not as alternatives to scientific knowledge.

The emphasis on the concept of experience is the key to Benjamin's relation to Marxism, for it is the means by which he confronts
a question basic, not only to Marxism, but to the whole tradition of
cultural history. It is the question of what connects different areas
of a culture, allowing us to see a common identity in their apparent diversity. In the German tradition it has led, as Ernst Gombrich
has put it, to "Hegelianism without Hegel" – attempts to preserve
the Hegelian idea of cultural unity emanating from a single center
without recourse to the metaphysics of speculative idealism. In the
context of Marxism, however, the problem arises in the specific form
of the relation between "base" and "superstructure": the nature of
the connection between the economic life of mankind as producers

of material goods and the ideological realm in which, according to Marx, economic life is both reflected and transfigured.

II

In a highly significant fragment from *The Arcades Project*, Benjamin proposes his own answer to this problem of the nature of the determination of the ideological superstructure:

At first sight it seems as though Marx only wanted to establish a causal connection between superstructure and base. But his remark that the ideologies of the superstructure mirror relationships in a false and distorted manner goes beyond this. The question is, in fact: if, in a certain sense, the base determines the thought- and experience-content of the superstructure, yet this determination is not a simple mirroring, how – leaving aside the question of its causal origin – is it to be characterized? As its expression. The economic conditions under which society exists come to expression in the superstructure. (*A* 392; *BGS* v.1, 495)

The question of Benjamin's relation to Marxism can thus be brought into focus in the form of a specific problem: how the existence of such an "expressive" relationship between base and superstructure can be accommodated within the framework of his conception of experience. The solution Benjamin proposes emerges most perspicuously in a short piece, "On the Mimetic Faculty," written in 1933. Here, once again, Benjamin pursues his challenge to the flattened, Enlightenment conception of experience. Even in the modern world, he claims (and Freud is just as important a witness to this as Marx) human beings show a disposition to structure their experience according to what he terms "non-sensible resemblances" – resemblances, that is, in which similarity is not just a matter of "mapping" or visible correspondence, and which may appear bizarre or even occult when measured against the standards of a worldview for which that is the only kind of experience imaginable.

Scholem (for whose reaction to the piece Benjamin waited with particular eagerness) regarded it as another instance of the Janus-face – a return (welcome to his mind) to the mystical stance of the early writings; it lacked, he said, "even the slightest hint of a materialist view of language."[9] But that is not how Benjamin himself saw things. Admittedly, the essay is quite at odds with modern scientific reductionism. But there is another sense in which the intentions behind "On the Mimetic Faculty" might reasonably be described as materialist: what the essay attempts to do is to undermine a perspective from which certain phenomena must either be dismissed, or, if they are acknowledged, treated as in some way occult or transcendent. Nowhere does Benjamin come closer to the ideas of Wittgenstein than here. Only because the "enlightened scientific" conception is taken as a norm are certain experiences made to seem supernatural; they are treated as such just because they go beyond the presupposed scientific perspective.

Benjamin drew parallels between this essay and an essay of Freud's on telepathy (from internal evidence, it seems likely that this essay now forms the second of Freud's *New Introductory Lectures on Psychoanalysis*). What impressed Benjamin was that, in this essay, Freud, like himself, takes seriously a phenomenon often dismissed; not treating telepathy as something occult, but seeing it, rather, as a type of perception, operating at a level not normally appreciated or acknowledged.

Mimetic experience is what allows us to identify "correspondences" between different areas of social life (see *A* 418; *BGS* v.1, 526) and makes plausible the idea of an expressive relationship between economy and ideology. The expressive relationship obtains because similarities have been transmitted by society's members (without, of course, their being aware of it) at the deepest, collective levels of their experience. The task of the social theorist is to reawaken that experience from its sedimentations and incrustations. Phenomena which seem the most dissonant and obscure – the interior exteriors of the *passages* themselves, the passion for roulette, the vogue for panoramas – may turn out to be the most revelatory. What Novalis once said of poetry is also true of Benjamin's *Urgeschichte*: the more personal, peculiar, temporal a phenomenon, the closer it may stand to the center.

Needless to say, this approach makes the concept of experience bear an enormous weight; there is, inevitably perhaps, a certain element of circularity. The "unseen affinities," referring, as they do, to a subterranean level of awareness, are not such as, immediately and unambiguously, to strike the uninstructed observer; and yet it is their existence that provides Benjamin's concept of experience with its only possible verification. Proof, thus, necessarily makes reference to the reader's own intuition – a point which Benjamin acknowledges in language quite strikingly reminiscent of Wittgenstein: "Method of this work: literary montage. I have nothing to say – only to show" (*A* 460; *BGS* v.1, 574). Yet there is always the worry that what are shown as the latent significance of cultural phenomena are, in point of fact, no more than subjective associations, made plausible by the shared political commitment of author and reader.

Furthermore, the necessary reference to intuition places a severe limit on how far Benjamin's "cultural Marxism" can be given expression in terms of the sort of scientifically oriented discursive theory characteristic of Marx's own "economic Marxism." If Benjamin's writing often seems "impressionistic" or unsystematic, then this is because its central purpose – the eliciting of correspondences – cannot be carried out in a methodical fashion. Hence, it is hard to see how he could, in principle, have responded to Adorno's criticism that his treatment of his material was insufficiently theoretical: "the work is located at the cross-roads between magic and positivism. This place is bewitched. Only theory can break the spell: your own fearless, good speculative theory."[10]

III

To appreciate fully the kind of theory Adorno is advocating – and the distance which separates it from Benjamin's own enterprise – one must compare the two men's understanding of one of Benjamin's key conceptions: the concept of the *aura*.

Benjamin introduces this concept originally as a way of identifying that quality of numinousness, traditionally acknowledged to be characteristic of the authentic work of art. As he writes in "The Work of Art in the Age of its Mechanical Reproducibility": "We define the aura of [a natural object] as the unique phenomenon of a distance, however close it might be. If, while resting on a summer afternoon, you follow with your eyes a mountain range on the horizon, or a branch which casts its shadow over you, you experience the aura of those mountains, of that branch" (*I* 224–5; *BGS* 1.2, 479).

So, for Benjamin, the aura is, in the first place, a quality of our experience of objects, not necessarily restricted to the products of artistic creation. In the case of the work of art, however, this exalted quality (what Benjamin calls its "cult-value") is closely tied to the

religious or quasireligious element in art – a remnant of that association between art and religion characteristic of premodern society.

However, the "desacralising" processes of modern civilization –
the development of industrial capitalism and the attendant rise of
the masses – have, hand in hand with the purely technical fact of the
increasing mechanical reproducibility of the artwork itself, diminished human beings' power to see and respond to this quality. Thus,
the *uniqueness* of the work of art becomes increasingly questionable,
and leads to the decline of its cultic function:

[The contemporary decay of the aura] rests on two circumstances, both of
which are related to the increasing significance of the masses in contemporary life. Namely, the desire of contemporary masses to bring things "closer"
spatially and humanly, which is just as ardent as their bent towards overcoming the uniqueness of every reality by accepting its reproduction. (*I* 225;
BGS I.2, 479–80)

At first sight this may appear as simply a Marxist version of the
conventional conservative lament for the erosion of high culture.
Thus it is important to emphasize that Benjamin does not *disapprove*
of this desacralising process. Given that the auratic values of uniqueness and authenticity were themselves, in fact, a perceptual legacy
from the work of art's cultic function, it follows, for Benjamin, that
their elimination will open the way to a political form of art, a transition which he welcomes: "[F]or the first time in world history,
mechanical reproduction emancipates the work of art from its para-
sitical dependence on ritual" (*I* 226; *BGS* I.2, 482). Benjamin fails to
make clear, however, what this political form of art might amount
to, and it is on this point that Adorno's objection to his analysis is
first raised. On one level, the objection is that Benjamin's dismissal
of the aura is too extreme: open as the traditional work of art is
to criticism, to sweep aside its auratic qualities entirely leaves no
basis for any distinction between art and propaganda. As Adorno
was, much later, to put it in his *Aesthetic Theory*: "The deficiency
of Benjamin's grandly conceived *theory of reproduction* remains that
its bipolar categories do not allow differentiation between the conception of art which has been fundamentally *disideologised* and the
abuse of aesthetic rationality for mass-exploitation and domination"
(*AT* 56; *AGS* VII, 90).

There is considerably more at stake here, however, than Adorno's
preference for Schoenberg over Brecht; it is the attitude which

Adorno takes to idealist aesthetics – and the transformation which he believes to be necessary to make the transition to a materialist perspective – which provides the key to his theoretical disagreement with Benjamin. To understand its basis, it is necessary to go back to the connection that Adorno takes to exist between Benjamin's concept of the aura and the German Idealists' characterization of art in terms of what they called *schöner Schein*. This apparent connection is asserted in the clearest possible terms by Adorno's pupil and collaborator Rolf Tiedemann (the editor of the collected works of both Benjamin and Adorno). Tiedemann writes:

The later, materialistic writings of Benjamin give a sociological derivation of the aura, perceiving in it "the transposition of a response common in human relationships to the relationship of the inanimate or natural object and man." Aura shows itself as the ideological investment [*Belehnung*] of the reified and alienated, with the capacity of "opening its gaze." At the same time, the "beautiful semblance" [*schöner Schein*], as ascribed to art by idealist aesthetics, rests on auratic *Schein*.[11]

Schein (which means both "semblance" and "sheen") is the identifying characteristic of fine art in the idealists' view: "the beautiful has its life in *Schein*," as Hegel puts it.[12] *Schein* is an index of art's characteristic as an epiphany, a mode of manifestation of truth – the *logos* underlying reality which Hegel calls the Idea: "art has the task of presenting the Idea for immediate intuition in sensible form."[13] Art *presents* the truth; it does not, that is to say, represent or, in some way, stand in place of it. It is, rather, like an *ikon*, a channel or a window through which to have access to what is universal and transcendent. This means that, ontologically (in their manner of being), works of art are not simply self-identical. The work of art also "points beyond itself," not by relating to a well-defined and specific further meaning, but by evoking what is transcendent in the shifting, unspecific form of *Schein*. In this sense, the work of art is a *symbol* of transcendence. Goethe, who was a pioneer of this theory, puts it as follows: "The objects presented [in authentic, symbolic art] appear to stand independently and are, again, most deeply significant, and this in virtue of the ideal which ever brings a universality with it. *If the symbolic utters anything apart from the presentation, then it does so in indirect fashion.*"[14]

For idealists, such authentic, symbolic art bears an intrinsic meaning, and stands in contrast to allegorical art, which they understand as an artificial way of importing meaning into art by means of life-less conventions. (Benjamin, of course, had polemicized against this dismissal of allegorical art in his *Origin of German Tragic Drama*; allegory was not conventional in expression, but the expression of convention.) This set of doctrines was developed in Germany, prin-cipally by Goethe and Schelling; it was, however, to become widely influential in nineteenth-century aesthetics. Coleridge, for example, presents a very orthodox – not to mention derivative – version of the theory in the following terms:

Now an Allegory is but a translation of abstract notions into a picture-language which is itself nothing but an abstraction from objects of the senses; the principal being more worthless even than the proxy, both alike unsub-stantial, and the former shapeless to boot. On the other hand a Symbol (ὁ ἔστιν ἀεὶ ταυτηγόρικον) is characterized by a translucence of the Special in the Individual or of the General in the Especial or of the Universal in the General. Above all by the translucence of the eternal through and in the temporal. It always partakes of the Reality which it renders intelligible; and while it enunciates the Whole abides itself as a living point in that Unity, of which it is the representative.[15]

For Hegel, however, it is just that duality between finite and infi-nite which is art's limitation. Being limited to the sensible, art is inadequate, to the extent that the truth expressed in it lacks full clarity or self-awareness: "Only a certain sphere and level of truth is capable of being presented in the element of the work of art," he writes.[16] As a consequence, as he puts it in a famous expression: "Thought and reflection have lifted themselves up above fine art."[17]

IV

Returning now to Adorno, it is important to note that his aesthetics has several crucial features in common with the idealist theory just described. He believes that authentic art does indeed have this qual-ity of "pointing beyond itself," and he agrees, too, that this is a form of manifestation of *Geist* (or Spirit). He writes: "That by which works of art, as they become appearance, are more than what they are: that is their Spirit" (*AT* 86; *AGS* VII, 134). What is more (although read-ers of Adorno have sometimes failed to appreciate the fact), Adorno shares Hegel's criticism of the limitation, which its sensible form imposes on art; it requires a higher, theoretical form to elucidate its truth-content: "[the truth-content of works of art] can only be attained by philosophical reflection" (*AT* 128; *AGS* vii, 193). Hence, the work of art's character as *Schein*, according to Adorno, is, at once, both true and false; it creates the illusion that the aesthetic quality of the work of art is a property without relation to nonaesthetic reality, but, at the same time (paradoxical though it may seem) it is what connects the work of art to a broader sphere of social meaning: "*Geist* is not simply *Schein*. It is also truth. It is not only the fraudulent image of an independent entity but also the negation of all false independence" (*AT* 108; *AGS* vii, 165–6). Thus, one could summarize Adorno's criticism of idealism as that, for him, it is not so much the structure of idealist aesthetics which is mistaken as its reference; the Idealists misunderstand the nature of *Geist* in imagining it to be original and independent. What, for Adorno, is necessary in order to submit idealist aesthetics to a "passage to materialism" is to reidentify *Geist*, to decipher it as a form of social labor: "*Geist* is no isolated principle but one moment in social labour – that which is separated from the corporeal" (*H* 23; *AGS* v, 270).

The idealist theory of *Geist*, thus, does not represent a simple illusion but is, rather, an accurate reflection of a certain form of social reality – one ruled by the division between mental and manual labor. The structure it describes really exists; the mistake is to ascribe its effects to the operation of a Neo-Platonic World-Spirit: "The World-Spirit exists; but it is no such thing," he writes in the *Negative Dialectic* (*ND* 304; *AGS* vi, 298).

The purpose of a philosophical aesthetics is, by its reflective activity, to "save" the *Schein* of works of art through the theoretical reconstruction of the sedimented layers of *Geist*'s activity:

no work of art has its content other than by the *Schein* in its own form. The [central part] of aesthetics would, thus be the salvation of the *Schein*, and the emphatic justification of art, the legitimation of its truth, depends on this salvation. (*AT* 107; *AGS* vii, 164)

Schein is not, as Benjamin would have it, to be eliminated. Whatever its associations with the cultic functions of the work of art is, *Schein* retains a progressive element, Adorno claims: "Magic itself, when emancipated from its claim to be real, is an element of enlightenment; its *Schein* desacralises the desacralised world. That is the dialectical ether in which art today takes place" (*AT* 58; *AGS* VII, 93).

In short, Adorno's aesthetics – indeed, I would argue, his entire philosophy – is based on a transformation, by means of the Marxist concept of social labor, of the idealist doctrine of *Geist*, and it is this which provides the intellectual substance behind his criticism of Benjamin. A letter written to Benjamin in 1940 was to make this crystal-clear.

You write in *Baudelaire* . . . "To perceive the aura of an appearance means to invest it with the ability to raise its gaze." This differs from earlier formulations by the use of the concept of *investment*. Is it not an indication of that aspect which, in Wagner, I made fundamental to the construction of phantasmagoria, namely, the moment of human labour. Is not the aura, perhaps, the trace of the forgotten human element in the thing, and does not therefore this form of forgetting relate to what you see as experience? One is almost tempted to go so far as to see the foundation in experience, underlying the speculations of Idealism, in the endeavour to retain this trace – in those things, indeed, which have become alien.[18]

This letter – characteristic in the manner of its attempt to lead Benjamin back towards Adorno's own ideas – gives expression to the two central elements in Adorno's theory that I have stressed: the association of the aura with the idealist doctrines of *Schein* and of *Geist*; and the transformation (but not the wholesale rejection) of those doctrines via the concept of social labor.

Adorno himself certainly considered the letter to be of major theoretical significance, since he reproduced it in a collection he published called *Über Walter Benjamin*. But even more illuminating, in my view, is Benjamin's reply, written only months before his death (though that letter Adorno did not reproduce), for in it Benjamin quite clearly and explicitly rejects this proposal of Adorno's:

But if, indeed, it should be the case that the aura is a matter of a "forgotten human element," then not necessarily that which is present in labour. The tree or the bush which are invested are not made by men. It must be a human element in things, which is *not* endowed by labour. On this I would like to take my stand.[19]

What this letter makes plain is that Benjamin, at least, was aware that he and Adorno had adopted quite different answers to the problem of the identity of cultures in their apparent diversity: for Adorno, it is social labor which – articulating itself like Hegel's *Geist* – produces a not always apparent unity between economic and noneconomic spheres of social reality. For Benjamin, it is the system of *correspondences*, the "non-sensible similarities" to which individuals respond without being aware of it, which gives expression to economic life in noneconomic reality. The conclusion must be that Adorno (and his followers) are wrong to read Benjamin in terms of the categories of Hegelian Marxism: these are incompatible with his theory and, as can be seen, he clearly rejects them.

V

What, then, of the decline of the aura? If, from Adorno's Hegelian-Marxist perspective, the doctrine of the aura is to be read as corresponding to the idealist concept of *Schein*, it follows that the disintegration of the aura implies the loss of art's potential for intrinsic meaning. So the *political* art, with which Benjamin hopes auratic art will be replaced, can, it would appear, be no more than instrumental. It will be purely a means to generate the appropriate, "proletarian" emotional responses.

But from Benjamin's own point of view – "Marxist-Kantian," one might call it – the alternative is not so simple. There is a parallel here to his rehabilitation of allegory: Benjamin rejected the opposition between the "intrinsic" meaningfulness of symbolic art and the "conventional" meaning of allegory, for allegory, he claimed, "is not a technique of image-play, but *expression*, as language is expression, indeed, as script is" (*OT* 162; *BGS* 1.1, 339). Similarly, in "The Work of Art in the Age of its Mechanical Reproducibility" he ascribes a distinctive experiential quality (what he calls, in contrast to "cult value," "exhibition value") to postauratic art. Thus, for Benjamin, it seems that the work of art in the age of mechanical reproduction *can* escape what appears to Adorno as an exhaustive alternative: it need be neither *Schein* nor pure propaganda.

The dispute between Adorno and Benjamin is, of course, important for the light it sheds on two original, influential – and notoriously difficult – thinkers. But it has, I believe, a broader significance. One of the most fundamental problems of Marxist theory has been how to conceive the nature of the relationship between base and superstructure – the more so because Marx himself gives the issue so little sustained treatment. To claim only that the superstructure "corresponds" to the base in the sense that the superstructure is such as to maintain (or, at least, to reinforce the preservation of) the base – which is where many Marxists leave the matter – is simply not enough. Marxism must also give an acceptable account of how the base is able to exert this apparently miraculous power of generating (the conscious awareness of the individual members of society notwithstanding) the superstructure it needs. To take up the parallel between Marx and Darwin which has recently become fashionable again: what made Darwin's theory a scientific breakthrough was *not* his claim that species had characteristics that were adapted to their needs – that was, after all, the merest commonplace of eighteenth-century biology – but his proposal of natural selection as a convincing causal account of how those properties might come to be acquired. Does Marxism have an equivalent account of the genesis of functional relationships?[20]

Since Lukács's early writings, it has been accepted by many Marxists that the most promising way of responding to this gap in Marxist theory is by a return to the Hegelian inheritance of Marxism. No one, however (and this includes Lukács himself), has followed through this strategy with greater rigor and consistency than Adorno.

To the question of how social systems come to achieve purposes that go beyond (or, indeed, against) the purposes of individuals, the Hegelian Marxist replies that we must look beyond the individual subject to a broader, social subject whose ends (like Hegel's "cunning of reason") are realized by and through individuals. For Adorno, this social subject – here, again, the parallel with Hegel is in order – is a source, not just of collective action but of *meaning*. Thus, what the interpreter of cultural phenomena aims at is an objective property of the object in question – not, to be sure, in the way that Locke thought that size and shape were objective properties, but as emanating from a social process which is, ultimately, nothing less than the circular process of the self-reproduction of the social whole.

Adorno's theory has the attraction – and the questionableness – typical of Hegelian theories. On the one side, it offers a comprehensive solution to a number of very real problems. It does so, however, at a price – that of accepting a central, overarching concept of social labor which may, one fears, prove no less metaphysically overambitious than Hegel's concept of *Geist* itself. Benjamin, on the other hand, is more usually seen as a brilliant (if somewhat mystical) aphorist, rather than as the proponent of an original and consistent social theory. Yet, his Marxist Kantianism does, it seems to me, have claims to be treated as equal in originality and significance to the more familiar Marxist Hegelianism represented by Adorno. Not that one should underestimate its difficulties. One cannot deny that Adorno was right to argue that the objectivity of Benjamin's theory rests on the claim of a shared, prediscursive level of collective experience, and it may be that this historicized version of the Kantian transcendental subject will prove just as problematic as Adorno's attempt to invoke the concept of social labor as a surrogate of Hegel's *Geist*. But, if neither Marxist Hegelianism nor Marxist Kantianism, what then? Once again, the chasm between "base" and "superstructure" yawns.

NOTES

* This chapter is based on material contained in chapter 7 of Michael Rosen, *On Voluntary Servitude: False Consciousness and the Theory of Ideology* (Cambridge, Mass.: Polity Press and Harvard University Press, 1996).

 1. Walter Benjamin, *Briefe*, 2nd rev. edn, ed. G. Scholem and T. Adorno (Frankfurt am Main: Suhrkamp, 1978), II, 523. I have often modified existing English translations of German texts. All other translations are mine.

 2. Gershom Scholem, *Walter Benjamin – Geschichte einer Freundschaft* (Frankfurt am Main: Suhrkamp, 1975), p. 246.

 3. Bertolt Brecht, *Arbeitsjournal – 1938–1942* (Frankfurt om Main: Suhrkamp, 1973), p. 16.

 4. *Adorno–Benjamin Briefwechsel 1928–1940* (Frankfurt-on-Main: Suhrkamp, 1994), p. 175.

 5. Ibid., p. 143.

 6. Ibid., p. 74.

 7. *Critique of Pure Reason*, Bxvi.

 8. Scholem, *Benjamin – Geschichte einer Freundschaft*, p. 77.

 9. Ibid., p. 260.

 10. *Adorno–Benjamin Briefwechsel*, p. 368.

 11. Rolf Tiedemann, "Aura," in *Historisches Wörterbuch der Philosophie*, ed. J. Ritter (Basel: Schwabes, 1971), I, 651–52.

12. Hegel, *Aesthetics: Lectures on Fine Art*, trans. T. M. Knox (Oxford: Oxford University Press, 1975), I, 4–5.

13. Ibid., I, 72.

14. Goethe, "Über die Gegenstände der bildenden Kunst," in *Gedenkausgabe der Werke, Briefe und Gespräche*, ed. E. Beutler (Zurich: Artemis, 1954), XIII, 124.

15. Coleridge, *The Statesman's Manual* (1816), in *S. T. Coleridge: Collected Works*, ed. R. J. White (London: Routledge and Kegan Paul, 1972), VI, 30.

16. Hegel, *Aesthetics*, I, 9.

17. Ibid., I, 10.

18. *Adorno–Benjamin Briefwechsel*, pp. 418–19.

19. Benjamin, *Briefe*, II, 849.

20. I have dealt with this issue in detail in *On Voluntary Servitude*, especially in chapter 6.

3   The dialectic of enlightenment

Horkheimer and Adorno's book *Dialectic of Enlightenment* was written in the concluding months of the Second World War. It is comparable with contemporaneous works by other exiled German-speaking philosophers, notably Popper's *The Open Society and its Enemies* and Lukács's *The Destruction of Reason*, in being what Popper himself described as his "contribution to the war effort." Comparisons are instructive.

Karl Popper was a philosopher of science and a resident of London. *The Open Society* traces – from the vantage point of western democracy – the way in which a certain kind of intolerant (and hence "unscientific") thinking reproduces itself in totalitarian political philosophies: Plato is the ancient representative of this tradition, while its modern representatives Hegel and Marx are discerned, despite their superficial political differences, as the authors of twentieth-century dictatorships of all colors. Györky Lukács, by contrast, wrote as a resident of the Soviet Union and as a metaphysician committed to socialism. For him, Marx, and to a substantial extent Hegel as well, were the fountainheads of an enlightened and humane political system. The strength of "scientific socialism" lay precisely in its incorporation of the insights of dialectical philosophy. *Dialectic of Enlightenment* differs from the other two works in that it reckons up not merely with philosophy under the Nazis, but also with the unashamed free market capitalism of its authors' temporary home, the United States. The book is a work of conservative cultural criticism, which, on a conceptual level, is by no means incompatible with work the Nazis were happy to tolerate. This is not to say that it is politically tainted. Of the three books mentioned, however, it offers the least clear alternative to the errors it castigates.

Despite this, *Dialectic of Enlightenment* has probably had a greater effect than either of the other two manifestos. Lukács's book commits itself in a verbose way to a socialism that was deeply compromised even then. Popper, however competent as a philosopher of science and despite his skill as a stylist, is out of his depth in the history of philosophy. Horkheimer and Adorno, by contrast, are argumentatively rigorous, systematically well founded, and draw judiciously on wide empirical knowledge.

Because of its conservatism, however, the book only achieved its impact long after the war had finished. It was "discovered" by the German student movement in the late sixties, when the original edition was handed round in innumerable bootleg reprints. At this point, in the middle of the Vietnam War, the book's anti-American sentiments had become acceptable in a way that would not have been the case in 1947, when it first appeared. For the authors themselves, who had now for many years been comfortably established in philosophical chairs in Frankfurt, this sudden revolutionary notoriety was, if anything, an embarrassment and led to bitter confrontations with radical students intent on holding them to commitments they believed were now being betrayed. These conflicts undoubtedly hastened Adorno's early death in 1969.

I now look in detail at what these commitments were and then consider the extent to which they can profitably be incorporated into a view of the contemporary scene.

CRITICAL IMPETUS OF *THE DIALECTIC OF ENLIGHTENMENT*

Dialectic of Enlightenment is directed above all against the "barbarity" of Nazi Germany (*DE* 1). The critique takes its cue from the oppression and physical atrocities perpetrated by the regime and seeks to explain these in terms of the wider philosophical background.

The particular ills identified by Horkheimer and Adorno include the "mythification" of philosophy by thinkers such as Borchardt, Wilamowitz-Moellendorff, and Klages, and the use of Nietzsche to justify the Nazis' moral nihilism. In addition to this, the authors' criticism broadens to include features of American capitalism, notably racketeering and other monopolistic abuses, on the one hand, and "amusement" – that is, the ideological dumbing-down of culture perpetrated by Hollywood and the entertainment industry – on the other. The authors combat these trends in two ways. One is, as the title of the book indicates, a critical investigation of the notion of "enlightenment." This discussion, which embraces a general analysis of the dangers implicit in enlightenment and specific investigations of two of the fields where enlightenment fails, namely the "culture industry" and anti-Semitism, is the thematic mainstay of the book. But in some ways the most striking measures, even though they are described as "excursions," are two adverse readings of classic cultural resources, namely of the *Odyssey* and of de Sade. The *Odyssey* is used to demonstrate that, contrary to German attempts to assimilate heroic culture to myth and legend, the emergence of social actors, of market exchange, and of *homo oeconomicus* is a conscious concern of pre-Hellenic culture, depicted with skill and subtlety by Homer in the *Odyssey*. The essay on de Sade is concerned with the collapse of morality under the impact of enlightenment. The authors seek to demonstrate that the formalized "I" envisaged by Kantian epistemology reduces to a procedural and ultimately vacuous concept of right action.

The essay which, apart from a collection of aphorisms, concludes the book is "Elements of Antisemitism. The Frontiers of Enlightenment." In this essay the authors attempt an ambitious psychotherapeutic derivation of the repressive consciousness they hold ultimately responsible for the many horrors of contemporary history. The book is described as "Philosophical Fragments," and is aphoristic rather than systematic in construction. The picture that emerges from it, however, is coherent and precise.

ALIENATION

The *Dialectic of Enlightenment*'s underlying theme is that of alienation. Alienation is the Marxist, psychotherapeutic, or indeed romantic notion that humankind is *estranged* from the natural world. Something does not fit; human beings are doing violence to nature, and ultimately to themselves. Workers spend their lives trapped in occupations they hate, creating products nobody needs and which destroy the environment they live in, engaged in futile and enervating conflicts with their families, their neighbors, other social groups, and nations. They are enslaved in orders of work and mindless hierarchies that prevent them from ever fulfilling themselves or pursuing their own ideas and creativity. They are torn out of the beauty of the countryside and cut off from the inspirations of culture and art. Human value is reduced to the values of the marketplace: you are what you earn. The supposed "liberation" represented by the modern epoch boils down to a change from one kind of slavery (being owned by the feudal lord) to another (being enslaved to the need to earn a wage). The consequences of this alienation are self-consuming: the more human beings struggle to maintain their artificial hell, the more they are beset by problems engendered by the struggle itself. Alienation is not merely the symptom of something seriously amiss in the world created by human beings, it is a fault that will lead, eventually, to a terminal implosion of the entire system. The beginnings of this catastrophe are visible in the horrors visited upon the world by fascism and Nazism. But they also appear in the miseries of dysfunctional sexuality and blunted sentiment evident at an individual level throughout the modern capitalist world – including, conspicuously, the United States.

THE *HIC ET NUNC*

Adorno and Horkheimer see the opposite of alienation in what they call the "sacredness of the *hic et nunc*" (*DE* 6; *HGS* v, 32). The here and now is the element from which alienation estranges us. It is the inability to see or feel what is here, now, in front of us that characterizes our inability to come to terms with our existence. Existence, ultimately, takes place now. As human beings, we have the capacity to think about our future and to incorporate the present and the past into schemes of life. However, our existence is only ever here and now. It can and does draw on the past, which is the sequence of heres and nows in which we have previously found ourselves. We are, with justification, reasonably confident that our existence will continue beyond this passing moment, and that this continuation will only cease at a boundary whose coming we can anticipate. Nonetheless, the "future" is an illusion based on the generalization of our memories of the past. To commit ourselves unreflectingly to this illusion is to give up our lives to a specter.

We spend so much time worrying about the future and about the web of plans and purposes in which we hope to ensnare it that we become unable to enjoy the only genuine reality we have – namely the moment of our existence right here and now. The character of this genuine reality, in the view of Horkheimer and Adorno, is intensely somatic. We "are" most adequately in the unmediated richness of sense. A particularly poignant example of this is the olfactory sense. When we smell, we are in a preconceptual realm of pleasure and pain. The most direct and powerful organs of sexual perception are smell and touch. And smell – as Marcel experienced with the *madeleines* – heralds contentments that do not recede into the abstract future of deferred gratification, but are located in and recoverable from a genuine past.[1]

Our relations with this genuine reality, according to Horkheimer and Adorno, are characterized not by striving and the achievement of purposes, but by "reconciliation." Human beings *are* purposeful; they are full of guile and scheming. They also constantly engage in struggles for power. These features, moreover, clearly can make the material circumstances of life more secure and more agreeable. But they represent a hubris which eternally calls for a return to the nature that has been ungraciously spurned and left behind. Human beings *must* be bodies as well as intellects, simple enjoyers as well as purposeful doers. If they define themselves as intellects alone, they condemn themselves to unhappiness and the perpetual risk of self-destruction.

EQUIVALENCE

The achievement of the market economy (this analysis derives from Lukács, at one remove from Marx's analysis of "commodity fetishism") is that it makes possible the organization of unlimited quantities of labor.[2] It thus enables human beings to carry out projects that would otherwise stretch their productive capacity to the limit. The market achieves this by defining objects (in the first instance) according to their abstract exchange value. Anything that can be sold comes to have a relation to any other sellable object. The question of whether anyone *wants* to acquire or dispose of a particular object becomes irrelevant: the market mechanism makes it possible to define and quantify the value of each object in isolation from its particular circumstances. Production, or the incentive to produce, becomes disengaged from individual desires and inclinations. It ceases to depend on any kind of personal relationship (for example, that the producer "belongs to" the person for whom he produces). All the manifold rituals attendant on work in any concrete case are reduced by the market to one simple relation: the exchange values of the entities offered by the market participants. This, moreover, embraces *any* tradable entity. It may be an item produced by a craftsman. But it may equally well be space (land) or time (the labor power of a worker). The more open and liquid the market – that is to say, the more participants engaged at any one time – the more efficient the market becomes at determining "correct" prices for the items traded on it. Items traded on a liquid market lose their character as individual entities and become *commodities*. Any one exemplar of a commodity can be directly substituted for another; anything tradable can as such be directly substituted for another commodity without diminishing or adversely affecting the trader's property interests. The commodity trader may trade coffee, wheat, or beef without ever seeing what she trades, and without the least conception of what raising cattle or growing crops might feel like. Some indication of future supply and demand are a useful aid to forming bids and offers, but essentially, commodity trading takes place in isolation from real world situations and needs.

In a modern market economy commodities are not merely physical items but human beings – or, more precisely, segments of human lives. Workers have a constant tendency to become commodities: they are commodities once their qualities (their "qualifications") and all the features that make them interesting to the capitalist who purchases them (especially their youth and fitness), can be determined in accordance with general norms. Capitalism needs predictable human commodities – individuals whose individuality becomes subordinated to the skill-sets specified for the various branches of production. Once individuals have acquired a "trade," they can allow themselves to be exchanged on the employment market just as the objects they produce are traded on commodity markets. Huge productive efforts can be built up, with the consent of all involved, at short notice and with absolute transparency. But this efficiency (say the critics of commodity fetishism) is bought at a high price. The subordination of individuality to market-defined function does not merely facilitate economic organization – it also destroys the identity and happiness of the human beings involved. It is not possible to alienate segments of one's life without also alienating oneself from the means of self-determination. The humanity that remains after the labor market has exacted its toll is no more than an empty husk.

The organizational techniques of the market are matched by a conceptual one: equivalence (*DE* 4; *HGS* v, 30). In syntactical terms, entities are equivalent if one can be substituted for the other without losing the truth of the statement. In the statement "Frozen rain makes the fields white," "snow" can be substituted for "frozen rain" without affecting the truth-value of the statement. Hence "snow" and "frozen rain" are equivalent. The two expressions say something quite different, their "intentions" are different, but they both enable the statement to perform the same role and to be usable in the same sort of way. This (Leibnizian) step, as Adorno and Horkheimer point out, enables conceptuality to dispense with individuality in favor of the ability to perform a *function* (*DE* 23; *HGS* v, 53) within a system. The function (the statement) is indifferent to the individual characters of the entities that enable it to perform its job. For the function, the only thing that matters is the *system* within which it operates. A system is a network of self-sufficient, preexisting statements. Because of this preexistence, every system is, as Leibniz described it, "windowless." It reaches out to the outside world only through the medium of functionality. This is its strength, from the point of view of instrumental efficacy. But in other respects (as Horkheimer and Adorno argue) it is a profound weakness. As far as the system is concerned, everything is already familiar: there is no real opening for the unique and the individual. The only difference a concrete thing can make, coming from the outside, is to trigger a "yes" or "no" value in some function. The function in the above case is "x makes the fields white." If the individual substituted for the variable x "works" – that is, enables the function to return a positive truth-value – then nobody cares about the specific details. "Snow," "frozen rain," "white paint," "detergent foam" – they are all satisfactory values for this particular "function," however much they may differ in themselves, essentially, or whatever.[3]

But the subordination of the individual to its functional context, though it may be liberating both in the context of logic and in the context of the labor market, makes humankind blind to the irreducible differences of individuals. The overweening arrogance of a calculus eclipses the genuine qualities of lived existence, and, moreover, it lends itself as instrument to the interests of power and repression.

Enlightenment is as totalitarian as any system can be. It is not, as its Romantic enemies have argued, that its analytical method, its recourse to elements, its dissolution through reflection make it untrue. What makes it untrue is the fact that, as far as Enlightenment is concerned, the trial is over before it starts. When in a mathematical procedure the unknown is converted into the variable of an equation, it is stamped with the character of the old and familiar even before any value has been derived. (*DE* 18; *HGS* v, 47)

POWER AND SELF-PRESERVATION

In an obvious sense, the reduction of individuals to their ability transiently to "substitute" for variables in functional contexts represents a radical disempowerment. The capitalist who buys individuals solely in terms of whether they can perform the job momentarily at hand exercises a dominion far more absolute than that of the feudal slave owner. What is less obvious is the consequence of this alienation for the concept of personal identity. Adorno and Horkheimer pursue this theme in their two "excursions" on the Odyssey and on de Sade.

The commentary on the *Odyssey*, as I have already noted, is concerned to subvert the sentimental and nationalistic readings of pre-Hellenic Greek culture hawked around by reactionary Germans. The *Odyssey*, according to *Dialectic of Enlightenment*, is a narrative of incipient modernity. Odysseus struggles with the terrors of undomesticated nature by means of tricks and stratagems. The central one of these are his games with identity. Identity involves, among other things, disengagement from the identity of the primitive or natural self in favor of a conceptual version (the Polyphemus myth; "My name is Nobody"), the foundation of a *historically* based identity to underpin that of the sentient present (the Sirens), and the installation of a repressive superego to enforce order on the newly emerged and unstable self (Calypso, Circe and the various themes of sexual discipline). The result of these maneuvers is an "identical, purposive and masculine character" (*DE* 26; *HGS* v, 56).

The comments on the *Odyssey* are basically approving. Among other things, Horkheimer and Adorno insist that the barbarity shown by Odysseus in relation to Melanthius the goatherd and to the maids who had cast themselves on the suitors is untypical and anomalous. Odysseus is a trickster, but he is not the "hard man" urged by

Prussian commentators. Odysseus's aim is to return home; and this "home," in terms of the commentary in *Dialectic of Enlightenment*, represents a genuine reconciliation with nature on the basis of unperverted individual identity. Odysseus is not a marauding blond beast, subduing nature and his fellows to some abstract obsession with power; he is a parable of that resourcefulness and cunning which goes just far enough to ward off the perils of natural existence, but no further.

The other source, which does indeed match the calls for moral "hardness" issued by Nietzsche and his followers, is de Sade. Here the perverse "capitalist" form of individual identity comes to full fruition in a cruel and inhuman order of morality.

In the argument of Horkheimer and Adorno, genuine morality is ultimately primitive and individual, not schematic. It articulates itself in emotions that are – from the point of view of any calculus of interests – pointless and futile: for example, in pity or remorse. "It's no use crying over spilt milk," says the "hard" moralist. But, say Horkheimer and Adorno, it precisely *is* the remorse over damage done to others that characterizes true moral sentiment, however "useless" it may be in any other perspective. Alienated morality, in their view, derives from the "dark thinkers" of the bourgeoisie, especially Machiavelli, Hobbes, and Mandeville (*DE* 71; *HGS* v, 113). These philosophers evacuate the natural core of morality and replace it with pure power. Moral content, from then on, is always ultimately arbitrary. *Cuius princeps, eius religio.* Moral rightness is a function of the interests it serves. The only axiomatic principle is self-preservation. The content of the "self" that is thereby preserved is immaterial; whatever it is, it defines itself in terms of power and articulates itself in the implementation of plans.

Self-preservation, clearly, is one of guileful Odysseus's goals. It is not, however, an end in itself, but merely a way of ensuring some continuity of the material self. It does not exclude the reconciliation of concept and nature at some terminal point. Under the regime of market equivalence, however, human concepts break free and acquire a momentum of their own. The object of the labor market is compelled now to preserve itself in terms of exchangeable attributes. These are a matter of inscrutable and seemingly random mechanisms: one year one needs computer programmers, the next year unemployment among such staff is the highest of any. The anatomical and moral gymnastics described by de Sade correspond with this view. Goals are, for de Sade, essentially neutral. Right action, or moral "value," resides in the completeness of the calculus that informs action. It does not matter what you do, so long as you do it with the requisite organizational polish. In this respect the sexual practices he describes occupy a point on a continuum from Kant to modern sport. For Kant, the self materializes through its role as center of the categorial system surrounding it (*DE* 68; *HGS* v, 109). But it has no role or being apart from that. The self is merely that entity which satisfies the function of accompanying all representations. The specific difference of any individual self is, at most, the "power" with which it engages its activities, or, perhaps, the degree and sophistication of the organization enveloping it. Exactly the same applies to the organized pointlessness of sport:

Sport, like all varieties of mass culture, is governed by concentrated and purposeful activity, even though less informed spectators may be unable to guess the distinction between the various combinations and the significance of the events as they unfold, for these are measured by arbitrarily fixed rules. Like the gymnastic pyramids of de Sade's orgies and the rigid principles of the early bourgeoisie's Masonic lodges – cynically mirrored in the strict regulation of the libertines in *120 Days of Sodom* – the peculiar architectonic structure of the Kantian system announces the fact that the organisation of life has now generally dispensed with substantive goals. (*DE* 69; *HGS* v, 111)

MIMESIS AND PROJECTION

Morality, then, has an intuitive basis, and alienation from this basis does not engender autonomy (as Kant would have it), but an abstract game whose only substantial content is power. Analogous arguments apply to knowledge itself.

In the view of Adorno and Horkheimer, knowledge has a "mimetic" origin. Mimesis is the assimilation of consciousness to reality. It does not involve reproduction or apprehension; it is, rather, a matter of unmediated organic intuition. Mimesis is "physical imitation of external nature." As such, it is not an intellectual process. Indeed, it is not even restricted to human beings. Mimesis is the expressive response of created things to their environment, and it acquires its origins with the capacity to *suffer*, which is something proper to all living beings: "[i]n the simultaneously chaotic and orderly flight responses of lower animals, in the figures created by their milling about, in the convulsive gestures of the tormented, something finds expression which despite everything cannot be quite dominated in poor nature: the mimetic impulse" (*DE* 151; *HGS* v, 213). Mimesis extends into the human realm, where it may be found in the impulse to picture and in acting. It is also, say Adorno and Horkheimer, an important component of primitive magic's striving to confront the hostile world of nature (*DE* 148; *HGS* v, 210).

The significant aspect of mimesis is its blend of perception and giving. In this respect it has a relation to the senses that differs from that of other forms of knowledge. While seeing, for example, distances the self from the object and leaves it untouched by the object, smell absorbs the self into the perceived object and unites the two:

Of all senses the act of smelling, which is attracted without reifying, bears most pregnant testimony of the urge to lose oneself in the other and to become identical with it. That is why smell, both as perception and as being perceived – both become one in the execution – is more expression than other senses. In sight one remains who one is; in smell one is absorbed. (*DE* 151; *HGS* v, 214)

A mode of knowledge which fails to blend the self and the object is one which, ultimately, converts everything into "mere nature" – an outside governed by inaccessible rules. In mimesis, by contrast, the self is carried into the outside and by that very token preserved as a free actor within it. This preservation within and despite the outside is a model of what Adorno and Horkheimer regard as the "reconciliation" of self and nature (*DE* 153; *HGS* v, 216).

The other model, namely a knowledge that insists on distance and the absolute distinction between self and object, is attacked by Adorno and Horkheimer as (false) enlightenment. "Enlightenment" knowledge is characterized by its attempt to thrust all known and knowable objects into the corset of systematic "science." It thus renders itself unable to accommodate the *hic et nunc*. But as the authors argue, the world, and everything in it, is essentially unique. No one thing is the same as another. Individuals truly are individuals, and not exemplars of a species (*DE* 6f.; *HGS* v, 32). Classification is no more than a *preparation* for knowledge, never its fulfillment (*DE* 182; *HGS* v, 250).

The source of this compulsion to "know everything in advance" (*Vorwegbescheidwissen*) is, according to the authors, partly psycho-pathic and partly the result of fear (*DE* 18; *HGS* v, 46). The fear is the primitive fear of nature, the hostile other which brings death. The psychopathic element is described as projection. Projection is, as Horkheimer and Adorno put it, an animal attempt to create instruments to master the outside world. It stabilizes what would otherwise be chaotic and formless. In itself, this is legitimate. It ceases to be legitimate at the point where a dogmatic insistence takes over that fixity is not merely a feature of instruments, but is a characteristic of the world in general. This insistence is no longer a particular combative response to the needs of survival; it becomes a generalized pathological response to the subject's sense of powerlessness when faced with a nature it perceives to be irresistible. Pathological – or paranoid – projection is convinced that everything is always the same. Only in this way can it cope with the fear that it is itself, eternally, the victim of omnipotent nature. The paranoid subject projects on to the outside world a conviction that all things circle within a closed system of eternal necessity; only thus can it survive its sense of absolute powerlessness. "The closure of the eternally same becomes a surrogate of omnipotence" (*DE* 157; *HGS* v, 220).

The exclusion of the self from the outside world, however, and the denial that free individuals can intervene to change anything in the circuitous mechanisms of "nature," is an illness. Unfortunately it is one that has extended deep into the thinking of modern cultures. It is particularly evident in the depredations of "science," which has done more than anything else to alienate humankind from nature. The nature depicted by "science" has become the object of a paranoid desire to dominate, and by that token, the human beings ejected from participation in nature really have become its victims. What Adorno and Horkheimer call "absolute realism," indeed, culminates in Fascism: it is "a special case of the paranoid illusion which depopulates nature and eventually the peoples themselves" (*DE* 159; *HGS* v, 223). The specific manner of this "scientific" projection is something I have already noted in the context of the market economy: it involves the evacuation of knowledge's human center in favor of systematic, procedural, and "functional" necessities. The substantive intuitions of true knowledge are replaced by the ghostly compulsions of deduction and all the "logical" hierarchies of systematic knowledge

(*DE* 16; *HGS* v, 44). These compulsions and hierarchies, of course, mirror those of the capitalist world. At the same time they convert material objects into values for functional variables, into elements of unremitting "subsumption" (*DE* 21; *HGS* v, 50).

REFLECTION AND THE EMANCIPATION FROM FALSE ENLIGHTENMENT

The core of the book's resistance to what it decries is the notion of "reflection." The failure of "Enlightenment" lies in its inability to see that the relation between subject and object is one of mutual giving and taking. The model of a *false* Enlightenment is provided, above all, by Kant. In Kant's philosophy, the subjects of knowledge and of morality become extensionless centers, abstract geometrical points of reference in systems where truth and falsity are determined exclusively by formal considerations. For Horkheimer and Adorno, truth involves awareness of the role taken in it by the subject, not as a paranoid tyrant projecting some rigid system on nature and humankind, but as the actor in a dialogical exchange with reconciliation, not dominion, as its goal. Consciousness, accordingly, has a "course" (*DE* 160; *HGS* v, 224). It happens in time, and can vary with the unique events and individuals it engages with. True thinking, according to Horkheimer and Adorno, is recognizable precisely in that it can abandon and supersede any previous convictions and conclusions. It does not stand on its imagined insights, but is essentially *negative* towards its own achievements. Consciousness projects systems, deductions, and conclusions, but reflection is always ready to relativize those conclusions once more. Reflection knows the individuality of the knower and of the known, so it is always ready to revise a standpoint as soon as it has reached it. Anything else is "madness."

The consequences of a reflective attitude would, it seems, encompass the following elements. First, it would lead to a more healthy sexuality. Sexuality, not least as an aspect of the book's psychotherapeutic perspective, plays a significant part in *Dialectic of Enlightenment*. There is a certain, though rather indistinct, critical angle to the comments on sexuality. The Nazis' technicistic attitude, and specifically their replacement of individual discretion with mindless collectivism, it would seem, predisposes them to be homosexuals (*DE* 210; *HGS* v, 285). Hitler himself, however, the archetypically "unmoved" paranoid, is on that account worshipped by women (*DE* 157; *HGS* v, 221). The book's own attitude to women is ambiguous. Although technical reason is spurned as "masculine," it is not necessarily apparent that feminine reason, whatever that might be, is to be preferred. The view that women capitulate too readily to repressive sexuality is prominent (*DE* 56; *HGS* v, 95). And moreover, it would seem, women have a pronounced inclination to compensate for this in pursuits even more futile than those of men: "The last female opposition against the spirit of male society peters out in the swamp of small-scale racketeering, of covens and hobbies, it transforms itself into the perverted aggression of social work and theosophical gossip, or the launching of small cabals in charity work and Christian Science" (*DE* 208; *HGS* v, 283). True sexuality, it would seem, contains the promise of reconciliation. This is not to be specifically or exclusively mediated by women, however. It is a reconciliation in the same spirit as that heralded by the sense of smell, the recollection of a primary happiness from the mists of time (*DE* 56; *HGS* v, 95). In sex, as in the purposeless eating of the lotos, the oldest and remotest happiness "flashes" before consciousness – as the book's Benjaminian phrase would have it (*DE* 50; *HGS* v, 87). Good sex as a recipe for political progress, however convincingly the book may present this argument, is not a particularly novel initiative. Indeed, right-wing philosophy of the time was itself not averse to promoting this road to health.

A second, more directly applicable model for practical action is to be found in the comments on justice. The insistence on calculability and on the subsumption of individual cases under general norms is, as Horkheimer and Adorno convincingly show, a feature of much modern justice (*DE* 4; *HGS* v, 29). A justice that refuses to look to the individual case is indeed one where, as the authors say, "Justice is swallowed by law" (*DE* 12; *HGS* v, 39). In a legal context, the thirst for equality ends in "repression" and ultimately in the promulgation of *injustice* (*DE* 9; *HGS* v, 35). The authors attribute this to false bourgeois enlightenment (*DE* 4; *HGS* v, 29). It is not clear, however, what they would put in its place. In response one would in any case need to point out that their strictures apply in the first instance not to "bourgeois" justice, but to the *civil law* tradition. The common law does not insist on "subsumption" as the primary act of the judge. On the contrary, common law judges are – paradigmatically – jurors, who are deliberately chosen from among the laity in order to *avoid* the kind of system-bound, "scientific" thinking promoted by civil law procedure. The jury is intended to have a direct and emotional engagement with the individual case, unclouded by the cynicism of the professionals. The jury, in common law, is the exclusive judge of fact. The professionals judge the law, but only in relation to matters which lay people, the jurors, have consigned to them as findings of fact. This division of responsibility is designed to maintain the supremacy of concrete facts and real particulars, to combat false assumptions of familiarity, and to preserve the courts' awareness that every case, ultimately, is unique. So in effect the American system of justice (which is pure common law, and is well founded in the philosophical debates of the eighteenth century and subsequently) might well have been an example of what Adorno and Horkheimer were searching for, had they but looked in the right direction while they had the opportunity.

The third, and most concrete, application of "reflection," at least for Adorno, lay elsewhere, namely in the field of *art*. False art, as is apparent from the essay on the culture industry, is merely an instrument of ideology, a means of suppressing the critical faculties of the masses. Ideology uses entertainment and "amusement," whose mendacious harmony and shallow humor merely reinforce the "steel rhythm" of industrial production. Genuine art, by contrast, refuses this appeasement. It recognizes humankind's "claim to happiness" (*DE* 124; *HGS* v, 181), but it does not celebrate reconciliation, which in this world is never more than a utopian image; on the contrary, proper art marks the "necessary failure" of conciliatory striving (*DE* 103; *HGS* v, 155). Art is like reflective thought in that it refuses the affirmative and points up the "negation" of all finite conclusions. Amusement perfidiously seeks to relieve people of this necessary burden (*DE* 116; *HGS* v, 170).

The theory of art goes further than this, for art is, it would seem, a form of knowledge (*DE* 25; *HGS* v, 56). Indeed, art, rather than faith (as Kant had claimed), is the true boundary of purposive knowledge (*DE* 14; *HGS* v, 42). Art allows the whole to appear in the part; as an expression of totality, claim the authors, art shares the dignity of the absolute (ibid.). Totality is never factually achievable or cognizable, but art gestures towards its place at the same time as it marks the boundary of the merely given. The dignity and worth of art thus

exceeds that of "science," and foreshadows the happiness and freedom which are the birthright of all human beings.

CONCLUSIONS

Dialectic of Enlightenment is a powerful manifesto for the fight
against modernist barbarity. It is, however, unclear whether it really
overcomes the essential conservatism that characterized so much
other German thinking of the time, including that of numerous
thinkers appropriated by "barbarity."

The book's resistance to modern Platonism and to the tyranny of
deduction is clearly opposed to thinkers such as Frege and Russell,
who were in the vanguard of the analytical tradition and explicitly
celebrated the possibilities of formal logic. They were not, however,
noticeably influential in reactionary political or cultural philosophy (despite Frege's unpleasant anti-Semitism in private). In fact,
the most vehement anti-Platonists of the first half of the twentieth
century were followers of Nietzsche such as Ludwig Klages and, at a
remove, Martin Heidegger – and the attractions of their thought for
National Socialism are well documented. Oddly, the most evident
alternative contemporary source of non-Platonistic thinking would
have been the empiricism flourishing in England and the United
States. Adorno and Horkheimer seem, however, to have regarded this
as a cynical, "pragmatic" formalism even worse than the Kantian
tradition they criticized in detail.

At the same time it is noticeable that – despite the lamentable per-
formance of *all* Germany's intellectual institutions under the Nazis,
including the universities, the arts, and the law – Horkheimer and
Adorno still hold to the Humboldtian notion that there is merit and
moral stability in state-monopolized ideological establishments (this
means, presumably, *Bildung* [*DE* 105; *HGS* v, 157]). Meanwhile, in
true German conservative manner, the problems of the age are diagnosed as an "illness of the spirit" (*DE* 165; *HGS* v, 230), which,
one imagines, the blessings of *Bildung* are to cure. Yet the prescrip-
tions for a new intellectual initiative, despite its rejection of "official
philosophy," seem disappointingly thin, however resoundingly they
call for resistance to "the administrators" (*DE* 201; *HGS* v, 275). By
contrast, Horkheimer and Adorno are fairly curmudgeonly when it
comes to American cultural alternatives. Humor in art, which can

have the most powerfully subversive political quality (e.g. Charlie Chaplin) is dismissed as the deception of "amusement": true joy lies in serious matters (*res severa verum gaudium*). Those who see through the falsehood cannot laugh: "Baudelaire is as humorless as otherwise only Hölderlin" (*DE* 112; *HGS* v, 166). American music, meanwhile, namely jazz, which is scarcely the kind of dumb amusement peddled by Hollywood, gets very short shrift.

In conclusion, it is difficult not to feel that much of the impetus behind *Dialectic of Enlightenment*, despite its breathtaking theoretical scope, is impatience and resentment at the myriad indignities of exile. The fact is that the English-speaking world did resist Nazism, both abroad and indeed at home, in a far more successful manner than Germany. Part of the reason for this, perhaps, lies in the intellectual institutions and traditions of that English-speaking world. This is not a moral judgment and it may be false anyway. But it is disappointing that two such gifted analysts could not have spent a little more time considering that question and the lessons, if any, that might have been learned from it.

NOTES

1. The emphasis on the here and now, and on the nondiscursive "instant," is classic Existentialism. See my *German Philosophy. An Introduction* (Cambridge: Polity, 1988), pp. 199–202. The same theme is important in the work of Ludwig Klages.
2. See Karl Marx, *Das Kapital*, I, 1 §4; Georg Lukács, "Reification and the Consciousness of the Proletariat," in *History and Class Consciousness*, trans. R. Livingstone (Cambridge, Mass.: MIT Press, 1971), pp. 83–222.
3. The Leibnizian project was carried into the twentieth century by Gottlob Frege and Bertrand Russell. Adorno and Horkheimer themselves trace its roots back as far as Parmenides (*DE* 4f.; *HGS* v, 29). For an assessment of the Leibnizian project in the twentieth century, see my *The Logic of Reflection* (New Haven: Yale University Press, 1992).

4   The marriage of Marx and Freud: Critical Theory and psychoanalysis

The members of the Institute for Social Research were the first group of philosophers and social theorists to take psychoanalysis seriously – indeed, to grant Freud the stature that is generally reserved for the giants of the philosophical tradition. In addition to Hegel, Marx, and Weber, Freud became one of the foundation stones on which their interdisciplinary program for a critical theory of society was constructed. It has often been observed that the Critical Theorists turned to psychoanalysis to make up for a deficiency in Marxian theory, namely, its reduction of the psychological realm to socioeconomic factors. This explanation, however, does not go far enough. With a few notable exceptions, the Left was not particularly interested in the modernist cultural movements of the past century – or, worse yet, denounced them for their bourgeois decadence. Though it may have proved to be an impossible project, the Frankfurt School – largely under Adorno's influence – sought to integrate cultural modernism with left-wing politics. And this is one of the places where psychoanalysis came to play an important role. For, despite Freud's own stolid lifestyle and aesthetic conservatism, his creation, psychoanalysis, made an incontrovertible contribution to the radical avant-garde that was transforming almost every realm of European culture.[1] *The Interpretation of Dreams* and *Ulysses* are cut from the same cloth.

Although Freud's views on sexuality had a broader impact on the general public, his critique of philosophy – no less than Nietzsche's and Marx's – played a major role in the death of the ontotheological tradition and the rise of postmetaphysical thinking. After Freud's intervention into the history of western rationality, many of the major traditional *topoi* of philosophy – authority, morality,

74

subjectivity, political association, indeed reason itself – could no longer be approached in the same way. The feeling that they stood on the other side of this *kulturhistorisch* divide must have contributed to the *élan* one senses among the early members of the Frankfurt School.

The intimacy between the Frankfurt School and psychoanalysis was more than theoretical. The Institute for Social Research and the Frankfurt Psychoanalytic Institute shared a building and held classes in the same rooms. Such eminent analysts as Anna Freud, Paul Federn, Hans Sachs, and Siegfried Bernfeld gave lectures to the general public, sponsored by the Critical Theorists. Max Horkheimer, the director of the Institute for Social Research, also sat on the board of the Psychoanalytic Institute. And Eric Fromm – a trained analyst and member of both institutes – helped the Critical Theorists educate themselves about the workings of psychoanalytic theory.[2] This contribution helped to prompt the Institute's groundbreaking studies on *Authority and the Family*.[3] The work was the first interdisciplinary empirical research that used psychoanalytic theory – in this case the theory of character – to investigate the relation between sociological developments and psychological phenomena.

After the war, the working relation between the Frankfurt School and psychoanalysis was reestablished when Horkheimer and Adorno returned to Germany. They gave their support to Alexander Mitscherlich's creation of the Sigmund Freud Institute, the institution in which psychoanalysis was rehabilitated in Germany after the debacle, which had left the country almost completely devoid of experienced analysts. Again, Horkheimer was on the board of directors of the psychoanalytic institute. And in the 1960s, Jürgen Habermas's discussions with Mitscherlich and Alfred Lorenzer, another prominent member of the Sigmund Freud Institute, played a major role in the philosopher's linguistic reinterpretation of psychoanalytic theory. Indeed, the influential Freud chapters in *Knowledge and Human Interests* were partly a product of those discussions.

HORKHEIMER AND ADORNO

There is nothing like a traumatic experience to shake up one's thinking. The shock of the First World War led Freud to radically recast his model of the psychic apparatus, introduce his new instinct theory – which now included the death drive – and ultimately write his late cultural works. Similarly, the news of Walter Benjamin's suicide and the "realization that Hitler's barbarism had exceeded even the most melancholy prognoses of the twentieth century's most melancholic thinkers,"[4] compelled Horkheimer and Adorno to reexamine the basic assumptions of their project. To be sure, their thinking had always been idiosyncratic. But prior to the 1940s, however heterodox, their work had remained basically within the Marxian framework and, therefore, the Enlightenment tradition, insofar as it sought to provide rational accounts of the phenomena it investigated, explaining them in terms of the material conditions, broadly conceived, that gave rise to them.

But now the Enlightenment itself – rationality and the rational subject – appeared to be implicated in the catastrophe that was engulfing Europe. The validity of reason as an *organum* for understanding that experience could therefore no longer be taken for granted. A "nonrational" as opposed to an "irrational" theory of some sort, which could get behind rationality and the subject and examine their genesis, had to be created.[5] To forge this new species of theory and write the "prehistory" (*Urgeschicte*) of reason and the subject, which meant writing the "underground history" of Europe and chronicling "the fate of the human instincts and passions which are displaced and distorted by civilization" (*DE* 231), Horkheimer and Adorno turned to psychoanalysis. The radical nature of the new task led them to take up some of the most controversial and speculative aspects of Freud's works, namely his psychoanthropological theories of culture and civilization.

In the *magnum opus* of the classical Frankfurt School, *Dialectic of Enlightenment*, Horkheimer and Adorno presented their version of the psychoanalytic account of (individual and collective) development through a commentary on Odysseus's wanderings, taking Nietzsche and Freud's closely related theories of internalization[6] as their point of departure. Their central thesis is that the subject[7] comes into being through "the introversion of sacrifice" (*DE* 55). Sacrificial practices derive from a central principal of mythical thinking, namely, the law of equivalence, which for Horkheimer and Adorno represents the magical origin of rational exchange. Every piece of good fortune, every advance, which the gods bestow on human beings, must be paid for with something of comparable value. Following this principle, early humankind attempted to influence the course of human and natural events by offering sacrifices to the gods in the hope that the deities would intervene on their behalf.

Odysseus sought to emancipate himself from the prerational and preindividuated world of myth and thereby escape the law of equivalence. His trials and adventures chronicle the stages in the emergence of the individuated, unified, and purposeful, which is to say, enlightened subject. Odysseus was already a transitional figure, somewhere between myth and enlightenment, for his incipient ego had developed to the point where he could make his basic calculation. He reckoned that by bringing the disorderliness of his internal nature under the control of a unified ego – that is, by repressing his unconscious-instinctual life – he could outwit the law of equivalence and survive the numerous dangers that awaited him on his journey home. These dangers represent the regressive pleasures of the archaic world – the forms of gratification offered by each stage of development – that threaten to divert the relatively immature ego from its developmental goals. The ego's main task, self-preservation, can only be achieved by staying the course. Moreover, every additional act of renunciation adds to the reality ego's consolidation and strength, further transforming it into a rational *qua* strategic subject who can manipulate the external world. And to the extent that external nature is reified, it is transformed into appropriate material for domination. Horkheimer and Adorno view Odysseus's legendary cunning, which is a "kind of thinking that is sufficiently hard to shatter myths" (*DE* 4), as the precursor of instrumental reason and the technical domination of nature.

There is, however, a flaw in Odysseus's strategy. And it becomes the "germ cell" (*DE* 54) out of which the dialectic of enlightenment unfolds. Although it is not directed outwardly, the renunciation of inner nature that "man celebrates on himself" (ibid.) is no less a sacrificial act than the ritual immolation of a bleating lamb. As sacrifice, it remains subject to the law of equivalence. A price must be paid for Odysseus's survival, that is, for victory over the dangers posed by external nature. That price is the reification of the self. Insofar as the ego distances itself from its archaic prehistory and unconscious-instinctual life, in one sense, it looses its mimetic relation to the world. In another, perverted sense however, mimesis is preserved in the process, for an objectified self mimics the reified world it has objectified.

Because Horkheimer and Adorno assume that the process they delineated represents the only path to ego formation, they equate the autocratic ego with the ego as such. For them the integration of the self is inherently violent: "Men had to do fearful things to themselves before the self, the identical purposive, and virile nature of man was formed, and something of that recurs in every childhood" (DE 33).[8] What is more, the violence involved in the ego's genesis remains attached to it throughout all stages of its development. To preserve its unity, its identity, the ego must vigilantly maintain its boundaries on two fronts, against inner nature and outer nature alike.[9]

Enlightenment was supposed to emancipate humankind from fear and immaturity and promote its fulfillment through the development of reason and the mastery of nature. As conceived by Horkheimer and Adorno, however, the whole process of ego formation, and hence the project of enlightenment, is self-defeating. It systematically eliminates the possibility of achieving its own goal. Enlightened thinking reduces the ego's function to the biological activity of self-preservation – "mere life" in Aristotle's sense – and the sacrifice of inner nature makes a fulfilled life impossible. The liberation of "desire" may not in itself constitute freedom, as many Marcuseans and French *désirants* believed in the heady days following '68. (Given desire's darker sides, it would in fact result in barbarism.) But at the same time an intimate and unconstricted relation with unconscious-instinctual life is an essential ingredient of living well. It not only enhances the vitality and spontaneity of psychic life, but it enables one to invest the everyday experience with fantasy, thereby fostering a more mimetic relation to the world. "It is creative apperception more than anything," as D. W. Winnicott observes, "that makes the individual feel that life is worth living."[10]

The French psychoanalytic tradition, deeply influenced by Heidegger, especially his critique of the Cartesian subject, tends to view the ego in unequivocally negative terms, as an agent of self-deceiving rationalization and an opponent of desire.[11] Despite their hostility to Heidegger, Horkheimer and Adorno share many of these same criticisms of the ego, especially with respect to the question of adaptation, but their position is more complicated. This is partly the result of political considerations. Fully aware of the price – the sacrifice of inner nature and the loss of a mimetic relation to nature – that was paid for the ego's emergence, they nonetheless believed that the formation of the modern subject also represented an undeniable advance. It marked the emancipation of the individual from its emersion in the quasinatural substance of premodern *Gemeinschaft* and the recognition of the new norm, autonomy, that, admittedly, has been only partially realized in modernity.

Whatever its deficiencies, the idea of the autonomous individual had to be defended on political grounds. For even if its "worldly eye" had been "schooled by the market," bourgeois individuality possesses a degree of "freedom from dogma, narrow-mindedness and prejudice," and thereby "constitutes a moment of critical thinking" (*MM* 72). And in the face of the hard totalitarianism of fascism and the soft totalitarianism of an administered world, Horkheimer and Adorno held that the "moment of critical thinking," of the capacity for independent political judgment, however limited, had to be preserved. They therefore reluctantly threw their lot in with the autonomous individual.[12]

On the basis of Horkheimer and Adorno's analysis, there is no way to break out of the dialectic of enlightenment from inside; only a utopian rupture of some sort could derail its seemingly relentless advance. And although Horkheimer and Adorno believed that a vision of redemption was necessary for illuminating the falseness of the world, they were opposed to the actual pursuit of utopian politics (*MM* 247).[13] As a result, they became imprisoned in a theoretical impasse from which they would never escape. Their political quietism – indeed, conservatism – that was partly the result of this impasse, only grew stronger over time. After the war, Horkheimer more or less moved away from psychoanalysis, but Adorno continued to pursue the psychoanalytic analysis the two had begun in *Dialectic of Enlightenment*. In the spirit of negative dialectics, he used psychoanalysis for exclusively critical ends, and objected to any attempt at envisioning a nonreified conception of the self. Theoretically, his proposition that the whole is the untrue prohibited him from indulging in such positive speculations. Any effort to picture "a more human existence," he argued, could only amount to an attempt at a "false reconciliation within an unreconciled world." "[E]very 'image of man' is ideology except the negative one."[14] Moreover, for him, the ego psychologist's celebration of adaptation as the *ne plus ultra* of psychic health constituted a retreat from Freud's emphasis on conflict.[15] In fact, it amounted to a rationale for social conformism masquerading as developmental theory.

As Albrecht Wellmer observes, there was one place where Adorno disregarded his apprehensions about false reconciliation and prohibitions on utopian speculation: in his aesthetic theory. Adorno claimed that new forms of synthesis, consisting in a nonreified relation between particular and universal, part and whole, had already been achieved in exemplary works of advanced art, especially in Schoenberg's music and Beckett's theatre. He suggested, moreover, that the sort of *aesthetic* integration manifested in these works might prefigure a postreified mode of *social* synthesis, which could possibly be realized in a future society. But for some reason – perhaps a lingering Marxian prejudice against psychology – Adorno never allowed himself the same speculative liberty with respect to the synthesis of the self. That is, he never attempted to extrapolate possibilities for new, less repressive ("nonrepressive" is too utopian) forms of integrating the self from the "nonviolent togetherness of the manifold" he thought he perceived in advanced works of art.[16] But this idea of a different form of psychic integration could have provided a way out of the dialectic of enlightenment.

Within *Dialectic of Enlightenment* itself, there are in fact several points where Horkheimer and Adorno allude to a possible, quasi-utopian way out of its impasse. The most suggestive refers to a renewed "mindfullness [*Eingedenke*] of nature in the subject" (*DE* 40), which could serve as an antidote to the domination of internal nature and the reification of the subject. Unfortunately, the concept is not further elaborated by Horkheimer and Adorno. A reconsideration of the relation between the ego and the id might provide some content to this enticing idea.[17]

At this point, a critical examination of Horkheimer and Adorno's central assumption, namely, that the ego is autocratic as such, is called for. Not only will such a critique undercut one of the key premises of the dialectic of enlightenment, it will also generate some content for the notion of minding inner nature. Furthermore, it allows us to envision a "less repressive" mode of psychic integration without resorting to utopian speculation. Relatively recent developments in theoretical and clinical psychoanalysis already offer considerable resources for adumbrating *"another relation* between the conscious and the unconscious, between lucidity and the function of the imaginary . . . another *attitude* of the subject between himself or herself."[18]

Considerable support for Horkheimer and Adorno's conception of the ego can be found in Freud. Freud's "official position," up to the 1920s at least, was that the ego's primary job was defensive and that the main function of the psychic apparatus was to reduce tension. The ego used repression, isolation, and projection to *exclude*, that is to say, "get rid of" excitation arising from inner nature.[19] The ego was considered strong and rational to the extent it maintained its solid boundaries and prevented the stimuli of instinctual-unconscious life from penetrating its domain. Freud's view of the ego, moreover, was tied up with his conviction that "scientific man," that is, the rational subject – the individual who has renounced magical thinking and been purified of the subjective distortions (*Entsellungen*) of fantasy and affect – represented "the most advanced form of human development."[20] Horkheimer and Adorno's acceptance of this mistaken position motivated their critique of the ego.

In a devastating observation, however, Hans Loewald notes that by adopting this view, psychoanalysis had "unwittingly taken over much of the obsessive neurotic's experience and conception of reality and . . . taken it for granted as 'objective reality.'"[21] The analysts had, in other words, equated a pathological mode of ego formation, namely, the obsessional, with the ego as such. And Horkheimer and Adorno's acceptance of this mistaken equation motivated their critique of the ego. But, as Loewald also notes, an ego that is "strong" in this sense is in fact only "strong in its defenses" – which means it is actually "weak."[22] On many topics, however, one can also find an implicit, "unofficial" position in Freud's thinking, and this is what Loewald does with respect to the ego. He extracts an alternative "inclusionary" conception of the ego from Freud's later structural theory. After 1924 the clinical experience and the immanent development of Freud's theory led him to a new problem. In addition to explaining defense – how things are gotten rid of – he found it necessary to elucidate how things are held together and preserved "in the realm of mind."[23] In direct opposition to the exclusionary model, the "optimal communication"[24] between the ego and the id was now taken as a sign of health, and the isolation of the two agencies from each other a mark of pathology. A truly strong ego, which is to say, an inclusionary ego, can open itself to the "extra-territoriality" of inner nature and "channel and organize it" into "new synthetic organizations."[25]

Adorno no doubt would have had little patience with this line of exploration. Not only does it attempt to envisage a positive conception of the self in an "untrue" world, but it places considerable emphasis on the notion of integration. Because of its potential threat to "the nonidentical," Adorno was always suspicious of the process of unification. But he was also steeped in Hegelian philosophy and therefore must have been familiar with the distinction between differentiated and undifferentiated forms of unification. In fact, he applied the notion of a differentiated whole in his discussion of the new forms of synthesis manifested in exemplary works of art. And insofar as the ego is exclusionary, that is, unified through the compulsive exclusion and repression of the otherness within the subject that is unconscious-instinctual life, it is, in fact, an undifferentiated unity. As such, Adorno's objections are justified. But Loewald's point is that the exclusionary model represents a pathological form of ego formation. He argues that a truly strong ego's unity consists in a differentiated and differentiating whole that grows by integrating its internal Other, thereby creating richer, deeper, and more complex synthetic structures.

Had Adorno been willing to extrapolate from the modes of synthesis he saw in advanced works of art to new possibilities of psychic integration, he might have attained a degree of freedom from the dialectic of enlightenment. But, then again, viewed from the standpoint of redemption, such piecemeal advances in human development – which are all Freud ever offered – appear inconsequential.

MARCUSE

Marcuse accepted the diagnosis of the dialectic of enlightenment as Horkheimer and Adorno formulated it, but where they held their hand, he was willing to play the utopian card.[26] Marcuse had briefly participated in the German Revolution of 1918 and was more disposed towards activism than were his two senior colleagues. Moreover, the fact that he remained in the United States after the war and became involved with the New Left – the authors of *Dialectic of Enlightenment* were always skeptical, indeed, even hostile towards the student movement – served to further Marcuse's activist proclivities. Indeed, Marcuse, who turned seventy in the fateful year of 1968, became something of an elder spokesman for the New Left. His deliberate and heavily accented pronouncements on the students' behalf seemed to confer some of the *gravitas* of the German philosophical tradition on their homespun radicalism. Marcuse's activism, however, was also tied up with a certain lack of theoretical restraint, which is one reason he could make the utopian move. In contrast to Adorno's exquisitely subtle dialectics, which could not have possibly resulted in a call to action, Marcuse often wrote in a declamatory style that is closer in spirit to the *Theses on Feuerbach* than to *Minima Moralia*.

The development of classical Critical Theory took place during the thirties and forties, the period that witnessed the Great Depression, the collapse of the Worker's Movement, and the rise of left-wing and right-wing totalitarianism. In spite of Horkheimer and Adorno's continued allusions to the radical transformation of society, these developments led them to become deeply suspicious of the Marxian project, which they began to see as itself only a variation within the Baconian project of domination. Marcuse, in contrast, wrote his two major works, *Eros and Civilization* and *One-Dimensional Man*, during the postwar boom years that followed, when "postindustrialist society" was in its ascendance; the capitalist economy was rapidly expanding, the labor movement seemed to have been integrated into the system, and a largely depoliticized consumer culture was colonizing the suburbs. It might be thought that these developments would also have led Marcuse to abandon Marxism. But this did not happen. Instead, he used neo-Marxian categories to explain the new historical constellation. And the tensions in his analysis – which, it could be argued, reflected tendencies within the object of his analysis – resulted from his neo-Marxian approach to the situation.

In *One-Dimensional Man*, Marcuse offered his version of the dialectic of enlightenment. However, rather than presenting it as a metahistorical narrative of the domination of nature and the triumph of instrumental rationality, he wrote a concrete socioeconomic analysis of the totally administered world, that is, the advanced capitalist society as it appeared to him in the 1950s. All significant "negative" thinking and radical political practice, he argued, were effectively neutralized insofar as the system implanted "false" consumerist needs in its members and continued to satisfy them through the steady production of superfluous commodities. Only a cultural revolution that undermined these false needs or economic crisis – it was not clear which – could disrupt this arrangement. But because of the advances in technocratic management, such crises could be indefinitely averted. What elements of negativity that remained within the society were confined to bohemians and minorities, and their marginality rendered them politically insignificant.

In the New Left spirit of the times – and unlike the other members of the Frankfurt School, who remained conspicuously silent on the subject – Marcuse also pointed to the postwar struggles against imperialism as a possible external source of negativity that could disrupt the international economic system. It is more significant for our concerns that, in *One-Dimensional Man*, Marcuse, who later praised the revolt of the instincts, argued that sexuality did not represent a potential source of political opposition. On the contrary, it had been effectively harnessed to help propel economic growth. Through its exploitation by the advertising industry, the "repressive desublimation" (*O* 56) of sexuality provided a powerful tool for marketing relatively superfluous commodities.

But, at roughly the same time that he wrote his version of *Dialectic of Enlightenment*, with its gloomy political prognosis, Marcuse also presented a philosophical thought experiment that could be used to support a program of utopian politics. Through an immanent critique of Freud, he sought to break the identification of civilization with repression and to prove that a "non-repressive" society was, at least in principle, possible (*EC* 35). He maintained that science and technology had developed to the point where they could, in principle, provide the material basis for a communist society. According to classical historical materialism, "the realm of freedom" could only be reached after the transition through socialism, during which the forces of production would be developed to their maximum (*FL* 62–82). Marcuse maintained, however, that this maturation had already taken place under capitalism. Rather than the conflict between labor and capital, the tension between unnecessary "surplus repression" (*EC* 35) and the potential for the radical reduction of repression – and "nausea as a way of life" – could provide the motivation for political action in advanced capitalist society. That is, abundance rather than impoverishment would be at the heart of political action. Furthermore, where the anti-utopian Marx refused to speculate about the nature of a future "realm of freedom," Marcuse used psychoanalytic concepts to provide some content for this utopian concept (see *EC* 5). But whereas in *Eros and Civilization* Marcuse only entertained these arguments as a theoretical thought experiment, in the 1960s he came to believe that these developments had actually begun to unfold in the radical movements of the day (*L* 1).

Marcuse's strategy, one which became the prototype for many Freudian (and Lacanian) Leftists who followed him, was to *historicize* psychoanalysis in order to combat Freud's skepticism about the possibility of radical change. Freud had argued that "the program of the pleasure principle," governing the operation of the human psyche, is at "loggerheads" with the requirements of civilized social life.[27] He maintained, moreover, that this conflict – one of the major causes of human unhappiness – is not the result of contingent social arrangements that might be altered by political action. Rather, it is rooted in humanity's biological endowment – its sexual and aggressive drives – and constitutes an immutable transhistorical fact.

Against Freud's claim, Marcuse set out to demonstrate that the reality principle, which he took as the principle governing social life, is historically contingent and can assume different forms under different social conditions. He began by granting that *to date* a conflict between the reality principle and the pleasure principle has always existed. In almost all known societies, economic scarcity (*Lebensnot*) has forced humans to devote the greater part of their lives to the struggle for survival. This in turn has required them to repress their instinctual life and to forgo the pursuit of "integral satisfaction" (*EC* 11). In other words, the reality principle, as it has historically existed, coincides with what Marx called "the realm of necessity." But now, Marcuse maintained, the science and technology created by capitalism can produce a qualitatively new level of abundance that can provide the basis for the utopian leap required to break the dialectic of enlightenment.

Like most sexual liberationists who make use of psychoanalysis, Marcuse relied on early Freud and the concept of repression. For the early Freud, repression is initiated by the societal demand for censorship of unconscious instinctual impulses. In one form or other, most sexual liberationists accept this picture and construe liberation as the emancipation of the unconscious-instinctual life – or desire – from the historically contingent requirements of social repression.

Freud observed that "with the introduction of the reality principle one species of thought activity was split off . . . kept free from reality-testing and remained subordinated to the pleasure principle alone. This activity is *phantasyzing*."[28] Marcuse took this to mean that phantasy, which "retains the tendencies of the psyche prior to its organization" (*EC* 142), is spared the influence of the reality principle and therefore represents an uncontaminated Other of the social order. Phantasy and the activities related to it, that is, mythology, sexual perversion and even artistic creation, can therefore supply a point of departure for utopian speculation (or phantasy) about "another reality principle" (*EC* 143) where instinctual life has been emancipated from historically superfluous repression. Because of their prelapsarian purity, phantasy and these phantasy-related ideas and activities foreshadow a form of life that could be created beyond the historical reality principle.

Like Horkheimer and Adorno, Marcuse believed that the unity of the self is intrinsically repressive. But in contrast to their ambivalent compromise, he was prepared to advocate the radical decentralization of the subject in the name of the "polymorphous perverseness" of inner nature. (In this, he anticipated the poststructuralist attempt to deconstruct the subject, which was based on similar assumptions about the necessarily violent nature of its unification.[29]) Although Horkheimer and Adorno did not directly refer to the relevant texts, especially "Mourning and Melancholia" and *The Ego and the Id*, they drew on Freud's later theories of internalization and the formation of the ego to argue for the repressive unity of the subject. But since Marcuse bases himself on early Freud, he primarily understands the integration of the self in terms of sexual development rather than ego formation. In 1905, Freud argued that the goal of libidinal development is to bring the partial drives under the dominance of genitality. The achievement of genitality was seen as the measure of psychosexual maturity and health.[30] Freud also used the same developmental theory to conceptualize sexual perversions, arguing that they represent the "inappropriate" continuation of pregenital sexuality into adult life. And no matter how much Freud and other analysts have tried to remain scientifically neutral and refrain from conventional moral judgments, it follows from this theory that the perversions must be categorized as pathological.[31]

Marcuse criticized the subsumption of "polymorphous perversity" – that is, the generalized erotism of the child's body – under genital supremacy as a form of the violent unification of the subject. Following his general strategy, he attempted to historicize Freud's position. Again, the subordination of the stages of psychosexual development to genitality is not the manifestation of an inborn biological program, as Freud had argued. It results, rather, from the socioeconomic necessity of fabricating unified purposive individuals, who are manageable and can carry out their assigned tasks in the productive process. Economic imperatives necessitate "the temporal reduction of the libido." Unless one is outside the process of production – either an aristocrat or a lumpenproletariat – sexual activity must be restricted to a limited number of time slots each week. Likewise, the creation of manageable subjects also requires the "spatial reduction" of libido – that is, "the socially necessary desexualization of the body" and the concentration of sexuality in the genitals (EC 48).

Given these considerations, Marcuse maintains that sexual perversions only assume a pathological status – only appear as the *fleurs du mal* – within the normative framework of our repressive society. Viewed differently, they can be seen as expressing "a rebellion against the subjugation of sexuality" demanded by contingent society, indeed, against its very foundations. Like phantasy, with which they are closely related, perversions remain loyal to an era of development prior to the establishment of the reality principle. As such, they also contain a *promesse de bonheur*, an intimation of happiness that might be achieved under different conditions.

Of the three theories under consideration, Marcuse's has been the least successful at weathering the storms of time. *Dialectic of Enlightenment* and *Knowledge and Human Interests* are living texts that still speak to contemporary philosophers. *Eros and Civilization*, on the other hand, strikes one as a document from another era. Because of their disabused realism and theoretical integrity, the Frankfurt School believed that "the 'dark' writers of the bourgeoisie" (PD 106),[32] such as Weber and Freud, could not simply be dismissed as the products of the class that produced them. The daunting challenge they posed to the progressive project had to be directly confronted. And this is what Marcuse attempted with his critique of Freud. When the influence of *Eros and Civilization* was at its height, Marcuse was seen as having accomplished a brilliant *coup de main*. If the dialectic of enlightenment, formulated with the help of Freud's pessimistic anthropology, requires a utopian solution, then Marcuse sought to provide it through an interpretation of Freud's own theories. He did not simply try to rebut Freud's arguments with rational counterarguments, as many perfectly respectable but less speculative critics have tried to do. Rather, using the Frankfurt School's favorite strategy, immanent critique, he tried to accomplish a dialectical reversal that transformed the profoundly anti-utopian psychoanalyst into a utopian thinker. Whatever its deficiencies, the boldness of Marcuse's approach deserves its due.

Today it is not only easy to spot the fallacies in Marcuse's reasoning, the whole stratagem appears mistaken. The central fallacy in Marcuse's "Freudo-Marxism" – or, perhaps more accurately, the "Marxification" of Freud – is the conflation of the idea of material scarcity with Freud's notion of *Ananke* (reality or necessity). There is no denying that, for Freud, the necessity of wrestling material survival from nature is an important reason for the harshness of life. The meaning of *Ananke*, however, is much broader in scope. Through inevitable loss, physical pain, and death, nature will always rise "up against us, majestic, cruel and inexorable" and remind us of our "helplessness and weakness, which we thought to escape through the work of civilization."[33] Whatever level of abundance might be achieved – and material well-being is nothing to scoff at – human beings will still be confronted with the "ineluctable,"[34] which will always administer an insult to our self-esteem.

One might dismiss these considerations as existential claptrap and argue that in a society that is not as atomized and anomic as ours the inevitable crises of life can be faced in a less anguishing way. And there is undoubtedly some truth to this assertion. Nevertheless, this overlooks some profound points not only of a philosophical but also of a *political* nature.

Psychoanalysis's objection to utopianism pertains not only to its idealizing assumptions about the goodness of human nature, it also considers utopianism to be undesirable in principle. The Freudian Left has often overlooked the fact that Freud was not only

concerned with the obstacles to human happiness that are created
by the conflict between the drives and the demands of civilization.
After he turned his attention to narcissism, he also became sensitive to the dangers that omnipotence posed for human existence.
And these dangers have only become more manifest with time. In
addition to the resolution of the Oedipus complex, the decentering of a child's omnipotence is a critical developmental task. (The
two are, of course, closely related.) Children must learn to accept
the existence of otherness and the finite nature of human life. A
part of this process is assuming one's place in a law-governed society, populated by a plurality of other decentered individuals. This is
an extremely painful developmental struggle, which we continue to
fight all our lives. If there is one thing that psychoanalytic political
theory on both the Left and the Right has taught us in the wake of
modernity's failed utopias, it is the danger of omnipotence. It is now
abundantly clear that a democratic society requires the renunciation of omnipotence (hubris) and the acceptance of self-limitation.
Given these considerations, Marcuse's suggestion that primary
narcissism "contains *ontological* implications," which point "to
another mode of being" (*EC* 107, 109), and that Narcissus and
Orpheus should become new cultural heroes is troubling. To be
sure, given the ecology crisis, envisaging and cultivating less Prome-
thian relationships towards the natural world is a matter of life or
death. But the pursuit of "integral satisfaction" (*EC* 11) that disavows
the incomplete and conflictual nature of human existence brings us
into the register of omnipotence and therewith raises the specter of
totalitarianism.

HABERMAS

Habermas came of age philosophically and politically in the years
following the Second World War. Throughout his career, his concern – indeed, obsession – has been to prevent the madness that
seized Germany from returning. For a young German of his generation, the aestheticized elitism and political quietism of Adorno
did not represent a viable alternative. And, unlike Marcuse and the
enragé students of the 1960s, Habermas was always wary of the revolutionary option. Instead, he pursued a path of radical reformism
and tried to create the appropriate theory to justify it. He took the

prewar critique of scientized reason articulated by Weber, Heidegger, Adorno, and others as a point of departure for developing a more comprehensive theory of rationality. Over the years, as the promise of socialism faded into the background, Habermas's defense of rationality became increasingly bound up with his defense of democracy.[35]

Habermas did not have to struggle to escape from the dialectic of enlightenment, for he rejected the way it was formulated in the first place. He suggests that the trauma of their situation led "Horkheimer and Adorno to commence their critique of enlightenment at such *depth* that the project of enlightenment itself is endangered." But since "we no longer share" this desperate mood, he maintains we can return to a more reasonable depth, which is to say, more conventional level of theorizing (*PD* 106, 114). Horkheimer and Adorno's impasse, he argued, resulted from their theoretical monism, that is, their attempt to conceptualize historical development in terms of only one dimension, namely, instrumental rationality (*TCA* 1.4; *PD* ch. 5). To counter their monism – and this was his decisive innovation – Habermas introduced a second dimension, communicative rationality. Philosophically, adopting the distinction between instrumental and communicative rationality made it possible to clarify the theoretical and normative foundations of the Frankfurt project, something the first generation of Critical Theorists were not particularly interested in doing. And politically, rather than ending up with the immobilization that followed from the dialectic of enlightenment, the more nuanced dualistic analysis made it possible, Habermas believed, to elucidate the progressive as well as the regressive aspects of modernity. This in turn allowed him to identify the strategic points where effective political intervention is possible.

Despite the differences in the various versions of the theory over his long and productive career, Habermas has stuck to his basic intuitions about communication with remarkable tenacity. As early as his inaugural address at the University of Frankfurt, he made the assertion that "autonomy and responsibility are posited for us" by the very structure of language. "Our first sentence," he argued, "expresses unequivocally the intention of universal and constrained consensus" (*KHI* 314; see also *TP* 142–69). Though this claim may have gone further than prudence dictates, causing him to later soften it, some such intuition has always guided his work. To this day, Habermas argues that language is the only place where normativity can be grounded after the demise of theology and metaphysics.

Despite the residue of Marcusean rhetoric in *Knowledge and Human Interests*, Habermas's interest in psychoanalysis was primarily methodological.[36] He believed it provided an actual instance of a successful critical science and could therefore serve as a model for Critical Theory. In line with his linguistic program, Habermas reinterpreted the critique of false consciousness – or the "hermeneutics of suspicion," as Ricoeur was christening it at roughly the same time[37] – as a theory of "systematically distorted communication."[38] This meant that as an actual critical science, psychoanalysis must also be a theory of systematically distorted communication. The false consciousness that psychoanalytic critique seeks to dispel – for example, the distorted manifest content of dreams, symptoms, and parapraxes – does not simply constitute a contingent mistake. It is rather the result of a process of obfuscation that interferes with an individual's attempt at self-understanding. Moreover, because of the systematic nature of the process, access to the true latent meaning underlying the manifest content is methodically blocked. The mere exertion of will, regardless of its intensity, is generally insufficient for overcoming the impasse. Something more than mere interpretation – technique – is required to remove the barriers.

But there is a problem lurking here and it proved to be of enormous import for the development of Habermas's theory. A theory of systematically distorted communication seems to require a concept of undistorted communication simply for those distortions to count as distortions. And the attempt to elucidate the nature of this normative underpinning in his theory, without falling into foundationalism, has plagued Habermas, one way or another, for the rest of his career.

Habermas had the right program, but when he moved away from psychoanalysis he gave up the means of fulfilling it. For unlike Adorno, he was willing to adumbrate a positive conception of the self. Indeed, using his communicative approach, he described a mode of self-organization that in general outline was strikingly close to Loewald's inclusionary model of psychic integration. The emergence of the ego, Habermas argued, takes place through the acquisition of language. It develops when children enter a linguistic community and internalize structures of ordinary language communication.

And as with Loewald (and late Freud), the goal of ego development is to maximize the ego's communicative openness towards
unconscious-instinctual life in order to expand and enrich itself
through the integration of its internal Other – its "internal foreign
territory," as Freud called it.[39]

Habermas suggested that to understand psychoanalysis we should
look to Freud's practice rather than to what he had to say about
it. For when the founder of psychoanalysis tried to provide a
methodological account of what he was doing, his "scientistic self-
misunderstanding" (*KHI* 246) – that is, his attempt to explain his
procedures in terms of energy, forces, displacement, discharge, and
so on – caused him to misinterpret his own work. In a position that is
close to Lacan's, Habermas maintained that the fault was not entirely
Freud's. For the crude state of contemporary neurology and the primitive state of linguistic theory made it impossible for him to properly explicate what he was doing. Freud simply did not have access
to the necessary theoretical resources, which only became available
with the maturation of the theory of language in the middle of the
twentieth century. To gain the proper perspective, Freud's scientific
conceptualization had, in short, to be reformulated with the help of
a theory of language.

That psychoanalysis ought to include the methods of linguistic analysis, however, does not mean it should be seen as a purely
hermeneutical enterprise, as many of the "linguistic reformulators"
have suggested.[40] At roughly the same time as *Knowledge and
Human Interests*, Habermas had written an explicit critique of a
purely hermeneutical, as well as a purely positivistic, approach in
the social sciences (see *LSS* chs. 7–9), and now he applied this critique to an exclusively linguistic interpretation of psychoanalysis.
He argued that, like the pure hermeneutics of the philologists, psychoanalysts aim at filling in gaps in understanding a text – in the
case of analysis, the text of an individual's life history. (Whether a
life history should be viewed as a text is another question.) But unlike
philologists, psychoanalysts do not believe that the gaps they deal
with are accidental. They are not the result of misfortune such as
the destruction of an important papyrus, which may occur in the
transmission of a classical text. The gaps in the texts of an individual's life history are products of specific defense mechanisms and
the defensive operation that created them in the first place. When

the attempt is made to fill those gaps in the psychoanalytic process the defenses assume the functions of obstacles, that is, resistances. The obstructions to understanding, originating in the individual's development, in other words, have meaning, which itself must be understood.

Freud insisted that the cognitive apprehension of the inaccessible, repressed information is not by itself therapeutically sufficient. The resistances themselves must also be worked through in order to realign the dynamic forces that produced them. For Freud, this dynamic approach is the only way therapeutic change of any significance is possible. And Habermas, it must be stressed, underscores the necessity of the dynamic point of view and even cites the relevant *aperçu* from Freud. Bypassing the resistances and merely presenting patients with the relevant information about their unconscious lives, Freud observes, would "have as much influence on the symptoms of nervous illness as a distribution of menu-cards in a time of famine has upon hunger."[41] Habermas grants, moreover, that the existence of the defenses and resistances – and the necessity of exerting effort to work against them – require that we posit force-like, which is to say, dynamic, nature-like (*naturwüschig*) phenomena functioning in the human psyche. And in order to apprehend these phenomena theoretically, psychoanalysis must employ causal-explanatory concepts similar to those used in the natural sciences.

In the analytic critique of false consciousness, the analyst must therefore be "guided by theoretical propositions" (*KHI* 120), which can decipher the nature and sources of those systematic distortions in order to outmaneuver them. Even if we assume that the goal of psychoanalysis is ultimately hermeneutical – and this is debatable – objectified blockages to insight must be removed to achieve understanding. These considerations lead Habermas to soften his charge of scientism against Freud and to admit that the latter's scientific self-understanding was not "entirely unfounded" (*KHI* 214).[42] In line with his general position on the social sciences, Habermas argues that clinical experience demands that psychoanalysis unite *"linguistic analysis with the psychological investigation of causal connections"* (*KHI* 217). Ricoeur goes even further and argues that psychoanalysis gains its very *raison d'être* through a "mixed discourse" that combines the language of energy with the language of meaning.

What Habermas gives on the clinical level he takes back on the meta-psychological level. Whereas, like Ricoeur, he insists on the necessity of combining explanatory and hermeneutical discourses for elucidating clinical experience, he slips into a linguistic monism in his theoretical account of repression. Developmentally, repression sets in, Habermas argues, in danger situations – that is, in situations where children feel it is too risky to express certain wishes publicly. And by "publicly," Habermas means in the intersubjective grammar of ordinary language. (This is his way of reinterpreting secondary processes.) Given their weak egos and the superior power of parental figures, children have no choice but to bar these forbidden wishes from the public domain, including the internal public domain of consciousness, and express them in a distorted and privatized form. Privatization is accomplished by "degrammaticizing" the wishes, which is to say, by removing their expression from the grammar of ordinary language and banishing them to a prelinguistic realm, namely, the unconscious. (These "degrammaticized" expressions are Habermas's way of interpreting the alogical thought of primary processes.) In this way children hide the "unacceptable" parts of themselves not only from others, but from themselves as well. The gaps that appear in an individual life history represent the points at which these repressions have disrupted the narrative.

Repression, then, is conceptualized as an entirely intralinguistic affair, consisting in the "excommunication" of forbidden ideas from the intersubjective realm of ordinary language. Habermas's attempted proof of this point borders on tautology: from the fact that repression can be undone in language (in the talking cure), he concludes that repression in practice is a linguistic process to begin with. But, as we saw Habermas acknowledge, the attempt to undo repression is not only a linguistic process, it encounters the force-like phenomena of resistances that must be combated with a powerful counterforce in clinical practice. The compulsion to think of everything in linguistic terms is so strong in Habermas, however, that he forgets his own observations, as well as his critique of Gadamer's linguistic monism.[43] This leads him to deny a crucial distinction in Freudian psychoanalysis: "The distinction between word-presentations and symbolic ideas," Habermas argues, "is problematic," and "the assumption of a non-linguistic substratum, in which these ideas severed from language are 'carried out,' is unsatisfactory" (*KHI* 241). But the distinction between word-presentations and thing-presentations is a hallmark of Freud's entire construction. It was meant to mark the difference between conscious rational thought and a radically different form of "archaic mental functioning"[44] – that is, the essential division of the self. To deny that distinction not only softens the heterogeneity between the two realms, but also radically diminishes the foreignness of the ego's "inner foreign territory."

During his apprenticeship in Frankfurt, where Freud was a standard author on the Institute's syllabus, Habermas undertook a deep *Auseinadersetzung* with psychoanalysis. But to the degree that he began separating himself from the first generation of Critical Theorists – especially from Adorno – and developing his own position, he also disengaged from psychoanalysis. Ultimately, Adorno and Freud are Enlightenment figures, but, along the way, they certainly gave anti-Enlightenment claims their due. Indeed, the perpetual conflict between the two positions animates their thinking.[45] For Habermas, however, the threat of the anti-Enlightenment was so profound that he had difficulty letting its spokesmen make the strongest case for their positions. In his discussions of Nietzsche, Heidegger, or Derrida, one always knew the outcome from the start. Thus, while Habermas was at home with Freud the *Aufklärer* – the champion of rationality, autonomy, and critique of idolatry – he found Freud's pessimistic anthropology and stress on the irrational uncongenial.

Habermas's interpretation of psychoanalysis as a theory of systematically distorted communication planted the seeds for his ultimate departure from Freud. It contained one of the germ cells that spawned the theory of communicative action, and, as he pursued that theory, psychoanalysis not only became increasingly superfluous but also something of a nuisance. Furthermore, when the defense of "the project of modernity" emerged as the centerpiece of Habermas's program, the cognitive psychologies of Piaget and Kohlberg, with their progressive theories of development, suited his purposes better than Freud's. A shift in the nature of critique was, moreover, implicit in this development, from Marx and Freud to Kant – that is, from the practical critique of concrete human suffering to the philosophical critique of the conditions of the possibility of communication. The hermeneutics of suspicion was quietly transmuted into the effort to justify the foundations of liberal democracy. With the Reagan–Thatcher counter-Reformation, the decline of the New Left, and the ambiguous rise of postmodernism, Habermas no longer trusted the vagaries of practical struggles as the medium of enlightenment. He now looked to "supra-subjective learning systems" to carry the "project of modernity."[46]

But Habermas made things too easy for himself. In principle, he advocates Reason's encounter with its Other as a way of undoing its reification – that is, of making itself richer, deeper, and more flexible. But the degree to which that process can succeed is proportional to the alterity of the Other to which Reason opens itself. Diminished Otherness results in the diminished potential for growth. With respect to the ego, the extension of the category of "the linguistic" to the unconscious lessens the foreignness of the ego's internal territory. This, in turn, reduces the split in the subject and the magnitude of the integrative task that confronts the ego. To the same degree, it also diminishes the ego's potential for growth. What Derrida said about the "dialogue with unreason" in Foucault, can also be said of the ego's encounter with its interior Other in Habermas. The whole process is "interior to *logos*";[47] *logos* never contacts its Other in any significant sense. It is telling that, though Habermas calls for the "linguistification" of inner nature, he does not suggest the "instinctualization" of the ego (*CES* 93).

CONCLUDING REMARKS

By the mid-1970s Critical Theory and psychoanalysis had gone their separate ways.[48] In defending the "project of modernity," Habermas and his circle became involved with the technical details of communication theory, the philosophy of law, and the foundations of liberalism in a more or less Rawlsian mode. To the extent that the communication theory of society required a psychology, Kohlberg's cognitive moral theory fitted the bill. Habermas believed that it lent credence to the strongly rationalist and progressivist direction of his thinking. Indeed, by the time Habermas's theory reached its mature form, it had become apparent that – despite his earlier interest in Freud – the pretheoretical intuitions guiding his project were, in fact, alien to the spirit of psychoanalytic depth-psychology. At the same time, psychoanalysts were engrossed in important but highly circumscribed questions of technique, having to do with the treatment of narcissistic and borderline personalities. The tradition of psychoanalytic social theory – which had extended from Freud's *Totem and Taboo* through the last chapters of *Knowledge and Human Interests* – was all but abandoned.

Today, is there any way for Critical Theory and psychoanalysis to productively reconnect? The work of the old Frankfurt School was a response to the rise of fascism. "Late capitalist society" provided the socioeconomic backdrop for the next generation of Critical Theorists. Today, the most pressing and dangerous issue that confronts us is fundamentalism – East and West, Christian, Islamic, and Jewish. Because psychoanalysis and Critical Theory both grew out of Feuerbach and the Enlightenment, their understanding of religion left much to be desired. Now that faith in reason and progress has been dealt a series of serious blows and the secularization thesis (which in the 1950s and 1960s held that the spread of a scientific culture would progressively lead to the elimination of religion) has proven incorrect, a less biased examination of religion might provide a fruitful topic for probing "the limits of enlightenment" (*DE* 137). (This is not to say that the religious position has proven to be valid, but only that the questions it raises are too ubiquitous and profound to be ignored.) If Critical Theory is going to take the topic of fundamentalism up in any adequate way, it will once again have to call on psychoanalysis. As it was with fascism, the primitive rage and sheer irrationality of the phenomenon require the resources of psychoanalytic depth-psychology. Nothing else will do.

NOTES

1. See *An Unmastered Past: The Autobiographical Reflections of Leo Loewenthal*, ed. M. Jay (Berkeley: University of California Press, 1987), 41. Peter Gay, referring to "the bourgeois as revolutionary," suggests that Freud required the safety and stability of his *bürgherlich* household in order to carry out his revolutionary and frightening exploration of inner reality. *Freud, Jews and Other Germans* (Oxford: Oxford University Press, 1978), pp. 60–1.

2. Many of Fromm's papers from the 1930s are collected in *The Crisis of Psychoanalysis* (New York: Holt, Reinhart, Wilson, 1970). Limitation

of space will prevent me from examining Fromm's important debate with Marcuse, which appeared in *Dissent* in 1955 and 1956, and his eventual break with the Frankfurt School. For an account of this history, see Martin Jay, *The Dialectical Imagination: A History of the Frankfurt School and the Institute of Social Research, 1923–1950* (New York: Little, Brown, 1973), pp. 86–106; Rolf Wiggershaus, *The Frankfurt School: Its History, Theories, and Political Significance*, trans. M. Robertson (Cambridge, Mass.: MIT Press, 1994), pp. 265–73.

3. *Studien über Authorität und Familie: Forshungberichte aus dem Institute for Sozialforschung* (Paris, 1936).

4. Anson Rabinbach, "The Cunning of Unreason: Mimesis and the Construction of Anti-Semitism in Horkheimer and Adorno's *Dialectic of Enlightenment*," in *In the Shadow of Catastrophe: German Intellectuals between Apocalypse and Enlightenment* (Berkeley: University of California Press, 1997), p. 167.

5. Rabinbach, "Cunning of Unreason," p. 85. To avoid a common postmodernist error, it must be stressed that Horkheimer and Adorno were as hostile to irrationalism as they were to instrumental reasons. See Rush, chapter 1 above. Although they recognized that it involved them in a self-contradiction, the two Critical Theorists remained "wholly convinced . . . that social freedom is inseparable from enlightened thought" (*DE* xiii). See also Jay, *Dialectical Imagination*, ch. 8; Wiggershaus, *Frankfurt School*, pp. 302–49.

6. See Friedrich Nietzsche, *On the Genealogy of Morals*, trans. M. Clark and A. Swensen (Indianapolis: Hackett, 1988), pp. 56–57; Sigmund Freud, *Civilization and its Discontents*, in *The Standard Edition of the Complete Psychological works of Sigmund Freud*, trans. J. Strachey (London: Hogarth Press, 1975), XXI, ch. 7 (hereafter *SE*).

7. Although there are distinctions to be made between them, for the purposes of this chapter I will use the terms "subject," "self," and "ego" more or less interchangeably.

8. See also Cornelius Castoriadis, *The Imaginary Institution of Society*, trans. K. Blamey (Cambridge, Mass.: MIT Press, 1987), pp. 300–1.

9. See *The Ego and the Id*, in *SE* XIX, ch. 5.

10. D. W. Winnicott, "Creativity and its Origins," in *Playing and Reality* (New York: Tavistock, 1986), p. 65; see also Hans Loewald, "Psychoanalysis as an Art and the Fantasy Character of the Psychoanalytic Situation," in *Papers on Psychoanalysis* (New Haven: Yale University Press, 1980), p. 352.

11. For the *locus classicus* of French poststructuralist psychoanalytic theory, see Jacques Lacan, *The Ego in Freud's Theory and in the Technique*

of Psychoanalysis (1954–1955), vol. II of *Seminars of Jacques Lacan*, trans. S. Tomaselli (New York: Norton, 1988).

12. In a counterintuitive move, Horkheimer and Adorno tied their defense of the autonomous subject to the most biologistic aspects of Freud's thinking. In fact, these two leftist philosophers criticized the progressivism of "neo-Freudian Revisionists," which sought to combat Freud's pessimistic anthropology by rejecting the importance of the drives and emphasizing the sociality of human beings. Against them, the Critical Theorists argued that their progressivism was too facile. Like much Whiggish leftism, it denied the moment of essential nonidentity between the individual and society – which is not only an antisocial phenomenon, but one that also safeguards individual freedom *vis-à-vis* the collective. Along with this, the progressives failed to adequately appreciate the danger of the integrative forces at work in modern society. Horkheimer and Adorno, in contrast, believed that the drives constituted an inassimilable biological core in the individual that could act as a barrier to those integrative forces.

13. See also Jay, *Dialectical Imagination*, pp. 3–40 and my *Perversion and Utopia: A Study in Pychoanalysis and Critical Theory* (Cambridge, Mass.: MIT Press, 1995), pp. 75–89.

14. Theodor W. Adorno, "Sociology and Psychology," trans. I. Wohlfatrth, *New Left Review* 47 (1968): 83, 86.

15. For the *locus classicus* see Heinz Hartmann, *Ego Psychology and the Problem of Adaptation*, trans. D. Rapport, Journal of the American Psychoanalytic Association Monograph Series, no. 1 (New York: International Universities Press, 1964).

16. See Albrecht Wellmer, "Truth, Semblance and Reconciliation" and "The Dialectic of Modernity." Both essays can be found in his *The Persistence of Modernity: Essays on Aesthetics, Ethics and Postmodernism*, trans. D. Midgley (Cambridge, Mass.: MIT Press, 1991). See also my *Perversion and Utopia: A Study in Psychoanalysis and Critical Theory* (Cambridge, Mass.: MIT Press, 1995), pp. 152–63.

17. In the chapter on anti-Semitism, Horkheimer and Adorno make several other comments, which might also help to envisage a way out of the dialectic of enlightenment. They identify fascism, which constitutes the culmination of the dialectic of enlightenment, as "pathological projection" (*DE* 193). This diagnosis seems to imply the idea of "non-pathological projection." And in the same chapter they also refer to "false projection" (*DE* 188), which similarly appears to presuppose the notion of an idea of "true projection." The implicit notion of a "nonpathological" form of projection points to a potentially crucial,

yet unexplored, area of research in Critical Theory. Such research would necessarily lead to the examination of key passages in Adorno's *Negative Dialectics*. See Honneth, chapter 13 below.

18. Castoriadis, *Imaginary Institution of Society*, p. 104.

19. Hans Loewald, "On Motivation and Instinct Theory," in *Papers on Psychoanalysis*, p. 119. On the critique of exclusion from a different direction, see Michel Foucault, *Madness and Civilization: A History of Insanity in the Age of Reason*, trans. R. Howard (New York: Pantheon Books, 1965), especially ch. 2.

20. Hans Loewald, "On the Therapeutic Action of Psychoanalysis," in *Papers on Psychoanalysis*, p. 228. See Sigmund Freud, *Totem and Taboo: Some Points of Agreement Between the Mental Lives of Savages and Neurotics*, in *SE* XIII, 88–90.

21. Hans Loewald, "The Problem of Defense and the Neurotic Interpretation of Reality," in *Papers on Psychoanalysis*, p. 30.

22. Loewald, "Therapeutic Action of Psychoanalysis," p. 241. See also Sigmund Freud, *Inhibitions, Symptoms and Anxiety*, in *SE* XX, 97.

23. *Civilization and its Discontents*, in *SE* XXI, 69. Clinically, Freud had discovered the importance of integration – the reabsorption of split-off ideas into the psyche's web of associations – during his work on hysteria. But, for complicated reasons that cannot be pursued here, several decades passed before he came to appreciate the importance of the ego's synthetic function. Its synthetic activity allows the ego to enlarge and integrate its unity by absorbing and integrating instinctual-unconscious material into its structure.

24. Loewald, "On Motivation and Instinct Theory," p. 108.

25. Loewald, *Sublimation: Inquiries into Theoretical Psychoanalysis* (New Haven: Yale University Press, 1988), pp. 5, 13.

26. See Jürgen Habermas, "Psychic Thermidor and the Rebirth of Rebellious Subjectivity," in *Habermas and Modernity*, ed. R. J. Bernstein (Cambridge, Mass.: MIT Press, 1985), pp. 74ff.

27. Freud, *Civilization and its Discontents*, in *SE* XXI, 76.

28. Freud, "Formulations on the Two Principles of Mental Functioning," in *SE* XII, 222 (emphasis in original).

29. Peter Dews argues that in order to criticize one of the basic flaws underlying the poststructuralist project, "the assumption that identity can never be anything other than the suppression of difference must be challenged." *The Logics of Disintegration: Post-Structuralist Thought and the Claims of Critical Theory* (London and New York: Verso, 1987), p. 170.

30. See Freud, *Three Essays on the Theory of Sexuality*, in *SE* VII *passim*.

31. Despite Freud's struggle to remain scientific and value-neutral on the subject, the very concept of "perversion" seems to imply reference norm and therefore entail a normative judgment. See J. Laplanche and J.-B. Pontalis, *The Language of Psychoanalysis*, trans. D. Nicholson-Smith (New York: Norton, 1973), pp. 306–7. This is not to say that, for Freud, pregenital sexuality did not have its acceptable place in the sexual life of the mature individual – namely, in foreplay. But if the indulgence of pregenital pleasures exceeds a certain duration in foreplay, or if the coupling does not culminate in genital intercourse, then the sex act crosses the line into perversion.

32. See also Max Horkheimer, "The Authoritarian State," in *The Essential Frankfurt School Reader*, ed. A. Arato and E. Gebhardt (New York: Continuum, 1978), pp. 95–117.

33. Freud, *The Future of an Illusion*, in *SE* xxi, 16.

34. Paul Ricoeur, *Freud and Philosophy: An Essay in Interpretation*, trans. D. Savage (New Haven: Yale University Press, 1970), p. 332.

35. See Baynes, chapter 8 below.

36. See Thomas McCarthy, *The Critical Theory of Jürgen Habermas* (Cambridge, Mass.: MIT Press, 1978), p. 195.

37. Ricoeur, *Freud and Philosophy*, pp. 32–5.

38. For a programmatic statement, see Jürgen Habermas, "Toward a Theory of Communicative Competence," in *Recent Sociology, No. 2: Patterns of Human Communication*, ed. H. P. Dreizel (New York: Macmillan, 1970), pp. 115–30.

39. Freud, "New Introductory Lectures to Psychoanalysis," in *SE* xxii, 57.

40. See Paul Ricoeur, "Image and Language in Psychoanalysis," in vol. iii of *Psychoanalysis and Language, Psychoanalysis and the Humanities*, ed. J. Smith (New Haven: Yale University Press, 1978).

41. Freud, "'Wild' Psychoanalysis," in *SE* xi, 225.

42. At roughly the same time, and out of similar theoretical motives, Paul Ricoeur argued that because the psyche objectifies itself in order to hide from itself, Freud's "objectivism" and "naturalism" are well grounded. See Ricoeur, *Freud and Philosophy*, p. 434; "Technique and Nontechnique in Interpretation," in *The Conflict of Interpretations*, trans. D. Ihde (Evanston: Northwestern University Press, 1974), p. 185.

43. In fact Habermas's position is, in the final analysis, virtually indistinguishable from Gadamer's. See my *Perversion and Utopia*, pp. 205–15.

44. Jonathan Lear, *Love and its Place in Nature* (New York: Farrar, Straus, & Giroux, 1990), p. 37.

45. See my "'Slow Magic': Psychoanalysis and the Disenchantment of the World," *Journal of the American Psychoanalytic Association* 50 (2003): 1197–218.

46. See Axel Honneth, *The Critique of Power: Reflective Stages in a Critical Social Theory*, trans. K. Baynes (Cambridge, Mass.: MIT Press, 1973), p. 284.

47. Jacques Derrida, "Cogito and the History of Madness," *Writing and Difference*, trans. A. Bass (Chicago: University of Chicago Press, 1978), p. 38.

48. The work of Axel Honneth represents an exception, inasmuch as it still tries to integrate the findings of psychoanalysis into a broader theory of society.

5 Dialectics and the revolutionary impulse

REVOLUTION

A story has it that during the storming of the Bastille in 1789, King Louis XVI, hearing the commotion, asked one of his courtiers what was going on, a riot (*émeute*) perhaps? "No, Sire," the courtier is said to have replied, "a revolution." One of several reasons for being suspicious of this story is that it seems to attribute to the courtier preternatural prescience. The nineteenth and twentieth centuries in Europe were to be the age of revolution, and this is at least as much a claim about intellectual history as it is about real political and social history. To be sure, the history of this period, from the Oath of the Tennis Court at the start of the first French Revolution to the fall of the Berlin Wall in 1989, can be told as the story of a series of radical transformations of the political and socioeconomic structures of various European societies. The nineteenth and twentieth centuries, however, were not just a period of actual instability and change, but one in which people acquired certain general ideas about the possibilities of large-scale social change and the human ability to unleash and perhaps control it. More or less spontaneous urban and rural violence, rebellions, *jacqueries*, uprisings of subjugated populations, conspiracies to seize established power, have been the stuff of much of human history for a long time, but events like this come to take on a new character altogether when the actual and potential participants (and the actual and potential opponents) acquire even a rudimentary general conceptual framework with which to understand their situation, the possible courses of action they could undertake, and the possible outcomes.

It is not that a revolution cannot take place unless the participants have the concept, nor that if they have the concept they will necessarily try to rise up against existing authorities, although opponents of the French Revolution did accuse various Enlightenment thinkers, especially Voltaire and Rousseau, of being at least partly responsible for it. In one sense, this is ludicrous. The starving poor do not need copies of the *Social Contract* to feel impulses of violence against their wealthy oppressors, and in a world of satisfied citizens, calls for revolution fall on deaf ears. It is true, however, that if people in a highly imperfect world do have an explicit concept of revolution – which, of course, requires that they have any number of other concepts and beliefs, too – then "revolution" will be on the agenda in a way in which it was not before. In the two hundred years that preceded the fall of the Berlin Wall, European political actors were obsessed with the need for radical social change (or with the need to prevent such change), and political thinkers were obsessed with the need to understand, explain, predict (if possible), and evaluate what seemed to be the phenomenon that defined the epoch – this very obsession was itself a political fact of some significance.

The idea of revolution had such a hold on the European imagination that, as the nineteenth century wore on, the term came to be used more and more widely. Thus it was extended metaphorically to designate other phenomena in realms outside politics. So one began to speak of an industrial revolution that changed the world of work, although "revolution" here designated a gradual, long-term process of (mostly) peaceful change, rather than an abrupt and violent upheaval. Eventually one could speak of a "revolution" in art, like those associated with Cézanne, Kandinsky, the surrealists, Mallarmé, Rimbaud, Wagner, or Schönberg. Today some people will even speak of a revolution in building techniques, dental technology, or marketing. At this point "revolution" and the whole set of terms that have grown up around it – "reaction," "reform," "counterrevolution" – seem to have become a potentially universal way of thinking about the realm of human politics, economics, and culture.

This is the intellectual and political context within which the thought of the members of the Frankfurt School must be located. Their theoretical work is a sustained reflection on revolutions in the modern world in all their complexity. They saw this work as part of a necessary process of preparation for revolution, and thought that theory could play its role only if it was "dialectical." This chapter will focus on the concepts of *revolution* and *dialectics* and will discuss the relation in which the members of the Frankfurt School thought these two things stood to each other.

The "Frankfurt School" is the term used for a loosely associated group of philosophers, historians, economists, literary critics, legal and social theorists, and psychoanalysts ranged around a set of interlocking institutions that were founded in Frankfurt in the late 1920s, and maintained their identity through a series of historical vicissitudes at least until the end of the 1960s. The institutions included the Institut für Sozialforschung (founded in Frankfurt am Main in 1923, moved to New York in the 1930s, then back to Frankfurt in the early 1950s) and the journal *Zeitschrift für Sozialforschung*. This group included centrally such figures as Max Horkheimer, Herbert Marcuse, Franz Pollock, and Leo Löwenthal. Theodor Adorno eventually came to belong to the inner circle, and even to become something of a dominating intellectual presence. Others, such as Erich Fromm, Franz Neumann, and Walter Benjamin, had a perhaps more distanced and idiosyncratic relation to the central group.

The members of this group used the term "Critical Theory (of Society)" to describe the intellectual project to which they were committed. For a number of reasons, including simplicity of exposition, I will concentrate in what follows on two figures of the first generation of Critical Theorists, Theodor Adorno and Herbert Marcuse.[1]

Radical, qualitative change

It is notoriously extremely peculiar that the term *revolution* established itself as the way to refer to political upheavals that result in large-scale changes in economic and social systems.[2] In modern usage a "revolution" is *radical* change in the system of fundamental institutions within a relatively short period of time, with the implication that it is archetypically at least, the genesis of something radically new and different from what went before. Originally, in ancient and medieval times, "revolution" had a rather different meaning; it designated a recurrent pattern of motion in which objects move in a fixed way so that they eventually *return* to their original place. The "revolution" of the heavenly bodies was thought to be a circular movement, embodying a certain continuing necessity. The sun rises each day in the east, moves through the sky and declines in the west, only to return to its initial position the next morning, and this was held to be not a mere accident, but in some very deep sense the way things are and will always be. The characteristic modern conception of a "revolution" is completely different from this. In calling the events in France in the late eighteenth century a "revolution," people were not in the least implying that the initial prerevolutionary state would eventually come round again in its turn, like the sun in the east every morning, that a new *ancien régime* would *necessarily* reestablish "the feudal system" after an appropriate period of further development. After the Revolution, most modern observers assumed, nothing would or could be the same as it was before – if the Bourbons did not realize that, this was seen even at the time as a sign of their unusual obtuseness.

Although there were no fully-fledged ideas of "revolution" in the modern sense before the late seventeenth century, there were patterns of thinking about possible radical transformations in the human world that would bring about qualitatively new forms of human life. Many of these, however, are encountered in the realm of religion. Thus early Christianity certainly had the sense that the unique historical event of Christ's Incarnation was the advent of a radically and qualitative new possible way of being human. This new form of life was completely different from anything that had gone before, and, although it had been "prophesied," it could in no sense have been "predicted"; it was also completely outside human control in that no human action could have brought it about. The Incarnation means the genesis of new human powers, made possible by divine grace, new forms of satisfaction, but also new criteria for judging good and bad. The new Christian worldview which the Incarnation makes possible is partly a transvaluation of existing values – positive virtues of the old, pre-Christian order such as dignity, patriotism, self-sufficiency, self-assertion, and so on are reconstrued as forms of human sinfulness, and previously despised character traits such as humility are advanced to the rank of positive values – and partly the invention of completely new "virtues" such as "faith" and "hope." After the Incarnation there is always the possibility of "conversion,"[3] which will allow the believer to throw off the Old Adam altogether and lead a radically new kind of life. This transformation is essentially an internal, spiritual one, a turning around of the soul and a change in its attitudes, powers, and possibilities, and as such it will not necessarily be immediately visible from the outside. Even at the end of the nineteenth century Tolstoy has Levin in *Anna Karenina* discover that despite his religious conversion, he will continue to live more or less the same outward life he always did, and will even continue to get angry at his coachman in the same old way. For traditional Christianity, at the end of time there will be a further, and perhaps parallel, collective transformation of the conditions of human life as a whole, as described, for instance, in Revelation. The New Jerusalem is not intended merely to be a very good, or even an "ideal *polis*," an optimal human social construction, but rather something completely different from any form of collective life humans could create by their own efforts alone. Neither conversion nor eschatology, however, is revolution, because conversion is the transformation of a single individual and eschatology is a result of divine intervention, not of human agency of any kind.

The two basic ideas about revolution, the older – patterned necessary recurrence – and the specifically modern – the historical eruption of the radically new – are in principle quite distinct, but one finds that some aspects of the older conception have remarkable persistence even into the modern period. This is easy to understand when one recalls the deep-seated fear humans have of the novel, the unknown, and the unexpected. To be able to fit potentially frightening historical upheavals into a pattern, even a retrospective pattern, might give us the sense that we had at least some cognitive control over them and might make them seem less threatening; to be able to fit them into a pattern of recurrence that would allow us to predict them would give us the chance to prepare ourselves appropriately and make them seem even less paralyzingly terrifying. This form of wishful thinking is an adequate explanation for the persistence of elements of the older view.

Necessity and prediction

If we have a perfectly comprehensible human need to try to get a cognitive grip on the phenomenon of revolution, one can ask how far it is possible to satisfy that need and in what way. Particularly in view of the fact that a revolution (in the modern sense) is thought to bring about a qualitative change in the way humans live, which is in each case distinctive, one may wonder whether it makes any sense to look for a *general* theory of revolutions, or whether each one is a unique historical event. Perhaps there is an explanation for each particular revolution in terms of a specific constellation of facts, but the different explanations of each individual revolution do not result from (or cohere to form a) single unitary theory of "revolution." A further possibility is that the general theory one could get of revolution was so thin that it gave us no real insight or was useless as a predictive tool. Suppose, for instance, that a pattern of recurrence exhibits itself only at a very abstract level such as that a revolution takes place when "dissatisfaction becomes intolerable and leads to action to remove the sources of dissatisfaction." It might still be the case that what counted as "dissatisfaction" (and as "intolerable") in different cases varied so much that it was impossible to say anything general and illuminating about it. Perhaps all one could do was describe the worldview and the situation of the population in question in as much detail and with as much sympathy as possible and narrate the events that lead to the upheaval. These narratives, however, might have only a family resemblance to each other.

A further related question is whether revolution(s) can be thought to be "necessary." Modern theorists take a number of different views about whether revolution may in certain circumstances be said to be or to have been "necessary," and if so in what sense one can speak of "necessity". Addressing this question properly raises extremely deep and difficult issues about the role of human action in history, about human intention, foresight, and control, and about freedom and the possibility of explanation.

One highly deterministic position derives from Marx's claim in the afterword to the second edition of *Das Kapital* that he was analyzing structures of social change that would take place "with natural necessity independent of will, desire, and consciousness of humans." A slightly weaker view would hold that there are "objective conditions" that are necessary but not sufficient for revolution. Whether the opportunity presented by the conditions will be seized or not is a matter of politics and free human action, not of strict prediction. Finally, some views emphasize that the "necessity" of revolution is in the first instance a moral necessity or the necessity of overwhelming practical reason, not a theoretical or predictive necessity. That is, the revolution is necessary because one "must" bring it about, in the sense in which one might think one "must" jump into the water to try to saving a person who is drowning or "must" plan ahead for retirement in a capitalist society in which pensions are privatized. The analysis of the "practical necessity" of revolution is not, on most views, disconnected and free-standing, but is connected first with an analysis of the "objective possibilities" of the situation on the one hand, and then second with various predictive claims on the other, but the meaning of "necessity" is distinct from that of a categorical prediction. First of all, to say that a situation is outrageous and "must" be remedied depends, many people might think, on it being possible for it to be remedied. There is no "practical necessity" in the appropriate sense to "end hunger" in a world in which there are no means for transporting surplus from one region to another. Hunger in late twentieth-century Latin America or Africa is objectively outrageous in a way in which it is not in Neolithic Europe. Second, if something actually is sufficiently morally outrageous and impinges in a sufficiently direct and harmful way on large numbers of humans, then they will be likely to notice it and become morally outraged, and if they are in a position to act, they will act.[4] The judgment that something is sufficiently outrageous for it to be the case that it "must" be changed thus has an indirect predictive component.

Directionality

I have up to now concentrated on a central feature of much of our usage of "revolution," that of radical, concentrated change producing fundamental novelty. There are, however, at least two further properties that are often associated with "revolution" in modern discussions. The first of these is directionality (or perhaps one might say "cumulativity") and the second extralegality (and, in the extreme case, violence).

It is, of course, perfectly possible to use the term "revolution" antiseptically to refer simply to any concentrated, swift major change without any commitment to the idea that the change in question fits into a larger historical pattern that exhibits a general historical directionality. Indeed this is, historically, the way the term is used throughout much of the eighteenth century, when the modern usage is still *in statu nascendi*. That is, it is at least in principle possible that the history of a certain region during a certain period of time was composed simply of a series of more or less random upheavals: traditional monarchy, unitary military dictatorship, a system of rule by independent local warlords, theocracy, and various kinds of authoritarian civilian government succeeding each other with interstitial periods of anarchy in a way that seemed overall to display no large-scale pattern at all. We might still refer to each change as a "revolution." For a large part of the nineteenth and early twentieth centuries, however, "revolution" was associated with an idea of history as moving cumulatively in a particular direction. The historical scheme that was most commonly imposed was a "progressivist" one of history as gradual evolution, punctuated by a series of revolutions, and moving cumulatively in the direction of increased human freedom, control over the world, and so on. It is, of course, perfectly possible to think that revolutions have a property of general directionality or even cumulativity without thereby being committed to endorsing that direction as good. Thus, one might agree that a certain chunk of history exhibited cumulative motion towards increased control over nature and economic productivity without committing oneself to the claim that this was in all respects a good thing. One might even in principle think of history as a series of successive and cumulative steps of falling away from some original good.

This general "progressivist" view lies at the basis of attempts to distinguish between "revolution" and "counterrevolution," a distinction that is of some importance for the members of the Frankfurt School (see generally *CR*, and, for the cultural domain, *PMM*). National Socialists described the seizure of power in 1933 as a "revolution," and the new regime certainly did represent a break with the political, social, and cultural reality of the Weimar Republic. Many of those on the political Left, however, insisted that one could not call National Socialism a "revolution" because although it was a radical break introducing a change in the quality of life, it was a movement "backwards," that is, in the wrong historical direction, away from freedom, individualism, and so on. It was not a "revolution," but a "counterrevolution."

The second feature often associated with revolution in the modern mind is extralegality. Perhaps the best approach to this slightly vague property is through reflection on the distinction between revolution and reform. This distinction, which is very important for certain theorists of revolution, is made along three dimensions. First, reform is distinguished from revolution in that a reform is construed as a change in relatively superficial rather than very basic structural features of the society. Second, a reform is thought to be a process of gradual transformation in contrast to abrupt revolutionary change. Finally, a reform is a transformation carried out by mobilization of forces not merely endogenous to the given political system, but recognized by it, that is, with an acknowledged place in it, whereas a revolution often, or even usually, depends on the action of forces that are in some sense not recognized as legitimate. Thus, a Parliamentary Commission may reform the Civil Services while exercising a mandate that satisfies all the conditions of legitimacy imposed by the existing political system; when the Soviets begin to exercise judicial functions in 1918, they do not have a mandate to do so that is recognized by the existing imperial or tsarist political system. This property of "extralegality" admits of degrees. The weakest would be the claim that the revolutionary process was "extraconstitutional," that is, that it depended on structures, institutions, groups, developments that are not part of the established and recognized regime of things, but were also not specifically forbidden. In most systems there are "grey areas" which are neither forbidden nor precisely endorsed, and since change is a regular feature of most European societies in the modern period, it is not surprising that the legal and political system does not always keep pace with reality, and simply overlooks the existence of certain forces and agents. Thus, for a long time political parties had no recognized status; they were the objects of a certain suspicion and disapprobation, but they were not strictly illegal. The same thing is true to an even greater degree of specifically proletarian parties at the end of the nineteenth century. In some countries they were in some sense not part of the acknowledged structure of political action, and were perhaps even subject to informal harassment, but they may not have been strictly illegal. A yet slightly stronger view would be that revolutions are always connected with activities that are strictly illegal. Action can, of course, be illegal but nonviolent. Finally, one can think that revolution must be inherently extralegal and violent. Human institutions, one could argue, are characterized by a natural conservatism or inertia, and only violence will allow one to make basic changes in them. If one thinks, in addition, that most socioeconomic formations up to now have been inegalitarian, then there will be a group that benefits differentially from the status quo. It will, then, not be surprising that those who so benefit will resist change as forcefully as they can.

Marx

In order to distinguish revolution as radical change from mere superficial reform one needs to decide what counts as a "radical" or "fundamental" change of an essential social structure. The members of the Frankfurt School had various criticisms of Marxism, especially of what they saw as its "vulgar" forms, but, with some qualifications which I will mention later, they accepted a basically Marxist account of the structure of society. Marx himself had a somewhat complex and differentiated, but very explicit, crisp, and clear account of what constituted the "essence" of a particular society. He distinguishes clearly between what he calls the "base" of a society and the "superstructure."[5] The more important part is the base, which is comprised of the sector of society that is responsible for the reproduction of "material" life, that is, for the cultivation and distribution of foodstuffs, the provision of housing and medicine, and so on. The "base" is essentially the available technology and the set of social relations of control over basic economic resources. The "superstructure" is comprised of everything else in society: laws, cultural phenomena, religions, political systems, and so on. The superstructure is obviously "dependent" on the base in that people who cannot eat cannot make music or practice religion.

Thus the essence of a modern western society is its economic base, capitalism, and a "revolution" was a change in the capitalist economic structure of a society. Capitalism for Marx is an interconnected system with three parts: (1) it is based on commodity production (i.e. production for sale or exchange rather than immediate use); (2) it is based on private ownership of the means of production, that is, in this system private individuals can own land and machines, which they employ others to cultivate or operate, while appropriating the products that these employees produce; and (3) it comprises a "free" labor market in which people who have no effective access to means of reproducing their lives on their own are forced to sell their labor power to others who employ them to operate privately owned machines. A class is a group of people who have a particular relation to the means of production. A capitalist society is a "class society" because it is divided into differential groups of persons having different relations to the means of production; as such, it is distinct from classless societies, like primitive hunter-gatherer or perhaps some tribal societies, in which all the people have roughly the "same" relation to the means of production – every adult has a bow or fishing net or digging stick, and each one uses his or her own to work. For Marx, then, as long as the capitalist structure remains intact, no revolution has taken place. Transitions between monarchy and parliamentary democracy, between liberal or fascist forms of government, or between systems with higher or lower provision of social welfare are mere superficial changes, at best reforms of no real historical significance.

Part of the theoretical attraction of Marx's position results from the fact that he had a view that was remarkably wide in its scope. Many theorists focus on only one or two aspects of society, but Marx had integrated views about four important areas in social philosophy. In addition to the analysis of the structure of society just described, Marx also had a predictive theory of socioeconomic development, a theory of a possible alternative form of economic organization, and a theory of the agency for radical social change in the modern world.

The predictive component of Marx's theory rests on his "productivist" worldview. He believed that humans were essentially "laboring animals" (homo faber) and that our self-realization took place in free, collective, meaningful work. He also believed that history exhibited an overall pattern in which social formations that fostered greater productivity displaced those that were less productive. Finally, he believed that capitalism had reached an unshiftable historical limit to its ability to develop productivity or to even maintain itself in a stable way, and that it had now entered into a period in which it would be subject to recurrent crises of increasing severity.

For reasons having to do with what he thought were the general limitations of human knowledge, Marx rejected utopian attempts to specify in detail how a better, future society could be organized, but he also believed it was possible to show that a modern society could organize itself without private ownership of the means of production and a free labor market, and to predict that such a form of organization would be classless, and both more stable and more productive than capitalism.

Finally, Marx thought he could show that there existed in modern society an agent with the power and the motivation to overthrow capitalism and introduce the new system of economic organization. The "proletariat," that is, the industrial working class, who were forced to sell their labor to live, was this agent. The upheaval the proletariat could produce would be a "revolution," not a mere "reform," because it would be a change in the basic structure of society.

Marx's view about the role of the sphere of "culture," of forms of social consciousness and ideology, and in general what he calls the "superstructure" of society are not very fully developed – he seems simply not to have been terribly interested in these matters. But at any rate his exoteric view is that important changes in the superstructure follow changes in the base and that a more advanced economic base, that is, one that has a higher level of productivity, means a higher standard of culture and civilization, and even the possibility of a fuller and more correct understanding of society itself.[6]

Vulgar Marxism of the type generally associated with western European social democratic movements at the end of the nineteenth and beginning of the twentieth centuries followed this lead, usually treating the realm of culture as "epiphenomenal," in some sense deeply dependent on "more basic" social-economic changes. This approach does not need to deny the possibility of a revolution in art, morals, or religion, but assigns it no historical significance, no causal role in the basic mechanism by which society lives.

Lenin

Although Lenin followed the official line about the dependence of culture and theory on economic conditions, in fact his early theoretical writings[7] and his practice indicate a slight deviation from it; he puts much more emphasis than Marx did on having the right theory, generating the right form of consciousness, and adopting the right organizational structure for a political party. The young Lenin worried about the loss of revolutionary *élan* in social democratic parties. In his view, excessive concern with straightforward economic issues could lead to the development of a kind of trade union consciousness that sacrificed possible long-term political progress for transient economic gains. The slaves of capital might succumb to the temptation of accepting an immediate minimal increase of their starvation rations rather than bringing about the abolition of slavery as an institution; similarly, no amount of unionization, reduction of working hours, increase of wages, or other benefits would necessarily change the basic structure of capitalism. Marx himself would not have felt the need to be concerned about this particular problem, because he subscribed to what has come to be called "the emiseration thesis" – namely, the view that the logic of capitalist production actually *requires* an ever greater reduction in real wages for the proletariat. For Marx, then, the choice between immediate economic gains and longer-term political ones was not one that would ever have presented itself in a serious way. Lenin would seem to have been motivated by a fear that the emiseration thesis was not true, at least in the short and medium terms. What if capitalism came to be capable of raising the standard of living of the workers rather than further depressing it? A trade union consciousness could then establish itself that was not inherently and irrevocably revolutionary, one that was itself, as Lenin claimed, a form of bourgeois ideology, that is, a form of consciousness that was itself a means through which the bourgeoisie could extend and solidify its domination over the working class. How could such embourgeoisement of social democracy be resisted and the revolutionary impulse maintained?

Lenin's answer was the creation of a party of full-time professional revolutionaries who would constitute a kind of political elite and who would be distinct from the mass of workers. The members of this party would have a correct knowledge of revolutionary theory and be free to engage in extralegal violence; they would be the vanguard of the revolution, leading while the rest of the working class followed.

DIALECTICS

The problem

The members of the Frankfurt School shared Lenin's fear. If Marx was right about the economy, why were the workers so docile? Could it be that capitalism was more flexible than Marx had anticipated; could it reach to providing at least for the immediate future something rather more ample than declining starvation wages for its slave labourers, the proletariat? Could it, furthermore, be that the power of the status quo resided *not* simply in its police force, army, and prison system, or even its factories, railways, and merchant ships, but in the power of its control over the human imagination? If that were true, then the realm of consciousness, culture, and "ideology" could be an important potential arena of political struggle in a sense not clearly envisaged by Marx himself.

To say that capitalism has a stranglehold on the imagination of the workers means two complementary things: that they have some of the beliefs and attitudes they do because of the society they live in, and these beliefs and attitudes are somehow inappropriately constrictive; and that they have some of the desires and needs they do because they live in a society of a certain kind, and that having these desires or needs inappropriately limits what they can imagine and thus what they can reasonably be expected to do.

Beliefs and attitudes

If I have a certain belief, this can constrict the space of possible actions I can envisage myself as performing. If I believe I am locked in a room, this belief can be construed as a limitation on how I can (reasonably try to) act. I think I know that I cannot simply turn the handle and exit in the usual way. I may, of course, not have full confidence in my belief and try the door handle to see if it is really locked, but that is another issue. It is not that I cannot "imagine" that the door is open, even if it is locked, or cannot imagine that I am powerful enough to break the lock and bolt simply by "effortlessly" turning the handle and pushing, although I am not actually strong enough to do that. Of course, I can "imagine" all these things, but this is a kind of idle counterfactual speculation rather than the concrete imaginative planning out of a realistic course of action before I embark on it. If my belief that the door is locked is true, and if I have adequate grounds for believing it to be true, then there can be no serious internal objection to the limitation it imposes on me – in fact that limitation could be seen as a liberation, as freeing me from pointless exertion which is doomed to failure.

When the members of the Frankfurt School claim that the workers in advanced western societies do not revolt in order to change the economic and political system because of some beliefs and attitudes they have, they do not *primarily* mean "false individual beliefs" or even false general beliefs of the usual empirical kind – although the workers may, of course, have some of these too. Thus, the members

of an oppressed class may have the false individual belief that the
police force in their region is more powerful and efficient than it is,
a belief the members of the police force may do their best to foster
and encourage, or, on a more banal level, they may believe that the
level of unemployment in their city is lower than it really is, or that
the food they get at the local shop – when they get any – is minimally healthful rather than genetically modified. They may also
have false general beliefs, such as that people everywhere drive on
the left-hand side of the road or that all children love chocolate. None
of these errors is necessarily unimportant, but the "(false) beliefs and
attitudes" the members of the Frankfurt School chiefly had in mind
are of a rather different kind from the more or less straightforward
empirical ones just cited. Thus, people who grow up in a commer-
cial society are likely to think that a tendency to "truck and barter"
is natural and inherent in all humans, not something acquired only
by people in a society with certain socioeconomic institutions and
a certain history. To say that a tendency to truck and barter is natural and inherent is to do more than merely to announce the result
of a sequence of observations; it is tacitly to accept it as part of the
unquestioned framework for thinking about society. Similarly, people who grow up in a modern, highly litigious society are likely to
find it plausible to think that all humans have a set of universal,
human rights which it is natural for them to stand on, and they will
be likely to hold this belief in a highly moralizing way that has very
significant effects on the way they shape their lives. The members of
the Frankfurt School are keen to understand the difference between
"normal" empirical beliefs (whether individual or general) on the one
hand, and the particular kinds of beliefs and attitudes they think are
the main mechanism of capitalist oppression on the other. They try
to do this by distinguishing between two possible general attitudes:
an objectifying one and a reflective one (*PDGS* 1–86). It is the first
of these two attitudes that they consider problematic, when agents
adopt it towards parts of the human social world.

Objectification and reflection

Human beliefs can be about any number of different kinds of things.
I can have a belief about the weather, about Gogol or Flaubert, about
the results of the recent German general election, about the best

kind of food for a cat of a certain type, and so on. When I adopt an objectifying attitude I treat my beliefs as if they were completely distinct from and external to the state of affairs to which they refer, and as if they were practically inert and had no effect on the state of affairs. If I think it will rain tomorrow, my belief and the weather are two distinct states of affairs. The weather is what it is regardless of what I might think. My belief itself is completely "external" to it and would not appropriately figure as part of the meteorological report. It is perfectly natural for us to adopt an objectifying attitude towards the nonhuman world of nature. The question is whether – and if so to what extent – it is also appropriate to adopt such an attitude towards a society of which I am myself actually or potentially a member.

The members of the Frankfurt School took a Hegelian view of human society that construes it as a self-reflexive, historically developing totality – that is, the beliefs and attitudes people in the society have about themselves and their society are themselves an integral part of the society. If everyone in a society, say early twenty-first-century Britain, thinks that people are universally selfish, then that belief is reflective in a way my belief about the weather is not. Since it is a belief about people in general, it includes the members of the society in question, and holding it will have an effect on that society. It is not simply a disembodied, external, speculative opinion. A society is a "totality" because in principle the beliefs and attitudes of the members could have an effect on *any* part of it (*PDGS* 9–16).

Because this point is both important and rather abstract, let me try to expand it slightly by discussing so-called "self-fulfilling" beliefs. A belief is self-fulfilling if believing makes what is believed true (or contributes in a substantial way to bringing it about that it is true). The classic example of this was the belief that members of a certain minority group are strike-breakers and ought not, therefore, to be permitted to join a labor union.[8] If enough people, especially union officials, hold this belief, then members of the minority group will be excluded from membership of labor unions, and will thus tend to be marginalized in the labor market and subjected to an extremely strong temptation to take what work they can get, even if that involves breaking a strike. The result then well may be that they become strike-breakers.

An "objectifying" attitude towards a belief isolates its strict observational content – such as that members of this minority group are strike-breakers – and treats it as if it were about an object in nature with given determinate properties. As I determine whether it is daytime or nighttime by opening my eyes and looking, or whether all swans are white by seeking out swans and observing them, so I determine whether the members of this minority group are strike-breakers by seeking out members of the group and seeing whether they engage in strike-breaking activities. "Strike-breaking" is a slightly more complex property than "being white," and observing it requires an ability to recognize certain social institutions ("a strike"), but for a person with an objectifying attitude, the basic principle is the same.

To treat a belief "as if" it were about a mere object in nature implies *both* something about how one can and should investigate it, and about how one can use it to argue, evaluate, and guide action. An "objectifying attitude" is closely associated with a merely instrumental use of reason.[9] An inert external object can sometimes be manipulated if I have sufficient knowledge of it. If I discover that the unwieldy sofa has a handle on the other side, I can perhaps grip and shift it, whereas before I could not. In doing this, of course, I need take no account of the beliefs or preferences of the object – it has none. If, on the other hand, I am dealing with a person or group of people, I can bring about change, using my knowledge, in a variety of different ways, including some that depend on changing the beliefs and preferences of the people in question. In the example above, the members and officials of the labor union have a nonreflective, that is, objectifying attitude towards a state of affairs – that members of a certain minority group break strikes – and use this to justify a certain course of action – excluding members of that minority from membership in the union. If I am an observer or a social theorist who has investigated this example and diagnosed it as a case of a self-fulfilling belief, I can tell the officials about my conclusion and how I reached it. By doing that I can perhaps persuade them to change their objectifying attitude to a reflective one, to see the fact of strike-breaking as a result (indirectly) of their own action, and thus as no grounds for the policy of exclusion. To be sure, the members of the Frankfurt School are not naïve about what it would take to bring about this result. After all, it is a basic part of their claim that everyone in our society is under maximal pressure to resist becoming reflective about their beliefs. Still, it is in principle possible to use my knowledge here in a way that is different from direct manipulation. What is going on here in the best of possible cases is rational persuasion; in bringing it about that a belief is held in a reflective rather than an objectifying way that I am not intervening manipulatively or "instrumentally." At the same time, this is a real change in the state of society. This way of using knowledge is not one that simply blanks out and ignores people's beliefs and preferences, but rather one that appeals to them as a basis for a change which they will themselves be able to agree has been in the direction of greater rationality.

The phenomenon of self-fulfilling beliefs is not a singularity that can be dealt with by a few simple methodological precautions; rather it tells us something fundamental about human beliefs in their social context. A reflective belief is *not* necessarily self-fulfilling; it may be self-defeating or have various other social effects. What is important is that one not see beliefs as mere disembodied contents, but realize that holding a belief is itself an act that will have social consequences, even if these consequences are minute, extremely hard to detect, diffuse, and indirect. On the view of the members of the Frankfurt School, all social beliefs are reflective and their consequences should be investigated. This is true both of the beliefs of normal, unsophisticated members of the society, who are absorbed in their daily business, and of the beliefs of theorists. It is people who create their own social world by their action, and their state of belief is a central component in determining how they will act. Anything that reduces the knowledge they have of their own power to structure their social world in a different way, to change what exists, contributes to their oppression.

Although the focus of the Frankfurt School is on "objectification,"[10] they see it as an instance of the more general phenomenon of inappropriate abstraction. One of the basic Hegelian conceptual structures with which the Frankfurt School operates is a contrast between "abstraction" and "concreteness," where "concreteness" means locating something appropriately within the social totality. To isolate a statement such as "Members of this group are strike-breakers," from its social context is to act *as if* it could continue to be true, and a good guide for action, even without being explicitly referred to, and thus qualified by, the more general context within which alone it is true. Another way of putting this is to say that objectification gives inappropriate precedence to "immediacy," to the appearances that present themselves directly to potential investigators. Objectifying thought is especially prone to false universalization for the obvious reason that it will encourage investigators to construe local phenomena as universal. Finally, objectification inclines one to take an ahistorical view of human society and to overlook the fact that the most interesting and important features of most social phenomena have the form they have because of their particular history, and are not fully comprehensible apart from that history. Objectification, false universalization, inappropriate abstraction, and ahistoricism are related deficiencies.

People in modern capitalist societies, then, are encouraged in a systematic way to have the wrong conceptual attitude towards their society, an attitude that stultifies their own possibilities of action. One especially important form of coercion in the modern world is the kind of intellectual conformism that consists in the widely shared belief, explicit or tacit, that there is no real alternative to the present. Causing people to have an objectifying attitude towards their own beliefs and society is a way of reinforcing this intellectual conformism, and preventing them from even envisaging a revolutionary change. This everyday objectifying attitude which capitalism encourages comes eventually to be elaborated theoretically into a philosophical doctrine. The term the members of the Frankfurt School sometimes use to sum up everything they reject about the intellectual superstructure of capitalism is "positivism."

Positivism

"Positivism," for the members of the Frankfurt School, is the ideology of capitalism; it is the explicit philosophical formulation and glorification of the incorrect, objectifying attitude people in capitalist society have towards their world (CT 132–88; PDGS 1–86; O 170–199). Positivism is both a reflection of the way people in our society tend to think – hence its apparent plausibility – and a justification of that way of looking at society. The Frankfurt School sees the intellectual history at least of the past two hundred years or so as a struggle between what they call "positivism" and negative, critical, or "dialectical" forms of thought (RR 323–9).

Traditional logical positivism[11] was committed to atomism – the view that reality can be fully depicted by a set of distinct facts, each separate from the others – to certain standards of clarity of linguistic usage, to the use of formal logic as a basic tool of philosophic analysis, and to the final grounding for all empirical knowledge in direct perception. The dialectical approach developed originally by Hegel and adopted by the members of the Frankfurt School rejects all of these commitments. They reject atomism and the view that all knowledge could be grounded in immediate sense perception because they believe that society is a historically constituted totality. What, however, about positivist standards of clarity and the role of logic?

Careful readers, especially those who have some acquaintance with traditional forms of philosophical analysis, may indeed find something unsatisfactory in the whole discussion of totality and reflexivity above. It seems to lack sharpness and definition, and to be constantly shifting its topic: sometimes what is at issue is belief as a possible linguistic content, sometimes the holding of the belief or even the acting on the belief; the relation between beliefs and attitudes is not specified clearly; sometimes a belief is said to be "objectifying" (or "objectivist"), sometimes people are said to be holding a certain belief in an objectifying way, and so on. This linguistic looseness and lack of formal definition is not a matter of inadvertency, but rather of policy. In this respect, too, the members of the Frankfurt School take their lead from Hegel, who rejects the view that linguistic clarity is an overwhelmingly important philosophical virtue (PDGS 51–4, 72–3). Partly this rejection results from thinking that clear definition of terms in the traditional sense is impossible in philosophical discussion, although perhaps both possible and unobjectionable in some other areas of human life. Hegel's own views on these matters are sufficiently peculiar, deviant, and highly articulated to be interesting in themselves, and they are so deeply embedded in the very basic texture of the Frankfurt view of the world that it is essential to understand them if one wants to attain a well-grounded comprehension of the Frankfurt project.

Hegel

A traditional series of basic assumptions about how to proceed in philosophy get their first formulation in Plato's representation of

Socrates at work. In various early Platonic dialogues Socrates argues that a certain kind of definition of key terms is a precondition to substantive philosophical discussion. First, he argues, we would have to define terms such as "piety" or "justice" or "courage" in a general abstract way, ideally *per genus et differentiam*, before we could move on to ask questions such as "What does piety require of us?" or "Is piety the same as or different from justice?" This way of proceeding later comes to be associated with a number of further assumptions, the most important of which is that the definition will give one the timeless, historically invariant "essence" of what is defined. "Piety" is "essentially" the same thing for Socrates's interlocutor Euthyphro (in the dialogue that bears his name) and for us, and a good definition will not only give us the meaning of a term, but will also circumscribe the "essence" of that which the term designates and will allow us to distinguish it clearly from the accidental accretions of time, superficial appearances, and contingent associations.

Hegel rejects the view that it is important to get formal definition of that which one wishes to discuss before starting a substantive discussion of it. He believes that for philosophically significant concepts, it is impossible to isolate an "essence" that can be given formal definition and distinguished sharply from "other" accidental features associated with it. The basic unit is not the individual word or concept with a fixed meaning, but rather a larger, in fact indeterminately larger, unit, the argument. A philosophical argument is essentially one in which the meaning of the central terms in question shifts during the course of the discussion; a good argument is one in which the semantic content of the basic concept involved changes in a structured way.

Thus Euthyphro in the aforementioned Platonic dialogue makes successive attempts to define "piety," each attempt is subjected to Socrates's argumentative discussion, and each fails. Plato thinks, or at any rate the generations of listeners and readers have thought they were being encouraged by Plato to think, that the essence, or definition, or meaning of "piety" is some abstract formula, such as "piety is the service of the gods," that Socrates and Euthyphro have, unfortunately, simply failed to find. Until they have a satisfactory definition, they cannot begin to discuss real philosophical questions such as whether or not Euthyphro should indict his father for killing a slave. Hegel holds that this way of thinking about philosophy is misguided. On his view, roughly, the essence or "definition" or meaning of "piety" is not a detachable formula that Socrates and Euthyphro could even in principle find or fail to find. Rather, if there is such a thing as a definition, it is precisely the whole series of arguments Socrates goes through in discussing "piety" with Euthyphro, including in particular the refutations of all the inadequate definitions. Or rather the essence of piety is revealed not in a formula, but in the course of an idealized dialogue in which an ideal "Socrates" and "Euthyphro" discuss and follow out the implications of a large number of arguments about piety. This discussion will exhibit a structure, or logic, or necessity, or rationality – it will not be simply a series of random, irrelevant, or merely causally sequential steps, but the "logic" in question will not be one that can be in any way interestingly formalized, and the structure is unique; that is, it cannot be reinstantiated in any way other than by simply *repeating* or *reenacting* the (ideal) discussion in question.[12]

Reason is inherently and irremediably a process, not a result. The "meaning" or "definition" of any term is nothing but its position in such an idealized process, and the process is too full of singularities (which, however, are instances of necessity) for it to be possible to summarize it in a way that would allow one to retain its philosophical substance. If philosophy is a structure of thought and argument *in irreducible motion*,[13] articulating this structure with any degree of sophistication and in any detail requires the use of language, that is, *some* use of *some* language, but *any* particular linguistic formulation of it can be at best approximate. There is, as it were, an inherent slack between language and the concept; the same kinds of pattern can be instantiated in different words, and what is important to see is the pattern – the set of steps of argumentative progression. Obsession with linguistic clarity, then, is in one sense a perfectly comprehensible part of philosophical activity. We constantly strive for clarity, and this striving is an important part of the motor of our philosophical progress, but eventually the philosopher will realize that the striving will never, and could never, be crowned with the success which one might have envisaged and desired at the outset, that of getting a definition of the essence of "piety" or "substance" that will represent a detachable formula. The members of the Frankfurt School add to this general Hegelian argument against linguistic clarity a further consideration of their own. Clarity will be the clarity of our existing, everyday language. That language, however, and the common sense associated with it, is an agency of conformist repression. To put great emphas s on clarifying language in fact means tacitly reinforcing the view hat the existing language is worth it and can be reformed so as no longer to be an instrument of oppression. If society as a whole needs revolutionary change, though, the language too needs to be charged wholesale, not "clarified." Literature, especially avant-garde literature, and other nonstandard forms of linguistic activity can be seen as attempts to escape the pressure towards conformism and can thus to keep open the idea of that which is radically different (*MM* §§5, 50; *O* 58–71, 170–99; *CR* 103).

Hegel is insistent that the method of mathematics, despite its unquestioned use in a variety of other areas, is no model for philosophy,[14] and there is little doubt that he would have thought the same thing to be true of modern logic. There is equally little doubt that all the members of at least the first generation of the Frankfurt School would have agreed fully with Hegel on this (*PDGS* 2; *RR* 144–5; *O* 139–43). Principles of (formal) logic, they assume, have application only when one already has particular terms and propositions that have a clear meaning which does not *change* during the course of the argument. If one thinks one has such propositions, this shows that one has missed the point completely and is not doing philosophy. Dialectics is thus no competitor to formal logic because the two operate, for Hegel, in completely different spheres. Positivism makes the mistake of trying to make formal logic such a competitor, of abstracting analytic clarity and formal logic from their proper subordinate place in philosophical discussion, and trying inappropriately to promote them to a position of unquestioned authority.

If "positivism," with its tacit glorification of the passive mirroring of the existing world as a set of atomistic facts, is a contributor to social immobilism and mystification, the members of the Frankfurt School think that dialectical thinking of the kind outlined by Hegel is more capable of undermining false "objectivism" and a politically charged fatalism. The dialectician need not deny the "facts," just as the social theorist who discovers the self-fulfilling nature of some beliefs does not deny the "fact," for instance that some members of a certain group act as strike-breakers. Indeed, the dialecticians had better not deny the facts, if they do not wish to enter the world of pure fantasy. They do, however, wish to change the focus of existing social research to some extent by demanding that the "facts" be placed in the widest possible context, and by scrutinizing the contribution to "constituting" the facts made by individual human subjects and by society as a whole considered as a kind of collective subject. This widening of the focus, they believe, will show "the facts" to be significantly less robustly grounded in brute nature than they might seem to be (*PDGS* 11, 112).

NEEDS. Describing positivism as the main ideological defense against social change suggests that the main problem is one of workers' *beliefs*. Society is a human creation, but that means a creation of human social animals acting together. These animals have desires, needs, emotions, habits of action, language, and also beliefs, but are not merely or essentially bearers of beliefs. My concentration on "beliefs" in the earlier parts of this chapter was an abstraction for the sake of perspicuous exposition. The control over the imagination that a capitalist society exercises does not operate through beliefs alone, but also operates at the level of people's desires and needs (*O* xv). It is not merely that workers believe in the universality of commodity production, "universal human rights," and so on but that they *need* and want the gadgets, fast food, mindless entertainment, and outlets for aggression capitalism provides for them. It is a basic tenet of Critical Theory that many of our needs and desires in a capitalist society are false, but that as long as we continue to have them, we will find ourselves locked into patterns of behavior that reproduce the capitalist system which produces them.

Positivists are not foolish enough to deny that humans have desires and needs in addition to having beliefs. True to their general commitment to what the members of the Frankfurt School call the principle of "immediacy," though, the positivists see human desires and needs simply as given, as facts like any others. They are thus loath to call any desires or needs "false." As far as needs are concerned, the basic notion of a "need" is a condition that must be satisfied if an organism is not to malfunction. This is a perfectly unobjectionable empirical concept. Thus one may say that humans have a need for water, meaning that they are not able to live without water. One can construe the notion of "malfunction" more or less widely. Without water I will die in a few days; without a nutritious diet I will perhaps not immediately die, only become lethargic, prone to illness, and so on. Still I can reasonably say I "need" to have a nutritious diet. Once, however, I have specified what "malfunction" means, then either I have a need of a certain kind or I do not, and there seems no room for application of the terms "true" or "false." To be sure, I can have a need without knowing that I have it – I may easily need some obscure trace element like selenium and yet have no idea that it is essential to my well-being. Therefore I can also have false beliefs about what I need, but then it is the belief that is false, not the need.

As far as desires are concerned, there is some sense in which positivists also could admit that philosophically we can do some-thing more than simply take them as brute facts to be accepted as they stand. Even positivists can admit some possibility of a limited "scientific criticism" of desires. For instance, one can judge them to be deficient by reference to some minimal principles of logical con-sistency and empirical adequacy. Thus, there is something wrong with the desire-set of a person who desires both A and not-A (or both A and some B which in fact will inevitably lead to not-A). One can also criticize the desire of someone who wishes to drink water which has, unbeknownst to them, been poisoned. Apart from these two modes of criticism, though, the positivist holds that as a social theorist one must take human desires as one finds them.

The members of the Frankfurt School reply to this that if posi-tivism does *not* present itself as a full theory of human rationality and a complete philosophical guide to living a human life, then it is a minor doctrine in a subordinate area of epistemology, and one must investigate its relation to wider issues, other areas of philosophy, more general principles, and so on. If, on the other hand, positivism is supposed to be itself a full-scale philosophy, the final framework for understanding our world and life, then it must at least tacitly be committed to the view that it tells us all we can know about how to live. This in turn implies that there is literally nothing to say about human desires and needs, other than seeing whether the agents under investigation actually exhibit the signs of having them, and whether, if they are desires, they are consistent and are minimally informed by correct empirical knowledge of the environment.

It should perhaps also be noted that the doctrine of "false needs" is a clear departure from traditional Marxist doctrine. Marx himself had a fully positive attitude towards the development of human needs.

A rich human society, he claims, is one rich in needs.[15] He has a complex theory of different kinds of need, their relation to human powers, and the interconnection between the development of powers and the development of needs, but he has no category of a "false need" since there was no interesting sense in which a need itself could be seen to be false or to be something that bound us to the present form of socioeconomic production. In fact, since the main reason for the demise of capitalism, according to Marx, was its inability to satisfy existing human needs, the more developed those needs became, the closer the capitalist system was to self-dissolution.

The concept of "need" used by the members of the Frankfurt School is slightly different from that described above in the discussion of positivism, in that the notion of "malfunction" is construed very broadly indeed. It includes not only the conditions of physical self-maintenance, vitality, and health, but also conditions that must be satisfied if psychic, social, or cultural health and vitality are to be maintained. Loss of a certain kind of self-respect (in a certain society) may not lead to physical illness, but it might well cause severe social malfunction, making the person afflicted with it unable to lead a vital, active social, political, and cultural life. Desire and need are usually construed as distinct. I can desire what I do not need – such as superfluous wealth – and need something I do not desire – such as selenium if I know nothing about it. The members of the Frankfurt School, however, generally tend to use "need" in such a way that desire of a certain kind can generate a corresponding need. I can internalize social pressures so fully and desire something so intensely that this desire becomes "second nature" to me and I will malfunction psychically if I do not satisfy it (L 10–11).

A false need is not one the satisfaction of which fails, or even fails systematically, to be gratifying, but rather one that the agents in question would not have developed had they been in a position to develop their need-structure freely (O 5). "Free development" here means development subject only to the conditions imposed by nature and the level of development of our forces of production. Thus, at a certain point in time the need for digging sticks might be a true need, because given the level of development of the forces of production at that time and the quality of the soil available and so on, sufficient food could not be produced without digging sticks. This need can count as a true need because people would starve without sufficient food, and, given that fact and the level of the development of their forces of production, without digging sticks they will "malfunction." This need can change over time with changes in technology; when hoes replace digging sticks, the need for digging sticks disappears. In contrast, members of late capitalist societies may not just want or desire large, new private cars of a certain brand, designer clothing, subservience from shop assistants, and salaries that are not merely "adequate," but visibly larger than those of people whom they see as their peers. They may genuinely "need" these things in that they pursue them as assiduously as they do true needs such as food and water, accepting no substitutes, and they (socially and psychologically) malfunction if sufficiently deprived of satisfaction. Nevertheless, the members of the Frankfurt School hold, although the needs may be experienced as perfectly genuine, they are false because they are needs that would not have been acquired if people had been allowed to develop their need-structure freely. They develop these needs not in response to natural imperatives, as mediated through the level of development of the forces of production, but in response to the specific pressures of a society based on repression, competitiveness, and compulsive accumulation. Once these "false" needs have been acquired, they stabilize the capitalist regime of repression from which they arose, because many of them, such as that for visible expression of one's standing in a hierarchical economic ordering, would not be satisfied in a postcapitalist society (L 11).

Distinguishing which needs are true and which are false is an extraordinarily delicate operation, which requires considerable powers of discrimination. In some societies (at some levels of development of the forces of production), usable cars of *some* sort are necessary, and having one is a true need, but new cars built by particular firms with particular extra equipment are not, and any "need" for them would be a false need. However, it is precisely one of the main tasks of a critical social theory, and in fact of any social theory that will be a good guide to human life, to try to make that discrimination. Research inspired by positivism can be useful in certain restricted areas, but since positivism does not provide the conceptual means to distinguish between true and false needs, it cannot be the final framework for a seriously critical social theory, one that could in principle be a guide to radical social change – revolution. To the extent to which positivism fails to make this distinction, so the members of the Frankfurt School claim, it tacitly contributes to embedding false needs more deeply into the collective psyche of the members of the society, thus making significant social change more difficult.

All this suggests, of course, that the project of criticizing existing society so as to produce an effective impetus towards revolution is more difficult than most eighteenth and nineteenth century social theorists thought. The false objectifying beliefs discussed in the last section are not just random "errors" that can easily be corrected, but rather are rooted in forms of wishful thinking which are in turn rooted in needs, in the satisfaction of which we have a deep psychic investment, given that we have grown up in this society. Capitalist society produces false beliefs – objectifying attitudes towards society – and false needs, and the conjunction is self-reinforcing. I come to need to see my society objectifyingly, and seeing it that way reinforces my need to retain my existing false needs. Revolution is supposed to bring about a "qualitative" change in the way people live. The basic form of a modern revolution, then, would be one in which people developed a qualitatively new set of human needs (L 4–23). Concretely, this means the genesis of a deep-seated intolerance of competitive, exploitative, and destructive forms of behavior, the development of new aesthetic needs and forms of self-realization, and so forth. If the capitalist system is self-reinforcing, where are these new needs to come from?

REASON AND REVOLUTION

Critique and utopia

"Dialectical" thinking begins its operation by trying to locate given "facts" in the social totality. The "social totality" however, for the members of the Frankfurt School, consists not merely of the economic institutions, but also of forms of consciousness and social ideals, in particular conceptions of the good life. These conceptions are not dictates of pure reason that inhabit a separate realm of thought, but are embedded integral parts of the social mechanism. Social institutions all have an inherent teleology – they are directed at contributing to the "good life" – and by analyzing their structure and their operation one can extract from them their "concept" in the technical sense in which Hegel uses that term: the internal teleological mechanism that governs their operation (*PDGS* 69). The juridical system is not merely a collection of codes, institutions, practices, and regularities, which exists and functions as an end in itself, but rather is a set of actions, events, and structures inherently directed at achieving certain ends: the administration of law, the regulation of criminal behavior, the attainment of justice. One can describe these ends at various levels of generality and in a number of different ways, but all of them can also be seen in turn as having the standing they do because they are assumed to contribute to realizing a certain kind of good (social) life. That is, if I ask about some detailed feature of the judicial system "Why do we do it like *that*?" I will perhaps sometimes get the answer, "What do you mean 'why?'; that is just the way we've always done it," but I will not always get this kind of answer from everyone about all features of the system. Rather, I will often get *some* answer of the form, "We do it this way because doing it this way contributes to the smooth administration of justice." If I keep repeating my question, I will eventually come to some answer that is tantamount to the claim that having a smoothly operating system for administering justice is a good thing for a society; it is part of what it is for a society to lead a good social life.

A serious difficulty arises here, though, from the fact that the more general my questions become, the less likely it is I will get a full, direct, definitive answer from a uniquely authoritative source. Where exactly would I look for an authoritative answer to the question why a particular judicial system is adversarial rather than inquisitorial? Who can tell me definitively what elements compose our historically embodied conception of "the good life"? There is no simple empirical way of determining the answer to these questions. One cannot simply take a poll, because, first of all, most people would have no idea what to answer, and second, even if they did all give a clear answer there is no reason to take that answer as authoritative. The conception of the good life in question is supposed to be the one really embedded in a historical formation of society, not whatever people *think* is the good for people in their society. After all, it is a major claim of the Frankfurt School that people are usually ideologically deluded about their society, so in asking them about "the good" one would elicit a lot of disjointed, indistinct, and contradictory nonsense as a response (*AGS* x.2, 573–94). The more general the questions get, then, the more likely it is that I will have to become active myself in constructing a theory about what exact conception of "the good life" the society is tacitly striving to attain, rather than simply reading it off from what the members themselves spontaneously say.

One very important resource for this construction will be the traditional subject matter of the humanities: works of art, cultural movements, religious and philosophical beliefs are highly condensed repositories of human aspirations and conceptions of the good life. Some of these, such as religious doctrines about universal equality, will have a discursive and general form; more generally they will present in a striking way individual images of good human lives (Achilles, the Buddha, Leopold Bloom) or bad human lives (Iago). Generally the deeply rooted human aspirations that are congealed in traditional works of art, religion, and philosophy have taken a "utopian" form: that is, they were aspirations that could not possibly have been realized in reality in the societies in which the works in question were produced. How could one have universal equality in a feudal society based on a mode of production that requires the distinction between lord and peasant? How many people in the Bronze Age had, like Achilles, relatives among the gods to give them invincible armor or talking horses to give them good advice? With the development of our forces of production, many of these ideals could now be realized, and thus stop being merely utopian fantasies. Even if we do not (yet) have talking horses, we do have a socioeconomic formation that is sufficiently productive, in the view of Marx and of members of the Frankfurt School, not to require gross social inequality.

The above is, of course, merely a first approximation of the Frankfurt view. Members of the School realized that in sophisticated art, the representation of lives as unmitigatedly "good" and "bad" gives way to more complex and subtle constructions. Still, they think the study of "culture" cannot be completely detached from moral and political concerns. Even highly formalist or abstract art can be seen as an expression of a laudable human desire to get beyond deceptive, everyday appearances and thus as a refusal to compromise with the existing corrupt capitalist world, and the romantic poet's gesture of turning away from society is something the moral value and political implications of which can be usefully discussed (NL 1, 37–55).

One important task of Critical Theory, then, is to extract from such traditional conceptions both positive images of the good life and negative images of lives that are not good, to translate them into a form which brings out as clearly as possible those parts of them that are no longer merely utopian, but could actually be realized, and to compare our present society with those images. This confrontation is a critique of our present. Dialectical thinking criticizes existing institutions, practices, or states of affairs simply by contrasting what they are with what they could be, and are in some sense striving to be but are not (ER 182; PDGS 69).

I have discussed two obstacles to revolution: agents in our society have false, objectifying beliefs that make change difficult, and they have false needs that tie them libidinously to the status quo. There is, however, a third obstacle. Specifically modern societies are attempting to discredit the whole idea of a conception of the good life against which our social reality can be measured, and often use positivism to support this discrediting (P 29–34; O 9–12). Conceptions of the good life, after all, do not have the clear "cognitive content" that is recognized and demanded by positivism. These obstacles seem overwhelming in their solidity. "Criticism" seems in comparison an extremely feeble force. How is revolution possible under these circumstances?

Politics

Marx and Lenin answered this question by specifying an agent, and showing how a situation could be predicted to arise in which that agent had the power and motivation to revolt successfully and revolutionize society. Marx's chosen agent was the industrial working class of advanced capitalist society. In the view of the Frankfurt School, however, capitalism had so deluded the classical proletariat that nothing could be expected from them. Lenin's revolutionary vanguard party could, under certain circumstances, seize political power, but its merely instrumental conception of knowledge means that the Leninist party would never be able to effect a *qualitative* revolution in the conditions of human life.[16] It would remain committed to, and foster, an "objectivism" of its own and the same kind of productivism one finds in Marx (which itself is a reflection and expression of one of the least attractive sides of capitalism, not an alternative to it) (*AGS* x.2, 15).

Political revolution, that is a change in the political structure of society together with a radical transformation of its economic and social structure, was always at the center of the thought of members of the Frankfurt School – none of them was a mere "cultural critic" in the sense in which that term is used today. Their analyses of music, literature, popular culture, and so on were always construed as part of a political project that would contribute at the very least to some kind of resistance to the capitalist mode of economic production. On the other hand, the proponents of Critical Theory resisted the temptation to construe culture *merely* as an epiphenomenal compensation for economic deprivation, if by that was meant that culture was or should become a pure instrument, not instantiating values of its own. Even the philosophical extraction of a "utopian kernel" from it by no means exhausts the significance or value of the work of art.

Of course, although the capitalist economic system operates to keep people's imaginations in thrall, it will be unlikely to operate perfectly and be universally successful in enslaving them. Some impulses of freedom and spontaneity will be overlooked and survive in odd places, although they may be rudimentary and inchoate. The prospects for revolutionary change, at least change that would bring qualitative improvement to human life, were bleak. What kind of politics, then, did the members of the Frankfurt School think was possible?

There are two extreme views, held respectively by Adorno and Marcuse. Adorno had by far the more pessimistic (and also self-indulgent) attitude – for him dialectics could be at best a defense against pressures of conformism, but without much hope that this could be more than a rearguard action. The only agents for this were the educated members of the European upper-middle class, who had enjoyed all the benefits of a privileged upbringing, which allowed them to develop and maintain some sensibility and spontaneity, and who could join the ranks of the artistic avant-garde – at any rate as spectators and sympathizers, if not as active participants. Non-Europeans ("Negro students of national economy" and "Siamese in Oxford," Adorno calls them in one memorable passage; *MM* §32) and those who did not grow up as members of the *grande bourgeoisie* could have no access to this culture, except perhaps in truly exceptional circumstances, and would play no role in the resistance. Since Adorno believes that society is a totality, the evil that is at its heart – capitalism and instrumental reason – pervades everything. As he never tires of repeating, there can be no "right" life in a false society (*MM* §18), no ethically or personally satisfactory life without revolution.

The members of the Frankfurt School are in general deeply committed to the principle of "negativity." Given the radical evil of the world, any form of affirmation, even of a highly mediated artistic or utopian kind, would be tantamount to complicity. The only course is relentless criticism of the present. Despite this, Adorno does occasionally give a glimpse of his view of what a good life in a fully emancipated society would comprise. I have been able to find three such suggestions. The first, minimalist one is that everyone should have enough to eat (*MM* §100); a perhaps slightly more advanced one that finds expression in the slogan, "To be able to be different without anxiety" ("*ohne Angst anders sein können*") (*MM* §§66, 128; see also §114); finally, there is liberation from the principle of productivity, "To do nothing at all like an animal" ("*rien faire comme une bête*") (*MM* §100). These are all surprisingly reductivist conceptions: no mention of string quartets, lyric poetry, *haute cuisine*, an *ars amatoria*, or easel painting. To be sure, these three suggestions themselves need to be read "dialectically" and not affirmatively. They are intended to *reject* any form of justification of high culture that depends on subjecting people to malnourishment, *Angst*, or forced labor, but nothing more than that. That seems unobjectionable. However, by the end of his life Adorno had maneuvered himself into a situation in which he seems to have thought that *any* projects for action were compromised by their implication in universal instrumental reason, and were thus evils to be avoided (*AGS* x.2, 786–99). At this point his continued verbal appeals for a radical politics begin to ring hollow.

Marcuse was more sanguine about the possibilities for the development of a potentially revolutionary "new sensibility": a spontaneously generated need for solidarity and aesthetic satisfaction, and an intolerance of repression and coercion (*L* 23–48). He saw this new sensibility arising within western capitalist societies among those who were not yet fully socialized, those who rejected the values of society by a kind of spontaneous act of will,[17] or those who for one reason or other were excluded. These were not members of the traditional Marxist working class, but students, hippies, and black inhabitants of North American ghettos. Marcuse is clear that these groups were *not* a new agent for revolution, but their existence and mode of life did suggest that the revolutionary impulse had not been completely eradicated (*FL* 69). He sometimes speculates about a political conjunction between these groups and third world movements. He also admits that he departs from the Frankfurt tradition in offering some slightly more concrete positive speculations about the content of a better human life (*L* 3–4). One major component of it is a reeroticization of all aspects of human life as a whole. At the end, though, he seems to think it is a genuinely open question whether capitalism, instrumental reason, and the forces of death will be able to maintain themselves, or whether they can be overthrown (*O* xv).

If the prospects for a traditional revolution, a radical change in the political structure in the direction of increasing substantive rationality, were grim in the 1930s or the 1950s, they are, if anything, much worse at the start of the twenty-first century. We also lack a belief in a unitary, teleologically structured history and the consolation of the "dialectic" (and its concept of "truth"). It is understandable under these circumstances that attempts to appropriate the Frankfurt School might concentrate on what might seem the only viable portion of their legacy, their cultural criticism in the narrow sense. This is perfectly understandable, but it is a mistake. Politics was the indispensable framework of their thinking. Nothing prevents us from having a different politics from theirs; it would not be difficult to find good reasons for that. And nothing prevents us from finding their extremely robust notion of "dialectical truth" exaggerated or misguided. Finally, no one will go to prison for treating history as a refuse tip from which one may salvage whatever scraps and fragments take one's fancy, paying no attention to their original context. Those who do find something of value in the work of the Frankfurt School, however, may reasonably want to know what held the various bits and pieces together. The attempt to connect the politics of revolution and culture, and a commitment to the distinction between "true" and "false," were the linchpins of their program (*PDGS* 3–4, 121–2); the parts of it, perhaps, that also have the greatest continuing vitality and relevance.

NOTES

1. The two best overall treatments of the history of the Frankfurt School are Martin Jay, *The Dialectical Imagination* (Boston: Little, Brown, 1973) and Rolf Wiggershaus, *The Frankfurt School: Its History, Theories and Political Significance*, trans. M. Robertson (Cambridge, Mass.: Polity, 1994). For discussion of the wider context, see Perry Anderson, *Considerations on Western Marxism* (London: New Left Books, 1976). See also Rush, chapter 1 above.

2. The best discussion of the history of the concept of "revolution" is still Karl Griewank, *Der neuzeitliche Revolutionsbegriff* (Frankfurt am Main: Suhrkamp, 1969). See also John Dunn, "Revolution," in *Political Innovation and Conceptual Change*, ed. T. Ball, J. Farr, and R. Hanson (Cambridge: Cambridge University Press, 1989) and Reinhart Koselleck, *Vergangene Zukunft: Zur Semantik geschichtlicher Zeiten* (Frankfurt am Main: Suhrkamp, 1979), especially chapters 1 and 3.

3. For more on the concept of "conversion," see A. D. Nock, *Conversion* (Oxford: Oxford University Press, 1933), Alain Badiou, *Saint Paul et la fondation de l'universalisme* (Paris: Presses Universitaires de France, 1997), and Alain Badiou, *L'Ethique: Essai sur la conscience du mal* (Paris: Hatier, 1998).

4. For qualifications, see Macur Olson, *The Logic of Collective Action: Public Goods and the Theory of Groups* (Cambridge, Mass.: Harvard University Press, 1965).

5. See G. A. Cohen, *Marx's Theory of History: A Defence* (Oxford: Oxford University Press, 1978).

6. Admittedly, there is a famous passage in Marx's introduction to the *Grundrisse* (Harmondsworth: Harmondsworth, 1973), pp. 110–11 that seems to contradict this, but this is not the place to discuss that.

7. Vladimir Lenin, *What Is To Be Done?* (New York: International Publishers, 1929).

8. Robert Merton, *Social Theory and Social Structure* (Glencoe: Free Press, 1957), pp. 475–90.

9. See Roberts, chapter 3 above.

10. In this they follow the Hegelian lead of Marx. See *Early Political Writings*, ed. J. O'Malley (Cambridge: Cambridge University Press, 1991), pp. 71–8, 132–3 and Georg Lukács, "Reification and the Consciousness of the Proletariat," in *History and Class-Consciousness*, trans. R. Livingstone (London: Merlin Press, 1971). The relation between "objectification" as discussed in this section, "alienation," and "reification" is too complex to discuss here, suffice it to mention that conceptual "objectification" stands in a relation of reciprocal determination to actual social reification. That is, people find it more plausible to think

of their world as an object to be manipulated, the more they are them-selves treated as mere objects to be manipulated, and the more they think of the world in these terms, the easier it is for them to find them-selves thus manipulated. See *PDGS* 43–4; *RR* 279–82.

11. The members of the Frankfurt School do not mean by "positivism" what contemporary analytic philosophers usually mean by the term. Their usage is much broader, including not only Comte and "logical empiricism," but also the late Schelling (and Heidegger, whom they treat as a late ideological dependent of Schelling). From their point of view, Heidegger, Soviet-style Marxism, and Carnap are all instances of the same thing, of a "positivism" that is committed to ignoring reflec-tion. Thus, despite individual reforms they might encourage, they are politically counterrevolutionary.

12. For Hegel, that is, the "logic" of being is very different from the "logic" of essence and from the "logic" of the concept. Hegel's intention in his philosophy is to "overcome" the distinction between form and content. That is why, strictly speaking, for Hegel there can be no "dialectical method." For there to be any such thing, it would have to be possible to separate form and content strictly, and to reduce different subject matters or different parts of philosophy to some relatively simple set of repeatable formal patterns, a thing Hegel thinks impossible (see also *ND* 144–6).

13. See Hegel, *Phänomenologie des Geistes*, in *Werke in zwanzig Bänden* (Frankfurt am Main: Suhrkamp, 1970), III, 25–7,46–63; *Phenomenology of Spirit*, trans. A. V. Miller (Oxford: Oxford University Press, 1977), pp. 11–13, 27–41.

14. See Hegel, *Phänomenologie des Geistes*, III 42–51; *Phenomenology of Spirit*, pp. 24–31.

15. See Agnes Heller, *The Theory of Need in Marx* (London: Allison & Busby, 1974).

16. To the extent to which members of the Frankfurt School depart from Marx and come to see the dominance of "instrumental reason" rather than specifically the capitalist mode of economic production as the main evil of the modern period, they will be committed to convergence between western societies and "really existing forms of socialism." See Roberts, chapter 3 above.

17. Marcuse sometimes speaks of "the Great Refusal" (*O* 255–6; *EC* 136 *et passim*).

6 "The dead speaking of stones and stars": Adorno's *Aesthetic Theory*

Unfinished, still a work-in-progress at the time of his death in 1969, *Aesthetic Theory* is arguably not only Theodor W. Adorno's masterwork, but perhaps the pivotal document of twentieth-century philosophical aesthetics. The book was to be dedicated to Samuel Beckett; and, at one level, the work can be construed as the philosophical articulation of the meaning of artistic modernism, as modernism brought to the level of the concept. Yet even these simple statements cannot be forwarded innocently: that a work of aesthetics stands at or near the center of the thought of Adorno's Marxism has always been cause for consternation and embarrassment; that western Marxism (in the writings of Ernst Bloch, Györky Lukács, Walter Benjamin, and Herbert Marcuse) has been from the outset bound to cultural critique and aesthetic theory can only deepen the puzzle. Some ground-clearing is thus necessary before a real start can be made.

PHILOSOPHICAL AESTHETICS AS A THEORY OF REASON

> Art is rationality that criticizes rationality
> without withdrawing from it   (*AT* 55)

Within western Marxism, aesthetics is not fundamentally concerned with the traditional questions thought to constitute philosophical aesthetics: what is art? what is beauty? is beauty a (non)natural property of objects or way of regarding them? what is it to adopt an aesthetic attitude? what distinguishes the beautiful from the sublime? can judgments of taste, aesthetic judgments, be objective? are aesthetic judgments cognitive or noncognitive?, and so on. While these

139

are not transparently bad questions, it is doubtful whether philosophical aesthetics was ever centrally motivated by the desire to
answer them, since they all take for granted what is truly puzzling,
namely, that human beings care inordinately about art and beauty,
that we are moved by aesthetic phenomena in a manner altogether
unseemly in comparison with how we think we should be moved
by things moral and political.[1] In banishing the poets from his ideal
state, Plato was acknowledging the depth of the claim of aesthetic
matters. Plato assumed that a routine effect of aesthetic phenomena
was to distract us from and so disorder the claims of reason, that
aesthetic modes of attention and appraisal were, in some sense, "the
other" of pure reason, and, finally, that the rule of reason necessary
for an ideal political order could not succeed if aesthetic matters
were permitted to be continuously formative in political life. Plato's
constellation of art, reason, and political culture has proven fateful
for critical aesthetics.

On the face of it, however, thinking of art or aesthetic awareness as the *other* of reason seems untoward – why not eating, sport,
sex, adventuring, sleeping, or dreaming? At least within the Platonic
dispensation, it would be more appropriate to say that *sensory
encounter* is the other reason, that for pure reason sensuous particulars are only instances of purely intelligible, rational forms, and
that originally philosophy, and now natural science, have the task
of revealing sense matters to be indeterminate illusions whose reality lay in what can be perceived by the mental eye alone: Platonic
forms, scientific laws. Conversely, art or aesthetic thinking would
be the encountering of sensuous particulars for their own sake, and
not as instances of nonsensible intelligibles. Hence, the question of
aesthetics concerns a certain *formation of reason*, of what does or
does not belong to reason, and how that matters.

Plato, Kant, Nietzsche, and Habermas all agree that formal or scientific reason necessarily surmounts and then excludes the authority of the sensible as its condition of possibility.[2] For Kant and
Habermas, the exclusion of sense from reason is driven by the presumption that the space of reason is normative, and thus necessarily a space of freedom, the very opposite of the domain of material
coercion and causality; and, conversely, that the sensible, whether
sensuous particulars themselves or bodily drives, inclinations, and
affections generally, all belong to the causal order of things. Reason

normatively binds the will while affects causally bend it. Although skeptical of the equation of freedom and reason (does not action belong to the purposive movements of living beings?), Nietzsche agrees that enlightened reason normatively excludes the passions and sensuous particulars, but worries at the problem from the side of a theory of action: how can reason *move* us to act if it is severed utterly from the intrinsic springs of action, namely, our desires and passions? Despairing of reason (he calls reason's own despair "nihilism"), Nietzsche seeks to promote the claims of the aesthetic as a fundamental world-orientation that contests the claims of desiccated, abstract reason. For Nietzsche, aesthetic reason in the form of a capacity for self-creation, for self-making and remaking, is the essential form of practical reason in its legislative ambition. The pure reason of the Kantians and the aesthetic self-making of the Nietzscheans are perfect mirror images of one another: they agree on the duality of reason and sense, norm and drive, but come down on opposite sides of the duality.[3]

For first generation Critical Theory, the question of aesthetics was indeed a question about the formation of modern, enlightened reason. However, in opposition to Kantian claims, they denied that the equation of freedom and reason entailed an opposition to a causally determined sense world – why should the claims of Newtonian physics constitute the ultimate ontological constitution of the natural and social world?[4] In opposition to Nietzsche and the Kantians, however, they denied that the rational and the sensible belonged to intrinsically incommensurable domains; on the contrary, the governing *animus* of Critical Theory aesthetics is to claim that sense is indeed the repressed or repudiated other of reason, not in the Nietzschean sense of an alternative to reason as a form of comportment towards the world, but rather as a repudiated and hence split off part of reason itself. For them, reason without sense is deformed and deforming (irrational in itself and thereby nihilistic), sensory matters belong intrinsically to reason. The domain of art (or, more widely, culture) is the social repository for the repressed claims of sensuousness, society's sensory/libidinal unconscious. Simultaneously, it is the social locale where the normative binding of reason and sense is forged, elaborated, and reproduced.

In Critical Theory, philosophical aesthetics is about reason, and only about reason. But then, if Critical Theory is a form of Marxist materialism, it should not be surprising that it sought to refute the idealist separation of reason and sense, and, since art and its elaboration, aesthetics, have been the repository of excluded sensory matters, that it sought to make aesthetics central to theory.

MARXISM AND AESTHETICS

The untruth attacked by art is not rationality but rationality's rigid opposition to the particular   (*AT* 98)

Alas, for traditional Marxism, aesthetics was as insignificant as it was for traditional philosophy – the materialism of aesthetic encounter a form of vulgar materialism. In this instance, the relegation occurs because it is presumed that the governing mechanism of society is its economy, the articulation of a body of productive forces by appropriate productive relations. Jointly, the forces and relations of production are taken to form the economic base of the society, while all else belongs to its superstructure. Call it inverted Platonism, only now the sensory world is illusory, a domain of ideology or false consciousness offering only distorted images of social reality, because detached from the real – material – mechanisms governing social reproduction.

Following the First World War and the Russian Revolution, the failure of the rest of Europe to follow the Russian example, despite severe social and economic crises, led to the thought that, perhaps, the deep economic structures of a society are not sufficient to explain its historical movement. Western Marxism developed from an initial questioning of the base/superstructure model of society. There are two basic aspects to this questioning and restructuring. First, rather than a causal model whereby the economic base produces certain ideas and beliefs, one may consider the domain of ideology as composed not only of false beliefs about the social world, but also of all the beliefs (images, ideas, affective dispositions) and practices social subjects must possess in order to successfully negotiate it. For this to work, one must shift to a broadly two-level, functionalist model of the social world. On the level of *system integration*, what is required is a functional integration of the consequences of social action, which must occur both within single social practices (as the idea of the "invisible hand" attempts to explain the integration of economic activities) and among institutional practices (e.g. education expands as the need for skilled workers rises). On the level of *social integration*, agents are able to coordinate their social actions by adopting harmonious action orientations, which itself involves adopting (internalizing and believing) the same or essentially complementary meanings, social rules, and values. If social integration is necessary for system integration (the functionalist equivalent of base/superstructure), then the two levels can be thought of as mutually conditioning one another, and the transforming of action orientations, hearts and minds, would be providential for social change. This would certainly give a fundamental role in political *Bildung* to art and culture.

Perhaps the most disappointing discovery of the past twenty years has been that social integration of a deep kind is not necessary for system integration, and that capital reproduction, whilst requiring social order, does not apparently require much in the way of doxastic support. From this angle, at least, the whole business of culture and ideology critique has come to seem irrelevant.

The second aspect of the interrogation of traditional Marxism focuses on its philosophy of history. The base/superstructure model left only the economic base as historical force: social change occurs as relations of production, class relations, develop in order to best maximize growing productive forces. While western Marxists remained content with the analysis of *Capital*, they came to think that the primacy of the economic base was not transhistorical and, therefore, not the deep motor of history but, in fact, a unique feature of capital itself: capital is defined by the economic becoming autonomous and the consequent relegation of other social instances, including the political, to the economic instance. The mechanism through which this occurs is not a dialectic of forces and relations of production but – said *sotto voce* – the long-term processes of occidental rationalization as theorized by Max Weber.[5]

Institutionally, rationalization involves social rules becoming more abstract, decontextualized, formal, impersonal, and means–ends rational, hence less traditional (historically bound) and less dependent on the character of reasoners and their relations with one another. Capital is the exemplary instance of this process; it is economic relations rationalized. In *Dialectic of Enlightenment*, Horkheimer and Adorno contend that what has happened to social rules and practices is, in fact, a component of a wider process of rationalization – the process of western enlightenment is nothing other than the *rationalization of reason* itself. The rationalization of reason is the process through which the sensory – the contingent, contextual, and particular – is first dominated and then repudiated as a component of reason, and the remnant, the sensory rump, dispatched into the harmless precinct of art and the aesthetic. According to Horkheimer and Adorno, this process commences from a fear of overwhelming nature, and is itself the discursive embodiment of the drive to self-preservation. We tame our fear of threatening nature when we see its terrors as components of recurring patterns, say the cycle of the seasons. But this mythic mode of adjustment is providential for instrumental engagement with nature generally, since we gain control over particular items by coming to see them as instantiations of recurring properties and concatenations of properties. Thus the general pattern of rationalization involves the *subsumption* of particulars under universals, and the *ascent* from narrow universals (which may remain dependent on particular sensory phenomena) to wider, more unconditioned ones. By means of this aeons-long process of abstraction, practical knowledge ("wood good for a boat") becomes mathematical physics, local exchanges become the capitalist subsumption whereby the qualitative use-values of all particulars are set within the uniform, quantitative system of exchange value (monetary worth), and reason itself is eviscerated from concrete social rules into method and deduction, a priori rules and universal principles. In each of these instances it is the same reason that is at stake, and the same mechanism of subsumption and ascent – the sacrifice of the particular to the universal – that is operative. The evisceration of reason is equally the evisceration – the domination, deforming, and injuring – of the objects of reason. When objects (including human beings) are seen, formed, and treated as representatives of a type of item (white swan, Coke, worker), then they each become ultimately replaceable, fungible, by another of the same kind or exchangeable against a monetary equivalent. The rational process through which the world was freed from superstition, the destruction of the gods, ends with the destruction of specific qualities. Even culture has become an industry subject to the same rationalizing processes.

For Adorno, this process not only has untoward, irrational consequences, but when taken as a whole is irrational in its endpoint because a part of reason – nature controlling, instrumental reasoning – is taken as the whole of reason. And this is self-destructive because this pure, autonomous, a priori constituted reason in fact has material and sensory conditions of possibility that it does not and cannot adequately acknowledge. The critique of the duality of sense and reason as bequeathed by the Platonic tradition, and accepted, however differently, by Kant and Nietzsche, overlaps exactly and completely with the critique of capital, once its central features (the domination of use-value by exchange value) are understood as the consequences and fulfillment of western rationalization.

If, by its own concept, art is bound to sensuousness, if art-making is, even in its representational phase, the accounting of the world in accordance with the material possibilities of a medium (stone, bronze, paint and canvas, sound, words, etc.), then in the context of western rationalization art becomes, increasingly, the marginalized habitat for the sensory-bound aspects of experience. The last *systematic* hold-out against the self-destruction of enlightened reason are the self-absorbed, hermetic works of high modernist art: the compositions of Schönberg, Berg, and Webern; the writings of Baudelaire and Mallarmé, Beckett and Joyce; the paintings of Cézanne, Picasso, Mondrian, and Pollock. Adorno's *Aesthetic Theory* is the elaboration of the traditional categories of aesthetic experience (beautiful, ugly, sublime, form, style, medium, expression, etc.) as reformed in the light of the practice and experience of artistic modernism. But these reformed categories represent nothing other than the claim of sensuous particulars and sensory encounter against dominating reason. Artistic modernism is the disenchanting and disenchanted return of the sensory repressed. In elaborating aesthetic categories in the light of modernism's disenchantment of art, we uncover the repudiated claim of sense for which art has secretly been the keeper and defender all along. Since sense is a component of reason, then aesthetics for Adorno is the study of integral or substantive reason in its alienated, aesthetic form; aesthetics for Adorno means to raise the claim of sensuously bound reason against its desiccated, instrumental form. In Critical Theory, philosophical aesthetics is about reason, and only about reason.

AUTONOMY: ART'S DOUBLE CHARACTER

[Art] epitomizes the unsubsumable and as such challenges
the prevailing principle of reality: that of exchangeability
(*AT* 227)

Modern art is characterized by its becoming autonomous; modernism is that increment in which art becomes self-conscious of its autonomy. Negatively, autonomy refers to the fact that art in modernity has lost any governing social purpose (political, religious, moral, epistemic); as modernism aged this lack of social purpose became ever more palpable and problematic. The starkness of art's social aimlessness is echoed in the very first sentence of *Aesthetic Theory*: "It is self-evident that nothing concerning art is self-evident, not its inner life, not its relation to the world, not even its right to exist" (*AT* 1).

Positively, "autonomy" can be taken to mean that the practice of each particular art is to be governed only by those norms discovered to be intrinsic to the practice itself; so, for example, modernist painting involves the extended interrogation of the minimum necessary conditions that must be satisfied if an object is to be a successful (good, authentic) painting in the light of the distinctive character of its medium. Historically, that interrogation preceded through a series of determinate negations: each later moment denying that the constitutive conditions for something to count as a painting posited in earlier painting really is necessary.

Now one might suppose that the negative loss of external purpose was a mere precondition enabling affirmative autonomy. But that would not explain the continuing disintegrating power of the negative moment – that even the right of art to exist is now in question. The overarching premise of Adorno's aesthetic theory is that art's autonomy is both a characteristic of works and practices, and, at the same time, a social fact. This is the "double character" of art: "something severs itself from empirical reality and thereby from society's functional context and yet is at the same time part of empirical reality and society's functional context" (*AT* 252). The double character of art entails that the affirmative and negative aspects of art's autonomy mutually refer to one another, and that hence, generally for all aesthetic phenomena there will be a purely aesthetic or internal way of regarding them and an external, social characterization.

Nonetheless, it is art's positive autonomy that is at the center of its critical significance. Again, the rationality of bourgeois society requires that every object be fungible; if society is a functional context, then fungibility involves suitability for fulfilling standardized social purposes. So an object can oppose social fungibility only if it is unique and nonsubstitutable; but an object can be nonfungible only through lacking a social purpose; autonomous works of art are unique objects of aesthetic attention that are purposeful in themselves (they are internally complex in normatively compelling ways) in and through lacking any imposed social purpose.[6] This tightens the connection between art's sociality and autonomy, since art may now be said to become social by its opposition to society, where that oppositional locale is conferred only through its autonomy:

> By crystallizing in itself as something unique to itself, rather than complying with existing social norms and qualifying as "socially useful," *it criticizes society by merely existing* . . . There is nothing pure, nothing structured strictly according to its own immanent law, that does not implicitly criticize the debasement of a situation evolving in the direction of a total exchange society in which everything is heteronomously defined. Art's asociality is the determinate negation of a determinate society. (*AT* 225–6; emphasis supplied)

Artworks are things whose value appears to lie in their very appearing; hence they appear as intrinsically valuable, valuable in and of themselves. In a context constituted by every object serving a purpose outside itself, the very existence of an artwork, through its utter uselessness (but also pointlessness, absurdity) is an indictment of that context – something Puritans and Philistines rightly sniff out and despise. But art's "purity" is more than formal; it derives from the social repudiation and repression of those features of sensuous particularity that, whilst intrinsic to artworks, are incompatible with the norms of societal rationalization. Hence what crystallizes in autonomous works in opposition to rationalization is precisely what rationalization has left behind in its progressive refinement; autonomous art is the return of the repressed.

Although the double character of art's autonomy is the conceptual key to *Aesthetic Theory*, hence implicit everywhere, here are four preliminary elaborations.

1. *Form versus content*   It is because Adorno locates art's opposition to society in the bald claim of art objects to be cognitively non-subsumable, unique objects of attention that he promotes the claim of pure, hermetic works against socially committed art like that of Brecht.[7] Socially progressive opinions are those useful to some group (working class, blacks, women), hence appropriable by some in opposition to others. However, if a social message is to be transmitted through an artwork, then it must be artistically formed; but nothing truly artistically formed is immediately social. Hence the aesthetic force of a social idea is discontinuous with its political truth. Conversely, the aesthetic force of a social idea is proportional to its artistic forming. But this is to say that form, not extra-aesthetic content, is the heartbeat of artworks: "Form works like a magnet that orders elements of the empirical world in such a fashion that they are estranged from their extra-aesthetic existence, and it is only as result of this estrangement that they master the extra-aesthetic essence" (*AT* 226). Since all contents of artworks are ultimately drawn from empirical reality, then the dominance of form in shaping social opinion holds generally between form and content; which leads Adorno to contend that in terms of its "microstructure all modern art may be called montage" (*AT* 155). Hence, again, what is "social about art is its immanent [formal] movement against society, not its manifest opinions" (*AT* 227).

2. *Fetishism and guilt*   The sublimation of content through the law of form that is art's resistance to society is itself something social. In this respect, artworks' presumption of being autonomous, spiritual items in opposition to the conditions of material production is a piece of false consciousness, indeed a form of fetishism. The fetish character of the commodity for Marx lay in relations between people appearing as if a property of the thing, its being worth "so-much." The fetish character of the artwork is its illusory claim to be a being in and for itself (to be a thing in itself). It is in virtue of this claim that artworks might be thought of as "absolute" commodities: they are social products that reject every semblance of being for society, unlike typical commodities. As an absolute commodity, the artwork seeks to slip past the ideology that clings to ordinary commodities, namely, of being for the consumer, designed to satisfy a real need of the consumer, rather than, in truth, being for the sake of capital expansion, a component of the production of exchange

value for its own sake. But while the artwork avoids the pretense of usefulness, its does not follow that it is not really a commodity or that it avoids ideological deception. It is exactly its uselessness that insures the absoluteness of the artwork's commodity status, its infinite vulnerability to the play of the market; on sale in the marketplace for whatever value the market decides without even the pretence of utility or the need to check the process. Hence, the very insistence through which art seeks to avoid commodification (its uselessness) makes it all the more subject to it.[8] There is no way around the problem.

What is true of the artwork as commodity, is equally true of its fetish character. Since to seek a compelling autonomy is the law of form governing modern art, then artworks must insist fetishistically on their coherence, that is, they must insist that they are really integral wholes valuable in and of themselves. To do otherwise would be either to renounce art's law of form (hence to renounce the claim to art as such) or to seek validating solace in, say, political commitment, which I have just shown to be is self-defeating. Artworks deploy fetishism against commodity fetishism, but there would be nothing like art at all without the pretense to be a whole. This is to acknowledge that the necessary guilt artworks bear of fetishism does not, and logically cannot, disqualify them "any more than it disqualifies anything culpable; for in the universally, socially mediated world nothing stands external to its nexus of guilt" (*AT* 227).

3. *Abstract and new*   If the autonomy of the work of art is to emblematize the possibility of real individuation in opposition to social heteronomy, then one might suppose that works somehow would be sensuously replete and thereby concrete in opposition to the abstract social relations of modern society; and further, that in art real novelty could emerge against the ever-same of commodity production. Successful particularization and the achievement of newness represent different aspects of a work being nonsubsumable, hence autonomous. But to make suppositions about concrete particularity and newness of this kind again involves conceiving of autonomy as independent from the conditions it opposes. If abstraction means retreat from explicit social content, then the "new art is as abstract as social relations in truth have become . . . [and] the artwork can only oppose this spell [of external reality over its subjects] by assimilating itself to it" (*AT* 31). Analogously, since artworks are

semblances, not real things, then the historically dynamic process of modernism in which each radical mode was succeeded by a further radicalism is in fact indicative of something eluding each work: being really new. "The new" in modernist art "is the longing for the new, not the new itself: That is what everything new suffers from. What takes itself to be utopia remains the negation of what exists and is obedient to it" (*AT* 32).

4. *Aporia of autonomy*   If its autonomy is modernist art's fundamental resource in opposition to administered society, it is a heavily qualified resource: thoroughly conditioned by what it opposes, verging on emptiness, complicit despite itself, and indefinitely vulnerable. Modernism's most consistent strategy for evading cooptation has been to make its products ever more difficult, hermetic, abstract, pure, leaving nothing that social leveling might get hold of. However, another way of describing this process of resistance would be to say that such works become increasingly empty: "The shadow of art's autarchic radicalism is its harmlessness: Absolute color compositions verge on wallpaper patterns . . . Among the dangers faced by new art, the worst is the absence of danger" (*AT* 29). The double character of art's autonomy entails that its situation is aporetic: "If art cedes its autonomy, it delivers itself over to the machinations of the status quo; if art remains strictly for-itself, it nonetheless submits to integration as one harmless domain among others" (*AT* 237).

IMAGELESS IMAGES: REMEMBRANCE OF NATURE IN THE SUBJECT

Natural beauty is the trace of the nonidentical in things
under the spell of universal identity   (*AT* 73)

Art does not imitate nature, not even individual instances
of natural beauty, but natural beauty as such   (*AT* 72)

Rationalized reason is that form of reason that conceives of itself as independent and self-determining; so understood, reason, again, must be fully independent of its bodily and natural situation. Such a conception of reason is most emphatically, self-consciously, and consistently realized in Kant's transcendental idealism and, to a lesser degree, in Hegel's objective idealism, which is why Adorno thinks that a philosophical critique of rationalized modernity can proceed through the immanent critique of idealism. If we place the idea of nonfungible particulars into this setting, then artworks will be construed as intuitions that are not reducible to a covering, classifying concept, or sensuous particulars for which no universal is adequate, remembering that for Kant the ultimate source of the unity of the concept is the unity of the subject (which is why Adorno always construes the reduction of particulars to universals as the domination of the particular [*viz.* nature] by the knowing subject). Artworks are neither universals with their elements simply coming "under" them, nor are they dumb particulars that would receive all their determinacy from whatever concepts are applicable to them (*AT* 83). Artworks protest the duality of universal and particular, concept and intuition, from the side of the particular. By exhibiting the current irreconcilability of universal and particular, artworks project their – utopian – reconciliation. Or, it may be said, artworks are exemplifications of a nonviolent synthesis in which there exists a mutual determination of the forming concept and the sensuous manifold. In order for any of this to run, the internal complexion of the artwork must be conceived as, somehow, intrinsically meaningful, as meaningful in itself (and thus not given meaning by what is external to or different from it). As much as anything, natural beauty instigates and so models such a notion of intrinsic meaningfulness. If that modeling were sufficient, art would not be necessary. A more oblique approach is thus necessary.

Hegel's shifting of the focus of aesthetics from natural beauty to art beauty was meant to underline reason's freedom from the authority of nature on the one hand, and, on the other, that in art what really occurred was spirit coming to know itself in the *alien* medium of sensuousness. Modernism contests these conceits: "Art's spirit is the self-recognition of spirit itself as natural" (*AT* 196). Art's sensuous manifold – called variously: the elemental, the diffuse, material, the nonidentical, the sublime – what is to be squared with universality, is a stand-in for repressed nature. *Pace* Hegel, art beauty cannot be thought without reference to natural beauty. In the course of his defense of the role of natural beauty with respect to art's beauty, Adorno contends that nowhere is the "devastation that idealism sowed" more glaringly evident than in its victims. He continues:

Perhaps nowhere else is the desiccation of everything not totally ruled by the subject more apparent, nowhere else is the dark shadow of idealism more obvious, than in aesthetics. If the case of natural beauty were pending, dignity would be found culpable for having raised the human animal above the animal. In the experience of nature, dignity reveals itself as subjective usurpation that degrades what is not subordinate to the subject – the qualities – to mere material and expulses it from art as a totally indeterminate potential, even though art requires it according to its own concept. (*AT* 62)

If the dignity of the subject is idealistically construed as its distance from animal nature – say, in the Categorical Imperative or the norms of communicative reason – then natural beauty will necessarily be found wanting, and this wanting will be transmitted into art. If spirit is to come to know only itself in artworks, then the materials from which works are made, the materials which, in part, constitute a medium, must be conceived reductively as mere "indeterminate potentials." This is contrary to art's own concept, to its being bound to a sensuous medium. If art's meanings were rational meanings in a wholly alien setting, then those meanings would be capable of being fully abstracted from their alien setting, and judged and communicated in exactly the same way as standard cognitive and moral claims, with the artistic "more" equal to nothing other than a rhetorical flourish. At first blush, this is implausible: the meaning of, say, *Antigone*, *King Lear*, *Endgame*, or *Lavender Mist* cannot be said in any other way without loss. Meanings conveyed in artworks are precisely those whose determinacy depends on the potentialities of the medium itself.

Art mediums are nature conceived of as a potential for human meaning. If color, for example, were a mere "indeterminate potential," then the limit case of the monochrome, which appears to be an empty vehicle licensing an indefinite explosion of possible meanings, would be the norm for art. It is just this that the great modern colorists seek to refute: the claim of Matisse's *The Red Studio* is precisely that its red is not reducible, as are the other elements in the painting, to artistic intention; and hence that the claim of the red, as the normative substance of the painting, instigates an objectivity that is incommensurable with the objectivity enjoined through the practices of drawing, forming, composing. Finding a painterly objectivity that might defeat the will as an arbitrary (subjective) source of meaning through the producing of intentionless appearances – images that are not images of anything – is a constant of modernism. Intentionlessness is secured through the producing of images whose meaning cannot be reduced to how or why they were intended (or, of course, from extant conventional assumptions). These images mark the limits of the constitutive, transcendental subject, a self-relinquishing of transcendental subjectivity, and so a relinquishing of the idea of the world as mere mirror of the subject. An impulse belonging to the deepest stratum of modernism is, thus, the extinguishing of the will in the object, a gesture whose realization has routinely been sought through the binding of works, their authority, to the shoreline of their medium.

The materiality of the medium is, of course, not the materiality of first nature direct: the red of *The Red Studio* does not, could not, mount its claim *anywhere else but in painting*. But that is in part Adorno's point: the nature that finds its way into painting, on which painting depends, and which is what is glimpsed in natural beauty ("nature can in a sense only be seen blindly"; *AT* 69), is a nature that is no longer an object of scientific knowledge, practical labor, or the travel industry, which jointly may be assumed to exhaust what nature may be (they are how nature has been constituted by us). What else of nature there is, art alone systematically interrogates. Hence, if art depends on this impossible nature for its objectivity, it is equally true that *only in the context of art is nature beyond its rationalized modes salvaged*.

Not too far down this path lies Adorno's most replete linking of art's beauty and natural beauty, art's beauty as the enlightened and so disenchanted version of natural beauty, and art as the attempt to make the mute language of nature eloquent:

Only what had escaped nature as fate would help nature to its restitution. The more that art is thoroughly organized as object by the subject and divested of the subject's intentions, the more articulately does it speak according to the model of a nonconceptual, nonrigidified significative language; this would perhaps be the same language that is inscribed in what the sentimental age gave the beautiful if threadbare name, "The Book of Nature". (*AT* 67)

Nature can only speak through art; but the kind of language that artworks seek, the kind of meaning necessary to defeat formal reason, is akin to what once was projected on to nature as its language. This will sound less puzzling if the properly epistemological notions of nondiscursive cognition and intrinsic meaningfulness are kept in mind.

If meaning and reason are to be bound to their material conditions of possibility, then the materiality in question cannot be flatly causal, but rather must represent a potential for meaning. That potential for meaning will only be intrinsic to the material if nondetachable from the material; and meaning that is nondetachable from its material embodiment when cognized is cognized nondiscursively. If intuitions, then, are to be meaningful in themselves and not solely through what concept they fall under, then it is necessary that some portion of cognition be nondiscursive; and, conversely, perhaps it is necessary for the possibility of nondiscursive cognition that meaning adhere to things, have a moment of nondetachability; and perhaps it is necessary in order to think of nondetachability that we have in mind the idea of a "nonconceptual, nonrigidified significative language."

Elsewhere, Adorno states the idea: "The logic of art, a paradox for extra-aesthetic logic, is a syllogism without concept or judgment" (*AT* 136). As paradoxical, indeed, as all this sounds, it follows directly from the original description of the autonomous artwork as being purposeful (internally complex) but without external purpose. The "non" of "nonconceptual" and "nondiscursive" is simply the claim that the meaning of a work is not reducible to any determination external to it: its internal ordering and complexion exhaust its claim to meaning. The most evident way this is manifest in modernism is through the destruction of genre, where genre assumptions are heteronomous conceptual determinations of what a work of art ought to be. Equally, the radicality of the new in modern art follows an analogous path: each "new" work interrupting the continuum of art history, denying that what till now has claimed to constitute art as art is exhaustive, negating previous accounts of what makes art art, and thus posing itself as something unknown, a claim to art with which no knowledge is equal. In both cases, the path of negative destruction is sought to free a work from external determination, and hence to insure that its claim was autonomous, deriving from its internal complexion alone.

When arguing for the rescue of a language of nature, it is human suffering Adorno has most in mind: remembrance of nature in the artwork is for him all but equivalent to the remembrance of suffering ("the artwork is . . . the echo of suffering"; *AT* 39). For Adorno, the relation between reason and suffering was exemplary of the *hybris* of reason and the domination of nature. The thought that the awfulness of suffering *depends* on the vindicability and acceptance of a principle of reason is, he avers, a denial of suffering, its awfulness. Even if that awfulness requires acknowledgment in order to orient significant action, it does not follow that the awfulness has the meaning it does because it is acknowledged by us: offering meaning to suffering is more a way of denying it, its insistence.[9] To claim that reason is not autonomous is in part to claim that even with respect to fundamental norms, pure reason is not their source nor the ultimate authority. If meaning can adhere to object, then factual states of affairs can be normative in themselves – it is this which the disenchantment of nature denies and what Adorno thinks is necessary in order to contest the hegemony of rationalized reason. It is equally just this which artworks exemplify through their nondiscursive meanings. So, now, the idea of a "nonconceptual, nonrigidified significative language" is of one in which reason is dependent on its object, in which there is a priority of the object over the subject.[10]

The more extreme the power of subjectivity, the more extreme in the opposing direction art must become. Art, for Adorno, positions us with respect to what is not up to us. Part of the difficulty in pursuing this idea is that the relation of the discursive to the nondiscursive in art is continually shifting; which is why, again, Adorno makes those hermetic, disintegrating works of late modernism exemplary for his conception of modernism in general.

His poetry is permeated by the shame of art in the face of suffering that escapes both experience and sublimation. Celan's poems want to speak of the most extreme horror through silence. Their truth content itself becomes negative. They imitate a language beneath the helpless language of human beings, indeed, beneath all organic language: it is that of the dead speaking of stones and stars. The last rudiments of the organic are liquidated . . . The language of the lifeless becomes the last possible comfort for a death that is deprived of all meaning . . . Celan transposes into linguistic processes the increasing abstraction of landscape, progressively approximating it to the inorganic. (*AT* 322)[11]

The "shame of art" is in miniature the shame of reason, the last velleity of idealism needing to be renounced. The form that renouncement takes in Celan is double: thematic in the disintegration of organic nature into inorganic nature; formal in the disintegration of "organic" language, language infused with intended meaning, into linguistic remnants – the latter accomplished through syntactic and semantic decomposition. Only through linguistic decomposition does that other disintegration become imaginatively compelling, where the image of inorganic nature is one of both what nature has become (what has been done to it) and how nature yet stands – nature beyond the will to mean. A broken word or an enjambed one interrupts communicative meaning for the sake of word meaning, where the elemental character of word meaning is to reverse language so that it becomes the agent of the thing spoken about rather than things being the merely intentional objects of linguistic subjects. The Book of Nature, stones and stars, nakedly appear as language effaces its own worlding, meaning-making powers. Celan's broken language registers each act of speech as a desecration of silence.

TRUTH CONTENT

Only what does not fit into this world is true.

(AT 59)

Adorno does not suppose, even for a moment, that Matisse's red or Celan's stones and stars are things in themselves. The claim is rather that artworks, a poem or painting, are illusory images of things in themselves in which, internally, there is carried out a curtailment of the meaning-constituting powers of the universal in the face of the sensuous particularity of the material elements of the medium. Modernist works attempt to prohibit their external conceptual appropriation, their neutralization through interpretation, through the explicit decomposing of their own imperative forms, thereby emancipating the elements of the medium as elements (words as words, paint as paint, etc.). One might say that, while in traditional art sensuous materials were to be in the service of the ideals represented, in modernist art form is to be in the service of the material elements of the medium – form is for the sake of the materials formed. Adorno thinks of this reversal as modernism bringing together in each work a moment of beauty (with its association of closure, harmony, perfection) and a moment of sublimity (the appearing of what exceeds and destroys form), the latter moment revealing the illusory

character of the former moment, so the moment of sublimity or dissonance in the modernist work is the moment in which even the
claims of aesthetic subjectivity are relinquished before and for the
sake of the object.

At least the broad parameters of Adorno's theory should now be
visible. The villain of the piece is instrumental reason. Instrumental reason is understood as the imposition of human subjectivity
on to nature. The mechanism of domination is the suppression of
the particular by the universal. Art stands out as a form of resistance to this process because meaning in art is meaning within the
materiality of a medium, and artworks' manner of claiming is as irreducibly unique items. Within works of art, universality is conveyed
through form while particularity is conveyed through moments of
dissonance or decomposition; hence, the dialectic of formation and
deformation (beauty and dissonance) within each work stands for the
possible articulations of universal and particular, subject and nature:
"In serene beauty [from which modernist art departs] its recalcitrant
other would be completely pacified, and such aesthetic reconciliation is fatal for the extra-aesthetic. That is the melancholy of art. It
achieves an unreal reconciliation [of universal and particular, subject
and nature] at the price of a real reconciliation" (*AT* 52).

Adorno thus wants to say that each authentic work of art, that
is, each work that lodges a compelling aesthetic claim, possesses a
truth-content. Adorno appears to designate a number of quite different phenomena under the heading of truth-content. Here are just
four examples:

1. *Nature.* "Nature, to whose imago art is devoted, does not yet
    in any way exist; what is true in art is something nonexis-
    tent." (*AT* 131)
2. *Society.* "Society inheres in the truth content. The appearing,
    whereby the artwork far surpasses the mere subject, is the
    eruption of the subject's collective essence." (*AT* 131)
3. *Ideology critique.* "The complete presentation of false con-
    sciousness is what names it and is for itself truth content."
    (*AT* 130)
4. *The philosophical concept.* "Philosophy and art converge in
    their truth content: The progressive self-unfolding truth of
    the artwork is none other than the truth of the philosophical
    concept." (*AT* 130)

Since artworks are not beholden to empirical experience for their legitimacy, it is almost universally assumed that artworks are noncognitive. Adorno does not dispute the distance from empirical experience. Rather, he thinks artworks are cognitive in almost the same way that philosophy is cognitive: philosophy – reflectively – investigates the relation of universal (concept) and particular (intuition) through the universal, while art – performatively – investigates the relation of universal and particular through the particular. Since in Adorno's lexicon, universal and particular are the epistemological/categorial equivalents of society and nature, subject and object, respectively, then the categorial truth about society and nature is ultimately going to be cashed out in an historically indexed, sociologically sensitive account of universal and particular. From Hegel, Adorno adopted the thesis that which forms of art and which individual arts are possible under specific historical and social preconditions is variable and broadly determinate. Artistic production (what it is possible to produce as a serious work of art) and judgment (what we can find authentic) are an index of what forms, with their specific powers of integration, are normatively possible at a given time. Form is the internal bearer of art's (external) sociality. Finding certain possibilities naïve or sentimental, shallow or kitsch or clichéd, is not a matter of fashion but of conceptual possibility – it speaks to the social fate of the concept at a given time. This was implicit in the claim that committed art now looks crude or shrill and sounds like special pleading, and, in the case of Celan's poetry, that only through something like the self-relinquishment of the lyric "I" could voice be given to the atrocity of the Holocaust.[12] This is why, in general now, Adorno takes artistic modernism as the performative transcendental interrogation of the relation of the universal and the particular. Said slightly more obliquely, "the truth content of artworks is not what they mean but rather what decides whether the work in itself is true or false" (AT 130). Assume that by "true or false" Adorno means authentic or inauthentic, then the truth-content of a work is what is revealed as determining its authenticity. So, for example, in the passage about Celan, when Adorno claims that the truth-content of the poems is negative, he means that their way of exhibiting the relation of universal and particular, form and nature, is through exhibiting – formally presenting – their emphatic irreconcilability; we experience the poems as authentic because they measure up to the demand of that concrete irreconcilability. To claim irreconcilability is the truth-condition of the poems is to claim, with respect to the phenomena in question, that the universal is the negation of the particular, and hence, for now, each universal that we might deploy in order to figure the extinction of those lives would appear as a betrayal of them. While such judgment with respect to particular works is always going to be contestable, Adorno binds his argument to the evolution of modernism as a whole.[13]

Since in artworks the moment of particularity is primary, since artworks perform rather than elaborate the disposition of universal and particular at a given time, then they cannot say outright that their particular complexion reveals the truth about universal and particular generally; which is why, for Adorno, artworks require philosophical elaboration. The ultimate stakes of art is the disposition of discursive reason, even if art's own concern is with the nondiscursive moment within it. Hence, one can think of the relation between art and philosophy in Adorno's aesthetic theory as itself analogous to the relation between concept and intuition in Kantian philosophy: philosophy gives conceptual expression to the claim of intuition, although it is only through intuition – aesthetic experience itself – that the claim emerges.[14] Within Adorno's modernist philosophy, philosophy depends on the experience of art for a content it can neither introduce nor authorize through itself – which is precisely the self-limiting character of conceptuality and rationality that is the ambition of the theory as a whole. The proximity of the truth-content of art to the philosophical concept is equally why the truth-content of a work negates the work: "Each artwork, as a structure, perishes in its truth content; through it the artwork sinks into irrelevance, something that is granted exclusively to the greatest artworks" (AT 131–2). Finally, although more indirectly, Adorno is supposing that one cannot take seriously the artwork's claim without that affecting the very idea of truth: correspondence, coherence, communicative, pragmatist notions of truth would all disallow the truth-claim of the work of art.

FRAGMENTS

1. *Praxis*. What makes modernism's critique of rationalized society possible is its distance from the demands of ordinary practice. Again,

its purposelessness and functionless character, its nonintervention in the empirical world, is the condition through which art takes a stand on society. It is thus natural to think of art as utterly opposed to praxis. But this cannot be quite right, since, minimally, works are actively produced, indeed, they are forms of synthesis. As forms of synthesis they exemplify a kind of relation of universal to particular; but each such kind of relation itself stands for a mode of comportment a subject may have towards an object-world. Some of this innervates the claim that "the process enacted internally by each and every artwork works back on society as a model of a possible praxis in which something on the order of a collective subject is constituted" (AT 242). Since forms of universality imply formations of sociality (how a social world stands to nature, and hence how each member stands to every other), then each configuration of a stance towards the world is at the same time a figure for a "We" (AT 167–8).

2. *Promise*. Even if it is conceded that modernist art models a conception of praxis, the obvious question arises as to the status of the model. And this question must reverberate back on to art's truth-content. Artworks are not real things, but semblances of real things; and it is because they are semblances that they can enact relations of universal and particular not possible in current empirical experience. "The appearance of the nonexistent as if it existed motivates the question as to the truth of art. By its form alone art promises what is not; it registers objectively, however refractedly, the claim that because the nonexistent appears it must be possible" (AT 82). By withdrawing from empirical possibility as it is now conceived, artworks open up another domain of the possible; because art forms are socially conditioned and are realized in socially determinate material mediums, then what they reveal as possible must be stronger than mere logical possibility, however much weaker than real, causal possibility they remain. Artworks are modally anomalous; they promise a future but can neither legislate what they promise nor vindicate it as potentially real. "It is not for art to decide by its existence if the nonexisting that appears indeed exists as something appearing or remains semblance" (AT 83).

3. *Fragment*. Even art's withdrawal from the demands of empirical practice may not be sufficient to explain and vindicate the authority of its reconfigurations of the relation of universal and particular, subject and object; even their promise of possibility exceeds the present.

"Artworks draw credit from a praxis that has yet to begin and no one knows whether anything backs their letters of credit" (*AT* 83). To the complicit conditioning of the artwork that we noted under its double character, we can now add that all artworks appear to be what they are not (wholes) and thus necessarily fail (to be real wholes); that they promise a possibility that they cannot secure as a real possibility; and that their capacity for resistance to social cooptation is purchased as the price of increasing emptiness. At their best, Adorno thought, artworks might attain the status of fragments since they are forms conceding what they cannot be and what they nevertheless want to be.

So saying, however, is a formal matter that does touch on what deserves the title of artwork; only whether a work "exposes itself to, or withdraws from, the irreconcilable" defines the rank of artwork (*AT* 190). Even as he wrote *Aesthetic Theory*, Adorno was aware that the modern was growing old (*AT* 342), that in a sense his work was as much memorial as critical defense, and that the fragments of which the work itself is composed were perhaps the only way in which exposure to the irreconcilable might be maintained. In this respect, my original contention that within Critical Theory philosophical aesthetics is about reason and only about reason is misleading, since if art is the criticism of rationality, then what tests the rationality of reason must be the same as what confers the rank of artwork. I hear a little of this as, in the closing sentences of *Aesthetic Theory*, Adorno contemplates the passing away of art: "it would be preferable that some fine day art vanish altogether than that it forget the suffering that is its expression and in which form has its substance" (*AT* 260). If this states why modernism cannot be regarded as just another art historical phase, a small twist in the history of forms and styles, just a passing moment, it equally, and perhaps terribly, announces an answer to the question with which the work opened – concerning art's right to existence.

NOTES

1. I am not denying that philosophical aesthetics proceeds *through* engaging with these questions. What the best writers on aesthetics all show is how the standard questions are really occasions for encountering pervasive but routinely repudiated features of experience.

2. Arthur Danto has nicely argued that from its very beginnings philosophical reason has legitimated itself by disenfranchising the claims of art and the aesthetic, as if the very goodness of reason became evident only in the light of the intrinsic awfulness (irrationality, illusioriness, transience) of the aesthetic. See Arthur Danto, *The Philosophical Disenfranchisement of Art* (New York: Columbia University Press, 1986), pp. 1–21.

3. Nietzsche thinks the claim of reason to purity is a metaphysical illusion, but his motivational critique does not require the metaphysical thesis. Max Weber, perhaps Nietzsche's most radical and thoughtful follower, elaborates the motivational critique without the metaphysical critique in "Science as Vocation," in *From Max Weber: Essays in Sociology*, ed. H. H. Gerth and C. Wright Mills (London: Routledge, 1991). This critique is also at the center of his account of western rationalization, on which see note 5 below.

4. In the background there is a more technical claim, namely, that causality and freedom are *not* contraries, only freedom and law are; and it is illegitimate to reduce natural causality to lawfulness. The duality of rational binding and causal bending is a constant target of Adorno's, and one he believes that artworks surmount: "in art there is no difference between purely logical forms and those that apply empirically; in art the archaic undifferentiatedness of logic and causality hibernates" (*AT* 137).

5. Max Weber, *The Protestant Ethic and the Spirit of Capitalism*, trans. Talcott Parsons (London: HarperCollins, 1991); *Economy and Society*, ed. G. Roth and C. Wittich, 2 vols. (Berkeley: University of California Press, 1991).

6. Given the previous discussion of reason and sense, wherever "unique" appears in these pages the reader should simultaneously hear "sensuously particular."

7. In his essay "What is Epic Theatre" (second version), Walter Benjamin briefly summarizes the point of Brecht's dramatic practice in these terms: "The task of epic theatre, Brecht believes, is not so much to develop actions as to present conditions. But 'represent' does not here signify 'reproduce' in the sense used by the theoreticians of Naturalism. Rather, the first point at issue is to *uncover* those conditions. (One could just as well say: *to make them strange [verfremden]*.) This uncovering (making strange, or alienating) of conditions is brought about by [represented] processes [of the represented actions] being interrupted." *Understanding Brecht*, trans. A. Bostock (London: New Left Books, 1977), p. 18.

8. But see Simon Jarvis, *Adorno: A Critical Introduction* (Cambridge: Polity, 1998), p. 118.

9. "Suffering remains foreign to knowledge; though knowledge can subordinate it conceptually and provide means for its amelioration, knowledge can scarcely express it through its own means of experience without itself becoming irrational. Suffering conceptualized remains mute and inconsequential" (*AT* 18).

10. "Artworks become like language in the development of the bindingness of their elements, a wordless syntax even in linguistic works" (*AT* 184). That is, the way in which form binds elements together has the force of a syntax such that the elements themselves take on the thrust of semantic items.

11. Here is a brief Celan poem that is exactly charting the liquidation into the inorganic, as if only the dead could witness what requires witnessing, and as if what requires witness is a landscape from which all life has been removed. Adorno considers this moment the extreme limit of rationalization: even death is no longer possible.

> WEISSGRAU aus-
> geschachteten steilen
> Gefühls.
>
> Landeinwärts, hierher-
> verwehter Strandhafer bläst
> Sandmuster über
> den Rauch von Brunnengesängen.
>
> Ein Ohr, abgetrennt, lauscht.
>
> Ein Aug, in Streifen geschnitten,
> wird all dem gerecht.

> WHITEGRAY of a
> steeply caved
> feeling.
>
> Inland, wind-
> driven dunegrass blows
> sand patterns over
> the smoke of wellsongs.
>
> An ear, severed, listens.
>
> An eye, sliced into strips,
> gives all that its due.

Selected Poems and Prose of Paul Celan, trans. J. Felstiner
(New York: Norton, 2001), p. 230–1.

In this passage Adorno is probably referring to "Radix, Matrix," which begins: "As one speaks to stone, as / you / to me from the abyss" (ibid., p. 167).

12. It is the weightiness of the pressures determining artistic possibility that lead Adorno to say that "great artworks are unable to lie" (*AT* 130). Hence for Adorno artistic authenticity and ideological deceit are in principle incommensurable.

13. I am here simply ignoring the question as to whether Adorno is correct in his judgment that the Holocaust represents the limit case of rationalized modernity rather than, as optimists hope, a particular and grotesque departure from it.

14. Albrecht Wellmer, "Adorno, Modernity, and the Sublime," in *Endgames: The Irreconcilable Nature of Modernity*, trans. D. Midgley (Cambridge, Mass.: MIT Press, 1998), pp. 156–7. For a concise handling of the formal, sociological, and philosophical moments in Adorno's account with respect to his musical theory, see Max Paddison, "Immanent Critique or Musical Stocktaking?," in *Adorno: A Critical Reader*, ed. N. Gibson and A. Rubin (Oxford: Blackwell, 2002).

7   Critique, state, and economy

The theorists who conceptualized Critical Theory's general framework set themselves a double task: they sought to critically illuminate the great historical changes of the twentieth century while reflexively grounding the possibility of their critique with reference to its historical context.[1] Most attempts to contextualize Critical Theory have done so in terms of contemporary historical developments, such as the failure of revolution in the West after World War One and the Russian Revolution, the development of Stalinism, the rise of Fascism and Nazism, and the growing importance of mass-mediated forms of consumption, culture, and politics.[2] Too often, however, such attempts do not consider that Critical Theory sought to make sense of such developments with reference to a superordinate historical context – an epochal transformation of capitalism in the first part of the twentieth century. In grappling with this transformation, the Frankfurt School theorists formulated sophisticated and interrelated critiques of instrumental reason, the domination of nature, political domination, culture, and ideology. Yet they also encountered fundamental conceptual difficulties. These difficulties were related to a theoretical turn taken in the late 1930s, in which the newer configuration of capitalism came to be conceived as a society that, while remaining antagonistic, had become completely administered and one-dimensional.

This pessimistic turn cannot be fully understood with reference to the bleakness of its immediate historical context in the late 1930s. It also resulted from the fundamental assumptions according to which that context was analyzed. Critical Theory's turn illuminates the limits of those assumptions inasmuch as it ultimately weakened both the theory's capacity to adequately grasp the ongoing historical dynamic of modern capitalist society and its reflexive character.

I

Central to Critical Theory was the view that capitalism was undergoing a fundamental transformation, entailing a changed relationship of state, society, and economy. This general analysis was formulated in various ways by Friedrich Pollock and Max Horkheimer, who belonged to the "inner circle" of Frankfurt School theorists, and Franz Neumann and Otto Kirchheimer, who did not. Whatever their differences, they all shared a fundamentally historical approach to questions of the state, law, politics, and economics. They did not accord ontological status to these dimensions of modern social life, but regarded political, legal, economic, and cultural forms to be intrinsically related, and sought to delineate their historical transformation with the supersession of nineteenth-century liberal capitalism by a new bureaucratized form of capitalism in the twentieth century.

The general analysis by these theorists of contemporary historical changes in the relation of state and society was, in part, consonant with mainstream Marxist thought. The new centralized, bureaucratized configuration of polity and society was seen as a necessary historical outcome of liberal capitalism, even if this configuration negated the liberal order that generated it. Hence, there could be no return to a *laissez-faire* economy or, more generally, a liberal order (Pollock, *ZfS* 1: 10, 15, 21 and *ZfS* 2: 332, 350; Horkheimer, *CTS* 78ff.; Neumann, *ZfS* 6: 39, 42, 52, 65, 66; Kirchheimer, *SPSS* 9: 269–89; Marcuse, *ZfS* 3: 161–95).

Nevertheless, the approaches developed by those close to the Institute and its house publication, the *Zeitschrift für Sozialforschung*, differed from most conventional Marxist understandings of capitalism's historical development in important respects. They did not, for example, regard the displacement of a liberal, market-centered order by a bureaucratized administered one to be an unequivocally positive development. All of the theorists involved – Pollock, Horkheimer, Neumann, Kirchheimer – considered important aspects of social, political, and individual life in liberal or bourgeois capitalist society to be more emancipatory, however equivocally, than the forms that superseded them. Similarly, they did not simply equate the individual with capitalism and the collective with socialism. Their approaches implied that a future, liberated society could not simply be a linear continuation of postliberal capitalism, but rather must retrieve and incorporate elements, however transformed, from the liberal past.

Instead of regarding the transition from liberal to bureaucratic state-centric capitalism as an expression of linear historical progress, these theorists analyzed it in terms of a shift in the nature of domination in capitalism. Their account of a shift in the nature of political culture became central to the better-known analyses by Horkheimer, Adorno, and Marcuse of transformations in the nature of culture and of personhood in the twentieth century. Friedrich Pollock, for example, regarded the market to be centrally constitutive of social relations under capitalism. The liberal order, however unjust, was characterized by an impersonal legal realm that was constitutive of the separation of private and public spheres and, hence, of the formation of the bourgeois individual. In postliberal capitalism, the state displaces the market as the central determinant of social life. A command hierarchy operating on the basis of a one-sided technical rationality replaces market relations and the rule of law (*SPSS* 9: 206–7, 443–9).

Otto Kirchheimer drew a similar historical contrast between liberalism and what he termed "mass democracy." In the former, money functioned as an impersonal universal medium of exchange; political compromise was affected among individual parliamentarians and between parliamentarians and the government under the informal aegis of institutions of public opinion. In the latter, central banks powerful enough to compete with governments superseded the impersonal universal medium; political compromise was effected between quasicorporate groups (capital and labor) whereby individual political and legal rights were sharply curtailed. This laid the groundwork for the fascist form of compromise where the state sanctions the subsumption of individual rights under group rights and the monopolies' private power and the state's public powers are merged. A form of technical rationality becomes dominant, according to Kirchheimer, which is rational only for the power elites (*SPSS* 9: 276–88, 456–75).

Franz Neumann also considered elements of the liberal constitutional state to be positive. Although formal general laws may have obscured the domination of the bourgeois class while rendering the economic system calculable, according to Neumann, the general character of law, the independence of the judiciary, and the separation of powers promoted and protected individual freedom and equality. He argued that these elements of the liberal order need not and should not be abolished with the overturn of capitalism. Neumann was very critical of the tendency for particularized substantive laws to be substituted for the formal and general laws of the liberal epoch, a tendency that, in his view, was an aspect of the transformation of capitalism in the twentieth century. This process, according to Neumann, reached its apogee under Fascism (*ZfS* 6).

In spite of the general agreement among these theorists, however, there were also important differences – particularly between Pollock and Neumann – that had significant theoretical and political consequences. These differences emerged openly in 1940–1 with regard to the nature of the Nazi regime. Pollock considered that regime to be an example of an emerging new configuration of capitalism, which he treated ideal-typically as "state capitalism." He characterized this new configuration as an antagonistic society in which the economic functions of the market and private property had been taken over by the state. Consequently, the sort of contradiction between production and private property and the market that had marked liberal capitalism no longer characterized state capitalism (*SPSS* 9: 200–25, 440–55). Neumann countered that Pollock's thesis was empirically incorrect and theoretically questionable. In *Behemoth*, Neumann's massive study of National Socialism, he argued that the Nazi regime was a highly cartelized form of capitalism in which heterogeneous ruling elites – Nazi party officials, capitalists, military officers, state bureaucrats – jostled with one another for power. He strongly rejected Pollock's thesis of state capitalism, and claimed that capitalism's contradictions remained operative in Germany even if covered up by the bureaucratic apparatus and the ideology of the *Volk* community (*B* 227–8). Indeed, Neumann claimed, the very notion of "state capitalism" is a contradiction in terms. Should a state become the sole owner of the means of production, it would be impossible for capitalism to function. Such a state would have to be described with political categories (such as "slave state," "managerial dictatorship," or "system of bureaucratic collectivism"). It could not be described with economic categories (such as "capitalism") (*B* 224).

The differences between Pollock and Neumann usually have been presented as a debate on the nature of National Socialism.[3] While this issue certainly occasioned this debate, the theoretical and political stakes of the differences between Pollock and Neumann were much higher.[4] They involved fundamental differences regarding the theoretical framework within which the transformation of capitalism was understood.[5] These differences had consequences for the way in which the new phase of capitalism was understood, the question of whether this new phase included the Soviet Union, and, reflexively, the nature of a critical theory adequate to those changes.

I shall focus on Pollock's argument inasmuch as it was adopted and shared by the inner circle of the Frankfurt School and was central to Critical Theory's pessimistic turn in the late 1930s and early 1940s. Before doing so, I shall briefly discuss the term "traditional Marxism" as I use it and elaborate on the significance of the notion of contradiction for a critical theory.

II

Pollock's analysis of the transformation of capitalism presupposes some basic assumptions of traditional Marxism. I use this term not to delineate a specific historical tendency in Marxism, but rather to characterize a general critical framework that regards private ownership of the means of production and a market economy to be capitalism's most fundamental social relations. Within this general interpretation, the fundamental categories of Marx's critique, such as "value," "commodity," "surplus value," and "capital" are understood essentially as categories of the market and of the expropriation of the social surplus by a class of private owners.[6] The basic contradiction of capitalism is considered to be between these relations and the developed forces of production, interpreted as the industrial mode of producing. The unfolding of this contradiction gives rise to the historical possibility of socialism, conceptualized as collective ownership of the means of production and economic planning.[7]

The notion of contradiction is not simply an important aspect of traditional Marxism; it is central to any immanent social critique. A critical theory of society that assumes people are socially constituted

must be able to explain the possibility of its own existence immanently; it must view itself as embedded within its context, if it is
to remain consistent. Such a theory does not judge critically what
"is" from a conceptual position that, implicitly or explicitly, pur-
ports to be outside of its own social universe, such as a transcendent
"ought." Indeed, it must regard the very notion of such a decontextualized standpoint as spurious. Instead, it must be able to locate
that "ought" as a dimension of its own context, as a possibility that
is immanent to the existent society. Such a critique must be able to
reflexively ground its own standpoint by means of the same categories with which it grasps its object, its social context. That is, the
critique must be able to show that its context generates the possibility of a critical stance towards itself. It follows that an immanent
social critique must show that the society of which it is a part is not a
one-dimensional unitary whole. An analysis of the underlying social
relations of modern society as contradictory provides the theoretical
basis for an immanent critique.

The notion of contradiction also provides the conceptual grounding for a central, historically specific, hallmark of capitalism as a
form of social life – that it is uniquely characterized by an ongoing,
nonteleological dynamic. In Marx's critique of political economy, the
contradictory character of the fundamental social forms of capitalism (commodity, capital) underlies that social formation's ongoing
directional dynamic. Such an approach elucidates this intrinsic historical dynamic in social terms, whereas all transhistorical theories
of history, whether dialectical or evolutionary, simply presuppose it.[8]
Grasping capitalism's basic social relations as contradictory, then,
allows for an immanent critique that is historical, one that elucidates
a dialectical historical dynamic intrinsic to the social formation that
points beyond itself – to that realizable "ought" which is immanent
to the "is" and which serves as the standpoint of its critique. Such
an immanent critique is more fundamental than one that simply
opposes the reality of modern capitalist society to its ideals.[9]

The significance of the notion of social contradiction thus goes
far beyond its narrow interpretation as the basis of economic crises
in capitalism. It should also not be understood simply as the
social antagonism between laboring and expropriating classes. Social
contradiction refers, rather, to the very structure of a society, to a

self-generating "nonidentity" intrinsic to its structures of social relations that do not, therefore, constitute a stable unitary whole.[10]
Social contradiction is thus the precondition of an intrinsic historical dynamic as well as of an immanent social critique itself. It allows
for theoretical self-reflexivity.[11]

   To be adequate, the fundamental categories of the critique of capitalism must themselves express its social contradiction. As categories of an immanent social critique with emancipatory intent, they
must adequately grasp the determinate grounds of domination in capitalism, so that the historical abolition of what is expressed by the
categories implies the possibility of social and historical freedom.
The adequacy of its categories allows the critique to reject both the
affirmation of the given, of the "is," as well as its utopian critique. As
I shall show, attempts by Pollock and Horkheimer to analyze postliberal capitalism revealed that traditional Marxism's categories do not
adequately express the core of capitalism and the grounds of domination in that society; the contradiction expressed by those categories
does not point beyond the present to an emancipated society. Nevertheless, although Pollock and Horkheimer revealed the inadequacies of the traditional critique's categories, they did not sufficiently
call into question the presuppositions underlying those categories.
Hence, they were not able to reconstitute a more adequate social
critique. The combination of these two elements of their approach
resulted in the pessimism of Critical Theory.

III

In the early 1930s Friedrich Pollock, together with Gerhard Meyer
and Kurt Mandelbaum, developed his analysis of the transformation of capitalism associated with the development of the interventionist state, and over the course of the following decade he
extended it. Both the increasingly active role played by the state
in the socioeconomic sphere following the Great Depression and the
Soviet experience with planning led Pollock to conclude that the
political sphere had superseded the economic sphere as the locus
of economic regulation and the articulation of social problems. He
characterized this shift as one towards the primacy of the political
over the economic (SPSS 9: 400–55). This notion, which later became

widespread in the 1960s, implies that Marxian categories may have been valid for the period of *laissez-faire* capitalism, but have since become anachronistic as a result of successful state intervention in economic processes.[12] Such a position may have appeared plausible in the decades following World War Two, but it has been rendered questionable by the subsequent global crisis of state-interventionist national economies. This crisis does not call into question Pollock's insight that the development of the interventionist state entailed far-reaching economic, social, and political changes. It does, however, suggest that the theoretical framework within which he analyzed those changes must be examined critically.

Pollock's analysis of the Great Depression and the transformation of capitalism developed in two, increasingly pessimistic, phases. In 1932–3, Pollock characterized capitalist development in terms of a growing contradiction, interpreted in the traditional Marxist fashion, between the forces of production and private appropriation mediated socially by the "self-regulating" market (*ZfS* 1: 21). This growing contradiction generated a series of economic crises culminating in the Great Depression, which marked the end of the era of liberal capitalism (*ZfS* 1: 10, 15 and *ZfS* 2: 350). There could be no return to a *laissez-faire* economy, according to Pollock (*ZfS* 2: 332); nevertheless, the development of free market capitalism had given rise to the possibility of a centrally planned economy (*ZfS* 1: 19–20). Yet – and this is the decisive point – this need not be socialism. Pollock argued that a *laissez-faire* economy and capitalism were not necessarily identical (*ZfS* 1: 16). Instead of identifying socialism with planning, he distinguished between a capitalist planned economy based on private ownership of the means of production within a framework of a class society, and a socialist planned economy marked by social ownership of the means of production within a framework of a classless society (*ZfS* 1: 18). Pollock maintained that a capitalist planned economy, rather than socialism, would be the most likely result of the Great Depression (*ZfS* 2: 350). In both cases the free market would be replaced by state regulation. At this stage of Pollock's thought, the difference between capitalism and socialism in an age of planning had become reduced to that between private and social ownership of the means of production. However, even the determination of capitalism in terms of private property had become ambiguous in these essays (*ZfS* 2: 338, 345–6, 349). It was effectively abandoned in Pollock's essays of 1941, in which the theory of the primacy of the political was fully developed.

In the essays "State Capitalism" and "Is National Socialism a New Order?," Pollock characterized the newly emergent order as state capitalism. He proceeded "ideal-typically," opposing totalitarian and democratic state capitalism as the two primary ideal types of this new social order (*SPSS* 9: 200).[13] Within the totalitarian form the state is in the hands of a new ruling stratum, an amalgamation of leading bureaucrats in business, state, and party (*SPSS* 9: 201). In the democratic form the people control it. Pollock's analysis focused on totalitarian state capitalism. When stripped of those aspects specific to totalitarianism, his examination of the fundamental change in the relation of state to civil society can be seen as constituting the political-economic dimension of a general Critical Theory of postliberal capitalism, an aspect which was developed more fully by Horkheimer, Marcuse, and Adorno.

The central characteristic of state capitalism, according to Pollock, is the supersession of the economic sphere by the political sphere. The state now balances production and distribution (*SPSS* 9: 201). Although a market, a price system, and wages may still exist, they no longer serve to regulate the economic process (*SPSS* 9: 204, 444). Moreover, even if the legal institution of private property is retained, its economic functions have been effectively abolished (*SPSS* 9: 208–9, 442). Consequently, for all practical purposes, economic "laws" are no longer operative and no autonomous, self-moving economic sphere exists (*SPSS* 9: 208–9). Political problems of administration have replaced economic ones of exchange (*SPSS* 9: 217).

This transition, according to Pollock, has broad social implications. Under liberal capitalism the market determined social relations; people and classes confronted one another in the public sphere as quasi-autonomous agents. However unjust and inefficient the system may have been, the rules governing the public sphere were mutually binding. This impersonal legal realm was constitutive of the separation of the public and private spheres and the formation of the bourgeois individual (*SPSS* 9: 207, 443, 447). Under state capitalism the state becomes the main determinant of social life (*SPSS* 9: 206). Market relations are replaced by those of a command hierarchy in which technical rationality reigns in the place of law. Individuals and groups, no longer autonomous, are subordinated to the whole, and the impetus to work is effected by political terror or by psychic manipulation (*SPSS* 9: 448–9).

Both the market and private property – capitalism's basic social relations (traditionally understood) – have been effectively abolished in state capitalism, according to Pollock. Nevertheless, the social, political, and cultural consequences of that abolition have not necessarily been emancipatory. Expressing this view in Marxian categorial terms, Pollock maintained that production in state capitalism is no longer commodity production, but is for use. Yet this did not guarantee that production served "the needs of free humans in a harmonious society" (*SPSS* 9: 446). Given Pollock's analysis of the nonemancipatory character of state capitalism and his claim that a return to liberal capitalism was impossible, the question became whether state capitalism could be superseded by socialism (*SPSS* 9: 452–5). This possibility could no longer be considered immanent to the unfolding of a contradiction intrinsic to a self-moving economy, since the contradiction had been overcome, according to Pollock, and the economy had become totally manageable (*SPSS* 9: 217, 454). He attempted to avoid the pessimistic implications of his analysis by sketching the beginnings of a theory of political crises.

Because state capitalism, according to Pollock, arose as a response to the economic ills of liberal capitalism, its primary tasks would be to maintain full employment and to develop the forces of production while maintaining the old social structure (*SPSS* 9: 203). Mass unemployment would result in a political crisis of the system. Totalitarian state capitalism, as an extremely antagonistic form, must, additionally, not allow the standard of living to rise appreciably, since that would free people to reflect critically upon their situation (*SPSS* 9: 220). Only a permanent war economy could achieve these tasks simultaneously, according to Pollock. In a peace economy, the system could not maintain itself, despite mass psychological manipulation and terror. A high standard of living could be maintained by democratic state capitalism, but Pollock seemed to view it as an unstable, transitory form: either class differences would assert themselves, pushing development towards totalitarian state capitalism, or democratic control of the state would result in the abolition of class society, thereby leading to socialism (*SPSS* 9: 219, 225). The prospects of the latter, however, appeared remote, given Pollock's thesis of the manageability of the economy and his awareness that a policy of military "preparedness," which allows for a permanent war economy without war, is a hallmark of the state capitalist era (*SPSS* 9: 220).

IV

Several aspects of Pollock's analysis are problematic. His examination of liberal capitalism indicated its developmental dynamic and historicity, showing how the immanent contradiction between its forces and relations of production gave rise to the possibility of a planned society as its historical negation. Pollock's analysis of state capitalism, however, was static; it merely described various ideal types. No immanent historical dynamic was indicated out of which the possibility of another social formation might emerge. We must consider why, for Pollock, the stage of capitalism characterized by the "primacy of the economic" is contradictory and dynamic, while that characterized by the "primacy of the political" is not.

We can elucidate this problem by considering Pollock's understanding of the economic sphere. In postulating the primacy of politics over economics, he conceptualized the latter in terms of the quasi-automatic, market-mediated coordination of needs and resources (*SPSS* 9: 203, 445ff.). His assertion that economic "laws" lose their essential function when the state supersedes the market implies that such laws are rooted in the market. The centrality of the market to Pollock's notion of the economic is also revealed by his interpretation of the commodity: a good is a commodity only when circulated by the market, otherwise it is a use-value. This implies an understanding of the Marxian category of value – purportedly the fundamental category of the capitalist relations of production – solely in terms of the market. Pollock, in other words, understood the economic sphere and, implicitly, Marxian categories of the relations of production in terms of the mode of *distribution* alone. He interpreted the contradiction between the forces and relations of production accordingly, as one between industrial production and the bourgeois mode of distribution (the market, private property).[14] This contradiction generated the possibility that a new mode of regulation, characterized by planning in the effective absence of private property, would supersede the old relations of production (*ZfS* 2:

345ff.; *ZfS* 1: 15). According to such an interpretation, when the state supplants the market as the agency of distribution, the economic sphere is essentially suspended; a conscious mode of distribution and social regulation replaces the nonconscious, economic mode (*SPSS* 9: 217).

It should now be clear why state capitalism, according to such an interpretation, possesses no immanent historical dynamic. The latter implies a logic of development, beyond conscious control, which is based on a contradiction intrinsic to the system. In Pollock's analysis, the market is the source of all nonconscious social structures of necessity; it constitutes the basis of the so-called "laws of motion" of the capitalist social formation. For Pollock, moreover, macroeconomic planning implies conscious control not limited by any economic laws. It follows that the supersession of the market by state planning signifies the end of any blind historical logic; historical development becomes regulated consciously. Furthermore, an understanding of the contradiction between the forces and relations of production in terms of the growing inadequacy of the market and private property to conditions of developed industrial production implies that a mode of distribution based on planning and the effective abolition of private property *is* adequate to those conditions; a contradiction no longer exists between such new "relations of production" and the industrial mode of production. Such an understanding implicitly relegates Marx's notion of capitalism's contradictory character to the period of liberal capitalism. Pollock's notion of the primacy of the political thus refers to an antagonistic, yet *noncontradictory*, society possessing no immanent dynamic pointing towards the possibility of socialism as its historical negation.

Pollock's analysis reveals the limits of a critique focused on the mode of distribution. In his ideal-typical analysis the Marxian category of value (interpreted as a category of the market) had been superseded in state capitalism and private property had effectively been abolished. The result did not necessarily constitute the foundation of the "good society." On the contrary, it could and did lead to forms of greater oppression and tyranny that no longer could be grasped adequately by means of the category of value. Furthermore, according to his interpretation, the overcoming of the market meant that the system of commodity production had been replaced by one of use-value production. Yet this was an insufficient condition of emancipation. For value and commodity to be critical categories adequate to capitalism, however, they must grasp the core of that society in such a way that their abolition constitutes the social basis of freedom. Pollock's analysis has the very important, if unintended, consequence of indicating that the Marxian categories, when understood traditionally, do not adequately grasp the grounds of domination in capitalism. Rather than rethink the traditional interpretation, however, Pollock retained that interpretation and implicitly limited the validity of Marx's categories to liberal capitalism.

As a result, the basic economic organization of both state capitalism and socialism is the same in Pollock's approach: central planning and the effective abolition of private property under conditions of developed industrial production. This, however, suggests that his traditional interpretation did not adequately grasp the capitalist relations of production. The term "relations of production" refers to what characterizes capitalism as capitalism. I have shown that capitalism – as state capitalism – could exist without the market and private property according to Pollock. These, however, are its two essential characteristics as defined by traditional Marxist theory. What, in the absence of those "relations of production," characterizes the new configuration as capitalist? The logic of Pollock's interpretation should have led to a fundamental reconsideration: if the market and private property are, indeed, the capitalist relations of production, the ideal-typical postliberal form should not be considered capitalist. On the other hand, characterizing the new form as capitalist, in spite of the (presumed) abolition of those relational structures, implicitly demands a different understanding of the relations of production essential to capitalism. It calls into question identifying the market and private property with the essential relations of production – even for capitalism's liberal phase. Pollock, however, did not undertake such a reconsideration. Instead he modified the traditional understanding of the relations of production by limiting its validity to capitalism's liberal phase and postulated its supersession by a political mode of distribution. This gave rise to theoretical problems that point to the necessity for a more radical reexamination of the traditional theory. If one maintains that the capitalist social formation possesses successively different "relations of production," one necessarily posits a core of that formation that is not fully grasped by any of those relations. This indicates, however, that capitalism's basic relations of production have not been adequately determined.

It is, therefore, not surprising that Pollock could not adequately justify his characterization of postliberal society as capitalist. He did speak of the continued importance of profit interests, but dealt with the category of profit indeterminately, as a subspecies of power (*SPSS* 9: 201, 205, 207). His treatment of profit merely emphasized the political character of state capitalism without further elucidating its capitalist dimension. The ultimate ground for Pollock's characterization of postliberal society as state capitalist is that it remains antagonistic, that is, a class society (*SPSS* 9: 201, 219). The term "capitalism," however, requires a more specific determination than that of class antagonism, for all developed historical forms of society have been antagonistic in the sense that the social surplus is expropriated from its immediate producers and not used for the benefit of all. A notion of state capitalism necessarily implies that what is being regulated politically is capital; it demands, therefore, a concept of capital. Such considerations, however, are absent in Pollock's treatment. What in Pollock's analysis remains the essence – class antagonism – is too historically indeterminate to be of use in specifying the capitalist social formation. These weaknesses again indicate the limits of Pollock's traditional point of departure: locating the relations of production only in the sphere of distribution.

V

It should be clear that a critique of Pollock, like Neumann's, that remains within the framework of traditional Marxism is inadequate. Neumann's critique reintroduced a dynamic to the analysis by pointing out that market competition and private property did not disappear or lose their functions under state-interventionist capitalism. On a less immediately empirical level, his critique raised the question whether capitalism could ever exist in the absence of the market and private property. However, Neumann's critique avoided addressing the fundamental problems Pollock raised regarding the endpoint of capitalism's development as traditionally conceived. The issue is whether the abolition of the market and private property is indeed a sufficient condition for an emancipated society. Pollock's approach, in spite of its frozen character and shaky theoretical foundation, indicated that an interpretation of the relations of production and, hence, value in terms of the sphere of distribution does not sufficiently grasp the core of domination in capitalism. This approach allowed him to include the Soviet Union within the purview of the critique of postliberal capitalism.[15] It is precisely because of these far-reaching implications that Pollock's approach was essentially adopted by mainstream Critical Theory. The problem with Pollock's approach was that it pointed to the need for a fundamental rethinking of the critique of capitalism that it did not adequately undertake. Nevertheless, to criticize Pollock from the standpoint of the traditional interpretation does not advance matters. It ignores the gains that Pollock's considerations of the problem of the twentieth-century state-centric configuration of capitalism represent.

In spite of the difficulties associated with Pollock's ideal-typical approach, it has the unintended heuristic value of revealing the problematic character of traditional Marxism's presuppositions. One can characterize that theory in very general terms as one that (1) identifies the capitalist relations of production with the market and private property and (2) regards capitalism's basic contradiction as one between industrial production, on the one hand, and the market and private property, on the other. Within this framework, industrial production is understood as a technical process, intrinsically independent of "capitalism." The transition to socialism is considered in terms of a transformation of the mode of distribution – not, however, of production itself. Traditional Marxism, as a theory of production, does not entail a critique of production. On the contrary, production serves as the historical standard of the adequacy of the mode of distribution, as the point of departure for its critique.

Marx's mature theory entailed a critical analysis of the historically specific character of labor in capitalism. The traditional interpretation, however, is based on a transhistorical, affirmative understanding of labor as an activity mediating humans and nature – what Marx critically termed "labor" – positing it as the principle of social constitution and the source of wealth in all societies.[16] Within the framework of such an interpretation (which is closer to classical political economy than it is to Marx's critique of political economy), Marx's "labor theory of value" is taken to be a theory that demystifies capitalist society by revealing "labor" to be the true source of social wealth.[17] "Labor," transhistorically understood, serves as the basis for a critique of capitalist society.

When socialism is conceptualized as a mode of distribution adequate to industrial production, that adequacy implicitly becomes the condition of general human freedom. Emancipation, in other words, is grounded in "labor." It is realized in a social form where "labor," freed from the fetters of "value" (the market) and "surplus value" (private property), has openly emerged and come to itself as the regulating principle of society.[18] This notion, of course, is inseparable from that of socialist revolution as the "coming to itself" of the proletariat.[19]

The limitations of this traditional framework become historically evident when the market loses its central role as the agency of distribution. Examining Pollock's analysis revealed that any attempt based on traditional Marxism to characterize the resultant politically regulated social order as capitalist remains inconsistent or underdetermined. By indicating that the abolition of the market and private property is an insufficient condition for human emancipation, Pollock's treatment of postliberal capitalism inadvertently showed that the traditional Marxist categories are inadequate as critical categories of the capitalist social formation. Moreover, Pollock's refusal to consider the new social configuration as merely one that is not yet fully socialist enabled him to grasp its new, more negative modes of political, social, and cultural domination as systematic rather than contingent. His analysis also revealed that the Marxian notion of contradiction as a hallmark of the capitalist social formation is not identical with the notion of class antagonism. Whereas an antagonistic social form can be static, the notion of contradiction implies an intrinsic dynamic. By considering state capitalism to be an antagonistic form which does not possess such a dynamic, Pollock's approach drew attention to the necessity of structurally locating social contradiction in a manner that goes beyond considerations of class.

An important consequence of Pollock's approach was that it implied a reversal in the theoretical evaluation of labor. I have shown that, for Pollock, central planning in the effective absence of private property is not, in and of itself, emancipatory, although that form of distribution is adequate to industrial production. This calls into question the notion that "labor" is the basis of general human freedom. Yet, Pollock's break with traditional Marxism did not really overcome its basic assumptions regarding the nature of labor in capitalism. Instead, he retained the transhistorical notion of "labor," but implicitly reversed his evaluation of its role. According to Pollock's analysis, the historical dialectic had run its course; "labor" had come to itself and the totality had been realized. That the result was anything but emancipatory must therefore be rooted in the character of "labor." Whereas "labor" had been regarded as the locus of freedom, it now implicitly became considered a source of domination.

VI

The reversal regarding "labor" implied by Pollock's analysis of the qualitative transformation of capitalist society was central to Critical Theory's subsequent association of "labor" with instrumental or technological rationality, and entailed a reflexive transformation of the immanent critique at the heart of Critical Theory. The broader implications of this transformation and its problematic aspects become evident when the development of Max Horkheimer's conception of Critical Theory is examined.

The transformation of Critical Theory has been characterized in terms of the supersession of the critique of political economy by the critique of politics, the critique of ideology, and the critique of instrumental reason. This shift has been usually understood as one from a critical analysis of modern society focused on only one sphere of social life to a broader and deeper approach. Yet an examination of Pollock's analysis suggests this evaluation must be modified. The theorists of the Frankfurt School, from the very beginning, viewed the economic, social, political, legal, and cultural dimensions of life in capitalism as interrelated. They did not grasp the critique of political economy in an economistic, reductionist manner. What changed theoretically in the period of 1939–41 was that the new phase of capitalism became understood as a noncontradictory social whole. The nature of the Frankfurt School's subsequent critique of ideology and of instrumental reason was directly related to this understanding of postliberal capitalism.

One can see the relation between the state capitalism thesis and the transformation of Critical Theory by comparing two essays written by Horkheimer in 1937 and 1940. In his classic 1937 essay,

"Traditional and Critical Theory," Horkheimer still grounded Critical Theory in the contradictory character of capitalist society. At the heart of this essay is the notion that perception and thought are molded sociohistorically; both subject and object are socially constituted (CT 201). On this basis, Horkheimer contrasts "traditional" and "critical" theory, analyzing Descartes as the arch-representative of the former. Traditional theory, according to Horkheimer, does not grasp the socially constituted character and historicity of its social universe, and, hence, the intrinsic interrelatedness of subject and object (CT 199, 204, 207). Instead, it assumes the essential immutability of the relation of subject, object, and theory. Consequently, it is not able to think the unity of theory and practice (CT 211, 231). In a manner reminiscent of Marx's analysis of various forms of "fetishism," Horkheimer seeks to explain this hypostatized dualism as a social and historical possibility by relating it to the forms of appearance that veil the fundamental core of capitalist society (CT 194–5, 197, 204).

At its core, capitalist society is a social whole constituted by labor that could be rationally organized, according to Horkheimer. Yet market mediation and class domination based on private property impart a fragmented and irrational form to that society (CT 201, 207, 217). As a result, capitalist society is characterized by blind mechanical necessity and by the use of human powers for controlling nature in the service of particular interests rather than for the general good (CT 229, 213). Although capitalism once had emancipatory aspects, it now increasingly hinders human development and drives humanity towards a new barbarism (CT 212–13, 227). A sharpening contradiction exists between the social totality constituted by labor, on the one hand, and the market and private property, on the other.

This contradiction, according to Horkheimer, constitutes the condition of possibility of Critical Theory as well as the object of its investigation. Critical Theory does not accept the fragmented aspects of reality as given, but rather seeks to understand society as a whole. This necessarily involves grasping what fragments the totality and hinders its realization as a rational whole. Critical Theory entails an immanent analysis of capitalism's intrinsic contradictions, thereby uncovering the growing discrepancy between what is and what could be (CT 207, 219). It thus rejects the acceptance of the given, as well as utopian critique (CT 216). Social production, reason, and human emancipation are intertwined and provide the standpoint of a historical critique in this essay. A rational social organization serving all its members is, according to Horkheimer, a possibility immanent to human labor (CT 213, 217).

The immanent dialectical critique outlined by Horkheimer in "Traditional and Critical Theory" is a sophisticated and reflexive version of traditional Marxism. The forces of production are identified with the social labor process, which is hindered from realizing its potential by the market and private property. Whereas for Marx the constitution of social life in capitalism is a function of labor mediating the relations among people as well as the relations between people and nature, for Horkheimer it is a function of the latter mediation alone, of "labor." The standpoint of his critique of the existing order in the name of reason and justice is provided by "labor" as constitutive of the totality. Hence, the object of critique is what hinders the open emergence of that totality. This positive view of "labor" and of the totality later gave way in Horkheimer's thought to a more negative evaluation once he considered the relations of production to have become adequate to the forces of production. In both cases, however, he conceptualized labor transhistorically, in terms of the relation of humanity to nature, as "labor."

Horkheimer wrote "Traditional and Critical Theory" long after the National Socialist defeat of working-class organizations. Nevertheless, he continued to analyze the social formation as essentially contradictory. In other words, the notion of contradiction for Horkheimer referred to a deeper structural level than that of immediate class antagonism. Thus, he claimed that, as an element of social change, Critical Theory exists as part of a dynamic unity with the dominated class but is not immediately identical with the current feelings and visions of that class (CT 214–15). Critical Theory deals with the present in terms of its immanent potential; it cannot therefore, be based on the given alone (CT 219, 220). Though in the 1930s Horkheimer was skeptical of the *probability* that a socialist transformation would occur in the foreseeable future, the *possibility* of such a transformation remained, in his analysis, immanent to the contradictory capitalist present.

Horkheimer did maintain that capitalism's changed character demanded changes in the *elements* of Critical Theory and drew attention to new possibilities for conscious social domination resulting from the increased concentration and centralization of capital. He related this change to a historical tendency for the sphere of culture to lose its previous position of relative autonomy and become embedded more immediately in the framework of social domination (*CT* 234–7). Horkheimer thereby laid the groundwork for a critical focus on political domination, ideological manipulation, and the culture industry. Nevertheless, he insisted that the *basis* of the theory remained unchanged inasmuch as the basic economic structure of society had not changed (*CT* 234–5).

At this point, the shift in Critical Theory's object of investigation proposed by Horkheimer – the increased emphasis on conscious domination and manipulation – was tied to the notion that the market no longer played the role it did in liberal capitalism. Yet, despite the defeat of working-class organizations by Fascism, Horkheimer did not yet express the view that the contradiction between the forces and relations of production had been overcome. His critique remained immanent and was not yet fundamentally pessimistic. Its character changed later, following the outbreak of World War Two, and was related to the change in theoretical evaluation expressed by Pollock's notion of the primacy of the political.

In "The Authoritarian State" (1940) Horkheimer addressed the new form of capitalism, which he now characterized as "state capitalism . . . the authoritarian state of the present" (*EFS* 96; translation emended). His analysis was basically similar to Pollock's, although Horkheimer more explicitly referred to the Soviet Union as the most consistent form of state capitalism (*EFS* 101–2). All forms of state capitalism are repressive, exploitative, and antagonistic according to Horkheimer. Although they are not subject to economic crises, inasmuch as the market had been overcome, they are, nevertheless, ultimately unstable (*EFS* 97, 109–10).

In this essay, Horkheimer expressed a new, deeply ambiguous attitude towards the forces of production. On the one hand, some passages in "The Authoritarian State" still described the forces of production, traditionally interpreted, as potentially emancipatory. For instance, Horkheimer argued that the forces of production are consciously held back in the interests of domination and claimed that using production in this way rather than to satisfy human needs would result in an international political crisis tied to the constant threat of war (*EFS* 102–3). Even in these passages, however, Horkheimer did not treat this crisis as expressing the possible determinate negation of the system, but rather as a dangerous result that *demands* its negation (*EFS* 109–11). The gap delineated here between what is and what could be were it not for the fetters on the forces of production highlights the antagonistic nature of the system, but no longer has the form of an intrinsic contradiction.

The dominant tendency of the essay, moreover, is to maintain that there is no contradiction or even necessary disjunction between the developed forces of production (traditionally understood) and authoritarian political domination. The forces of production, freed from the constraints of the market and private property, have not proved to be the source of freedom and a rational social order (*EFS* 112). On the contrary, Horkheimer now skeptically wrote that, although the development of productivity *may* have increased the possibility of emancipation, it certainly *has* led to greater repression (*EFS* 106–7, 109, 112).

"The Authoritarian State" signaled a turn to a pessimistic theory of history. Horkheimer now maintained that the laws of historical development, driven by the contradiction between the forces and relations of production, had only led to state capitalism (*EFS* 107). He, therefore, radically called into question any social uprising based on the development of the forces of production (*EFS* 106) and reconceptualized the relation of emancipation and history by according social revolution two moments:

Revolution brings about what would also happen without spontaneity: the societalization of the means of production, the planned management of production and the unlimited control of nature. And it also brings about what would never happen without resistance and constantly renewed efforts to achieve freedom: the *end of exploitation.* (ibid.)

Here Horkheimer fell back to a position characterized by an antinomy of necessity and freedom. He now presented history deterministically, as an automatic development in which labor comes to itself, but not as the source of emancipation. He treated freedom, on the other hand, in a purely voluntarist fashion, as an act of will against history (*EFS* 107–8, 117).[20] Horkheimer now assumed that (1) the material conditions of life in which freedom for all could be fully achieved are identical to those in which domination of all is realized, (2) those conditions automatically emerge, and (3) they are essentially irrelevant to the question of freedom (*EFS* 114). Not having fundamentally reconsidered the traditional Marxist reading of the categories, Horkheimer was no longer able to consider freedom a determinate historical possibility, but rather had to regard it as historically and socially indeterminate: "Critical Theory . . . confronts history with that possibility which is always visible within it" (*EFS* 106). Horkheimer's insistence that a greater degree of freedom had always been possible did not allow for a consideration of the relation among various sociohistorical contexts, different conceptions of freedom, and the sort (rather than the degree) of emancipation that can be achieved within a particular context. His notion of the relation of history and emancipation had become indeterminate.

In conceptualizing state capitalism as a form in which the contradictions of capitalism had been overcome, Horkheimer came to realize the inadequacy of traditional Marxism as a historical theory of emancipation. Yet he remained too bound to its presuppositions to undertake a reconsideration of the Marxian critique of capitalism that would allow for a more adequate historical theory. This dichotomous theoretical position, expressed by the antinomial opposition of emancipation and history, undermined Horkheimer's earlier, dialectically self-reflective epistemology. If emancipation is no longer grounded in a determinate historical contradiction, a critical theory with emancipatory intent must also take a step outside of history. I have shown that Horkheimer's theory of knowledge in 1937 assumed that social constitution is a function of "labor" which, in capitalism, is fragmented and hindered by the relations of production from fully realizing itself. In 1940, however, he considered the contradictions of capitalism to have been no more than the motor of a repressive development, which he expressed categorially by claiming that "the self-movement of the concept of the commodity leads to the concept of state capitalism just as for Hegel the certainty of sense data leads to absolute knowledge" (*EFS* 108). Horkheimer now argued that a Hegelian dialectic, in which the contradictions of the categories lead to the self-unfolded realization of the subject as totality, could only result in the affirmation of the existing order. Yet, he did not reformulate the categories and, hence, their dialectic in a manner that would go beyond the limits of that order. Instead, retaining the traditional understanding, Horkheimer reversed his earlier position. "Labor" and the totality had previously constituted the standpoint of the critique and the basis of emancipation; they now became the grounds of oppression and domination.

The result was a series of ruptures. Horkheimer not only located emancipation outside of history, but, to save its possibility, now introduced a disjunction between concept and object: "The identity of the ideal and reality is universal exploitation . . . The difference between concept and reality – not the concept itself – is the foundation for the possibility of revolutionary praxis" (EFS 108–9). This step was rendered necessary by the conjunction of Horkheimer's continued passion for general human emancipation with his analysis of state capitalism. As indicated above, an immanent social critique must show that its object – its social context – and, hence, the categories that grasp that object, are not unidimensional. The notion that the contradiction of capitalism had been overcome implies, however, that the social object has become one-dimensional. Within such a framework, the "ought" is no longer an immanent aspect of a contradictory "is." Hence, the result of an analysis that grasps what is would necessarily be affirmative. Because Horkheimer no longer considered the whole to be intrinsically contradictory, he now posited the difference between concept and actuality in order to allow room for another possible actuality.

Horkheimer's position – that critique cannot be grounded upon any concepts (such as "commodity") – necessarily posits indeterminacy as the basis of the critique. According to such a position, since the totality does not subsume all of life, the possibility of emancipation, however dim, is not extinguished. Yet this position cannot point to the possibility of a determinate negation of the existing social order. Similarly, it has no way of accounting for itself reflexively as a determinate possibility and, hence, as an adequate Critical Theory of its social universe.[21]

Horkheimer's Critical Theory could have retained its reflexive character if only it would have embedded the affirmative relation it posited between the concept and its object within another, more encompassing set of categories that still would have allowed theoretically for the immanent possibility of critique and historical transformation. Horkheimer, however, did not undertake such a reconsideration. The disjunction of concept and actuality rendered his position similar to that which he had criticized earlier in traditional theory: theory is not understood as a part of the social universe in which it exists, but is accorded a spurious independent position. Horkheimer's concept of the disjunction of concept and reality cannot explain itself.

The dilemma entailed by Horkheimer's pessimistic turn retrospectively highlights a weakness in his earlier, apparently consistent epistemology. In "Traditional and Critical Theory" the possibility of fundamental critique, as well as of the overcoming of the capitalist formation, was grounded in the contradictory character of that society. Yet that contradiction was interpreted as one between social "labor" and those relations that fragment its totalistic existence and inhibit its full development. According to such an interpretation, Marxian categories such as "value" and "capital" express those inhibiting social relations – the mode of distribution; they ultimately are extrinsic to "labor" itself. This means that when the concepts of commodity and capital are understood only in terms of the market and private property, they do not really express the contradictory character of the social totality. Instead, they grasp only one dimension of that totality, the relations of distribution, which eventually comes to oppose its other dimension, social "labor." The categories, so interpreted, are essentially one-dimensional from the very beginning. This implies that, even in Horkheimer's earlier essay, the critique is external to, rather than grounded in, the categories. It is a critique of the social forms expressed by the categories from the standpoint of "labor." Once "labor" no longer appeared to be the principle of emancipation, given the repressive results of the abolition of the market and private property, the previous weakness of the theory emerged overtly as a dilemma.

In spite of its apparently dialectical character, then, Horkheimer's earlier Critical Theory did not succeed in grounding itself as critique in the concepts immanent to capitalist society. In discussing Pollock, I showed that the weakness of his attempt to characterize postliberal society as state capitalism reveals that the determination of the capitalist relations of production in terms of the market and private property had always been inadequate. By the same token, the weakness of Horkheimer's reflexive social theory indicates the inadequacy of a critical theory based on a notion of "labor." That Horkheimer became aware of the inadequacy of such a theory without reconsidering its assumptions resulted in a reversal of, rather than an advance beyond, an earlier traditional Marxist position. In 1937, Horkheimer still regarded "labor" positively as that which, in contradiction to the social relations of capitalism, constitutes the ground for the possibility of critical thought, as well as of emancipation. By 1940 he began to consider the development of production as the progress of domination. In *Dialectic of Enlightenment* (1944/47) and *Eclipse of Reason* (1947), Horkheimer's evaluation of the relationship between production and emancipation became more unequivocally negative: "Advance in technical facilities for enlightenment is accompanied by a process of dehumanization" (*ER* vi). He claimed that the nature of social domination had changed and had increasingly become a function of technocratic or instrumental reason, which he grounded in "labor" (*ER* 21). And although he did assert that the contemporary decline of the individual and the dominance of instrumental reason should not be attributed to technics or production as such, but to the forms of social relations in which they occur, his notion of such forms remained empty (*ER* 153). He treated technological development in a historically and socially indeterminate manner, as the domination of nature. Hence, in spite of Horkheimer's disclaimer that the dominance of instrumental reason and the destruction of individuality should be explained in social terms and not be attributed to production as such, it can be argued that he did indeed associate instrumental reason with "labor" (*ER* 21, 50, 102). This association, implied by Pollock's notion of the primacy of the political, reverses an earlier traditional Marxist position. The optimistic version of traditional Marxism and Critical Theory's pessimistic critique share the same understanding of labor in capitalism as "labor."

The pessimistic character of Critical Theory should not, then, be understood only as a direct response to the transformations of twentieth-century industrial capitalism. It is also a function of the assumptions with which those transformations were interpreted. Pollock and Horkheimer were aware of the negative social, political, and cultural consequences of the new form of modern society. The bureaucratic and state-centric character of postliberal capitalism and the Soviet Union provided the "practical refutation," as it were, of traditional Marxism as a theory of emancipation. Because Pollock and Horkheimer retained some basic assumptions of the traditional theory, however, they were not able to respond to that "refutation" with a more fundamental and adequate critique of capitalism. Instead, they developed a conception of an antagonistic and repressive social totality that had become essentially noncontradictory and no longer possessed an immanent dynamic. This conception called into question the emancipatory role traditionally attributed to "labor" and to the realization of the totality, but ultimately did not get beyond the horizon of the traditional Marxist critique of capitalism.

The limits of the critique of traditional Marxism undertaken by Pollock and Horkheimer have been made more evident in recent decades by a new historical transformation of capitalism, beginning in the early 1970s, that dramatically highlighted the limits of state-interventionist forms, East and West. This historical process, entailing the supersession of the "Fordist" accumulation regime of the mid twentieth century by neoliberal global capitalism, can be viewed, in turn, as a sort of "practical refutation" of the thesis of the primacy of the political. It retrospectively shows that Critical Theory's analysis of the earlier major transformation of capitalism was too linear and did not grasp adequately the dynamic character of capital; it strongly suggests that capitalism has indeed remained two-dimensional.

An advance beyond the bounds of traditional Marxism would have required recovering the contradictory character of the Marxian categories by incorporating the historically determinate form of labor as one of their dimensions. Such a reconceptualization, which differs fundamentally from any approach that treats "labor" transhistorically, would allow for a historical critique that could avoid the problematic aspects of both traditional Marxism's and Critical Theory's understandings of postliberal society. More generally, it would allow for a critique of capitalism able to fulfill the task Critical Theory set for itself – critically illuminating the ongoing historical dynamic of the present in a theoretically reflexive manner. The critical pessimism so strongly expressed in *Dialectic of Enlightenment* and *Eclipse of Reason* evinces an awareness of the limitations of traditional Marxism, but one that does not lead to a fundamental reconstitution of the dialectical critique of what remains a two-dimensional form of social life.

NOTES

I would like to thank Spencer Leonard for his assistance and critical feedback.

1. Often interpreters of Critical Theory argue that the Frankfurt School replaced political economy with philosophy and neglected historical analysis. See, for example, Perry Anderson, *Considerations on Western Marxism* (New York: New Left Books, 1976); Goran Therborn, "The Frankfurt School," in *Western Marxism: A Critical Reader*, ed. G. Steadman Jones (New York: New Left Books, 1976); Tom Bottomore, *The Frankfurt School* (London: Tavistock, 1984). But this overlooks Critical Theory's fundamental contextual character – that it wrestled with a far-reaching epochal transformation of modern, capitalist society in a way that entailed the reflexive transformation of the critical theory of that society. Such interpretations tend to translate historical issues of structural transformation into more static ones of the strength of working-class movements.

2. See, for example, Andrew Arato, "Political Sociology and Critique of Politics," in *The Essential Frankfurt School Reader*, ed. A. Arato and E. Gebhardt (New York: Continuum, 1978), pp. 3–25; Seyla Benhabib, *Critique, Norm, and Utopia: On the Foundations of Critical Social Theory* (New York: Columbia University Press, 1986); Helmut Dubiel, *Theory and Politics: Studies in the Development of Critical Theory*, trans. B. Gregg (Cambridge, Mass.: MIT Press, 1985), pp. 99–112; David Held, *Introduction to Critical Theory: Horkheimer to Habermas* (Berkeley: University of California Press, 1980), pp. 16–23, 46–65, 398–400; Martin Jay, *The Dialectical Imagination* (Boston: Little, Brown, 1973), pp. 3–30, 356, 279; Douglas Kellner, *Critical Theory, Marxism and Modernity* (Baltimore: Johns Hopkins University Press, 1989), pp. 9–12, 19–21, 43–4, 55, 65–6, 104–20; Rolf Wiggershaus, *The Frankfurt School: Its History, Theories, and Political Significance*, trans. M. Robertson (Cambridge, Mass.: MIT Press, 1994).

3. See, for example, Jay, *Dialectical Imagination*, pp. 143–72; Wiggershaus, *Frankfurt School*, pp. 280–91.

4. Andrew Arato recognizes this (although his interpretation of the stakes is different than that presented in this chapter). See "Political Sociology and Critique of Politics," pp. 10–13.

5. Horkheimer clearly expresses this view in a letter to Neumann, agreeing that, empirically, the situation in Germany is nowhere near that of state capitalism. Nevertheless, he maintains that society is moving toward that situation, which proves the value of Pollock's construct in providing a basis for discussing current historical tendencies. Letter

from Horkheimer to Neumann, August 30, 1941, cited in Wiggershaus, *Frankfurt School*, p. 285.

6. Cf. Paul Sweezy, *The Theory of Capitalist Development* (Oxford: Oxford University Press, 1942), pp. 52–3; Maurice Dobb, *Political Economy and Capitalism* (London: Routledge & Kegan Paul, 1940), pp. 70–1; Ronald Meek, *Studies in the Labour Theory of Value* (London: Lawrence & Wishart, 1973), p. 303.

7. For a critique of traditional Marxism based upon a reconceptualization of the categories of Marx's critique of political economy and, hence, of his conception of capitalism's most fundamental social relations, see my *Time, Labor, and Social Domination* (Cambridge: Cambridge University Press, 1993). The analysis developed there provides the standpoint of the critique of Pollock and Horkheimer outlined in this chapter.

8. Ibid., pp. 286–306.

9. Opposing the reality of society to its ideals is frequently considered the central hallmark of an immanent critique, also within the tradition of Critical Theory. See, for example, Adorno, "On the Logic of the Social Sciences," in *PDGS*. This approach is not the same as the understanding of immanent critique presented here, which seeks to explain historically and socially both the ideals and the reality of society, rather than calling for the realization of its ideals.

10. This point is elaborated in my *Time, Labor, and Social Domination*, pp. 87–90, 286–306. It should be noted that "structure" is not used here as it is within the framework of structuralism with its constitutive dualism of *langue* and *parole*, structure and action. Rather, "structure" here refers to historically specific congealed forms of practice, forms that are constituted by and constitutive of practice.

11. The possibility of theoretical self-reflexivity is intrinsically related to the socially generated possibility of other forms of critical distance and opposition – on the popular level as well. That is, the notion of social contradiction also allows for a theory of the historical constitution of popular forms of opposition that point beyond the bounds of the existent order.

12. Habermas presents a version of this position in "Technology and Science as 'Ideology,'" in *TRS*. See also Daniel Bell, *The Coming of Post-Industrial Society* (New York: Basic Books, 1976).

13. In 1941 Pollock included the Soviet Union as a state-capitalist society (*SPSS* 9: 211 n.1).

14. For Marx, property relations as well as the market are aspects of the mode of distribution. See *Time, Labor, and Social Domination*, p. 22.

15. One weakness of traditional Marxism is that it cannot provide the basis for an adequate critique of "actually existing socialism."

16. Marx, *Theories of Surplus Value*, trans. R. Simpson (Moscow: Progress Publishers, 1968), II, 164. When enclosed in quotation marks, the term "labor" refers to a conception, criticized by Marx, which transhistorically ontologizes labor's unique role in capitalism.

17. See Dobb, *Political Economy and Capitalism*, p. 58; Martin Nicolaus, "Introduction" to Marx, *Grundrisse* (Harmondsworth: Penguin, 1973), p. 46; Paul Walton and Andrew Gamble, *From Alienation to Surplus Value* (London: Sheed & Ward, 1972), p. 179.

18. Cf. Rudolf Hilferding, "Böhm-Bawerks Marx Kritik," in *Die Marx-Kritik der österreichischen Schule der Nationalökonomie*, ed. H. Meixner and M. Turban (Giessen: Verlag Andreas Achenbach, 1974), p. 143; Helmut Reichelt, *Zur logischen Struktur des Kapitalbegriffs bei Karl Marx* (Frankfurt am Main: Europäische Verlagsanstalt, 1970), p. 145.

19. It should be noted as an aside that, whereas labor in capitalism is the object of Marx's critique of political economy, traditional Marxism affirms it as the standpoint of the critique. To the degree that this reversal is considered historically, it cannot, of course, only be explained exegetically, that is, that Marx's writings were not properly interpreted in the Marxist tradition. By the same token, a historical explanation would also have to outline the conditions of possibility of the reading outlined in this chapter.

20. This antinomial opposition of historical necessity and freedom, rooted in the state capitalism thesis, paralleled that expressed by Walter Benjamin in "Theses on the Philosophy of History" (*I* 253–64).

21. This weakness of later Critical Theory is characteristic of poststructuralist thought as well.

8 The transcendental turn: Habermas's "Kantian pragmatism"

HABERMAS'S "KANTIAN PRAGMATISM"

Habermas's philosophical career can easily and instructively be read as a succession of attempts to appropriate the achievements of Kant's critical philosophy without being drawn into its commitment to a "philosophy of the subject." Even *Knowledge and Human Interests* (1968), whose task is described as the continuation of epistemology by other means (e.g. social theory) and which is perhaps the work most philosophically distant from Kant, opens with an appreciation of Kant's enterprise: "The critique of knowledge was still conceived in reference to a system of cognitive faculties that included practical reason and reflective judgment as naturally as critique itself, that is, a theoretical reason that can dialectically ascertain not only its limits but also its own Idea" (*KHI* 3). Similarly, Habermas's later conception of philosophy as (in part) a "reconstructive science" that seeks to make explicit the pretheoretical know-how of speaking and acting subjects – expressed most clearly in the project of a formal or universal pragmatics – shares many features with other roughly contemporaneous attempts to deploy transcendental (or "quasitranscendental") arguments without the trappings of transcendental idealism.[1] Finally, and perhaps most obviously, the project of discourse ethics, first outlined in the early 1980s, is explicitly conceived as a defense of a Kantian conception of morality (e.g. categorical imperatives that bind us solely in virtue of our capacity for rational agency) within the context of his theory of communicative action.[2]

It is therefore not surprising that in some of his most recent essays Kant and Kantian themes emerge even more clearly. At one point, he describes his work as a form of "Kantian pragmatism" and he pursues the suggestion, first made by Tom McCarthy, that the various idealizing suppositions implicit in the idea of communicative action be considered analogous to Kant's "ideas" of reason introduced in the "Transcendental Dialectic" of the *Critique of Pure Reason*: Kant's ideas of a single world, the soul, and the "unconditioned" (or God) would thus correspond to the suppositions, in Habermas's work, of a common world, accountable subjects, and context-transcending validity claims.³ This "return to Kant" is nonetheless striking, since elsewhere he strongly criticizes Kant for his reliance on the philosophy of the subject and, in particular, the "spontaneity of a subjectivity that is world-constituting yet itself without a world" (*PT* 142). This tension at least raises the question of the extent to which one can follow Kant without likewise embracing the philosophy of the subject (or consciousness). In what follows, I propose to take Habermas at his word and examine his most significant philosophical contribution – the account of communicative action introduced in *The Theory of Communicative Action* and importantly presupposed in *Between Facts and Norms* – as such a project. The interpretation should help to locate Habermas in relation to some of the contemporary philosophical figures he has critically engaged – Dieter Henrich, Richard Rorty, Robert Brandom, and Hilary Putnam. More importantly, however, it will show his proximity to some recent developments in the philosophy of action where, I believe, a similar "return to Kant" can also be discerned (Donald Davidson, Christine Korsgaard, and Brandom). It will also, I hope, help to clarify some of the distinctive features of Habermas's own "Kantian pragmatism."

It will be useful to first sketch, in very broad strokes, an interpretation of Kant's project with which Habermas would be largely sympathetic. First, Kant's "critique of reason" is arguably not "foundationalist" but "coherentist" or "constructivist."⁴ That is, he does not attempt to ground the nature and limits of our cognitive powers (reason) through a form of deductive argument that appeals to certain self-evident axioms or principles. Rather, Kant seeks to defend the broadly human capacity for reason (theoretical and practical) against "empiricism" (that is, broadly naturalist accounts that would inevitably lead to skepticism) and "dogmatism" (that is, metaphysical accounts that allow a much greater scope for knowledge than Kant believes is warranted).⁵ His project can be called "constructivist" in that it seeks to establish the basic principles and "ideas" that reason is more or less obliged to acknowledge in its efforts to reflect critically on its own exercise. It thus neither assumes the skeptical (Humean) position that we lack a capacity for (anything other than instrumental) reason nor does it appeal to something beyond our capacity for reason in order to justify its claims. Moreover, Kant's "critique of reason" concedes a certain primacy to practical over theoretical reason. In the preface to the second *Critique*, Kant states that freedom is the "keystone" for the entire edifice of reason. It is our capacity for freedom or, in his words, to "set ends" – that is, to think and act on the basis of considerations ("reasons") that one can reflectively endorse – that is central to Kant's account of human reason. Though at times he describes this capacity as our "spontaneity" and suggests it discloses our membership in a noumenal world, the core idea, I believe, is the idea that freedom, and hence reason, are irreducibly normative concepts. Thus, an adequate account of our capacity for reason cannot be given in terms of the natural sciences (in fact, the latter presuppose the exercise of reason normatively understood), but neither does this capacity need to be seen as entailing any more metaphysically obscure notions than our capacity to be "reasons-responsive." Rather, what is required is showing how a normative account of agency (and hence reasoning generally) entails the presence of a "logical space of reasons" that, however much it supervenes upon the world known by the natural sciences, nevertheless cannot be reduced to it.[6] A central feature of this normative (and ultimately "compatibilist") reading of Kant, I believe, depends on an interpretation of his claim that, in acting freely, an agent must "incorporate" or take up a desire into the maxim of his action or, as it has been recently expressed, the agent must treat the desire as a reason for action. Finally, Kant's somewhat later doctrine of the "fact of reason," as others have shown, need not be construed as a desperate attempt to keep the critical enterprise from collapse. Rather, it again shows the roots of Kant's critique in a conception of practical agency and in the exercise of common human understanding.

The account of Habermas's "Kantian pragmatism" to be developed here exhibits a great deal in common with this sketch of Kant's critical project. In fact, one of the distinctive contributions of the theory of communicative action is to provide the contours for a conception of agency (and related notion of incorporation) that helps make that conception more intelligible. More specifically, on Habermas's model, normativity does not depend on a voluntaristic notion of the capacity of an agent to give a law to itself. Rather, it is specifically *within* social practices of "reciprocal recognition," where individuals mutually ascribe the status of reason-giver to one another, that the notion of an agent as a "law-giver" (and hence the source of normativity) must be located. Thus, in contrast to the philosophy of the subject, it is not the agent's reflection on his own capacity for thought or "end-setting" that, so to speak, "transports" him into the logical space of reasons.[7] Rather, to formulate it somewhat sharply, the social practice of reason-giving (which "institutes" the logical space of reasons) presupposes (in order to make that practice intelligible as reason-giving) that agents possess a defeasible, first-personal authority with respect to many of their mental states. It also presupposes the defeasible capacity to "set ends" or, in Habermas's related terminology, to take a "yes/no position" with respect to the claims raised in their utterances and actions (*PT* 43). Habermas's account of agency is thus at one level closest to Kant's "Kingdom of Ends" formula of the categorical imperative. More immediately, the interpretation of communicative action proposed here also parallels in many respects Robert Brandom's account of normative pragmatics. The idea common to both projects is that rational agency is fundamentally a normative status dependent on social practices and the attitudes displayed by, or ascribed to, individuals in the context of those practices: the capacity for incorporation, "reflective endorsement," or treating as a reason is a function of practices in which actors already find themselves (but which it is also practically impossible for them to imagine doing without).

COMMUNICATIVE ACTION AND
THE DELIBERATIVE STANCE

In *The Theory of Communicative Action* the concept of communicative action is introduced in the context of a historical review of concepts of action within social theory (e.g. Weber, Durkheim, Marx, Talcott Parsons) and the challenges posed for a Critical Theory of society. According to Habermas's preferred typology of social action, the basic distinction is between "consent-oriented" (or communicative) and "success-oriented" (or purposive-rational) action (*TCA* 1, 285). Within the latter class he distinguishes further between strategic and instrumental action. Instrumental actions are goal-oriented interventions in the physical world. They can be appraised from the standpoint of efficiency and described as the following of technical rules. Strategic action, by contrast, is action that aims at influencing others for the purpose of achieving some particular end. It too can be appraised in terms of its efficiency and described with the tools of game theory and theories of rational choice. Many instrumental actions can also be strategic, and some types of strategic action can be instrumental. However, communicative action, according to Habermas, constitutes a distinct type of social action. The goal or *telos* of communicative action is not expressed or realized in an attempt to influence others, but rather in the attempt to reach an agreement or mutual understanding (*Verständigung*) with one or more actors about something in the world. Thus, while all action is teleological or goal-oriented in a broad sense, in the case of communicative action any further ends the agent may have are subordinated to the goal of achieving a mutually shared definition of the agent's situation through a cooperative process of interpretation (*TCA* 1, 76, 80, 101). In acting communicatively, individuals more or less naïvely accept as valid the various claims raised with their utterance or action and mutually suppose that each is prepared to provide reasons for them should the validity of those claims be questioned. In a slightly more technical (and controversial) sense – and one tied more directly to specifically modern structures of rationality – Habermas also holds that individuals who act communicatively self-reflectively aim at reaching understanding about something in the world by relating their interpretations to three general types of validity claims that are constitutive for three basic types of speech acts: a claim to truth raised in constative speech acts; a claim to normative rightness raised in regulative speech acts; and a claim to truthfulness raised in expressive speech acts (*TCA* 1, 319–20). For the purposes of this chapter, I will focus on the claim to normative rightness, or what, in *Between Facts and Norms*, Habermas now refers to as the "principle of (practical) discourse": a norm of action is justified only if it could be agreed to by all affected as participants in a discourse (*FN* 107–9). The central claim, as I understand it, is not that actors always act communicatively, or that a clear line can always be drawn between when individuals are acting communicatively and when they are acting strategically, but rather that in order to interpret behavior as meaningful or rational *action*, we must, at least as an initial default position, assume that individuals generally act under these idealizing suppositions – and, indeed, that all of their action is only intelligible as action relative to these idealizing suppositions.

What I believe is easily missed in this account of communicative action is that it amounts, essentially, to a claim about normative statuses that are ascribed to actors in the context of certain social practices – specifically, the practice of the exchange of reasons. Utterances can count as an exchange of reasons – and actions can count as actions done *for* reasons – only if they are seen as issuing from agents who occupy a normative status; similarly, agents occupy the status they do as a result of the attitudes that are adopted towards them (or that they adopt towards one another). In other words, the claim concerning both the existence and presuppositions of communicative action is essentially a claim about what it means for an agent to be located within what Wilfred Sellars called the "logical space of reasons." The validity claims identified by Habermas (together with the idea of agents as accountable) are, in effect, constitutive rules for the practice of reason-giving – rules that the interpreter must assume in order to interpret action as rational. But they are also rules that the agents must be assumed to view each other as acting under, insofar as they view themselves as rational agents, that is, as capable of giving and responding to reasons.

The further ideas of communicative freedom and communicative reason are then introduced in connection with this notion of communicative action. Communicative freedom, as Habermas defines it, refers to the capacity of individuals to take a yes/no position (or to abstain from taking a position) with respect to the claims raised in contexts of social interaction (*FN* 119). Whether individuals have such freedom is not simply an empirical question. It too refers to a status ascribed to individuals in order to make rationality intelligible and in this sense it is similar to the related status of first-personal authority.[8] Likewise, communicative, in contrast to strategic or instrumental, reason refers generally to the process of the exchange of considerations in support of one or more of the basic validity claims (and the "subjective capacities" this process entails); however, "reason" too denotes primarily a set of normative practices.

Some have suggested that communicative action with its idealizing suppositions is a mere fiction, or that there is no such thing. How might one respond? Clearly, this does not seem to be a question that can be settled empirically. The thesis I would like to defend is that acting under these (and possibly other) idealizing suppositions is a condition of rational agency or, to use Jonathan Lear's terminology, a condition of being "minded" at all. The claim, again, is not that all actions are performed under such suppositions, but that to understand individuals as acting for reasons, they must generally be interpreted as acting under these suppositions, and to view them as agents is, in effect, to suppose that they view each other as acting under these idealizing suppositions. It requires adopting what I will call the "deliberative stance." The claim, then, is that to see agents as "rational" or "minded" requires viewing them from the deliberative stance, to see them as acting under the idealizing suppositions of communicative action.

How might such a thesis be supported? One strategy – suggested by Donald Davidson, Daniel Dennett and others – is to identify the assumptions that are required for rational interpretations, and see how far these lead. To be "minded" on this approach is (first) to be a subject to whom intentional states (beliefs, desires, and other proattitudes) are ascribed. However, as holists such as Davidson and Dennett have argued, to be "minded" requires more than the ascription of individual beliefs and other intentional states. It is also necessary that the intentional states (and the agent's actions) stand in a relation to one another in accordance with various norms or principles (e.g. a norm of rationality or a norm of continence). It also assumes a principle of "first-personal authority": to view an individual as rational requires that she be aware (conscious) of the beliefs and desires that rationalize or guide her action. Thus, to be minded is to be viewed from the perspective of a framework constituted by these interpretive norms and principles. But is this framework something that exists only in the "eye of the beholder," that is, the interpreter? And does this framework also include the idealizing suppositions of communicative action?

In the case of what Dennett calls "simple" intentionality, we ascribe beliefs and desires to another agent and interpret it under certain norms of rationality. My dog nudges her food dish with her nose because she *wants* her dinner and *believes* this will get my attention. Sometimes, however, we ascribe more complex forms of intentionality to other intentional systems as well: we attribute to them not only rationality, but also the capacity to view others as intentional systems as well – what Brandom calls the "discursive-scorekeeping stance."[9] It is also possible to view other intentional systems as not only capable of ascribing (simple) intentionality to others, but as also capable of acting from (and viewing others as capable of acting from) considerations ("reasons") they can reflectively endorse. This stance involves seeing systems as significantly "active" and not just passive with respect to their desires. They are able to ask whether they have reason to act upon (ground-floor) desires, where this question is settled not solely by an appeal to other desires, but also with reference to the norms and principles they can endorse.[10] Finally, from the perspective of the deliberative stance, agents or complex intentional systems are seen (and see themselves) as capable of acting for reasons that they can justify to other codeliberators. In fact, this feature is central, I believe, to a constructivist conception of reason: something ultimately can count as a reason not in virtue of some property it possesses independent of the practice of reason-giving (as in some forms of moral realism), nor solely in virtue of its endorsement by an agent, but as a result of its status within the normative practice of the exchange of reasons.

Thus far I have made the limited suggestion that the deliberative stance is required only if we want to develop rational interpretations of a certain sort (ones that view agents as codeliberators). Can an argument be given to show that the deliberative stance is required for any rational interpretations at all? And can an argument be provided to support the claim that the deliberative stance is not "just" in the eye of the beholder, or that, if it is, why it is not contingently so – that is, why we must nonetheless take it up? There are, I believe, two arguments that might be proposed and both can be found in Habermas's writings at various points. The first I will call a transcendental argument; the second, by contrast, appeals to the *practical* impossibility of disregarding the "deliberative stance."

One way in which the claim that we "must" adopt the deliberative stance (towards ourselves and others) might be defended is through a form of transcendental argument. The claim is that the idealizations that collectively define the "deliberative stance" are presupposed by – "conditions of possibility for" – agency, or practical rationality, even in the more minimal sense of the capacity to act on the basis of beliefs and desires. The argument strategy is similar to Kant's attempt in the *Groundwork for the Metaphysics of Morals* to show that practical reason presupposes freedom. What Kant refers to as the "capacity to set ends" would then parallel the capacity to act under the idealizations of the deliberative stance (e.g. from reasons that could be justified to others). Of course, Kant also argued, in connection with his "reciprocity thesis," that practical agency in general also presupposed the moral law, but that is a further claim that need not be pursued here.[11]

The transcendental argument begins with the claim that, even in standard cases of agency, more is presupposed than Dennett's account of simple intentional systems. Ascriptions of agency involve not only the assumption that the agent's conduct can be predicted via beliefs and desires attributed to him, but also four other steps. First, the agent must be assumed to be appropriately sensitive or responsive to reasons – this is crucial to the view that an agent acts not only in accordance with a rule or norm, but also from a rule or norm. Second, conceiving an agent to be sensitive to reason, in the relevant sense, requires conceiving of the agent as "active" and not merely passive with respect to her desires. Third, the notion of an agent as "active" and not merely passive entails something like the capacity on the part of the agent for critical reflection, or for what Korsgaard calls "reflective endorsement" – the ability to step back from a potentially motivating desire and ask whether one endorses it or wants to treat is as a reason for action. Fourth and finally, the capacity for reflective endorsement is best understood in connection with the "sociality of reason" – roughly, the idea that reflective endorsement is not a solitary endeavor but something that requires social practices of justification that include other reason-givers or "codeliberators." An agent can identify with or reflectively endorse a desire only if she sees it as one that (as appropriate) she could justify to others. Agency, or acting for reasons, in even its simpler sense would thus seem to presuppose the capacity to act under the stronger idealizations of the deliberative stance – though it of course does not mean that agents always do act in view of those idealizations.[12]

A second approach takes the form, not of a transcendental argument about the conditions of agency, but of an appeal to what, given certain social practices, is extremely difficult (or even impossible) to imagine doing without. It parallels an argument that can be found in P. F. Strawson's influential essay, "Freedom and Resentment" and also bears a strong similarity with Kant's doctrine of the "Fact of Reason."[13] According to standard interpretations of this doctrine, Kant abandons the attempt to provide a transcendental argument *for* freedom. In the second *Critique* he instead treats it as a "fact" to which appeal can be made to help make explicit what is already implicitly known in practice or, in Kant's words, already known by "common human understanding." Thus, rather than an independent transcendental argument for freedom, the doctrine of the "fact of reason" helps us to better understand (and to resist naturalist or skeptical objections to) what, from a practical point of view, is already familiar to ordinary humans.

At various points in his writings, Habermas invokes both sorts of argument. For example, the transcendental argument offers the best way to understand his claims in *The Theory of Communicative Action* that strategic action is parasitic upon communicative action (*TCA* 1, 292). It can also be found in his more recent response to Richard Rorty's contextualist "ethnocentrism" as well as in his criticisms of Dieter Henrich's version of a philosophy of the subject that treats the paradoxical notion of a nonreflective self-awareness as basic.[14] At the same time the more "modest" argument, which appeals to what is (nearly) unimaginable from a practical point of view, is most clearly seen in his remark that we are all "children of modernity," that is, products of historical and thus contingent traditions which are, nonetheless, practically inescapable for us. As Habermas has recently expressed it: "Communicative reason, too, treats almost everything as contingent, even the conditions for the emergence of its own linguistic medium. But for everything that claims validity *within* linguistically structured forms of life, the structures of possible mutual understanding in language constitute something that cannot be gotten around" (*PT* 139–40). In fact, the two approaches need not be mutually exclusive. It might be that while skepticism or what John MacDowell calls "bald naturalism" with respect to human behavior is theoretically possible, viewing others (and ourselves) as "minded" is so deeply embedded in a wide range of practices that abandoning it is simply not a practical alternative for us. If this is so, then the idealizing presuppositions of communicative action will be relatively secure and the transcendental argument from the conditions of agency helps us to see why.

I would like to consider further steps three and four in the "transcendental argument" presented above, for I suspect that these are the most controversial. Does a conception of practical agency require something like the capacity of reflective endorsement (step 3) and does the capacity for reflective endorsement entail the "sociality of reason" (step 4)? Addressing the first question requires a brief survey of various notions of critical reflection that have received a good deal of attention in recent literature on agency. The second question, by contrast, brings us closer to Habermas's distinctive contribution, though parallels to it can also be found in Brandom's and other "neopragmatist" readings of Hegel. It is the clearest "pragmatic" component in Habermas's "Kantian pragmatism." Before pursuing these questions, however, I would like to show their relevance by indicating where they fit in with Habermas's account of communicative action.

REFLECTIVE ENDORSEMENT AND
MUTUAL RECOGNITION

In *The Theory of Communicative Action* Habermas introduces the concept of the life-world as a correlate to his concept of communicative action. The idea is, roughly, that action always occurs within a broad nexus – the life-world – of cultural meanings, normative expectations, and patterns of individual socialization.[15] According to Habermas, the life-world is also "experienced" by agents in two ways: as something that supports (and constrains) actors from *behind*, and as something that *confronts* them as a conflict or problem to be solved. It is, in his terms, both a "resource" on which they draw and a more or less explicitly problematized "topic" about which they can seek to reach agreement with others. The idea of the life-world as "resource" (or "background") should be relatively familiar from wider discussions of the role of the background (and holism generally) in the literature of belief-ascription. What individuals can mean (and thus believe, desire, etc.) is not solely up to them, but depends importantly on the symbolic order(s) in which they live and act. The idea of the life-world as "topic" is, I think, also relatively familiar. Individuals can experience particular aspects of the life-world as problematic and, if they choose, take them up as issues to be questioned, debated, and, at least at times, renegotiated. What is particularly of interest for the present, however, is Habermas's further claim that an individual's relation to the life-world should be viewed as a circular process: "Action, or mastery of situations, presents itself as a circular process in which the actor is at once both the *initiator* of his accountable actions and the *product* of the traditions in which he stands, of the solidary groups to which he belongs, of socialization and learning processes to which he is exposed" (*TCA* II, 135).[16] This reference to a "circular process," while instructive, must be interpreted cautiously, for if individuals are construed as "products" of the process it is not clear how they can be agents. At the same time, we need a more precise characterization of what it means to be an "initiator" of one's actions if this is not to be understood in an excessively voluntaristic manner. Habermas thus importantly remarks that, in this circular process, the reproduction of the life-world is "not merely routed *through* the medium of communicative action, but is saddled *upon* the interpretative accomplishments of the actors themselves" (*TCA* II, 145; *PD* 342; *FN* 324). It is at this point that the idea of communicative freedom (as a particular take on reflective endorsement) is introduced. The notion of an "interpretative accomplishment" refers to the view that actors can actively adopt a yes/no position with respect to the various validity claims raised in speech and action. Insofar as the life-world serves as a "resource" that supplies the agent with potential *reasons* for action, the various considerations or motivations that it provides must, in some appropriate sense, be taken up and *treated* as a reason by her. Otherwise, we will lose our grip on an appropriate sense in which she can be an agent ("initiator") of her actions. The account of communicative freedom in *The Theory of Communicative Action* – the capacity to take a yes/no position on claims – is thus offered as a plausible account of agency able to avoid the charge of an "overly socialized" individual or "cultural dope," on the one hand, and an overly intellectualized or "voluntarist" notion of deliberation and choice, on the other. Considerations, as potential reasons for action, are elements found within (or constructed from) the individual's life-world (including as well her "inner world" of needs and desires).[17] However, whether these considerations can become *reasons* for action depends on the "yes/no" position that actors take up or adopt towards them.

Specifying the appropriate conditions of agency – stating when an action is in the relevant sense "one's own" – is a topic that has received a great deal of attention in recent literature in action theory. New interpretations of Kant's doctrine of "incorporation" by Henry Allison and Onora O'Neill, accounts of "identification" inspired by Harry Frankfurt's work, and Christine Korsgaard's notion of "reflective endorsement" represent important proposals. A central challenge for each of these accounts is to avoid, on the one hand, an excessively voluntaristic model that risks viewing the "decision to treat as a reason" as an isolated act, more or less removed from the agent's wider motivational set, and, on the other hand, a regress of ever "higher order" endorsements that is at some point arbitrarily broken off. The second danger is especially prominent among hierarchical accounts of the will, such as Frankfurt's, whereas the first is a particular challenge to Kantian models of "incorporation" or "reflective endorsement."[18]

Frankfurt's response to earlier criticisms provides at best a mixed response to this second challenge. In order to bring the possibility of regress to a halt, the agent's higher-order identification with her lower-order desire must be "wholehearted" and the agent must be appropriately "satisfied" with his decision.[19] It must "resonate" throughout the agent's motivational structure and be a condition that, on reflection, the agent has no interest in changing. However, Frankfurt's discussion of these notions suffers from an ambiguity that threatens to undermine its aim to provide an account of when motivating desires are genuinely the agent's own. On the one hand, "wholeheartedness" suggests the idea of a resolute *decision*. To identify with lower-order motivating desires is to endorse them in a way that brings to an end the need for higher-order endorsements because the agent (even on reflection) sees no reason for change. The decision itself thus "establishes a constraint by which other preferences and decisions are to be guided," and identifying with them makes them "authoritative" for the self.[20] On the other hand, though, Frankfurt also states that whether the agent is satisfied in the appropriate sense – whether the endorsement is one she can live with or not – is to a great extent not up to her: "We are not fictitious characters, who have sovereign authors; nor are we gods, who can be authors of more than fiction . . . We can be only what nature and life make us, and that is not so readily up to us."[21] However accurate this may be as a description of how many of us sometimes experience the world, it would seem to undermine any attempt to specify the conditions under which a desire could be genuinely or authentically one's own. At best, it leads to the somewhat paradoxical conclusion that whether a desire is the agent's own has little to do with her "active," reflective self. Frankfurt, indeed, seems to have become more convinced in this latter position in his most recent remarks.[22] What in particular is absent from this account is how various higher-order considerations (including principles, norms, and policies) serve to structure the reflective self.[23] Frankfurt embraces a largely Humean conception where what an agent has reason to do (and what can be a reason for her) is ultimately settled by contingent desires within her motivational set and over which she seems to have little control.

Korsgaard, by contrast, develops the Kantian idea of "incorporation" and attempts to defend it against the charge of voluntarism. The danger of this approach, to repeat, is that it views the agent as potentially able to incorporate any desire he has into a maxim for acting, thus making him responsible for everything he happens to do. There is no practically available criterion, it seems, for distinguishing between desires that happen to motivate him and those reasons that are genuinely his own. On Korsgaard's interpretation, however, "reflective endorsement" (incorporation) is not an isolated event separate from what she calls the agent's "practical identity." What an agent is able to endorse is shaped (and constrained) by this practical self-conception and though, as on Frankfurt's view, these conceptions are not simply "up to us," they are "constitutive" of the self and not simply factors outside the self. Further, what an agent can endorse is not fixed simply by higher-order, though still contingent, desires. Included within an individual's practical identity are also norms, principles, and policies and what she can reflectively endorse is partly set by the norms constitutive for that practical identity. This distinguishes Korsgaard's position from Frankfurt's in that the self (or its practical identity) includes not simply an ordering of desires with which the agent is in some sense "satisfied" – what Charles Taylor calls a "thin self" – but a more "thickly constituted" self whose identity is (at least in part) structured by the norms, principles, and policies implicit in a practical identity.[24] Finally, what an agent can reflectively endorse is not simply up to her in another sense: to treat a desire as a "reason" is to grant it a kind of generality such that if any similarly situated agent were to reflect, she too would find it to be a reason she could endorse. In this way, Korsgaard also attempts to highlight the public or "shareable" character of reasons for action.[25] Thus, for a consideration to be appropriately the agent's own, it must be one that she could and would endorse on reflection as issuing from her practical identity and for it to be a "reason" for her it must, in a suitable way, also be a reason that is public or can be shared. Though these are both constraints on what can be a genuine reason for an agent that are in some sense not simply up to her, in contrast to Frankfurt's formulation, they do not undermine an account that seeks to clarify when it can count as genuinely her own in the relevant sense.

To turn now to step 4 from above, we need to examine further the ideas of reflective endorsement and practical identity and their connection to the notion of the sociality of reason. Two points are especially relevant. First, to have a practical self-conception is (minimally and among other things) to have various commitments and entitlements. Thus, to have a practical conception of one's self as a professor, parent, or friend is to assume the various entitlements and obligations related to those roles. In an important sense, then, the "content" (commitments and entitlements) of one's practical self-conception is not up to the agent who has it; rather, it depends on the understanding of the larger community of which she is a member.[26] Secondly, to reflectively endorse a desire as a reason is, as I have shown, to acknowledge it as issuing from one's practical identity. However, to "acknowledge" a commitment/entitlement, to treat it as a reason (as justifying), also presupposes that one is located in the space of reasons and thus seen as a reason-giver. Indeed, whether even a particular desire can count as a reason – and hence whether you can acknowledge it as a reason – depends again on the more specific commitments and entitlements one has acquired within the "space of reasons" or, as Brandom has expressed it, within the game of deontic scorekeeping.

It is important here not to confuse two features of this social practice. On the one hand, an important norm of the practice of reason-giving itself is a principle of first-person authority. Thus, the fact that the agent avows a particular desire as a reason is a *prima facie*, though defeasible, reason to consider it a reason for her action. Indeed, the ascription of first-personal authority is a fundamental assumption of the practice of reason-giving. On the other hand, as I have claimed, whether a desire can (objectively) be treated as a reason by her is not exclusively up to her: it also depends upon the (socially defined) content of her practical identity and on her socially recognized status as a reason-giver. This suggests the possibility that an agent can (mistakenly) treat as a reason something that (given her practical identity) cannot be a reason for her – that is, it is not a consideration that she could justify to (the appropriate) others – as well as the possibility that she may not (on any particular occasion) recognize something that is (objectively) a reason for her.[27] Nonetheless, even in these cases, the claim is that when an agent "reflectively endorses" a desire or treats it as a reason, she is committing herself to being able to justify (to others, as appropriate) the commitments and entitlements (the content of the desire) she thereby acknowledges. Acting for a reason, in sum, requires viewing the agent from the deliberative stance.

Let me summarize the claims of this section. To view an agent as acting for reasons requires ascribing to her the capacity to be reasons-responsive. This capacity is best construed as the capacity to take a yes/no position on validity claims raised in speech and action. An adequate interpretation of this capacity (and what Korsgaard calls "reflective endorsement") requires recognizing both the "sociality of reason" and, within the practice of reason-giving, the principle of first-personal authority. A person can act for reasons – and hence be viewed as accountable – only under the idealizing suppositions of communicative action (e.g., she is assumed to be able to provide justifying reasons for her actions).

RATIONAL INTERPRETATIONS, NORMATIVITY, AND THE INELIMINABILITY OF THE "SECOND PERSON PERSPECTIVE"

The account sketched thus far closely aligns Habermas's theory of communicative action with the idea of rational interpretations, or rational explanations, found, for example, in Davidson and Dennett. Like them, it asks what must be supposed in order for interpretation to be possible. It extends those accounts in suggesting that, to interpret the actions of others as rational, we must also adopt a "deliberative stance" towards them: we must view others as also moving within the "logical space of reasons" and as acting under the idealizing suppositions of communicative action, including the obligation to provide justifying reasons for their conduct.

However, it might be objected that this account of Habermas's aim is too limited. Habermas is not only interested in the (otherwise legitimate) question of how rational interpretations are possible, but also in the more ambitious goal of developing a deeper grounding for the normative features required for a critical theory of society, given that, as he once expressed it, "bourgeois consciousness has become cynical" (CES 97). This objection is certainly correct. Nonetheless, the argument about what rational interpretations presuppose also lays the groundwork for the more ambitious goal. I cannot hope to fill in all the relevant steps here, but I would like to mention some differences with other approaches to the question of rational interpretations in order to at least indicate the direction such a filling-in would take. Pointing out these differences will also show how Habermas remains closer to the Kantian conception of reason outlined earlier. Central to these differences is both the "primacy of practical reason" and the ineliminability of the participant's or second-person perspective.

First, on the view most closely associated with Davidson and Dennett, the point of developing rational interpretations could be described as primarily theoretical. Its aim is to make reasonably accurate predictions about how others will behave and thereby "explain" their action. This aim is certainly important. However, Habermas's interest in rational interpretations – and reason generally – is not primarily this theoretical one. His aim, I believe, is practical and is at least equally concerned with questions of deliberation such as "What should I do?" or "Who shall I be?" In viewing another from the deliberative stance – viewing them as complex intentional systems – we see them (like ourselves) as concerned with questions such as "What is the right thing to do?" or "What kind of person do I want to be?" In short, then, the "decision" to adopt a deliberative stance is practical and adopting the deliberative stance is to view others (like ourselves) as having a fundamental interest in these practical questions.

Second, and perhaps more importantly, Habermas's account of communicative action has important consequences for an analysis of the source of normativity – one that, best understood, can be seen as "constructivist" or Kantian. According to Habermas, to adopt the deliberative stance is to view the conduct of others (like ourselves) as norm-guided. Norms, on this view, are embedded in practices and practices are reflected in the relevant attitudes of social actors. In viewing others from the deliberative stance, we treat them as guided by norms and as themselves instituting norms via the attitudes they adopt towards one another. In other words, in viewing them not only from the "intentional stance" (as simple intentional systems) but also from the "deliberative stance" (as complex, discursive scorekeepers) we not only see their practices as normative, but see them as instituted through the attitudes the actors themselves take up towards one another (in the eye of the beholder "twice-removed," one might say). However, and this goes to the core of Habermas's approach, this means we must view ourselves as "virtual participants" in the practices we consider from the deliberative stance. That is, we see them as reason-givers whose reasons must convince us and (again, at least virtually) as entitled to reasons for our interpretations in response.[28] In other words, on Habermas's view, adopting the deliberative stance is ineliminably second-personal, and this second-person, or participant's, perspective is important for his account of normativity, since the norms are instituted through the (participants') attitudes – both those of the interpreter and those of the (interpreted) actors.

The question of whether normativity requires a second-person or participant's perspective – that is, attitudes involving certain specifically interpersonal expectations – emerges explicitly in a recent exchange between Habermas and Brandom.[29] The exchange is particularly significant given the apparently deep agreement between their respective projects. Like Habermas, Brandom also locates the source of normativity in the attitudes adopted by actors in the context of social practices: "Now it is a fundamental claim of *Making it Explicit* that normative facts of the sort appealed to in making explicit defining features of discursive practice – those pertaining to *commitments* and *entitlements* – should be understood as *socially instituted*. That is, apart from our scorekeeping attitudes of attributing and acknowledging such deontic statuses, there are no such statuses, and hence no corresponding normative facts about them."[30] Nonetheless, in his review of Brandom's book Habermas suggests that Brandom's account falls back into "methodological individualism" and hence fails to due justice to the role of the second person. More specifically, he claims that "on closer examination [of his account], it becomes evident that the act of attributing, which is of fundamental importance for discursive practice, is not really carried out by a *second* person." Rather, the attitudes that institute normativity – fundamentally, taking or treating another as a discursive scorekeeper, or treating another as undertaking a commitment – are, on Brandom's account, attitudes that are *attributed* to another from a "third-person" perspective – that is, from the perspective of one not considered to be a participant in those practices. In his reply, Brandom accepts this characterization of his account and suggests that it reflects an important motivation: namely, to explain the normativity intrinsic to intentionality (e.g. he "ought" to go because he promised) without already presupposing it or, as he has elsewhere expressed it, its aim is "to make intentional soup out of non-intentional bones."[31] The weakness of Habermas's account of communicative action, according to Brandom, is that it presupposes the normativity intrinsic to intentionality rather than explaining it. In acting communicatively, actors are prepared or "intend" to make good their claims and they "expect" others to provide reasons for the claims they make. On Brandom's view, these second-person attitudes are intentional in character and are consequently to be eschewed in an explanation of intentionality.

At least two questions can be raised in connection with this exchange. Does the account of the second-person attitudes central to communicative action presuppose intentionality? And, is it possible to explain (intentional) normativity from a conceptually prior (nonintentional) normativity that Brandom identifies with the *third-person* attitudes of treating as scorekeepers (assuming here that treating as a scorekeeper is just to attribute a more complex set of entitlements and commitments to the actors being interpreted)? Distinguishing these two questions also exposes a different motivation behind the two projects. Habermas is not primarily interested in explaining how "intentional soup can be made from nonintentional bones." Rather, he is concerned to show how the (normative) resources for coordinating social action can be derived from the pragmatic suppositions of "mutual understanding" or communicative action. (And, if the argument I have sketched here is sound, in showing – in a roughly Kantian fashion – how these idealizing suppositions of communicative action must be presupposed insofar as we treat others as "acting for reasons" at all.) It is, of course, also true that in opposing the "philosophy of the subject" Habermas is interested in developing an account of action (and meaning) that does not treat a particular model of intentionality – the intrinsic directedness of private mental states – as a fundamental starting point for developing an account of normativity, but begins instead with the "intersubjective" recognition (via mutual ascription, on my view) of ego and alter as "reason-givers." But this social practice – in which ego and alter are, so to speak, "coposited" – is still not equivalent to the project outlined by Brandom in his response. That is, it may be that Brandom is correct that the "second-person" attitude identified by Habermas does assume (rather than explain) intentionality (and its distinctive normativity).

On the other hand, one can also ask whether, in ascribing normative status to others, Brandom's third-person perspective is really able to avoid the second-person perspective described by Habermas. Brandom describes the perspective as one in which the interpreter *attributes* (but does not *acknowledge*) a range of commitments and entitlements to another.[32] But is it possible for an interpreter to attribute a commitment to another without himself having some grasp of what a commitment (or entitlement) is, or without having some idea of what it is to undertake or acknowledge a commitment himself? If not (as seems likely), then this description of the "third-person" perspective as one of attributing but not acknowledging a commitment does not represent a genuine alternative to Habermas's notion of a virtual participant. In treating another as a discursive scorekeeper, one treats her as a "reason-giver" who is (at least virtually) within the same logical space of reasons as the interpreter, that is, subject to the same sorts of commitments that one would oneself acknowledge (and not only attribute to another). Brandom might reply that whether the third-person interpreter is himself a discursive scorekeeper who acknowledges (as well as attributes) scorekeeping attitudes is itself a question that can only be answered from the perspective of yet another, higher-order scorekeeper who attributes the relevant attitudes to the lower-order interpreter. But this would surely open up an unsatisfying regress of attributions.

A second response open to Brandom – one that suggests a possible reconciliation between the two projects – can be found in some remarks in a recent essay where he adopts a more ecumenical approach to the study of intentionality.[33] He distinguishes again between the normativity specific to intentionality (what he hopes to explain) and a prior conception of normativity instituted via the practical know-how (and corresponding attitudes) concerning proprieties, commitments, entitlements, and the like. The idea, as he summarizes his project there, is to explain intentionality with reference to this (normative) practical know-how.[34] This description of the project rejects more ambitiously reductivist attempts to explain the normative on the basis of the nonnormative – the intentional on the basis of the natural – but retains the ambition of "making intentional soup from non-intentional bones." However, though this "practical know-how" is not intentional, it could nonetheless be "participatory" or "second-personal" – and indeed this seems likely. A practical (not semantically explicit) grasp of what is appropriate in a situation, or of what one is committed or entitled to do or say, would seem to depend upon practical expectations about the responses of others that arise in the course of social interactions. It involves attitudes that treat others not simply as objects but, at least in some primitive sense, interaction partners. In fact, in an admittedly rather speculative account in *The Theory of Communicative Action*, Habermas has proposed a genetic reconstruction of Mead's notion of "taking the position of the other" along just these lines (see *TCA* II, 8ff.).[35] Brandom's strategy could then be preserved to the extent that intentionality is explained from the (now also second-personal) know-how required for the adoption of discursive scorekeeping stance towards others (and oneself).

To conclude, I have argued that our interest in developing rational interpretations – or rational explanations – is not an exclusively (or even primarily) theoretical task. First, to the extent that we see ourselves as deliberators, as concerned with who we are and what we should do, our interest in rational interpretations is also practical. Further, we interpret the actions of others as also practical in this sense. Second, the account of rational interpretations – and the claim that it involves idealizing suppositions – is relevant for the larger question of the origin or source of normativity. Habermas, like Brandom, locates normativity in the attitudes we suppose actors to take up towards one another – there is no normativity apart from the statuses instituted via these attitudes. For Habermas, these attitudes are importantly and irreducibly second-personal in the sense that to adopt the deliberative stance is to treat them as "coparticipants" in the "space of reasons." In adopting the deliberative stance, we view others as at least virtual participants in the exchange of reasons that must convince us as well. So construed, the deliberative stance – and Habermas's account of communicative action, generally – can be seen as a "pragmatic" rendering of Kant's claim that, insofar as we view ourselves as capable of acting for reasons at all, we must view ourselves as acting under the idea of freedom.

NOTES

1. See, for example, Habermas's remarks in "Philosophy as Stand-in and Interpreter" and "Reconstruction and Interpretation in the Social Sciences" in *MC* and his summary comment: "All species competences of subjects capable of speech and action are accessible to a rational reconstruction, if, namely, we recur to the practical knowledge to which we intuitively lay claim in tried-and-true productive accomplishments" (*PT* 14). This strategy of preserving transcendental arguments without transcendental idealism, of course, is much indebted to the work of P. F. Strawson. See *The Bounds of Sense* (London: Methuen, 1966).

2. See Jürgen Habermas, "Discourse Ethics: Notes on a Program of Philosophical Justification" and "Morality and Ethical Life: Does Hegel's Critique of Kant Apply to Discourse Ethics" in *MC*.

3. Jürgen Habermas, "From Kant's "Ideas" of Pure Reason to the "Idealizing" Presuppositions of Communicative Action," in *Pluralism and the Pragmatic Turn: The Transformation of Critical Theory*, ed. W. Rehg and J. Bohman (Cambridge, Mass.: MIT Press, 2001), pp. 11–39. The description of his work as a form of "Kantian pragmatism" occurs in the preface to *Kommunikatives Handeln und detranszendentalisierte Vernunft* (Stuttgart: Reclam, 2001), p. 5; and in his "Reply," in *Habermas and Pragmatism*, ed. M. Aboulafia (New York: Routledge, 2002), p. vi.

4. For a defense of this reading of Kant, see Onora O'Neill's, *Constructions of Reason* (Cambridge: Cambridge University Press, 1989) and "Vindicating Reason," in *The Cambridge Companion to Kant*, ed. P. Guyer (Cambridge: Cambridge University Press, 1992), pp. 280–308.

5. For this important and influential interpretation of Kant's project, see Dieter Henrich, "The Concept of Moral Insight and Kant's Doctrine of the 'Fact of Reason,'" in *The Unity of Reason* (Cambridge, Mass.: Harvard University Press, 1994), pp. 55–88 and John Rawls, "Some Themes in Kant's Moral Philosophy," in *Kant's Transcendental Arguments*, ed. E. Forster (Stanford: Stanford University Press, 1989), pp. 81–113.

6. The notion of the "logical space of reasons" is due to Wilfred Sellars, "Empiricism and the Philosophy of Mind," in *Science, Perception and Reality* (London: Routledge & Kegan Paul, 1963), pp. 127–96. It has more recently been defended by John McDowell, Robert Brandom, and, at least on some interpretations of his anomalous monism, Donald Davidson. For an earlier important compatibilist (and Davidsonian) reading of Kant, see Ralph Meerbote, "Kant on the Nondeterminate Character of Human Actions," in *Kant on Causality, Freedom and Objectivity* (Minneapolis: University of Minnesota Press, 1984), pp. 138–63.

7. For one of the most ambitious attempts to work out this assumption of the philosophy of the subject, see Henrich's "Fichte's Original Idea," in *Contemporary German Philosophy*, vol. 1, ed. D. Christensen (University Park: Pennsylvania State University Press, 1982), pp. 15–54 and "Self-Consciousness: An Introduction," *Man and World* 4 (1971): 3–28; see also "What is Metaphysics – What is Modernity? Twelve Theses against Jürgen Habermas," in *Habermas: A Critical Reader*, ed. P. Dews (Oxford: Blackwell, 1999), pp. 281–319.

8. See Richard Moran, "Interpretation Theory and the First Person," *Philosophical Quarterly* 44 (1994):154–73 and Tyler Burge, "Reason and the First Person," in *Knowing our own Minds*, ed. C. Wright *et al.* (Oxford: Clarendon Press, 1998), pp. 243–70.

9. Robert Brandom, *Making it Explicit* (Cambridge, Mass.: Harvard University Press, 1994), p. 628; see also Daniel Dennett, *The Intentional Stance* (Cambridge, Mass.: MIT Press, 1987), pp. 240ff.

10. See Christine Korsgaard, *The Sources of Normativity* (Cambridge: Cambridge University Press, 1997).

11. See H. Allison, *Kant's Theory of Freedom* (Cambridge: Cambridge University Press, 1990), pp. 201–13. Habermas pursues a similar line of argument in "Discourse Ethics."

12. See Habermas, "From Kant's "Ideas" of Pure Reason," p. 25, where he refers to situations in which communication breaks down and the suppositions become "indirectly defeasible."

13. See Jürgen Habermas, "Freedom and Resentment," in *Free Will*, ed. G. Watson (Oxford: Oxford University Press, 1982), pp. 59–80.

14. For Habermas's response to Rorty, see "Richard Rorty's Pragmatic Turn," in *On the Pragmatics of Communication*, ed. M. Cooke (Cambridge, Mass.: MIT Press, 1998), pp. 343–82. For his critique of Henrich, see especially "Metaphysics after Kant" (*PT* 23f.).

15. As this threefold characterization suggests, for Habermas the lifeworld is not comprised solely of cultural systems (including language), but also includes normative orders and personality structures

(motivations). Thus, in contrast to the "linguistic idealism" he attributes to, for example, Gadamer, the life-world is not only about "meaning" but also about normative orders and motivational resources as well. This threefold characterization raises some important questions that cannot be taken up here.

16. See also Jürgen Habermas, "Remarks on Communicative Action," in *Social Action*, ed. G. Seebass and R. Tuomela (New York: Reidel, 1985), p. 167.

17. This last claim, of course, connects with Habermas's "hermeneutic" approach to psychoanalysis proposed already in *KHI*. For Habermas, "our need-based nature [*Bedurfnisnatur*] is communicatively structured" (*CES* 93).

18. For an account of Kant's notion of "incorporation" and some of the problems associated with it, see especially Henry Allison, "Autonony and Spontaneity in Kant's Conception of the Self," in *Idealism and Freedom* (Cambridge: Cambridge University Press, 1996), pp. 129–42.

19. See especially Harry Frankfurt, "The Faintest Passion," in *Proceedings of the American Philosophical Association* 66 (1992): 5–16.

20. Harry Frankfurt, "Wholeheartedness and Identification," in *The Importance of What We Care About* (Cambridge: Cambridge University Press, 1988), p. 45.

21. Frankfurt, "Faintest Passion," p. 10.

22. See especially Frankfurt's replies to the essays by Bratman, Scanlon, and Herman in *Contours of Agency*, ed. S. Buss and L. Overton (Cambridge, Mass.: MIT Press, 2002).

23. This point is nicely developed by Michael Bratman, "Hierarchy, Circularity and Double Reduction," in ibid., pp. 65–85; see also his "Identification, Decision, and Treating as a Reason," in *Faces of Intention* (Cambridge: Cambridge University Press, 1999), pp. 185–206.

24. Charles Taylor, "Self-Interpreting Animals," in *Philosophical Papers*, vol. 1 (Cambridge: Cambridge University Press, 1985), pp. 45–76.

25. For a sympathetic, yet critical discussion of this position, see my "Practical Reason, the "Space of Reasons," and Public Reason," in Rehg and Bohman (ed.), *Pluralism and the Pragmatic Turn*, pp. 53–85.

26. This claim, of course, is indebted to the thesis of "wide-content" or semantic externalism. For a very helpful discussion, see Cynthia MacDonald, "Norms and Externalism," in *Current Issues in the Philosophy of Mind*, ed. A. O'Hear, Royal Institute of Philosophy Supplement, no. 43 (Cambridge: Cambridge University Press, 1998), pp. 273–302.

27. A significant tension or ambiguity is still preserved in this sketch between what an agent *could* endorse and what she on reflection *would* endorse. These two may not always coincide: the first depends

on whether, given the content of the agent's practical identity, the desire *could* be reflectively endorsed by the agent. Whether the agent is accountable (whether the action is "hers") *additionally* depends on whether the agent, on reflection, *would* endorse it.

28. I would like to add that I believe this is something like a "default position" in adopting the deliberative stance. Of course, given the addition of much other empirical information – that is, about what knowledge was available to them at the time, and so on – we do not think the reasons they could give are reasons that would convince us. Nonetheless, in viewing others, from the deliberative stance, as reason-givers, we must begin from this default position. This is, I believe, not only true of the interpretation of "other cultures," but, equally, in the interpretation of ourselves – though here the sorts of considerations that might move us off the default position will be different.

29. See Jürgen Habermas, "From Kant to Hegel: On Robert Brandom's Pragmatic Philosophy of Language," *European Journal of Philosophy* 8 (2000): 322–55 and Robert Brandom, "Facts, Norms and Normative Facts: A Reply to Habermas," in ibid., pp. 356–74.

30. Brandom, "Facts, Norms and Normative Facts," p. 365.

31. Ibid., p. 364.

32. Ibid., p. 367.

33. Robert Brandom "Modality, Normativity, and Intentionality," *Philosophy and Phenomenological Research* 63 (2001): 587–609.

34. Brandom, "Facts, Norms and Normative Facts," p. 364.

35. We would also need to distinguish, then, between the second-person or participant's perspective of actors who share propositionally differentiated speech (and intentionality) and the second-person or participant's perspective associated with a conceptually earlier stage of "symbolically mediated interactions."

9   The politics of Critical Theory

It has long been commonplace to point out that the Critical Theory of Horkheimer and Adorno has no politics.[1] This is usually meant in three senses. The first is that Critical Theorists of this time explicitly refused to engage in party politics, voice opinions about current events, propose reform agendas, or indeed talk about political institutions in any specific way. The second sense in which early Critical Theory has no politics is that its critique focused more and more on a realm of culture and aesthetics detached from politics. For some this merely led to abstraction, while others thought it led to irrelevance.[2] Finally, and most significantly, early Critical Theory has no politics because its diagnosis of the times is so pessimistic as to make any political action, or indeed any attempt to break out of the logic of instrumental reason, futile. Thus, to the question "What is to be done?" Horkheimer and Adorno appear to answer, "Alas, nothing."[3]

Contemporaries of Horkheimer and Adorno, such as Marcuse, as well as later thinkers such as Habermas and Honneth, have tried to make up for the political deficit within the *Dialectic of the Enlightenment*. Despite these attempts, the accusation of weak or nonexistent politics persists until today. An evaluation of these accusations suggests, however, that there are many competing views of politics at work here. In this chapter I attempt to sort out and untangle the various ways in which Critical Theory's political credentials have been put into question. Nevertheless, the story always seems to come back to the famous question: "What is to be done?" This is not surprising, as Critical Theory was born in the conviction that social theory should embrace normative, and pursue moral, ends. Thus for every evaluation of an "is," Critical Theory suggests an "ought."

What Critical Theory has not always been good at is suggesting how we get from the "is" to the "ought."

THE POLITICS OF ENGAGED WITHDRAWAL

We should not be too quick to dismiss early Critical Theorists for having no politics to speak of. For one thing, they continued writing even during their most pessimistic stage. One can still ask what they thought they were *doing* in pursuing critical social theory. For another, the relationship between early Critical Theory and politics is complicated by its own attempt to forge a new relationship between theory and practice. This new relationship is nothing less than a new definition of the political and as such would put into question the original accusation.

The redefinition of politics gets one of its earliest articulations in the essay "Traditional and Critical Theory." Traditional theory for Horkheimer encompasses many disparate schools of thought from idealism and phenomenology to positivism and pragmatism. According to Horkheimer, all these theoretical approaches make a fatal error by splitting the subject matter under discussion from the process of knowledge formation. For idealists and phenomenologists, this means social phenomena are external to the thinker. The philosopher relies on reason alone, independent of experience, to generate laws and principles that are then "brought" to reality. Positivists represent the flip side of this problem. Again, social phenomena are viewed as external to the observer. The "brute facts" of reality are seen as containing all that is necessary to generate a theory and reason and understanding are simply neutral procedures: mills for the grist of data.

Although idealism and phenomenology come under attack, Horkheimer's real target is positivist social science. The upshot of the problematic understanding of the relationship between reason and reality is a science that (1) can only systematize and classify brute facts, (2) mistakenly thinks that brute facts are the transparent, self-evident, and independent foundations of objective science, and finally and most importantly, (3) can never go beyond the given. Positivist social science cannot set ends for itself. All it can do is reproduce existing goals and ends that are presupplied by the present social structure. Thus it is complicit in (and sometimes central to) the stability of existing social structures. Despite claims to neutrality, positivism has normative effects – it "does" something in the world. This critique of positivism is an attempt to show that science and knowledge are political in an analogous way that feminists remind us that the personal is political. Claiming to be apart in a separate private or value-free sphere is not only false, the insistence that there is a value-free zone is itself a value-laden move that has an implication in the political world.

In the face of this diagnosis, Critical Theory set out to do two things. Firstly, to show the internal relationship between knowledge and experience. Facts are socially constructed both in how we perceive them and in their own right, that is, to the extent that social facts are not natural accidents but products of human activity. The second and much more complicated task that Critical Theory set for itself was to use the interconnectedness of knowledge and experience to break out of the given and project normative goals and ends. Thus Critical Theory is envisioned as political in the sense of embracing the unavoidably political nature of all theory and attempting to direct it towards rationally chosen ends. It is this second task that appears to be stymied by Critical Theory's own analysis of the contradictions of modernity.

Critical Theory has a normative agenda. Its stated interest is the emancipation of humanity from injustice. What justifies this particular interest over some other? Horkheimer argues that this interest is the product of applying negative dialectics to the contradictions of social reality. Two basic contradictions anchor the normative ends of Critical Theory in reality so that it cannot be accused of idealism (spinning normative ends out of the arbitrariness of pure thought) and yet is not weighed down and imprisoned by existing conditions (as is positivism). The first contradiction manifests itself at the level of political economy and ideology, while the second points to a deeper level and involves the confrontation of human reason and nature. The contradictions of political economy involve the confrontation between the professed goals of the bourgeois economic revolution and what that revolution had become. Critical Theory's "content is the transformation of the concepts which dominate the economy into their opposites: fair exchange into deepening of social injustice, a free economy into monopolistic control, productive work into rigid relationships which hinder production, the maintenance of society's life into the pauperization of the peoples" (*CT* 247). Over and over again one can identify the inversion of liberal values into their opposites. At the center of this negative dialectic stands the individual whose freedom, once extolled and apostatized by liberals, shrinks and contracts to nothing under the forces of commodification until "the individual no longer has any ideas of his own" (*CT* 237). In this way, the critique generates a new understanding of the object from within a historical context. This new understanding is then supposed to open up the possibility for radical change. But that change is again only articulated in the negative. Critical Theory does not propose positive programs for change: "true theory is more critical than affirmative" (*CT* 242). In identifying contradictions, we can turn away from them or try to lessen that contradiction. One pursues the path of least contradiction. But negative dialectics, itself, undermined the possibility of there being such a path.

As Horkheimer's and Adorno's diagnosis of contradiction began to take on ever grander and all-encompassing proportions, it became more and more difficult to imagine anyone breaking out of the logic of domination.[4] Action itself appeared to entangle the actor in negative dialectics beyond her control. To enter the world of action is to enter a world saturated by commodification and fully reified; it is to have one's actions hijacked by overwhelming powers of management. The fully administered society "embraces those at war with it by coordinating their consciousness with its own" (*MM* 206). Thus it appears not simply that Horkheimer and Adorno had no politics in the sense that they were unwilling to recommend plans of action, they also appear to deny the very possibility of autonomous political action. All action *in* the world is immediately contaminated *by* the world.

What about theory? What about the idea that theory *does* something in the world – that it is political in and of itself? Despite their pessimism, Horkheimer and Adorno continued to theorize. One of the ways of understanding their continued commitment to theory is to suggest that they replaced the question "What is to be done?" with the much older one of "How should one live one's life?" This is not to be understood as analogous to the inward withdrawal of Hellenistic philosophy. Horkheimer is quite clear that although he has chosen philosophy over action, "Philosophies that look exclusively to an inner process for eventual liberation end as empty ideologies . . .

Hellenistic concentration on pure inwardness allowed society to become a jungle of power interests destructive of all the material conditions prerequisite for the security of the inner principle" (*ER* 184). Horkheimer argues, however, that philosophy should stay out of the business of issuing commands to action. In the middle ground between pure inwardness and action stands the reformation of theory. Clear thinking and the correction of error and confusion within theory were the tasks set for Critical Theory. Thus, like Socrates in the *Gorgias*, we see an embrace of truth over the *demos* and, again, like Socrates, this is understood as ultimately political.[5]

Socrates claims that he is "one of the few Athenians (not to say the only one) who has attempted the true art of politics," despite the fact that he avoided public office and democratic politics whenever he could.[6] Care for the community or the true art of politics seeks truth and the improvement of souls through Socratic interrogation. In a similar fashion, Horkheimer and Adorno think that personal rectitude and moral criticism based on what truth can be grasped under the conditions of late capitalism is the only authentic politics available to them, that is, the only way to care for the community. Horkheimer and Adorno were committed to a Socratic enterprise of cranky admonishment and moral dressing-down. From the student movement to contemporary music, everything came under their dour and critical eye. Thus, to the question "How should I live my life?" they did not answer, as Epicureans had in the face of a changing and cruel world, "I shall live my life in quiet contemplation of the good and calm things of this world." Instead they answered as Socrates had: "teaching of the good life" (*MM* 15), even to those who do not wish to learn. Their political stand could be called *engaged withdrawal*. Although politics as *paideia* has a long and respected pedigree, it is not very satisfying for those who crave for a more concrete answer to the question "What is to be done?"

THE GREAT REFUSAL

Herbert Marcuse is a curious and ambiguous figure in this story. On the one hand, many of his best-known writings, in particular, *One-Dimensional Man*, fall squarely into the category of engaged withdrawal. On the other hand, these writings inspired the engaged activism of the New Left and the student movements of the 1960s.

One-Dimensional Man is a deeply pessimistic work that maps the thorough triumph of instrumental reason in the modern world. Advanced capitalism has succeeded in creating individuals with such misshapen needs and ideas of happiness that they are incapable of taking up an authentically critical perspective on the world that furnishes their satisfaction. It is impossible to cultivate a revolutionary consciousness under these conditions. The question "What is to be done?" becomes "how can administered individuals – who have made their mutilation into their own liberties and satisfactions, and thus reproduce it on an enlarged scale – liberate themselves *from themselves* as well as from their masters? How is it even thinkable that the vicious circle be broken" (*O* 251). Marcuse's answer is bleak: "Dialectical theory is not refuted, but it cannot offer the remedy . . . It defines the historical possibilities, even necessities; but their realization can only be in the practice which responds to the theory, and, at present, the practice gives no such response" (*O* 253). He concludes the book with the famous and close to despairing words: "The critical theory of society possesses no concepts which could bridge the gap between the present and its future; holding no promise and showing no success, it remains negative. Thus it wants to remain loyal to those who, without hope, have given and give their life to the Great Refusal." Marcuse follows this with Walter Benjamin's words expressing the tragic irony presented to those who would theorize against Fascism: "It is only for the sake of those without hope that hope is given to us" (*O* 257). For Marcuse, a new form of totalitarianism was in place and there was very little we could do about it except weather the storm in the personal moral rectitude of the Great Refusal.

What was the Great Refusal? It involved a refusal to be drawn into the life of late capitalism. And this included, indeed especially meant, not being drawn into reformist politics. Marcuse rejected, and continued to reject until the end of his life, the idea that transformation could be accomplished, furthered, or even aided by working within the existing democratic institutions: "The democratic process organized by this structure is discredited to such an extent that no part of it can be extracted which is not contaminated" (*L* 67).[7] Thus, the Great Refusal was a refusal to engage in liberal democratic politics. But it also seemed a refusal to engage in any type of politics or action. This is certainly how some contemporary commentators understood the concept: "Marcuse displays that basic hostility to politics which is the curse of too many German thinkers for too many years. Its effects spill over into the only type of political action he sanctions today: the Great Refusal, a complete rejection of the mechanics of political change presented by the system . . . (and a) rejection of politics as such."[8]

On paper, the Great Refusal looks like a great withdrawal; its political life, however, belied this conclusion. The pessimistic and apolitical message of *One-Dimensional Man* inspired a generation of radical activists. Published in 1964, it quickly catapulted Marcuse into the heady politics of the 1960s. Paul Breines, a New Left intellectual writing in 1968, noted that Marcuse "is the most widely discussed thinker within the American Left today."[9] Todd Gitlin, in his memoir of the sixties, tries to articulate how Marcuse's pessimism could have been such an inspiration to action:

We were drawn to books that seemed to reveal the magnitude of what we were up against, to explain our helplessness. Probably the most compelling was Herbert Marcuse's *One-Dimensional Man*, with its stark Hegelian dirge for the Marxist dream of an insurgent proletariat . . . Gradually its reputation swelled among the New Left for its magisterial account of a society that, Marcuse argued, had lost the very ability to think or speak opposition, and whose working class was neutered by material goods and technology. Some unimaginable radical break, some "Great Refusal," was apparently impossible but deeply necessary. Impossible and necessary: that is how we felt about our task.[10]

Although settled in the United States, Marcuse achieved a high profile among German students as well, even earning the sobriquet "father" of the student movement.[11] Throughout the tumultuous years 1966–9, Marcuse was a frequent figure on podia, roundtables, and other organized student and New Left events. He was clearly an inspirational figure for many activists; nevertheless, his relationship to the politics of the sixties is ambiguous. While expressing unwavering solidarity and participating in "events" in a way shunned by Horkheimer and Adorno, it is not clear what connection can be made between Marcuse's writings and the student movement. Marcuse himself insisted on a number of occasions that he was a philosopher and not a strategist or even an activist.[12] Furthermore, like his Frank-furt School contemporaries, he was suspicious of the idea that theory could be translated directly into practice.[13] There was very little in his pre-1965 writing that could have given students any clear ideas about how they should be organizing, what they should be demand-ing, or to whom they should be appealing. Even his more "politi-cal" writings could not be directly translated into concrete political action.

Rather than Marcuse's influence on the student movement, it might be more accurate to talk about the student movement's influ-ence on Marcuse.[14] From 1965 to 1970 Marcuse's writings take a decidedly upbeat and practical turn. His three major publica-tions of this period, "Repressive Toleration," *An Essay on Libera-tion*, and *Counterrevolution and Revolt*, "glow with revolutionary optimism."[15] This optimism is founded on the emergence of spe-cial groups capable of breaking with the totally managed society. To be sure, he had voiced something similar in earlier writings, but only in passing and with little enthusiasm. Now Marcuse appeared to embrace the view that students, blacks, and certain third world liberation movements were sufficiently nonintegrated into the one-dimensional society to be able to develop a new sensibility and awareness of the suffocating nature of the capitalist system. Marcuse never mistook student and black protest for revolution, and never believed that a revolutionary moment was at hand (*L* 10).[16] Instead, he appeared genuinely inspired by the radical spirit spreading across campuses and through civil rights groups. It was his hope that this spirit could lead to new fissures in culture and ultimately allow for the development of new needs and instincts. Even at the height of the student rebellions, Marcuse retained a consciousness-centered view of change as opposed to an institutional or political view of it. The modification that was required was very deep and added up to nothing less than a qualitative change in "the infrastructure of man" (*L* 14). Our very biology, in the sense of instincts and needs, required transformation before we could even contemplate intuitional trans-formation: "the rupture with [the] self-propelling conservative con-tinuum of needs must *precede* the revolution which is to usher in the free society but such a rupture itself can be envisaged only in a revolution" (*L* 27). Thus, although a supporter of direct action, this was not for the sake of reforming institutions or changing the rules so much as for the effect such action might have on consciousness. What was required was a rupture of some sort that could shake individuals loose from the false needs and free them to get in touch with deeply buried authentic ones. In this way, direct action was understood as playing an indirect role in bringing about the true revolution.

By the 1970s the force of the student movement appeared spent, and as it waned, so did its place within Marcuse's writings. Although he never repudiated the idea that certain groups had a special opportunity to develop a new sensibility, by the end of his life he had turned away from direct action and towards art (see *AD passim*). In art we can experience the free play of the imagination and so in art we can escape the "given." Art is the refuge of rebellious subjectivity and the outlet for utopian energies. The focus on art rather than political action is more in keeping with Marcuse's pre-1965 analysis of late capitalism. Indeed, some have suggested that his "political" phase is in deep contradiction with the general thrust of his social critique. Habermas, while noting that there is something appealing in Marcuse's "chiliastic trust" in the emergence of true needs, nevertheless adds that Adorno, in his lack of trust, "was the more consistent thinker."[17]

Ultimately, Marcuse is squarely within first generation Critical Theory on the question of politics. The issue here is not so much pessimism as the level of analysis that makes all political action in the world seem beside the point. It was not a political regime that needed overthrowing, so much as the Enlightenment itself. What was called for was a deep, historical transformation akin to the transformation that took place from the Middle Ages to the modern world. Asking Critical Theorists to propose policies or a political program to bring about this transformation would be like asking Francis Bacon to suggest policies to bring about the Enlightenment. They saw themselves as contributors to a body of knowledge that might (but more likely would not) one day be part of a history of transformation. The rejection of politics as superficial and ultimately collaborationist is repudiated in the next generation of Critical Theory and in particular in the work of Jürgen Habermas. His alternative view of politics was crystallized during the student protests of the late 1960s.

At first sight it would appear that the student movement in Germany caused a split in Critical Theory, with Marcuse on one side expressing full solidarity with the students and Habermas, Adorno, and Horkheimer on the other, having a problematic and, at times, highly critical relationship with the students. But on closer examination this picture does not fit. Horkheimer and Adorno remained aloof from the events. In contrast, both Habermas and Marcuse were deeply engaged with the student cause. But here is the telling difference. While Marcuse voiced a general and enthusiastic support for the movement, he was not engaged at the level of suggesting political or pedagogical reforms, on the one hand, or specific tactics and strategies, on the other. Habermas, in contrast, was involved at the level of proposals and strategies and this led to conflict and tension with certain elements of the movement. Although vocally supportive of many of the demands and positions of the movement, Habermas was at the same time critical of elements in the movement that appeared to him to have embraced a type of actionism, that is, disruptive action for its own sake. What many of the more radical elements in the movement lacked, according to Habermas, was any clear idea of the ends to be achieved by action.[18] His misgivings and frustration with the activists who mistook the student uprisings for a revolution, led to his infamous and also unfortunate reference to "Left-Fascism" at a student-led conference in June 1967. This remark caused such a stir and made Habermas such a controversial figure that from that moment on it become difficult for him to continue as a leading figure within the movement, even though he had developed, and was indeed the only prominent Critical Theorist to have developed, a detailed program of university and political reform. It was Habermas's embrace of politics, leading to a subsequent dispute over politics, that caused the rift between him and the students; for Marcuse, it was his lack of politics that allowed him to stay clear of arguments concerning "what is to be done."

Marcuse, although personally committed to actual and real political movements, could not endorse reform within the system because of his evaluation of Enlightenment reason. This meant that his politics would always be, to use Martin Jay's formulation, "Metapolitics, which is no politics at all."[19] Marcuse's idea of transformation entailed some unimaginable but hoped for rupture with the present that somehow would let agents of the revolution circumvent existing institutions and bring about the rational society via wholly untainted means. In the end, Marcuse's Critical Theory offers no more of an answer to the question "What is to be done?" than do Horkheimer's and Adorno's, despite his ringing endorsement of what was done by students and civil rights activists in the sixties. In a sense, he had no theoretical reasons to make such an endorsement.

THE POLITICS OF CONSTITUTIONAL DESIGN

Has later Critical Theory been able to overcome the pessimistic immobility of the first generation? Habermas certainly sees his work partially as a corrective to this immobility. He rejects the total critique of Horkheimer, Adorno, and Marcuse, and instead argues that Enlightenment reason presents a Janus face of possibilities, some good and some bad. This allows him to envision emancipation, not as a historical overcoming of the Enlightenment, but rather as requiring the identification of forces within the Enlightenment that can be put into the service of emancipation and autonomy. Some of those forces will be found in the existing institutional possibilities presented by constitutional democracy. Thus, ordinary politics in the form of a reform of democratic institutions is squarely on the Habermasian agenda. The irony is that for some critics, Habermas's revision of Critical Theory has replaced one form of the apolitical with another; Habermas is criticized both from within Critical Theory as well as without for not being political enough. The internal criticism is that he is not radical enough; the external criticism (coming from postmodernism) is that in placing consensus at the center of his democratic vision, he is trying to displace or transcend politics. I will offer a brief map of his social and political theory and then turn to these criticisms.

The road from the Frankfurt School to Habermas has two important turning points. The first is a linguistic turn in which the culture critique of earlier Critical Theory is joined to a theory of communication and social evolution.[20] The second turn is what could be called a liberal Kantian turn, which sees Habermas defending some core liberal characteristics of civil society while at the same time maintaining a critical perspective.[21]

Habermas's revision of the Critical Theory tradition begins in the 1960s with *The Structural Transformation of the Public Sphere*. In this book he tracks the rise of bourgeois civil society, paralleled by the rise of a corresponding pubic sphere, in which private citizens first come together to form a public. The proliferation of political clubs, journals, and pamphlet-writing – as well as regular but informal political meetings in coffeehouses, salons, and the like – serve as venues for the formation of a public opinion that is not simply the aggregation of private opinions about public matters. Opinion is "public" in three senses: it is about public matters; it is in the public domain; and it is produced by a public, that is, by private citizens interacting in the public sphere.

At first, the political function of public opinion is simply public criticism. But as state actors come to heed the voice of public opinion, a new and stronger role is envisioned: "Since the critical public debate of private people convincingly claimed to be in the nature of a noncoercive enquiry into what was at the same time correct and right, a legislation that had recourse to public opinion thus could not be explicitly considered as domination" (STP 82). Critical debate in public becomes a test of rationality and right. By making public the grounds for state action and subjecting these grounds to the critical force of public debate, one can insure that the state has just reasons for its actions as well as that citizens believe that these reasons are just. Following Kant, this has come to be known as the principle of publicity.[22] The optimistic assumption at work here is that injustice and domination cannot survive the scrutiny of an enlightened and civic-minded public.

Although sympathetic to the ideal of publicity, in his early writings Habermas nevertheless argues that such a principle inevitably succumbs to the contradictions of the liberal/capitalist order (STP 141–235). Kant's public might have been critical but it was also very bourgeois, both in the sense that it was restricted to property owners and that it primarily pursued economic interests in the public sphere. Inclusiveness, however, brought a degeneration of the quality of discourse. Critical debate gets replaced by the consumption of culture and an apolitical sociability. Participation is fatally altered and the public sphere becomes an arena of advertising rather than a site of criticism. This pessimistic diagnosis is very much in keeping with Habermas's Frankfurt School roots. His later career, however, has seen the development of a theoretical approach that is much more optimistic about the possibility of rekindling the emancipatory potential of the public sphere first identified by Enlightenment thinkers of the eighteenth century. Much of contemporary Critical Theory has taken his lead in this matter, finding the possibility of emancipation in a revitalized and democratized principle of publicity.

How can we transform the public sphere into an arena of critical autonomous debate that is insulated from the distorting effects of power and money? Habermas understands this task as developing a procedurally centered theory of deliberative democracy: "[D]iscourse theory does not make the success of deliberative politics depend on a collectively acting citizenry but on the institutionalization of corresponding procedures" (IO 248). Legal and constitutional safeguards that roughly correspond to existing liberal systems of rights become a precondition for an emancipated public sphere. Much of Habermas's political theory can be understood as offering a discourse-theoretic reinterpretation of liberal constitutionalism.[23] This discourse-theoretic reading of constitutionalism would then suggest ways in which we could develop the liberal democratic framework to make it more democratic, that is, to give citizens more power and autonomy in steering and determining both their collective and individual lives. Thus, at its crudest, the politics of deliberative democracy involves taking the liberal state as it stands now in most western liberal democracies and expanding the public sphere in such a way as to involve citizens to a greater degree in a process of public opinion and will formation. The idea is to take citizens out of the narrow competitive model of politics so often found in western democracies and place them in a deliberative politics where their opinions are formed in critical concert with others. Not only do collective opinions epistemically benefit from rational debate, but citizens are also empowered through public sphere participation.

Deliberative democracy is a two-tier model of democracy. The relatively formal institutions of representative democracy form one tier; the informal interactions of a public forming their opinion in a well-ordered public sphere forms the other. Although informal, these interactions must take place under certain conditions in order for the opinion formation to be authentic and noncoerced. These conditions include certain levels of equality and respect and make up the content of a well-ordered public sphere. A democratized or well-ordered public sphere should offer everyone, and especially marginalized groups, the opportunity to participate in shaping, influencing, and criticizing public opinion. Just as liberal individualists have stressed the centrality of universal suffrage, so deliberative democrats stress the centrality of universal voice: each and every citizen should have the opportunity to have their voice heard and responded to. But can every voice speak, let alone be heard, under conditions of advanced capitalism? This is a question often put to Habermas and it contains the charge that, despite developing a political theory that goes well beyond Horkheimer and Adorno, Habermas is still not very comfortable with politics – or at least with the question "What is to be done?"

SOCIAL JUSTICE, ACTIVISM, AND AGONISTIC PLURALISM

The charge that Habermas avoids politics comes from three not unrelated directions. The first involves claims that the politics of Critical Theory should be about social justice and that Habermas has completely failed to accord that concern sufficient weight.[24] The second criticism is that, in concentrating on constitutional and procedural design, Habermas has failed to see that deliberative democracy is a call to action and a form of insurgency.[25] Finally, postmodernists argue that, in privileging consensus, Habermas tries to transcend "the political," which is defined (by postmodernists) as essentially contestatory and agonistic.[26]

Habermas acknowledges that a well-ordered deliberative democracy would have to address social inequality. Social inequality is a serious barrier to the ideal that all members of the political community are able to participate in the generation of political power. Although Habermas acknowledges this fact, he does not specifically address it, thus leading to the charge that he has failed to follow through on the radical potential of deliberative democracy.[27] That potential lies in spelling out the ways in which the capitalist system, globalization, and consumerism are undermining authentic democratic participation. Habermas has a real problem here: his own radical democratic bent has boxed him into a corner.

Habermas believes that if sincerely committed to democracy, we must also be committed to persuading citizens to reevaluate the relationship between the economy and politics along social-democratic lines. Those who challenge him on this issue must answer the "vanguard question." They appear to preempt deliberation and debate by saying that we cannot take democratic voices seriously until we have the right conditions. Habermas is faced with the opposite problem: not vanguardism but democratic deference seems to paralyze him. Habermas is a committed empirical proceduralist. Procedures must be undertaken in the real world and philosophers cannot preempt them.[28] Habermas cannot predict what would be agreed to in a full democratic debate, although he could speculate on the broad boundaries of outcomes. But a theory of deliberative democracy does not yield a principle of distribution, as does Rawls's idea of the original position, for example. That is ultimately left up to us, to citizens. But this leads to a circle that might be vicious. What if it is the case that present-day socioeconomic conditions are such that the public sphere is stacked against any egalitarian outcome? Perhaps those likely to make the most persuasive arguments in favor of egalitarianism are severely handicapped by existing conditions. Conversely, perhaps those most likely to distort the economic facts have the most access to the public sphere. Campaign financing is a good example, even if it touches only the tip of the iceberg. As long as people who benefit from the system are those in power, we will never change the system. But we will never get other people in power until we change the system. Habermas's dilemma is the following: we must find a way of talking with each other as equals about the elimination of systemic inequality before we can eliminate it.

In his unwillingness to speak for the people in fear of preempting their own deliberation, Habermas is unable to offer any substantive principles of social justice. By being a radical procedural democrat he is unable to be radical social democrat – at least, that is, while he is acting the philosopher and social theorist. Despite what looks like grand theory building, Habermas actually makes very modest claims on behalf of philosophy. Philosophy cannot tell us what the world ought to look like. It can offer some guiding rules that ought to apply as we go about the business of figuring out how the world should be. Philosophy can offer insight into broad questions of design that encompass constitutional essentials and the principles underlying the basic structure of liberal democracies. Ultimately it is not as philosophers and academics that we will change the world, but as activists, citizens, and participants in the hurly-burly of politics. In this realm, theory does not always have the answer. Habermas's unwillingness to go beyond proceduralism is a call to philosophers to step out of that role and enter the fray as citizens.

Some theorists have questioned the sincerity of this call. They argue that the division of labor between philosophy and engaged citizenship is a red herring. The real problem is that philosophy threatens to make political activism pointless. A constitutionally centered understanding of deliberative democracy privileges "politics as usual" over politics as radical critique. The constitutional model highlights the possibility of a people collectively shaping and steering society according to democratically elaborated principles or values. Thus, although public opinion is shaped in civil society, the focal point is the translation of that opinion into legitimate law via the old liberal representative institutions. For Habermas, emancipation is understood as the authentic exercise of popular sovereignty. In contrast, theorists such as John Dryzek, James Bohman, and Mark Warren, all of whom have Critical Theory backgrounds, are developing more genuinely postsovereignty models of democracy that do not rely on traditional ties that bind a *demos* or a collective civic identity.[29] Democracy is centered not in a collective will but rather in making institutions, elites, and governments accountable to a plurality of voices often joined together by issues, interests, or causes, rather than by culture or history. This model eschews traditional notions of sovereignty that need a clear and constituted authority to stop the buck and offers in its place the conception of a "decentered democracy" consisting in a plurality of grass-roots forces engaging in global campaigns of discursive harrying. Decentered democracy places the democratic voice in a largely uncoordinated civil society and public sphere.

To be sure, Habermas also places much stock in civil society, but the difference is that ultimately the opinions formed in the crisscrossing debates of civil society and the public sphere are to be funneled into representative institutions that coordinate our shared life. A fully decentered view of democracy focuses on the way any holder of power, from representative institutions to multinationals, answers to the multiple and uncoordinated voices of civil society. The accusation is that Habermas "has turned his back on extra-constitutional agents" and fails to see the critical and progressive potential of "protests, demonstrations, boycotts, information campaigns, media events, lobbying, financial inducement, economic threats, and so forth."[30]

The issue at stake for theorists such as Dryzek is the type of democratic action that can move a progressive agenda forward. At the forefront is grass-roots activism that can, for example, directly challenge the World Trade Organization to justify its policies to the public without having to go through representative institutions. For Habermas, it is the possibility of establishing a legal order that is democratically legitimate. While the activist model is democratic in the sense that it is grass roots, it too faces charges of vanguardism when placed in the context of the general public. When envisioning the Battle of Seattle as an essentially democratic event, one wants to ask, who elected the masked avengers in turtle suits seen so frequently on the news reports?[31]

While theorists such as Dryzek lament an unwillingness to engage in progressive and genuinely emancipatory politics, others on the Left argue that Habermas's political philosophy is so optimistic in its emancipatory vision that it bypasses, displaces, or transcends politics altogether. This criticism is typically leveled by postmodernists who understand politics to be a sphere of conflict, competition, struggle, confrontation, contestation, and antagonisms.[32] Procedural theories like Habermas's are intent on designing procedures that would channel and subdue these unruly forces of politics. Indeed, consensus is here understood as the ultimate overcoming of politics: who needs politics if we achieved a full consensus?

Chantal Mouffe, for example, argues that the Habermasian project of "how to arrive at a consensus without exclusion" implies "the eradication of 'the political.'"[33] By "political" she means "the dimension of antagonism that is inherent in human relations." "Politics," in turn, is the set of institutions and arrangements that organize the political – it "aims at the creation of unity in a context of conflict and diversity."[34] The entire enterprise of envisioning a power-free public sphere or domination-free social relations is suspect not simply because it is utopian, but also because the ideal itself inevitably turns into its opposite. "We have to accept that every consensus exists as a temporary result of a provisional hegemony, as a stabilization of power, and that it always entails some form of exclusion. The ideas that power could be dissolved through a rational debate and that legitimacy could be based on pure rationality are illusions which can endanger democratic institutions."[35] Here we see the claim that Critical Theory has no politics to be the mirror image of the accusation leveled at first generation Critical Theorists. With Horkheimer and Adorno, the concern was that there was no clear emancipatory vision that could, at the very least, inspire us to action. Now the accusation is that any emancipatory vision is apolitical because it attempts to transcend politics itself, and in transcending politics it attempts to silence the deepest forms of pluralism, difference, and otherness. Mouffe suggests we should think of democracy in terms of agonistic pluralism rather than deliberative democracy. Democracy is all about skirmishes rather than decisive battles.[36] Our world will always be full of irreconcilable differences. Rather than striving for agreement, we need to ensure that our disagreements are manageable. Our aim, according to Mouffe, should be to "to transform *antagonism* into *agonism*." The former is a struggle between enemies and the latter is struggle between adversaries.[37] By "warning us against the illusion that a fully achieved democracy could ever be instantiated," agonistic pluralism "forces us to keep the democratic contestation alive."[38]

Mouffe is very vague, however, about what agonistic politics would really look like and, more importantly, how it would concretely differ from deliberative politics. What differences in institutional arrangements or political action follow from these two models, for example? A Habermasian view can certainly accommodate protest and struggle and Mouffe nowhere implies that we should do away with representative institutions. In order to get a clearer picture of how these different theoretical views of politics might lead to a different set of actions or institutions, we need to go beyond Habermas and postmodernism towards more concrete formulations of Critical Theory. Here we see that third generation Critical Theorists have attempted to reconcile the strongly universalist view of Habermas with an openness to difference, diversity, and struggle.

The politics of recognition

How do third generation Critical Theorists answer the question "What is to be done?" Like Habermas, many if not most of this younger generation concentrate on articulating the conditions necessary to achieve authentic democracy. There are, however, significant differences. Although not for the most part agonistic in their approach to democracy, third generation Critical Theorists often see the world as an essentially messier and more fragmented place than does Habermas.[39] Their social theory is much more likely to take account of the disruptive and contestatory forces of difference and differentiation. The result is to counterbalance what sometimes appears to be Habermas's one-sided universalism.

Axel Honneth has developed a variant of Critical Theory that, although indebted to Habermas's work, also departs from it in significant ways.[40] While communication stands at the center of Habermas's social theory, recognition stands at the center of Honneth's. The conditions of agreement and understanding are what Habermas aims to uncover, but Honneth is after the conditions of healthy identity formation. Following Hegel, Honneth argues that we develop our sense of self, and in particular our sense of self-worth and self-confidence, in intersubjective relations of recognition with others. Rather than tracing ideal forms and conditions of recognition, Honneth describes the ways in which the process of identity formation can be distorted through actions and attitudes that deny recognition. Three broad categories emerge: violation of body; denial of rights; and denigration of ways of life. Extreme forms of these would be rape, enslavement, and ethnic cleansing. But one can also identify less extreme forms of distortion that are more relevant to life in western liberal democracies. In particular, the last form of distortion, which speaks to group identity and solidarity, has hit a chord in contemporary theory.

Honneth's social theory leads to a critical perspective focused on the personal and psychological dimensions of domination and emancipation in a way that Habermas's approach does not. For Honneth, personal integrity (wholeness) and undamaged development are essential for leading an emancipated life. What of the politics to come out of this perspective? Honneth is not a political theorist and, so far, the political implications are vague:

For the fact that the possibility of a positive relation-to-self emerges only with the experience of recognition can be interpreted as pointing to necessary conditions for individual self-realization. As in other contexts, a negative approach provides a preliminary justification: unless one presupposes a certain degree of self-confidence, legally guaranteed autonomy, and sureness as to the value of one's own abilities, it is impossible to imagine successful self-realization.[41]

Whereas Habermas concentrates on conditions for authentic citizenship, Honneth focuses on the conditions for authentic personhood that must precede citizenship. Rather than a procedural conception of law, Honneth develops what he calls a "formal conception of ethical life."[42] But the specifics of this formal conception are not developed in any systematic way and it is not self-evident where they would lead politically.

In some ways, Honneth's social theory speaks more to transitions to democracy than to the conditions within well-established liberal democracies. This is not surprising. His social theory is explicitly historically oriented, given his interest in the way struggles for recognition can be seen as the motor of history. Honneth, however, is talking about fundamental, almost primordial prerequisites for building democratic societies. For example, the discussion of rape and the damage such violation does to self-confidence and integrity, although clearly relevant for our world in which women are still violated and in which there is an underground "entertainment/pornography" industry that includes rape in its repertoire, speaks more to areas of the world in which rape is regularly and openly used in military and strategic actions by states, pseudostates, and other organized groups. Here we see the real cost, in human terms, of a failure to see the other as a person at all.

Although Honneth's greater awareness of contemporary global political reality makes his characterization of injustice and struggle more concrete than Habermas's, he is no more "political," if to be political is to offer an answer to the question "What is to be done?" Furthermore, if one did try to work out what followed politically from his theory of recognition, the result might appear highly problematic. This, at any rate, is the argument that Nancy Fraser, another third generation Critical Theorist, develops in response to Honneth. Fraser challenges Honneth on two fronts.[43] On the first, she questions the displacement of redistribution that his theory of recognition implies and, on the second, she questions a dangerous essentialism contained in this approach. By stressing recognition, Honneth locates the epicenter of injustice in misrecognition. This is then given political content, mostly via identity theory,[44] by looking at the stratification of cultural communities: "As a result of repeated encounters with the stigmatizing gaze of a culturally dominant other, the members of disesteemed groups internalize negative self-images and are prevented from developing a healthy cultural identity of their own."[45] The politics to emerge from this perspective centers on contesting "the dominant culture's demeaning picture of the group."[46]

Honneth argues that struggles for recognition and selfhood are the driving force in historical development. This would imply that economic inequalities are not only secondary but also dependent on this first and more essential differentiation in society. Fraser challenges this assumption. In particular, she points out that we live in a time of aggressive marketization that leads to "at least a partial decoupling of economic mechanisms of distribution from cultural patterns of prestige."[47] Thus, cultural hierarchies and misrecognition do not fully determine economic injustice. The politics of Critical Theory, if still directed at injustice, must proceed on both fronts. Indeed, it plays into the hands of the forces of marketization to concentrate on cultural wars and leave the economic sphere to itself. It is not that culturalism, as she calls it, is apolitical (a charge sometimes leveled at Horkheimer and Adorno's "culturalism"), it is that *by itself* it is bad politics.

Fraser's second challenge to recognition is deeper and speaks to an internal contradiction within the perspective: "The identity politics model of recognition tends also to reify identity. Stressing the need to elaborate and display an authentic, self-affirming and self-generated collective identity, it puts moral pressure on individual members to conform to a given group culture."[48] Thus, identity politics, while setting out to eradicate one form of domination embedded in misrecognition, often perpetuates a form of domination saddled with essentialism. Who gets to decide what it means to be Native Canadian, a woman, or an African American? Each of these groups contains struggles and disputes within it over its self-definition. Are patriarchal marriage regulations part of an authentic Native Canadian way of life requiring recognition, or are opposing claims made by women natives, who can also claim to be authentic, to be recognized? Now, it must be noted that Honneth does not elaborate an identity politics per se. His model of recognition, however, lends itself to identity politics – one might even say that identity politics flow logically from his position.

Seyla Benhabib has recently tried to untangle some of the issues raised by theories of recognition.[49] I will call her approach "constructivist" in the sense that both identities as well as collective norms are understood as constructed within a deliberative framework. Within Critical Theory debates, Benhabib places herself squarely within the universalist camp and believes that central to a viable critical stand *vis-à-vis* society is the ability to "distinguish a consensus, rationally and freely attained among participants, from other forms of agreement that may be based on power and violence, tradition and custom, ruses of egotistic self-interest as well as moral indifference."[50] At the same time she develops this idea of consensus alongside the acknowledgment that "we live in a globalized world of uncertainty, hybridity, fluidity, and contestation."[51] This fact about us is neither to be celebrated nor overcome. Like many aspects of modernity, it brings with it pluses and minuses, potentials for living freer and more satisfying lives as well as barriers to achieving such lives.

Like Habermas, Benhabib's model of deliberative democracy is two-tiered – "dual-tracked," as she calls it – with formal legislative institutions forming one track while the more informal deliberations of the public sphere form the other. But it is also "two-tiered" in another sense. Deliberation moves back and forth between ethical questions and moral questions. Deliberation can be about many different things, indeed one of the most significant differences between deliberation and Rawls's idea of public reason is that in deliberation there are no restrictions on what may be introduced into the conversation either as a topic or as a reason. Only some topics and disputes will be open to possible consensus and, further, only some of our disputes require consensus. For Habermas and Benhabib, only the most broadly understood principles of justice rest on consensus. As we move away from questions of justice, and away from both the need for and the possibility of consensus, we move into ethical as opposed to moral questions.[52] Ethical deliberation speaks more to identity formation, for such questions have to do with finding meaning in the lives we have chosen or been given. There are no universal answers to ethical questions.

Habermas has always been most interested in moral deliberation and the relation between moral norms and legal norms, thus his political theory is primarily a constitutional theory of design in which participants are thought of as equal citizens. Benhabib has turned her attention to the ethical debate. She questions any attempt to draw a hard and fast line between moral and ethical dimensions. Our conversations naturally flow back and forth and arguments and reasons put forward in one dimension will also be salient in the other. Cultures are in a constant process of flow and change in which groups and individuals reformulate narratives and bring new or altered meanings to the fore: "discourses are processes through which such resignification and narrative retelling will alter the line between the universalizable content of moral discourses and the ethical discourses of the good life without erasing them altogether."[53] Identities and norms are always under construction – they are always to be understood as works in progress. At any one time a group identity will be riddled with internal contestation and contain multiple understandings and narratives. The same can be said for a shared moral/legal framework: constitutional essentials regularly come under scrutiny, are questioned and contested, and require new justifications to answer new claims.

Benhabib's fluid constructionism partially answers the postmodern criticism. Consensus is still a regulative ideal for deep questions of legitimacy but, as all existing consensual understandings are by their very nature partial, they are always corrigible and fallible. Thus *contra* Mouffe, it is not the case that deliberative theory "is unable to recognize that bringing deliberation to a close always results in a *decision* which excludes other possibilities"[54] Deliberation is never brought to a close – it is an ongoing project of construction. There remains a significant difference of opinion between Benhabib and Mouffe, however. Mouffe thinks that every consensus is the result of a "provisional hegemony" and reflects a "stabilization of power." The Critical Theorist wants to know if we can distinguish better provisional hegemonies from worse ones. We might be unable to fully eradicate power and coercion in our imperfect world, but surely we want to be able to criticize some forms of power or be able to claim that some decisions are more legitimate than others. This appears impossible from the postmodern viewpoint. Here we have an old and well-documented quarrel between postmodernism and Critical Theory.[55] Critical Theory is intent on criticizing society from a normative vantage point. The postmodern perspective appears to erase such a vantage point. And to the question of "What is to be done?" the postmodern answer appears to be: struggle against any and all hegemony because the very act of struggle, regardless of the substantive issue, shakes things up and loosens the general hold of hegemony. Mouffe does go a little farther by trying to make a distinction between a political "enemy" and an "adversary."[56] But what is unclear is how exactly we proceed in an adversarial way as opposed to an antagonistic way.

Benhabib, by contrast, develops a procedural model from which to criticize provisional hegemonies and, in particular, the various ways in which claims for recognition have been addressed. She argues that, as long as arrangements do not violate the principles of egalitarian reciprocity, voluntary self-ascription, and freedom of exit and association, then they are compatible with a universalist deliberative democracy model.[57]

Democratic theory should be focused on the design of "impartial institutions in the public sphere and civil society where struggle for the recognition of cultural differences and contestation for cultural narratives can take place without domination."[58] From this vantage point she critically evaluates a number of hard cases and recent legal precedents drawn from various political and legal contexts. These cases include Muslim women in Europe, First Nations in Canada, Druze in Israel, and the Hmong community in the USA. The analysis is concrete and normative, focusing on the dual goals of democratic empowerment and autonomous identity formation without doing damage to ways of life. Cultures are not sacrosanct, but nor is it legitimate to assume smooth assimilation into the dominant culture. The recognition of difference and identity must be made compatible with the universalist and emancipatory aspirations of Critical Theory. Benhabib has gone some way in achieving this. Her approach acknowledges that struggle, contestation, contingency, and partiality characterize all our decisions and rulings. Nevertheless, we can criticize decisions and rulings if the people affected were not given a chance to speak, be heard, and have their claims and objections answered.

CONCLUSION

Where does this leave us on the general question of politics? There are two senses in which theorists such as Fraser and Benhabib have a more robust political content than early Critical Theory and Habermas. First, they are more concrete, and in two ways. They are more concrete in that they are more concerned with others rather than in a generalized conception of "the Other." The individuals who populate their theories have identities and lives, whereas Habermas's individuals are more abstract and generalized. Additionally, Fraser's and Benhabib's theories are more concrete in the very mundane sense of dealing with real context-specific cases: they enter political controversies and take sides in democratic disputes. Furthermore, they do not shy away from suggestions for institutional reform. Thus they come the closest to having a programmatic agenda, one that focuses primarily on expanding and enhancing democratic procedures and conditions. The question that animates this politics is: "What is needed to give people voice?" The second sense in which these theories are more political is in the way they address and take into account "the political" as it is understood by postmoderns. Struggle and contestation, pluralism and difference are not phases on the road to socialism. They are constitutive parts of our public life. Even if one retains consensus as an ideal, one must acknowledge that every empirical consensus is corrigible, fallible, and subject to change. Furthermore, this does not preclude one from recognizing that power and coercion are permanent parts of public life, nor does it entail the defeatism of giving up taking stands from which we can criticize particular structures of power and coercion and seek to lessen their hold on our lives.

Nevertheless, there is sense in which third generation Critical Theory is caught in the same bind as the first and second generation. In giving up vanguardism for democracy, Critical Theory will always be limited by the democratic will. As Benhabib puts it, "Discourse ethics does not present itself as a blue print for changing institutions and practices; it is an idealized model in accordance with which we can measure fairness and legitimacy of existing practices and aspire to reform them, *if and when* the democratic will of the participants to do so exists."[59] Such democratic self-limitation is a good thing, but it can also be a frustrating thing.

NOTES

1. Martin Jay, *The Dialectical Imagination: A History of the Frankfurt School and the Social Institute of Social Research, 1923–1950* (Boston: Little, Brown, 1973); see also Joan Always, *Critical Theory and Political Possibilities: Conceptions of Emancipatory Politics in the Works of Horkheimer, Adorno, Marcuse, and Habermas* (Westport, Conn.: Greenwood Press, 1995).

2. Leszek Kolakowski, *Main Currents of Marxism: 3 – The Breakdown*, trans. P. S. Falla (Oxford: Oxford University Press, 1978), p. 376.

3. Helmut Dubiel, *Theory and Politics: Studies in the Development of Critical Theory*, trans. Benjamin Gregg (Cambridge, Mass.: MIT Press, 1985).

4. The classic statement of this is to be found in Horkheimer and Adorno's *Dialectic of Enlightenment*.

5. For the tension between truth and democratic politics, see the exchange between Socrates and Callicles in *Gorgias* 481a–522b and especially 481b–482a.

6. *Gorgias* 521d.

7. See also Helmut Dubiel, "Democratie und Kapitalismus bei Herbert Marcuse," in *Kritik und Utopie im Werk von Herbert Marcuse* (Frankfurt am Main: Suhrkamp, 1992), pp. 61–73.

8. Martin Jay, "Metapolitics of Utopianism," *Dissent* 17 (1970): 348. In a review by someone with "Old Left" leanings, *One-Dimensional Man* was described as "a sustained exercise in Olympian despair" leading to "quietism" that reinforces the existing state of affairs. The review was aptly entitled "The Point is Still to Change It," echoing a certain frustration felt by the organized Left with the "romanticism" of the Frankfurt School. Karl Miller (pseud.), "The Points is Still to Change It," *Monthly Review* 17.2 (1967): 51. The title refers to Marx's eleventh thesis on Feuerbach. See "Theses on Feuerbach," *The Marx–Engels Reader*, ed. R. Tucker (New York: Norton, 1978), p. 145.

9. Paul Breines, "Marcuse and the New Left in America," in *Antworten auf Herbert Marcuse*, eds. J. Habermas *et al.* (Frankfurt am Main: Suhrkamp, 1968), p. 137.

10. Todd Gitlin, *The Sixties: Years of Hope and Rage* (New York: Bantam Books, 1987), p. 246.

11. Clemens Albrecht *et al.*, *Die Intellektuelle Gründung der Bundesrepublik: Eine Wirkungsgeschichte der Frankfurter Schule* (Frankfurt am Main: Campus, 1999), p. 317. On Marcuse and the student movement in Germany, see ibid., pp. 317–27; Rolf Wiggershaus, *The Frankfurt School: Its History, Theories, and Political Significance*, trans. M. Robertson (Cambridge, Mass.: MIT Press, 1994), pp. 609–36; Douglas Kellner, *Herbert Marcuse and the Crisis of Marxism* (Berkeley: University of California Press, 1984), especially pp. 276–319.

12. See especially Wiggershaus, *Frankfurt School*, pp. 622–36.

13. Ibid., p. 634.

14. Kellner, *Marcuse and the Crisis of Marxism*, p. 280; Jürgen Habermas, *Die Nachholende Revolution* (Frankfurt am Main: Suhrkamp, 1990), p. 27.

15. Kellner, *Marcuse and the Crisis of Marxism*, p. 285.

16. For comments on this see Wiggershaus, *Frankfurt School*, p. 622 and Jay, "Metapolitics of Utopianism," p. 347.

17. Jürgen Habermas, "Psychic Thermidor and the Rebirth of Rebellious Subjectivity," in *Marcuse: Critical Theory and the Promise of Utopia*, ed. R. Pippin (Massachusetts: Bergin & Garvey, 1988), pp. 9–10.

18. Jürgen Habermas, "Die Scheinrevolution und ihre Kinder," in *Kleine Politische Schriften*, vols. I–IV (Frankfurt am Main: Suhrkamp, 1981), pp. 249–60; see also Habermas, *Nachholende Revolution*, pp. 27–8.

19. Jay, "Metapolitics of Utopianism," p. 350.

20. For more on this subject, see Albrecht Wellmer, "Communications and Emancipation: Reflections on the Linguistic Turn in Critical Theory," in *On Critical Theory*, ed. J. O'Neill (New York: Continuum, 1976), pp. 231–63.

21. On Habermas's liberal Kantianism, see Kenneth Baynes, *The Normative Grounds of Social Criticism: Kant, Rawls, and Habermas* (Albany: SUNY Press, 1992) and chapter 8 of this volume.

22. "Perpetual Peace," in *Kant's Political Writings*, ed. H. Reiss (Cambridge: Cambridge University Press, 1970), p. 130; "On the Common Saying: 'This may be true in theory, but it does not apply in practice,'" in ibid., p. 85.

23. See generally *FN*.

24. William Scheuerman, "Between Radicalism and Resignation: Democratic Theory in Habermas's *Between Facts and Norms*," in *Habermas: A Critical Reader*, ed. P. Dews (Oxford: Blackwell, 1999), pp. 153–77; Nancy Fraser, "Rethinking the Public Sphere: A Contribution to the Critique of Actual Existing Democracy," in *Habermas and the Public Sphere*, ed. C. Calhoun (Cambridge: Cambridge University Press, 1993), pp. 109–42.

25. John Dryzek, *Deliberative Democracy and Beyond: Liberals, Critics, Contestations* (Oxford: Oxford University Press, 2000).

26. Chantal Mouffe, *The Democratic Paradox* (London: Verso, 2000); D. Villa, "Postmodernism and the Public Sphere," *American Political Science Review* 86 (1992): 712–21; Jean-François Lyotard, *The Postmodern Condition: A Report on Knowledge*, trans. G. Bennington and B. Massumi (Minneapolis: University of Minnesota Press, 1984).

27. Scheuerman, "Between Radicalism and Resignation," p. 161.

28. Thus, one of his long-standing criticisms of Rawls is that, in deducing outcomes to the original position, Rawls preempts real debate. See "Reconciliation Through the Public Use of Reason: Remarks on Rawls' Political Liberalism," *Journal of Philosophy* 42 (1995): 109–31.

29. Dryzek, *Deliberative Democracy and Beyond*; James Bohman, "The Globalization of the Public Sphere: Cosmopolitan Publicity and the Problem of Cultural Pluralism," *Philosophy and Public Criticism* 24 (1998): 399–416; Mark Warren, "What can Democratic Participation mean Today?," *Political Theory* 30 (2002): 677–702.

30. Dryzek, *Deliberative Democracy and Beyond*, p. 27.

31. "Battle of Seattle" refers to the antiglobalization protest against the World Trade Organization which took place in December 1999 in Seattle and has since become an inspiration for antiglobalization movements.

32. Mouffe, *Democratic Paradox*; Bonnie Honig, *Political Theory and the Displacement of Politics* (Ithaca: Cornell University Press, 1993).

33. Mouffe, *Democratic Paradox*, p. 101.

34. Ibid.

35. Ibid., p. 104.

36. There is a difference between postmodern agonism and the decentered model defended by Dryzek. Dryzek is still a theorist of deliberative democracy in that he believes that criticism, accountability, and debate can (partially) dissolve power constellations.

37. Mouffe, *Democratic Paradox*, pp. 102–3.

38. Ibid., p. 105.

39. Joel Anderson, "The 'Third Generation' of the Frankfurt School," *Intellectual History Newsletter* 22 (2000): 6.

40. Axel Honneth, *The Struggle for Recognition: The Moral Grammar of Social Conflicts*, trans. J. Anderson (Cambridge, Mass.: MIT Press, 1996).

41. Ibid., pp. 173–4.

42. Ibid., p. 171.

43. Nancy Fraser, "Rethinking Recognition," *New Left Review* 3 (2000): 107–20; see also Fraser and Honneth's exchange on these issues in *Redistribution or Recognition? A Philosophical Exchange* (New York: Verso, 2003).

44. See, for example, Iris Marion Young, *Inclusion and Democracy* (Oxford: Oxford University Press, 2000).

45. Fraser, "Rethinking Recognition," p. 109.

46. Ibid., pp. 109–10.

47. Ibid., p. 111.

48. Ibid., p. 112.

49. Seyla Benhabib, *Claims of Culture: Equality and Diversity in the Global Culture* (Princeton: Princeton University Press, 2002).

50. Ibid., p. 37.

51. Ibid., p. 186.

52. There is a third form of deliberation that covers pragmatic questions of means-ends – for example, how best to achieve full employment if that is a chosen end. Democratic deliberation naturally flows back and forth between these three.
53. Benhabib, *Claims of Culture*, p. 13.
54. Mouffe, *Democratic Paradox*, p. 105.
55. See, for example, the collection of essays entitled *Critique and Power: Recasting the Foucault/Habermas Debate*, ed. M. Kelly (Cambridge, Mass.: MIT Press, 1998).
56. Mouffe, *Democratic Paradox*, pp. 98–105.
57. Benhabib, *Claims of Culture*, p. 19.
58. Ibid., p. 8.
59. Ibid., p. 115.

10 Critical Theory and the analysis of contemporary mass society

REVOLUTION IN THE MEANS OF COMMUNICATION

In February 1848 Karl Marx and Friedrich Engels's *Manifesto of the Communist Party* appeared in London's *Red Republican*. This treatise was the one and only celebration of the revolutionary power of the new, bourgeois age. Marx and Engels were expecting from the bourgeoisie and its epoch not only the freeing of *all* productive forces of humankind, but also the permanent revolution of *all* relations of production and, what is more, of *all* social relations:

> The bourgeoisie cannot exist without continually revolutionizing the instruments of production, hence the relations of production, and therefore social relations as a whole . . . The continual transformation of production, the uninterrupted convulsion of all social conditions, a perpetual uncertainty and motion distinguish the epoch of the bourgeoisie from all earlier ones. All the settled, age-old relations with their train of time-honored preconceptions and viewpoints are dissolved; all newly formed ones become outmoded before they can ossify. Everything feudal and fixed goes up in smoke, everything sacred is profaned, and men are finally forced to take a down-to-earth view of their circumstances, their multifarious relations.[1]

Premodern societies always had only one solution for the notorious poverty of the great masses – namely, *caritas* organized from above.[2] Industrialization and the improvement of the means of communication through extensive commerce – together with their tremendous accelerating effects – first allowed independent, concerted actions of the large majority of the population, which had until then been condemned to political passivity. As Marx and Engels ask in the *Manifesto*, what promotes the "unification of workers" in solidarity? Not the local sympathy of shared association, the friendly affection of equally well-off citizens in a *polis* that is readily comprehensible, but rather the "railway," "extensive commerce," and "the improved means of communication that are created by modern industry and that place the workers of different localities in contact with one another . . . The unification that took centuries for the workers of the Middle Ages to attain, given their miserable highways, is being achieved by the modern proletariat in only a few years, thanks to the railways."[3]

As it would be similarly asserted in the democratic pragmatism of John Dewey a little later, Enlightenment and technological progress were thought to form a continuum together with the "practical-critical," "revolutionary activities" of social and political actors.[4] There could be no egalitarian freedom, no democracy of the masses, and no socialism without technologically induced economic growth.[5] This assumption ties Marxism with pragmatism, and, despite all of their radical alterations, revisions, and revivals of it, it is an assumption that Horkheimer, Adorno, and Habermas never relinquish.

Walter Benjamin's claim that the technological reproducibility of the artwork destroys the aura of affirmative class art and releases through that destruction the revolutionary energy of a saving critique is exemplary in this regard. According to Benjamin, such a critique is supposed to make possible the reappropriation of the messianic promise of redemption, a promise merely hidden under the "bourgeois" glow of the aura (*I* 217–51; *BGS* 1.2, 435–67).[6] True, the messianic emphasis on salvation that is always already addressed to the exploited and maltreated masses *by means of* technological progress and thus through *mass culture* – particularly through the cinema – is clearly more conservative here than it is with Marx. For Benjamin, it is not only a matter of leaving behind in the course of the communist revolution (which he still expected in the 1920s) the arduous "tradition from all the dead generations" that "weighs like a nightmare on the brain of the living."[7] Nor is it simply a matter of breaking the power of the past over the present along with the enlightened thinkers Marx and Freud. Benjamin also wanted to seize the messianic promise of redemption – and here is where he is in agreement with Adorno, despite their many differences – from the "detritus" of the past, from the "names, battle cries, costumes," the "disguises" and the "borrowed languages" of the semantic inheritance that Marx only disdains as "tradition." More-over, for Benjamin the universalism of this messianic promise of redemption would extend further chronologically than the universal-ism of Marx, which was limited to present and future generations.[8]

Even Adorno adopts the thesis of the unity of technology and free-dom when he explains the technological progress in the "mastery over the material" in modern art – and, in this respect, contrary to the more classically and conservatively thinking Marx[9] – as the nec-essary condition of all aesthetic gains in freedom (AT 35, 66, 134, 186, 208–12, 248, 285, 288f.; AGS VII, 59, 104, 202, 278, 310–16, 368, 424, 428f.; NLI, 260; AGS XI, 303; PMM 34, 64–6, 185–6; AGS XII, 40, 65–6, 169–70). Adorno understands modern art as the emanci-pation of its productive powers. The "anti-traditionalistic energy" of autonomous works is to be released only after the mastery of the productive powers has reached the most technically advanced level (AT 280; AGS VII, 416). "Technique" is "constitutive" for art, and "only through technique, the medium of its crystallization," does art distance itself from the "prosaic and factically existent" (AT 213, 217; AGS VII, 317, 322; cf. PMM 7, 36, 42, 52; AGS XII, 16, 42, 47, 55). Even in the somber critique of technology and in the account of the "culture industry" that Horkheimer and Adorno develop in the *Dialectic of Enlightenment,* Adorno shows himself to be fascinated by the "most prodigious productive power" (DE 102; AGS III, 150) that emerges in the industrial production of exoteric mass culture and communes – in subterranean ways – with the esoteric art of the aesthetic avant-garde. Democratized mass culture "reveals" the sup-posed "genuine style" of all past art "as the aesthetic equivalent of domination," and in this respect it corresponds to the "great artists' suspicion of style" – here Adorno names Mozart, Schoenberg, and Picasso (DE 94–5, 95–6, 99, 103, 105f., 125–6; AGS III, 141, 143, 147, 151, 154f., 178; cf. DE 115; AGS III, 166).

The avant-garde and the culture industry come together in the practically executed suspicion of "unity" and "genuineness of style" in classical art as an art of the ruling class (DE 103f.; AGS III, 151f.). For Adorno, it is a necessary condition of the totalitarian-leaning "tri-umphs of advertisement" that the "consumers" "see through" the socially determined form of the "cultural products" as such (DE 136; AGS III, 191). At least in this constitutive feature of disenchantment the culture industry is progressive. It forces human beings to see their relations "with sober senses" (Marx). There is no freedom *without* alienation, mechanization, or "mediatization" (*DE* 73; AGS III, 112; see also *EC* 241f.). That is the "point of no return" of even the most negative dialectic. Adorno also regularly distances himself from conservative culture critique with the view "that the devastation wrought by progress can be made good again, if at all, *only by its own forces*, never by the restoration of the preceding conditions that were its victim" (*AA* 138; *AGS* x.2, 630). This claim fundamentally distinguishes Adorno from Heidegger and Hannah Arendt, who "think back" (*nach-denken*) to the source – be it poetic or political – *before* the productive powers are freed.

Marx remains the central reference of the Critical Theory of mass culture. With the "discovery of America" and the "rounding of the Cape," write Marx and Engels in the *Manifesto*, the general dependence of nations on each other came to its end, and the new technologies – not least the "electric telegraph," which would make "communications infinitely easier" – would most certainly in the end "draw all, even the barbarian nations, into civilization" and "rescu[e] a significant part of the population from the idiocy of living on the land."[10] With increasing insight into global interdependence, the provincial, European world perspective is decentered:

In place of the old local and national self-sufficiency and isolation we have a universal commerce, a universal dependence of nations on one another. As in the production of material, so also with intellectual production. The intellectual creations of individual nations become common currency. National partiality and narrowness become more and more impossible, and from the many national and local literatures a world literature arises.[11]

Indeed, the later Adorno helps himself to the same arguments even in defense of the enlightening power of television – of which he otherwise was rather skeptical and suspicious – not in order to promote the revolution but rather to save what still could be saved. In the much read essay "Education after Auschwitz," he writes that the universal dissemination of these means of communication would be able to help mitigate the worst barbarism of rural life through appropriate broadcasts (*AA* 24–5; *AGS* x.2, 680).

The *means of mass communication*, so the central thesis of the *Manifesto* claims, are the medium both of the capitalist-dominated globalization *and* of the emancipation of the masses from all relations of domination, capitalist as well as precapitalist. For Marx, Ernst Bloch, Adorno, and Marcuse technology stands on the side of the *"tired* and *burdened,"* the *"downtrodden* and *degraded."*[12] In the *Dialectic of Enlightenment,* which deals at length with this latter subject, Horkheimer and Adorno hold firmly to the idea that it is the universalism of objective truth that is embodied in "instruments" and "machines" and that would *also* always serve to remove those instruments and machines from their one-sided use on behalf of particular forms of domination. The "instrument," "weapon," "language" (including those of mass culture) – like "law and organization" (including the "law and organization" of the culture industry) – require the propertied classes equipped with them to subject their interests to a moment of generalizability:

Domination, in becoming reified as law and organization . . . has had to limit itself. The instruments of power – language, weapons, and finally machines – which are intended to hold everyone in their grasp, must in turn be grasped by everyone. In this way, the moment of rationality in domination also asserts itself as something different from it. The thing-like quality of the means[,] . . . its "objective validity" for everyone, itself implies a criticism of domination. (*DE* 29; *AGS* III, 60)

Certainly the tone of 1945, when the full extent of industrially produced mass death was known, is infinitely more defensive than it was almost one hundred years previously, at the beginning of the European year of revolution, in 1848. Exemplary textual passages, such as those cited above, demonstrate that the thesis regarding the internal connection between technological growth and egalitarian freedom remains the same at its orthodox core. Horkheimer and Adorno also hold that the culture industry has the same technology-led capacity for decentering particularized domination and promoting general autonomy: "Against the will of those controlling it, technology has changed human beings from children into persons" (*DE* 125; *AGS* III, 178).[13]

There is a strong tendency among the first generation of Critical Theorists (Benjamin, Marcuse, Horkheimer, Adorno, Leo Löwenthal) to denounce social democratic progress towards egalitarian mass society as a "one-dimensional," "technocratic," and "positivistic" duplication of "what already is the case" and to denounce the equality that has been achieved as an equality of bondage (*O* 19ff., 144ff.;

I 258–61; *BGS* I.2, 698–701; *ND passim*; *AGS* VI *passim*; *HGS* V, 377–95; *FL* 44–61; *MS* VIII, 60–78; *DE* 118–19; *AGS* III, 170). So long as the relations of production remain determined by the capitalist law of the free market – Marx's "form of value"[14] – mass society tends to turn all human beings into bondsmen. *After* the experience of the radio becoming "the universal maw of the *Führer*" "in fascism," Adorno puts forward the provocative thesis that the "immanent tendency of radio" is to transform the dialogical speech act of "recommending" into "commanding" – a thesis that stands at a clear distance from the earlier Benjamin and from Brecht's socially optimistic theory of radio (*DE* 128f.; *AGS* III, 182f.). At the Frankfurter Soziologentag of 1968, Adorno was still citing the elitist Nietzsche in order to bring to expression the repressive equalization resulting from mass culture: "A flock, but no shepherd" (*AA* 116; *AGS* VIII, 360). And, towards the end of the 1930s, Benjamin describes the "social democratic progress" without much ado as one, single catastrophe" (*I* 257, 258, 260; *BGS* I.2, 697, 698, 700).

But despite such seemingly unambiguous statements, social democratic progress remains the *indispensable presupposition* of all attempts at culture critique in the circle surrounding Horkheimer. The effusive, crypto-theological idea of Benjamin's "true progress" remains empty and insubstantial without the mediation of the profane "social democratic" concept of the factical "progress of the mastery over nature," technology, and the means of communication: "Both concepts of progress communicate with each other, not only in averting the ultimate disaster, but rather in every actual form of easing the persistent suffering" (*AA* 138; *AGS* X.2, 630).[15] The egalitarian level of mass culture can be undercut only at the price of relapsing into worse relations of domination. Marcuse writes:

The critique of the Welfare State in terms of liberalism and conservatism (with or without the prefix "neo-") rests, for its validity, on the existence of the very conditions which the Welfare State has surpassed – namely, a lower degree of social wealth and technology. The sinister aspects of this critique show forth in the fight against comprehensive social legislation and adequate government expenditures for services other than those of military defense. (*O* 50)

In his aphoristic way, Adorno turns these ideas of egalitarian solidarity into an ideological critique of the bourgeois understanding of art: "The bourgeois want art voluptuous and life ascetic; the reverse would be better" (*AT* 13; *AGS* VII, 27).

DIALECTIC OF MASS CULTURE

In the *Manifesto* it often sounds as if freedom, equality, and solidarity were the intrinsic purpose and the historical *telos* of the growth of the modern means of communication. Freedom and solidarity are in no way, however, the intrinsic *telos* of the historical growth of the productive forces and means of communication. They represent only the *conditions for the possibility* of egalitarian freedom. Marx's commentaries on the ongoing events of the Paris revolution of 1848 show him overcoming the teleological scheme of a material philosophy of history at the point at which he refers directly to the contingent multiplicity of historical events. *Event history (Ereignisgeschichte)*, whose success and failure must be ascribed by human beings themselves, is in no way determined ahead of time through the logic of the *developmental history (Entwicklungsgeschichte)* – or *evolution* – of productive forces and relations of production.[16] From the perspective of event history, the *potential for freedom and solidarity* that grows with the unbounded dissemination of ever newer means of communication is accompanied by the shadow of a no less considerable *potential for repression and manipulation*.

In June 1848, just at the moment when the French translation of the *Manifesto* appeared in Paris, an uprising of Parisian workers was bloodily put down and the workers' interest in a revolutionary regime of a constitutionally sanctioned national assembly disappeared with their leader into prison. The "real movement" of communism that Marx wanted to call forth both performatively and prophetically in the *Manifesto* seemed to revert to the "specter" with whose disenchantment Marx and Engels had opened the publication in February of the same year.[17] The projected "red specter" had frightened the ruling classes of Europe to such an extent that the "state of being under siege" that was feigned in June in Paris "found its way across the entire continent" in a matter of weeks.[18] From this moment on, Marx and Engels began to write about the revolution *and* counterrevolution. Immediately after the *coup d'état* of President Louis Bonaparte on December 2, 1851, Marx composed over the winter in his London exile a work which begins straightaway with a discussion of the "great tragedy" of the 1789 revolution and which silences the emphasis on progress from the winter of the 1848 revolution.[19] In its place appeared a first chapter of the *Dialectic of Enlightenment*.

Just as Adorno in 1944 notes the "liquidation of tragedy" in the transition from bourgeois autonomous art to the socially inclusive culture industry, so Marx had begun his polemic of the year 1852 with the observation of the change of revolutionary politics from the "great tragedy" of the 1789–1814 revolution to the "shabby farce" of the years 1848–51 (*DE* 124; *AGS* III, 177).[20] What Marx describes in *The Eighteenth Brumaire of Louis Bonaparte* is the petering out of the revolutionary vigor of both of the great progressive classes of civil society – namely, the bourgeoisie and the proletariat. And he describes this twofold historical defeat – of the proletariat in June 1848 and of the bourgeoisie "on one beautiful morning" in December 1851 – as a relapse of enlightenment into superstition, of autonomy into heteronomy, indeed, as the "liberation" of "civil society from the trouble . . . of ruling itself."[21] Here the outlines of the thesis that Horkheimer and Adorno develop in the *Dialectic of Enlightenment* become visible.

In the language of the *Dialectic of Enlightenment* Louis Bonaparte was the first "master" of the "culture monopoly" (*DE* 96; *AGS* III, 143) and at the same time its "character mask": a "synthesis of Beethoven and the Casino de Paris" (*DE* 107; *AGS* III, 157).[22] He won election campaigns and garnered popular support through the manipulative utilization of the new means of communication celebrated by Marx and Engels in the *Manifesto* as the medium of proletarian solidarity. The sobering realization of the *Eighteenth Brumaire* is that the new means of communication evidently accelerate not merely the solidarity of the exploited masses but also that of their masters. Bonaparte used not only the accelerating effect of mass publication and the telegraph but, above all, the speed of the railways to establish in France a style of electioneering that was highly innovative, thoroughly organized in terms of its propaganda, entirely state-wide – indeed, campaign-like, in the military sense. With such means he was able to establish his presence in the entire country and to organize plebiscites whose acclamation was achieved through manipulation.[23] If one combined into a negative dialectical concept

Marx's observations with Adorno's *Stichwort*, one might say that, for the first time in Europe, *enlightenment as mass deception* was carried out on a large scale.

It was possible, however, to use the new means of communication in the interest of those in control and to convert them into the political power of the dictator only because modern relations of production and the coinciding universal establishment of private property produced a segmentation of society into politically "organizable *classes*" and an unpolitical, "inorganic *mass*" of atomized individuals – an economically "superfluous population."[24] Both the "inorganic mass" of the (minority) "*Lumpenproletariat*" in the quickly growing cities and the (majority) impoverished farming masses of the lowlands had been freed by the Napoleonic *Code civile* from all feudal chains; yet they had nothing, no self-consciousness of their own, with which to counter the large-scale manipulation of the culture industry.[25]

Marx does not yet, however, give to the thesis of the *Dialectic of Enlightenment* that autonomy is collapsing into heteronomy the paradoxical and aporetic form that it later takes with Adorno. Two important differences come to mind.

1.   To begin with, it is only the *backward* rural population that, under the special circumstances of impoverishment (for which modern, equalizing private property has created the very basis), can become the presiding dictatorship for the atomized base of the masses. The urban proletariat does not yet grasp the degeneration of the organized class to the atomized masses (with the exception of the minority, but militant, *Lumpenproletariat*). Yet, it is this shocking observation that prompts Horkheimer and his friends and coworkers at the Frankfurt Institute for Social Research to generalize the thesis of atomization to the entire society with the coming to power of Hitler in 1933. This thesis, which is now supported by its own empirical investigations, had by that time already developed further, from a broad discussion of culture critique and social psychology into a phenomenon of the "masses."[26] It is not the backward farming population but rather the *most advanced* and best organized classes of society, including the urban proletariat, that are collapsing into atomized, manipulable masses under "those in control of the system" (*DE* 131; *AGS* III, 185) and that internalize external

authority without developing at the same time the strength to turn what is being internalized into resistance against the external. From the decline observed in the emancipatory potential of the new means of communication and the simultaneous rise in its repressive potential, Horkheimer, Marcuse, and Adorno conclude that there is no longer a revolutionary opening in the negative totality of history at hand. Rather, at the end of the 1930s, in American exile, they replace the positive with a negative overgeneralization. The positive philosophy of history – overcome by Marx in the face of his negative experiences, but subsequently renewed in orthodox Marxism – turns into its opposite: a *negative philosophy of history.*

"Culture today," as the chapter on the culture industry begins, "is infecting everything with sameness. Film, radio, and magazines make up a system" (*DE* 94; *AGS* III, 141). This system forms a unity with the "culture monopoly" that extends over the entire society and which, in turn, forms such a unity with the "economic system" (*DE* 96f., 105, 111; *AGS* III, 143f., 154, 161). The negative message of the chapter is that the reduction of society to one single system is in danger of becoming complete, both as a result of mass culture enabled by technology and organized by capitalist industry and as a result of the inclusion of "spectators" – *in itself* democratic and egalitarian – in the liquidation of the private sphere (*DE* 104f., 110; *AGS* III, 153f., 160). "Manipulation and retroactive need" form a "cycle" which "is unifying the system ever more tightly" (*DE* 95; *AGS* III, 142). In fact, it becomes so tightly unified that the "explicit and implicit, exoteric and esoteric catalog of what is forbidden and what is tolerated" extends so far "that it not only defines the area left free but wholly controls it" (*DE* 101; *AGS* III, 149). The techniques of normalization of the culture industry "produce, steer, and discipline" the individual (*DE* 115; *AGS* III, 166; see also *DE* 116–17, 121; *AGS* III, 168, 173). Adorno describes "existence in late capitalism" as a "permanent rite of initiation. Everyone must show that they identify wholeheartedly with the power which beats them" (*DE* 124; *AGS* III, 176). The power makes itself invisible – so one could say, employing a variation of Brecht's thought – by assuming dreadful proportion.[27] In a language that has "become totalitarian" one can no longer hear "the violence done to the words" (*DE* 135; translation modified; *AGS* III, 190).

Much of this not only reminds the present-day reader of Foucault's theory of power, which has before its eyes the similar phenomenon of dedifferentiating penetration – "wholly controlling" versus "defining" (see *DE* 101; *AGS* III, 149) – of the collective social body with the techniques of power and control. It also brings to mind more recent feminist theory of the subject and how it develops, above all, following Foucault and Althusser, in the work of Judith Butler.[28] Her thesis is that the power *over* the subject consists in the ultimately *voluntary* adoption of the standpoint of power *by* the subject. Only through such an involuntary adoption can power increase (even in nontotalitarian political regimes) to totalitarian limits. But that requires that it make itself at the same time dependent on the subject's own contributions – a subject that has been subjugated this power. Human beings are "appendages of the machinery" (Marx) only because they have made "*themselves*," as Adorno also says, "the apparatus meeting the requirements of success" (*DE* 136; *AGS* III, 191). Moreover, the power *over* the subject that has increased to its upper limit *is* – and on this point the theses of Butler and Adorno coincide – power only as power (*potentia*) *of* the subject. Power constitutes itself according to Butler's thesis insofar as the subject exercises power on itself and in this way first gains, through submission, room for autonomy in general.

Adorno's thesis of a "cycle" between manipulation and need is structured in a very similar way to that of Butler's. Insofar as the need of a bodily subject unites with the manipulatively ensnaring power in a systematically closed "cycle," power becomes total, but in the unity of the cycle the one-sidedness of causal manipulation is overcome (see *DE* 95; *AGS* III, 142). The "deceived masses" "have their aspirations" (*DE* 106; *AGS* III, 155). The catch is that the aspirations too remain mistaken and "under pressure" from the system (*ND* 283–4; *AGS* VI, 279). "They insist unwaveringly on the ideology by which they are enslaved. The pernicious love of the common people for the harm done to them outstrips even the cunning of the authorities" (*DE* 106; *AGS* III, 155). Without the subject's own independent contribution, power does not function and the bodies whose power has been subjugated cannot "show" in any way that they "identify" *themselves* "wholeheartedly" with the power (see *DE* 124; *AGS* III, 176). *The dependence remains, even in its totality, reciprocal as well.* "Individuality is a product of the pressure as well as the center of power that resists it" (*ND* 283, translation modified; *AGS* vi, 279). As I shall show in the next section, it is this idea upon which Adorno draws when it comes to the search for a way out of the "cycle" of autonomy.

But, for the negativists Adorno, Horkheimer, and Marcuse, the dominant tendency of late capitalism is towards a system of identity that makes everything that is not already assimilated to it become so, and that effectively prevents any deviation or any resistance. The new media of mass culture that achieve this assimilation include sound film, radio, magazines, photography, short stories, cartoons, automobiles, stunt films, popular biographies, box office hits, movie stars, pop songs, soap operas, sports, air raid drills, modern propaganda, totalitarian sloganeering, close-ups, functional architecture, television, jazz, advertising, and easy listening music (*DE* 94ff., 105ff., 128, 130–1, 132–3, 134–5; *AGS* iii, 141ff., 154ff., 182, 184, 187, 189). The beginning of their globalization seems to level even fundamental differences constitutive of freedom, that is, those between democratic and authoritarian regimes (*DE* 94, 99–100, 121–2, 134–5; *AGS* iii, 141, 147, 174, 189).

Not only does "control of the system" seal itself off against all resistance here. Critical Theory also fixes itself in upon a negative philosophy of history that scientific critique can no longer touch, for positivist science – much as the late Heidegger has it – has long since fallen under the spell of the system too (*DE* 131; *AGS* iii, 185). Although the tendency towards self-immunization in Critical Theory has been unmistakable since the 1940s, one should not lose sight of the thesis claiming the internal connection of technological growth, equality, and freedom that was presented in its constitutive parts in the first section above. This has always remained the leading premise of the Frankfurt School's critique of culture. Adorno's warning of the gloomy other side of technological and "democratic" progress leads in a different direction than the often very similar sounding warning of conservative culture critique. The problem is not the culture industry's freeing of technological-productive forces or mass culture's egalitarianism of democratic inclusion. It is, rather, the danger of regressive *dedifferentiation* that increases simultaneously with technology, the division of labor, and the functional differentiation and which results from the crisis-ridden dove-tailing of technology, equality, and class domination.[29]

2. For Marx, the thesis of the relapse of autonomy into heteronomy does not just lie far below the threshold of a negativistic claim of totality; it is above all an *empirical* thesis. For Horkheimer and Adorno, on the other hand, this thesis is meant in its strongest version to be *conceptual*. This means that enlightenment and autonomy not only *can* relapse into mass deception and heteronomy under certain circumstances – like those that Marx describes in the *Eighteenth Brumaire* (atomized masses, particular class domination, dictatorially organized executive power, a self-contradictory constitution, state of siege, etc.) – but that they are *necessarily* bound up with mass deception and heteronomy because of their internal structure.[30] For this reason the history of philosophy is much more important for Adorno than for Marx. Hence, in the *Negative Dialectics* of 1966, for example, it no longer matters at all what the empirical *conditions* are under which autonomy and heteronomy are relapsing. Adorno attempts in the famous Kant chapter entitled "Freedom" to show, instead, that there can be no *concept* of autonomy that does not have heteronomous consequences (*ND* 211ff.; *AGS* vi, 211ff.; see also *DE* 63ff.; *AGS* iii, 100ff.). Such a radical version of the thesis of dialectical relapse runs into the danger, however, of an *individualistic materialism* for which general concepts are ultimately *unthinkable* or self-contradictory. Nevertheless, whenever they *are* thought and transformed from the atomized masses into behavioral schemata, this is only a sign of the ubiquitous "false consciousness" produced by the culture industry. ("False consciousness" is a term that Adorno takes over from Marx, which is, however, removed from the empirical network of Marxist social theory and transposed, as the explosive charge of ideological critique, into the conceptual network of a priori arguments – which is to say, into philosophical discourse.) For this reason Adorno also calls false consciousness *identifying thought*. And correspondingly, the negative and intrinsically paradoxical *consciousness of the nonidentical*, whose function appears restricted to disturbing a "common sense that has become sick with its health," takes the place of the no longer possible *true consciousness*.[31] In the logical terminology of the identical/nonidentical, Adorno then formulates his famous paradox of autonomy:

subjects are free . . . insofar as they are conscious of themselves and identical with themselves; and then again are not free in such an identity insofar as they remain under and perpetuate the constraint of that identity. As non-identical and diffuse natures they are not free, and yet, as such, they are free because their overpowering stirrings – for the non-identity of the subject with itself is nothing but that – rid them of identity's constraining character. (*ND* 299, translation modified; *AGS* vi, 294)

DIALECTICAL CONSTELLATIONS

Mass culture appears in many formulations by Horkheimer, Adorno, and Marcuse as false consciousness through and through. Where enlightenment becomes indistinguishable from mass deception, the constraint of "identifying thought" no longer allows any way of "escape" for the nonidentical, any "possibility of resistance," or any "room to move" (*DE* 112, 113; *AGS* iii, 162, 164). Freedom without "room to move," without alternatives, is not freedom. It becomes illusory and thus indistinguishable from captivity (*DE* 135; *AGS* iii, 190). At the very outset of the *Dialectic of Enlightenment*, Horkheimer and Adorno call an enlightenment "totalitarian" that is no longer capable of making such distinctions (*DE* xv; *AGS* iii, 12).

   Because theory just *is*, for Critical Theory from Horkheimer to Habermas, "critique" in the twofold sense of Marx's *Critique of the Political Economy* – that is, reflexive critique *in* the theory and *of* its object – a *critique* of mass culture, which in its most extreme formulation identifies enlightenment with totalitarianism and mass deception, deprives itself of its very basis. If all enlightenment is totalitarian and if the system puts everything under its spell, how is Critical Theory still to distinguish between true and false thinking and acting? How in a "false" life, where according to Adorno's famous aphorism there is consequently "nothing true," is Critical Theory capable of offering a critique of that which is false? Or, to take another famous aphorism, does not the proposition that the whole is untrue belong to this whole (*MM* 50; *AGS* iv, 55)? Whence does Critical Theory get the competence to enlighten us on the totalitarianism of the enlightenment? Horkheimer and Adorno have always forbidden themselves and their closest companions and students from taking the Platonic God's eye view – "the view from nowhere" outside the system of society – and defended this prohibition with arguments that to a large extent correspond with the critique of metaphysics and dualism put forth by American pragmatism.

The modern, functionally differentiated, posttraditional society can no longer be criticized from the outside as can the premodern, stratified, and traditional aristocratic society of Platonic or Christian philosophy; rather, it can be criticized now only from the inside. For this reason, the Hegelian dialectic becomes a useful instrument for critique. It is particularly well-suited for revealing the negative aspect of that which is (allegedly) positive, yet it remains nonetheless *dialectical* as it also makes the constitutive moment of the positive visible *in* the negative (as the negation of the negative). This procedure of determinate negation is also suited for self-reflexive radicalization and thus for the adjustment to conditions in which the teleological explanatory scheme of self-unfolding reason in history – in its idealist version with Hegel yet also in its weaker, materialist version with Marx – has lost all historical plausibility and is also no longer scientifically convincing.

Of the founding generation of Critical Theory only Adorno persistently pursues this program of a *negative dialectic*, which, while holding on to determinate negation *with* Hegel and Marx, is at the same time directed *against* the positivism, however latent, inherent in their teleological views of history. Benjamin falls back on the fragmented trappings of monotheistic theology at precisely the point where social democratic progress is transcended. By contrast, the late Horkheimer, faced with the task of immanence, practically gives up and contents himself with a negative philosophy of history in decline. At one time there existed a strong ego that was a product of paternal repression and maternal affection, but, with the end of the upper-middle-class family, weakness of the ego became ubiquitous (*HGS* v, 377–95). At one time there existed objective reason and great art, but now all subjective reason is but one of the economic powers that have disposition over the subject, and art *qua* culture industry is now only the eternal redoubling of the same (*ER passim; HGS* vii, 81–103). Such theses do not go beyond an *indeterminate negation* of the existing order. Yet, if one rejects – as the late Horkheimer does – the relapse into the most highly questionable, positive characterizations of metaphysics, only the negative theological hope of the imageless, and thus of the wholly other, remains.

Marcuse, on the other hand – and in contrast to Adorno and Horkheimer – holds on to the idea of a politically revolutionary *praxis*.[32] But his impressive attempt to *determine* the possibilities of a revolutionizing of late capitalist society by reverting to the prepolitical potential of a "rebellious subjectivity" that was to be recognized as the *source* of natural human drives, falls back just as obviously as it does tacitly on strong ontological premises (*EC* 144–57, 203–16). A return to potentiality could no longer be predicated on the historical development of productive forces, means of communication, or social relations. Such a return leads to a critique that attempts – in a philosophically effusive way – to take up a point of view beyond society, a society that we cannot abandon when speaking or writing, as *One-Dimensional Man* shows (*O* ix–xvii, 58ff., 124ff., 128–9, 203ff., 215–16; 217–18). If the critique is genuinely political, as it is with Marcuse, then there is hardly any other way left open to it than that of revolutionary decisionism. It sees itself compelled – in a philosophically consistent way – to place its bet on the revolt of "outlaws and outsiders" who rise up *against* the majority population that are irrecoverably bound up in the system of one-dimensional mass culture and *against* the ubiquitous conformism of a "society without opposition" that is "sealed off" by the workings of the culture industry and by the forces in control (*O* ixff., 19ff., 247ff., 256–7). It may appear as if the desperate "revolt" changes nothing with respect to the triumph of the "counter revolution." But, to the contrary – as Marx had claimed in his time in regard to the nineteenth-century state – "every revolution" "reinforce[s]" the counterrevolutionary "machine." Nothing remains in the end but the "defensive embassy of the beautiful" (*CR* 79–128; *AD passim*).

In a different way from Horkheimer, Benjamin, or Marcuse – and less politically than the latter – Adorno attempts to mediate the radically negativistic construction of history with the method of determinate negation and to show in an intricately worked out theory of modern art and culture how false consciousness drives "out beyond itself" (*AA* 138; *AGS* x.2, 630). In his critique of Veblen's "Theory of the Leisure Class" it is stated programmatically that "the existing society and the other society do not have two different kinds of truth; rather truth in this society is inseparable from the real movement within the existing order and each of its moments" (*P* 92; *AGS* x.1, 94; see also *AA* 124; *AGS* viii, 368–9).

Here one can still recognize the trace of Marx's thesis from February 1848 that communism (the "other society") is not a "specter" but rather an "actual movement" in the history of modern society (a "real movement within the existing order and in each of its moments"). This movement, however, positions itself *in* the existing society – indeed, in each of its moments *against* this society. Regarding society, Adorno claims that it is "controlled through and through" by *identifying thought* (*DE* 101; *AGS* iii, 149). The most highly ambivalent contribution of identifying thought lies in the subjugation of "subjects" that can behave towards themselves only as bodily entities – not as Cartesian "ghosts in machines" (Gilbert Ryle) – under the "constraining character of identity" that commands subjects from the outside (*ND* 299, translation modified; *AGS* vi, 294). The fully realized false consciousness would be a condition under which subjects, with all the "diffuse" "stirrings" of their spontaneous impulses, would be wholly subsumed and in which they would become "mere intersections of universal tendencies" (*DE* 125; *HGS* iii, 178).

Since the individual "of material relations" (Marx) is, however, too complex to be completely controlled at any time, a moment of the "nonidentical" always extracts itself from external control. Adorno likes to ground this *first*, inherent limit of disciplinary power by referring to Leibniz's dictum: *individuum est ineffabile*.[33] The identifying cognition can never completely penetrate and control the "inert masses" (Sartre) or the ever-changing versatility of material bodies. Irreducible ambiguity puts it beyond the clutches of total control.

The social power of discipline and normalization can therefore only be raised to the limit of total power of disposition *over* subjects when those subjects carry out *on their own initiative* the practices of discipline, control, and normalization expected of them by external authority – as was seen above in the second section, in the comparison of Adorno with Butler. Yet, the moment they internalize the perspective of power, they gain from that same power that suppresses them the *potentia* of autonomous action, and thus are "free . . . as far as they are identical with themselves" (*ND* 299, translation modified; *AGS* vi, 294). Such freedom, however, is still defective in that it allows the freedom of spontaneous stirrings to emerge only along the narrow paths permitted to a subject identical with itself (and with societal imperatives) and, moreover, disciplines them as soon as they threaten to break out of these paths. Is it possible to dissolve this paradox and thus to escape from the dominating "cycle" of "manipulation" and "need" with which the disciplinary power of the culture industry beats down the subject? (*DE* 95–6; *AGS* III, 142). Adorno sees two possibilities, yet only the second leads to a variant of determinate negation.

1. The first attempt to dissolve the paradox of autonomy lies along the path of dualistic metaphysics. It transforms that paradox into the "hedonistic utopia of a complete satisfaction of human drives."[34] In such a utopia, theory and practice collapse platonically and the nonidentical becomes the cipher of a "whole that is no longer untrue."[35] This utopian state would be reached if the nonidentical had wholly and definitively removed the "constraining character of identity" (*ND* 299, translation modified; *AGS* VI, 294). The false freedom of identity-ridden mass culture – the "freedom to be perpetually the same" – would have died out along with the "existing... society," and the true freedom of "stirrings" that "overpower" subjects identical with themselves would have risen up from the dead. But with such freedom the old Augustinian dualism of two kingdoms would have risen as well (*DE* 136; *AGS* III, 190; *ND* 299; *AGS* VI, 294). The "absolute . . . as metaphysics imagines it," writes Adorno in *Negative Dialectics*, "would be the non-identical that only emerges after the constraint of identity dissolves" (*ND* 406, translation modified; *AGS* VI, 398). Thus only now, at the moment of metaphysics' Fall, could it emerge – that is to say, at the end of all days (of prehistory) (*ND* 408; *AGS* VI, 400).

Although Adorno carefully approaches the concept of a hedonistic utopia in *Minima Moralia*, it remains completely indeterminate as the negation of that which exists: "he alone who could situate utopia in blind somatic pleasure, which, satisfying intention, is intentionless, has a stable idea of truth" (*MM* 61; *AGS* IV, 68). Adorno's hedonistic utopia is a utopia of *good dedifferentiation* but, as such, is uncritical because it blurs, in the fog of the perpetually same, all distinctions on which it depends in the real life of the one and only existing society. Democracy and Fascism, apolitical "advertisements" and "totalitarian slogans," "popular song" and "*Blitzkrieg*" are then not much more than "the same things" – as Heidegger's culture critique, which is motivated by an originary philosophy, has it (DE 96, 105–6, 134–5; AGS III, 143, 154, 189).[36]

Adorno's *hedonistic* utopia clearly lacks the complexity of his paradox of freedom, which takes as its starting point a *unified* concept of freedom. Moreover, Adorno uses this concept of freedom, which comprehends both sides of the subject – the identical and the nonidentical – to ground the many places in the text where he denounces the *regressive* utopia of a total freedom from the constraint of identity as "the horror of the diffuse" (ND 158; AGS VI, 160). His own understanding of good dedifferentiation is, however, no longer distinguishable from such a regression to the bad. For this reason, a "weak messianic power" (I 254; BGS 1.2, 694; see also MM 247; AGS IV, 283) – a power that is at no one's disposal – is required by what is *unspeakable* in existing society for the *unsayable* distinction between regressive and good dedifferentiation, and thus for the *determination* of the utopian achievement of negating "blind somatic desire" (NL I, 245; AGS XI, 286; AT 204–5; AGS VII, 304–5).[37]

2.   On the other hand, Benjamin's concept of *dialectical constellation*, which Adorno takes as a basis for his aesthetic theory, clears the way for a dissolution of Adorno's paradox of freedom that is *internal to society*. For Adorno, this concept is always a constellation (following Hegel's logic) between the *universality* of identifying thought – a thinking that is materially embodied in the growth of the productive powers and means of communication – and the *particularity* of the "nonidentical" "diffuse nature" of "stirrings" that "overpower" the always only bodily existing subject (ND 299; AGS VI, 294). Such universality in the controlling clutches of identifying thinking on the subject is the first component in the dialectical constellation that, taken by itself, is false and abstract: the "false identity of society and subject" (DE 124; AGS III, 177). The anarchical revolt of the "blind somatic desire" of individual subjects scattered in the masses – subjects who believe themselves to be capable of the *practical* actualization of the hedonistic utopia – is the second element in the constellation that, considered in isolation, is equally false and abstract (MM 61; AGS IV, 68; cf. PMM 46–7; AGS XII, 51). It is the "horror of the diffuse" (ND 158; AGS VI, 160) of the indeterminate negation.

The solution of the quandary lies in a mediation of both "extremes" that brings their potential for freedom into a constellation that allows both sides – the *extreme* of identifying thought and the *extreme* of the nonidentical – to follow from one another. According to the side of identifying thought (and here the orthodox Marxist starting thesis resurfaces), the most developed level of society's productive powers and means of communication must be raised to "extreme mastery over the material." And as a result of the way in which this happens, the other side – the nonidentical of spontaneous impulses – should reach unobstructed and thus free "expression" (*AT* 43ff.; *AGS* VII, 70ff.).

The successful works of "great artists" are Adorno's classic examples of such constellations, which free the productivity of the antinomy of freedom in the process of dissolving it. They are the product of a technical-constructive rationality, raised to its extreme, which consists in the "rational power of the works over everything heterogeneous in them" – that is, over the nonidentical (*AT* 24, 36–7, 57–8, 212–13; *AGS* VII, 43, 62, 91–2, 316). In order to realize the abstract possibilities of art, so Adorno says, "every authentic artist" must be "obsessed" "with technical procedures" (*AT* 44; *AGS* VII, 72). In successful works, the point of the technical construction, which indeed is a way in which identifying thought appears, is in no way simply to make possible the liberation of "diffuse nature" from "the constraining character of identity." Technical construction does not stand in the service of a hedonistic utopia. Rather, it sets free the liberating power of "stirrings" that "overpower" the subject by once again producing its nature as second nature – namely, as the *startling, incalculable, innovative result* of a construction that is strictly adhered to (*ND* 299; *AGS* VI, 294). "What in artworks opposes spirit [construction, identifying thought] is, however, on no account what is natural in their materials and objects; they constitute merely a limiting value in artworks. They bear what is opposed to them in themselves" (*AT* 344; *AGS* VII, 512). Adorno illustrates how this is to be understood with an example from the culture industry – namely, functional architecture – where the exoteric mass culture (functional architecture) corresponds with the esoteric art of the modern period (orchestral music): "Functionalism today, prototypically in architecture, would need to push construction so far that it would win expression through the rejection of traditional and semitraditional forms." With Adorno, this means to liberate the "nonidentical" from the "constraining character of identity" in a nonregressive way. "Great architecture gains its supra-functional language," in which the nonidentical produces freely, "when it works directly from its purposes, effectively announcing them mimetically as the work's content. H. B. Scharoun's Philhar-monic Hall in Berlin is beautiful because, in order to create the ideal spatial conditions for orchestral music, it assimilates itself to these conditions rather than borrowing from them" (*AT* 44; *AGS* vii, 72–3).

This achievement of aesthetically successful functional architec-ture is an example of determinate negation that *forces out beyond itself* the *false consciousness* of the "perpetually same" of "well-organized" "living cells" and of the "bright monumental structures shooting up on all sides" (i.e. Los Angeles *circa* 1944) that "repre-sent" nothing more than "the systematic ingenuity of the state-spanning combines" (*DE* 94; *AGS* iii, 141; see also *AA* 138; *AGS* x.2, 630).[38] Even without hedonistic utopia and "weak messianic power," the *real movement within the existing order* (*P* 92; *AGS* x.1, 94), through which successful functional architecture separates itself from the unsuccessful, is capable of saving us from the night-mare of "messianic poverty" in a society that has become bereft of meaning.[39]

Adorno is, of course, fond of analyzing examples of advanced art as productively irritating "configuration[s] of mimesis and rational-ity" (*AT* 127; *AGS* vii, 192) and, moreover, freights these examples with a (higher) concept of truth that could be redeemed only as a realized utopia of the "absolute . . . as metaphysics imagines it" (*ND* 406, translation modified; *AGS* vi, 398). This view is grounded in the negative philosophy of history towards which Adorno's theory of mass culture had always tended, and which could now be over-come only by "weak messianism" and no longer by "revolution-ary, practical-critical activity" (Marx). If one puts aside the sense in which it refers to a program of determinate negation relieved of an empty utopianism, then Adorno's comment from a letter to Benjamin that Schoenberg and American film were the "torn apart halves of one freedom" can be translated first and foremost into a program of an egalitarian critique for which the objects of mass cul-ture and of advanced art are equally important.[40] At least Adorno still sees both in the extreme polemicizing against blind mass culture's "most prodigious productive powers" and in the "compulsion of the technically conditioned idiom" of the "revue films" and the "grotesque" – nuances "so fine as to be almost as subtle as the devices used in a work of the avant-garde" (*DE* 102, 114; *AGS* iii, 150, 164; cf. *AT* 106; *AGS* vii, 162). The heirs of Adornian culture critique start with this transposition of Adorno's program of a determinate negation of mass culture, which does without any bourgeois elitist reservations, however covert they might be.[41] In this way, Critical Theory has effected a turn in the science of culture without resuming the original Marxist program of a critique of mass culture *as social theory*.

BACK TO SOCIAL THEORY

Jürgen Habermas has resumed this program. He qualifies the concept of culture – following Durkheim and Parsons – in terms of a functional division between society, on the one hand, and culture and the persons of the life-world, on the other (*TCA* ii, 140–52). Society is now thoroughly defined (as with Nikolas Luhmann) by the concept of communication, where (contrary to Luhmann *and* Adorno) the distinction between communicative and functionalistic reason is supposed to make possible a critique of society that need no longer content itself with the *aporia* of removing the paradox of what, in the end, is only technical rationality ("identifying thought" or "systematic rationality") (*TCA* i, 1ff., 273ff.; *TCA* ii, 119ff., 199ff.).[42] For Adorno (as it is for Weber), the pluralization of the *one* rationally purposive reason at the height of progress of the technical "mastery over material" is an unmistakable sign of its simultaneous and necessary decline. Habermas, however, is able to describe the pluralization the other way around, as the evolutionary liberation of a *communicative* reason *from* the domination of purposive rationality.[43] The distinction between evolution and history can be used to supplement empirical research, replacing a philosophy of history founded on historical concepts.[44] Historical materialism can then be reconstructed as a theory of social evolution, and reason (as it is in pragmatism) is downgraded from its former position as the good or evil mistress of history to an empirically effective or ineffective moment of evolution.[45]

Because of these theoretical presuppositions, brought to a programmatic formulation in *Knowledge and Human Interests* – namely, that "radical critique of knowledge" is now only "possible as social theory" – Habermas too remains committed, no differently than Adorno does, to the Hegelian program of *determinate negation*. This version of determinate negation works on the normatively interesting contradictions internal to what Hegel termed *objective spirit* and no longer on the contradictions between the existing social order and the ideal or *absolute spirit* of practical reason. The critique of pure reason becomes (with Marx) the self-critique of society (*KHI* vii).[46] As a result of the return from culture to society, the critique restricts itself to "mass culture" and "culture industry," which had silently replaced the critique of society and the entire spectrum of its value systems and subsystems in the work of Horkheimer, Adorno, and Marcuse. As with Marx at the time he wrote the *Eighteenth Brumaire*, culture was turning back into *one* aspect of the process of revolution and development *amongst others*.

The evolution of modern society gains its momentum through the differentiation of the economic subsystem. It is formed just as much through the disenchantment of the world picture as through both the secondary education of classes dependent on the market and their social struggles. And it is stabilized through its differentiation from politics organized by the state and from positive law. But through the simultaneous transformation of social struggles into politically organized, constitutional ones, social existence achieves fluidity before it can "ossify."[47] In the *Eighteenth Brumaire*, Marx analyzes the concrete relation of functional evolution and revolutionary "event history" across the entire range of social phenomena, and Habermas has from the very beginning steered Critical Theory back to this path. Even after the turn in thought that he energetically brought about, art and culture – with and without the masses – have an important, indeed irreplaceable, role in the evolution of *modern* society. They disrupt the self-evident, provoke through newness, and as the avant-garde, they prefigure each development. They act in an "antitraditionalistic" fashion (Adorno) as the saving critique for the semantic legacy. They manipulate and lie, yet finally are indispensable – both as a diagnosis of the times and as an early recognizable symptom of them.[48] But, in the social theory of communication, art and culture are *displaced from the center of concern*. They have at times an affirming effect and at times a revolutionary one – for this is an empirical question – but they lose their status as placeholder for the revolution to end all others.

Already in Habermas's postdoctoral thesis on the structural transformation of the public – rejected by his supervisor, Horkheimer – the political and legal concepts of this transformation occupy the place that Horkheimer and Adorno reserve for the closed system of mass culture. There Habermas supplements the classical concept of the political in order to demarcate from the start the modern understanding of the public from the classical (*TP* 41–120). While Horkheimer in particular identifies mass culture with "democracy" and sharply differentiates, according to a theory of decline (and in a similar way to Carl Schmitt), "democracy" from the "liberalism" of the bourgeois elite culture that has not yet completely bound itself to "those in control of the system," "the public" for Habermas is a watchword with which the democratic self-organization of society begins in "liberalism," even if it actually remains restricted to middle-class property owners (cf. *HGS* IV, 303–31, V: 293–319; *DE* 104ff., 106–7, 124–5; *AGS* III, 153ff., 156, 176; *STP* 81ff., 89ff., 204, 206, 210, 212). His idea of democratic self-organization breaks with the old European understanding of political representation that grounded Carl Schmitt's and Horkheimer's concepts of liberalism. This former understanding defines representation in terms of *ruling* – a representation of the whole in terms of the part (*STP* 5–14). With the statement "everything for the people, nothing by the people" – Lincoln's formulation reversed – Habermas cites the Prussian king, Friedrich II, as one of the last embodiments of the classical model (*STP* 219). In democratic representation, on the other hand, and as Marx writes in the *Eighteenth Brumaire*, the people are no longer "represented" as subjects "by" their "ruler," but rather the free and equal citizens "represent" "themselves" in the very organs of political power.[49]

In the model of egalitarian representation made possible by culture critique, the thesis of mass culture – which the early Habermas still wholly shares with Horkheimer and Adorno, and which he introduces in the concept of a transformation from the "culture-sustaining" to the "culture-consuming" public – must be ascribed a completely different status than it has in *Dialectic of Enlightenment* (*STP* 159–74). The manipulative incursion of the culture industry into public life no longer appears now as *a leveling decline* of liberalism *towards* mass democracy. Rather, it appears as an oppressive *deformation* of the egalitarianism of mass democracy having to do with domination, the idea of which was presupposed in the liberal constitutional state – namely, in the *socially inclusive* rule of law – even when there was still no universal voting rights and no general literacy.

Additionally, the public that is constituted by legal institutions, which, with regard to fundamental rights, is anchored in the unprecedented separation of private and public autonomy and stabilized systemically by political parties and organizations, is immune from the direct, external control of mass culture. The structural weakening of mass culture's potential for manipulation that is bound up with such a public guides the diagnostic eye to further, systemic sources of deformation. For instance, the hegemonic concentration of political power to organize (big business, administrative machinery, associations, parties) obstructs the free and public formation of the will of all affected legal subjects, at least to the extent that the now merely *relative* power of control over the culture industry does. But, without this power of organization, no empirical will can be formed in mass democracy. With this new source of deformation, the focus upon the dialectic of enlightenment is postponed in the new chapter that Habermas adds to this seminal work of the twentieth century. *The empirical conditions of the stabilization of the public formation of the will become recognizable as the conditions of its restriction and of its distortion by domination.*

On the one hand, this means "colonization of the life-world" – adopting the language of Habermas's *Theory of Communicative Action* – by those functional systems, such as the market economy, administrative politics, and positive law, that simultaneously stabilize and maintain the communicative infrastructure of the modern form of life (*TCA* II, 332ff.).[50] Even money, power, and law are the mass media of communicative exchange. On the other hand, the shift in focus of the dialectic of enlightenment from the closed system of culture to complex and differentiated society offers new and hopeful perspectives for the reformation of a deformed public. "Public organization," "repoliticization," "institutionalization of discourses," "communicative power," and "civil society" are the key concepts running through the whole work (see, e.g. *STP* 200 n. 49, 208–11; *TP* 25–8; *FN* 329–87; *TRS passim*).[51]

The program of a critique of a public deformed by dominating forces remained the leading impetus for theory formation, extended by Habermas in the 1970s through the integration of functionalist sociology and systems theory, on the one hand, and normative theories of development, on the other. It is for this reason that, in the attempt to integrate the Marxist theory of crises into current research work, theories of *crises in legitimization and motivation* move to the foreground (*LC* 68ff., 75ff.). In Marcuse's striking formulation in *One-Dimensional Man*, the welfare state not only dissolves all social classes into one atomized mass of happy consumer-slaves, despite continuing, enormous differences in distribution. It also drives the rational demand to solve politically the problems resulting from the growth of capitalism, solutions that far outstrip the capacity of the administrative state, which lacks active participation of the citizenry (*O* 1–18; *LC* 69). The technocratic "maneuvering room" is in truth "narrowly limited, for the cultural system is peculiarly resistant to administrative controls: *there is no administrative production of meaning*" (*LC* 70, translation modified).

Making culture egalitarian by means of the welfare state can therefore be understood not only as a possible threat to *private* autonomy, but also as a chance for increased *public* autonomy (*LC* 111ff.). The one-sided emphasis on the danger to freedom, which Marcuse, Horkheimer, and Adorno share with conservative authors such as Arnold Gehlen or Helmut Schelsky, is ultimately a consequence of the *conceptual* reduction of rationality to purposive rationality. For this reason their theories remain insensitive to the communicative potential of rationality peculiar to mass democracy. Only by supplementing pragmatist thinkers such as C. S. Peirce, George Mead, and John Dewey with Critical Theory reformulated in terms of a dialogue-oriented, communicative rationality does it become possible to gain insight into the increasing chances of democratization from the absolutely undeniable dangers to freedom of mass culture, while at the same time overcoming the (at the very least, latent) antidemocratic confrontation between freedom and democracy. For, only to the extent that the democratic self-organization of society is successful can dangers to individual freedom be limited by possible manipulation of mass culture, a possibility that increases with every technological revolution. This is the thesis of Habermas's *Between Facts and Norms* (1992).

The possibility of manipulating mass culture finds its ultimate limit in the unavailability of communicative power. It is the "living productive force" (Marx) with whose mobilization inside *and* outside the representative organs of power the egalitarian regime of parliamentary democracy stands and falls. Habermas's late philosophy of right, dating from 1992, coincides precisely at this point with the political theory of the still relevant, young Marx of 1852.

If it saw "peace and quiet" endangered by every stirring of life in society, how could it want to retain at the head of society a *regime of unrest*, its own regime, the *parliamentary regime*, a regime that, as one of its spokesmen put it, thrives on conflict? The parliamentary regime lives by discussion, so how is it to forbid it? Every interest, every social organization is transformed into a generality, debated as a generality, so how is an interest, any kind of institution, to transcend thinking and to impose itself as an article of faith? The war of the orators at the rostrum evokes the war of the printing presses; the parliamentary debaters are necessarily supplemented by debaters in the salons and saloons . . . representatives who make constant appeals to public opinion license public opinion to express itself openly in petitions. The parliamentary regime leaves everything to majority decision, why then should the great majorities outside parliament not want to make decisions? When you call the tune at the pinnacles of power, is it a surprise when the underlings dance to it?[52]

Seen in this way, the democratic constitutional state is, if not *the*, then at least *an* institutional embodiment of the positive concept of enlightenment that Horkheimer and Adorno wanted to formulate in their philosophical fragments during that dark and forbidding year of 1944.

NOTES

This chapter has been translated from the German by James Hebbeler.

1. Karl Marx and Friedrich Engels, *Later Political Writings*, ed. and trans. T. Carver (Cambridge: Cambridge University Press, 1996), p. 4.

2. See my *Solidarität. Von der Bürgerfreundschaft zur globalen Rechtsgenossenschaft* (Frankfurt am Main: Suhrkamp, 2002), pp. 40ff. (English translation forthcoming, MIT Press, 2004).

3. Marx and Engels, *Later Political Writings*, p. 9.

4. "Theses on Feuerbach," in *Early Political Writings*, ed. and trans. J. O'Malley and R. Davis (Cambridge: Cambridge University Press, 1994), p. 116 (Thesis I).

5. I thank Rudolf Stichweh for discussion of the general meaning of this thesis.

6. On the idea of a saving critique, see Jürgen Habermas, "Bewußtmachende oder rettende Kritik – die Aktualität Walter Benjamins," in *Zur Aktualität Walter Benjamins*, ed. S. Unseld (Frankfurt am Main: Suhrkamp, 1972), pp. 173–223.

7. *The Eighteenth Brumaire of Louis Bonaparte*, in Marx and Engels, *Later Political Writings*, p. 32.

8. In Benjamin one finds the unguarded and affirmative remark that the Communist revolution ultimately comes down to "waking the dead and piecing together what has been shattered." Benjamin does not, however, mean this in the sense of a sacred, but rather of a peculiarly "profane illumination" (1, 253–64; BGS I.2, 691–704). He calls this illumination "profane" because it refers not theologically to the literal *restoration* of shattered remnants (which is not within our means), but rather to its capacity to be cited (inherent in human speech acts): "only a redeemed mankind receives the fullness of its past – which is to say, only for a redeemed mankind has its past become citable in all its moments" (1, 254; BGS I.2, 694). What Benjamin imagines is an "emancipation of . . . art *from* tradition [that] brings about the emancipation *of* tradition." David Roberts, *Art and Enlightenment. Aesthetic Theory after Adorno* (Lincoln: University of Nebraska Press, 1991), p. 22. So, of course, Benjamin could hardly have had postmodernism in mind as the image of redeemed humanity. The immediate adoption of theological discourse in a no longer theological context is precisely what keeps him from this.

9. Cf. Marx, *Grundrisse*, trans. M. Nicolaus (Harmondsworth: Penguin, 1973), p. 111.

10. Marx and Engels, *Later Political Writings*, pp. 2, 5.

11. Ibid., p. 5.

12. Ernst Bloch, *Naturrecht und menschliche Würde*, 2nd edn (Frankfurt am Main: Suhrkamp, 1975), p. 13.

13. What immediately follows, of course, is the debit sheet that reflects the cost of progress. See also, the second section below.

14. Marx, *Capital*, vol. 1, ed. E. Mandel and trans. B. Fowkes (Harmondsworth: Penguin, 1990), pp. 138–77.

15. Adorno is referring to the example of the Titanic, which was an early model for the intertwinement of technological progress, the staging of the culture industry, and the conservative culture critique that

ensued. Adorno objects to this sort of conservative culture critique: "Whoever rubs his hands smugly while remembering the sinking of the Titanic, because the iceberg supposedly dealt the first blow to the idea of progress, forgets or suppresses the fact that this accident, which, incidently, was by no means fateful, occasioned measures that in the following half-century protected sea voyages from unplanned natural catastrophes" (*AA* 138; *AGS* x.2, 630).

16. Jürgen Habermas, "Geschichte und Evolution," in *Zur Rekonstruktion des Historischen Materialismus* (Frankfurt am Main: Suhrkamp 1976), pp. 200–59; cf. *LC* 30–1. For a contemporary consideration, see my "Evolution und Revolution – Hat die Evolution des politischen Systems eine normative Seite?," in *Das System der Politik*, ed. K.-U. Hellmann, K. Fischer, and H. Bluhm (Wiesbaden: Westdeutscher Verlag, 2003), pp. 326–35.

17. See *Manifesto of the Communist Party* in *Later Political Writings*, pp. 1–12 and *Eighteenth Brumaire*, pp. 33–4.

18. *Eighteenth Brumaire*, pp. 46–7.

19. Ibid., pp. 31–2.

20. See also ibid.

21. Ibid., pp. 46–7.

22. On character masks, cf. ibid, pp. 66–7; *Capital*, I, 170.

23. *Eighteenth Brumaire*, pp. 77–92.

24. Ibid., p. 50.

25. Ibid.

26. Cf. Siegfried Kracauer, "Das Ornament der Masse" and "Die Angestellten. Aus dem neuesten Deutschland," in *Schriften* (Frankfurt am Main: Suhrkamp, 1990), I, 203–304; v.2, 57–67; Erich Fromm, *Arbeiter und Angestellte am Vorabend des Dritten Reiches* (Stuttgart: DVA, 1980).

27. Brecht's statement reads in the original, "Stupidity makes itself invisible by assuming dreadful proportion."

28. See, for example, Judith Butler, *The Psychic Life of Power: Theories in Subjection* (Stanford: Stanford University Press, 1997). On Foucault and Adorno, see Axel Honneth, *The Critique of Power: Reflective Stages in a Critical Social Theory*, trans. K. Baynes (Cambridge, Mass.: MIT Press, 1991).

29. In this respect older Critical Theory shows itself to be the negative of functionalistic sociology, which, from Durkheim through Parsons and on to Luhmann, emphasizes above all the tendency toward the increasingly comprehensive differentiating of autonomous spheres of society, but which only occasionally thematizes the risk of regressive dedifferentiation that runs parallel to it. Only with the recent inclusion

of peripheral societies ("the third world") in the globalization debate
does this seem to have changed.

30. For a criticism, see *PD* 106–30.
31. For discussions of the idea of identity and nonidentity thinking, see
    Josef Früchtl, *Mimesis* (Würzburg: Königshausen & Neumann, 1986);
    Anke Thyen, *Negative Dialektik und Erfahrung* (Frankfurt am Main:
    Suhrkamp, 1989); Albrecht Wellmer, "Adorno, Anwalt des Nicht-
    Identischen. Eine Einführung," in *Zur Dialektik von Moderne und Post-
    moderne* (Frankfurt am Main: Suhrkamp, 1985), pp. 135–67; Herbert
    Schnädelbach, "Dialektik als Vernunftkritik. Zur konstruktion des
    Rationalen bei Adorno," in L. Von Friedeburg and J. Habermas, *Adorno-
    Konferenz 1983* (Frankfurt am Main: Suhrkamp, 1983), pp. 66–91; and
    my *Theodor W. Adorno. Dialektik der Moderne* (Munich: Piper, 1990),
    pp. 15ff., 242ff.
32. Jürgen Habermas, "Die verschiedenen Rhytmen von Philosophie und
    Politik. Herbert Marcuse zum 100. Geburtstag," in *Die postnationale
    Konstellation* (Frankfurt am Main: Suhrkamp, 1998), pp. 232–9.
33. See my *Adorno*, pp. 29–30.
34. Schnädelbach, "Dialektik als Vernunftkritik," p. 91.
35. Ibid.
36. For Heidegger's views on the sameness (*Selbigkeit*) of the superficial
    contradictions of mass culture (e.g. "Americanism" vs. "Bolshevism"),
    see "The Age of the World Picture," in *The Question Concerning Tech-
    nology and Other Essays*, trans. W. Lovitt (New York: Harper & Row,
    1977), pp. 115–54.
37. For Adorno's differentiation of the unspeakable (*das Unsägliche*) from
    the unsayable or inexpressible (*das Unsagbare*), see Michael Theunis-
    sen, "Negativität bei Adorno," in Friedeburg and Habermas, *Adorno-
    Konferenz 1983*, pp. 45, 48–50.
38. Admittedly, the risk of breakdown, and thus of relapse into complete
    negativity, is *no less* with the most progressive avant-garde music
    than it is in mass culture. "One may ascribe to "twelve tone tech-
    nique" the double character of the emancipation of the nonidentical *and*
    of the "violence of mastery" as "domination," whose bad "infinity lies
    in the fact that nothing heteronomous remains which is not absorbed
    into the continuum of this technique" (*PMM* 66; *AGS* xii, 66).
39. See Jacques Derrida, *Specters of Marx: The State of the Debt, the Work
    of Mourning, and the New International*, trans. P. Kamuf (London
    and New York: Routledge, 1994), p. 89. Derrida's negative reference to
    the negation "messianic poverty" shows that Benjamin's and Adorno's
    talk of a "weak messianic force" is still too affirmative. On semantic

stultification in a culture of messianic poverty, see Habermas, "Bewußt-machende oder rettende Kritik?"

40. Cited in Albrecht Wellmer, "Wahrheit, Schein, Versöhnung," in Friede-burg and Habermas, *Adorno-Konferenz 1983*, p. 169.

41. See, for example, Christine Eichel, *Vom Ermatten der Avantgarde zur Vernetzung der Künste. Perspektiven einer interdisziplinären Ästhetik im Spätwerk Adornos* (Frankfurt am Main: Suhrkamp, 1993); Gertrud Koch, *Was ich erbeute, sind Bilder. Zum Diskurs der Geschlechter im Film* (Frankfurt am Main: Stroemfeld, 1989) and *Die Einstellung ist die Einstellung. Visuelle Konstruktionen des Judentums* (Frank-furt am Main: Suhrkamp, 1992); *Kracauer zur Einführung* (Hamburg: Junius, 1996); Miriam Hansen, *Babel and Babylon: Spectatorship in American Silent Film* (Cambridge, Mass.: Harvard University Press, 1991); Martin Seel, *Ethisch-ästhetische Studien* (Frankfurt am Main: Suhrkamp, 1996); Richard Shusterman, *Pragmatist Aesthetics: Living Beauty, Rethinking Art* (Oxford: Blackwell, 1992); Albrecht Wellmer, "Kunst und industrielle Produktion," in *Zur Dialektik von Moderne und Postmoderne* (Frankfurt am Main: Suhrkamp, 1985), pp. 115–34.

42. This is admittedly not unproblematic. What still poses a threat here – as the discussion about the theory of communicative action immediately shows – is the outbreak of new dualisms (e.g., life-world vs. system) that both Dewey, by reconceiving the Aristotelian distinction between *technē* and *praxis* as lying on a continuum, and Luhmann, by reducing it to the concept of functional equivalence ("comparative reason"), can avoid. For Luhmann's views, see *Grundrechte als Institution* (Berlin: Duncker & Humblot, 1965), p. 8.

43. Particularly insightful for Adorno's concept of reason is *PMM* 29–133; *AGS* xii, 36–126; *NL* i, 241–75; *AGS* xi, 281–321. For an explanation of the differentiation of aesthetic, rationally evaluative, and rationally pur-posive "spheres of significance" as the freeing of the productive power of communication, see especially the critique of Max Weber in *TCA* i, 157ff.

44. Habermas, "Geschichte und Evolution," pp. 200ff.

45. Habermas, *Zur Rekonstruktion des Historischen Materialismus*, pp. 9ff., 129ff.

46. Since the 1980s Habermas has been increasingly received as a kind of neo-Kantian – a misunderstanding to which his more recent students have not insignificantly contributed. They have isolated the theory of discourse from its social-theoretical context and transformed it into a free-standing, practical philosophy. As a result, the connections to his-torical materialism and to functionalist social theory (which also remain fundamental to his late philosophy of right) have been overlooked in the

reception and further development of Habermas's theoretical program. This amounts to a reversal of foundation and structure.

47. *Manifesto of the Communist Party*, in *Later Political Writings*, p. 4; cf. *Eighteenth Brumaire*, pp. 40ff., 55–7, 67ff., 84ff., 93ff., 114ff.

48. Cf. Jürgen Habermas, "Preface," "Theodor W. Adorno: Urgeschichte der Subjektivität und verwilderte Selbstbehauptung," and "Herbert Marcuse über Kunst und Religion," in *Politik, Kunst, Religion* (Stuttgart: Reclam, 1978), pp. 3–10, 33–47, 96–102; "Bewußtmachende oder rettende Kritik?"; *PD passim*.

49. *Eighteenth Brumaire*, p. 117.

50. This is the thesis of the *Dialectic of Enlightenment*, translated into the vocabulary of systems and communication theory: whatever secures self-preservation of the autonomous subject and unscathed intersubjectivity (i.e., systematic stabilization) endangers it through its own form of communicative blindness (i.e., colonization of the life-world).

51. See also Habermas, "Hannah Arendts Begriff der Macht," in *Politik, Kunst, Religion*, pp. 103–26.

52. *Eighteenth Brumaire*, p. 71. See *FN* 185, n 54, where Habermas cites this passage against Schmitts's dualistic division between liberalism and democracy.

11   Critical Theory and poststructuralism: Habermas and Foucault

At the center of the contentious debates that have engaged second-generation Critical Theorists and poststructuralists since the publication of Habermas's "Modernity: An Unfinished Project" (1980) and *The Philosophical Discourse of Modernity* (1985) lie several embattled epistemological and political presuppositions: on the one hand, the normative validity claims underpinning Habermas's theory of communicative action; on the other, the antifoundationalism of poststructuralism. In the wake of modernity's "legitimation crisis," Habermas argued for the retention of the Enlightenment legacy of reason, vowing to complete the unfinished project of *political* modernity, whose anatomy was radically different from the *aesthetic* modernity initiated by Baudelaire, from Nietzsche's aestheticism, or even from a "presentist" culture of the "now." Poststructuralist thinkers, by contrast, rejected the principles of universalism and consensus formation, together with the defunct narratives of rationality, legitimacy, and normative justification, either in the name of a postmodern agonistic pragmatism (Lyotard), a postmetaphysical deconstruction (Derrida), or a critical genealogy of the historical vicissitudes of reason (Foucault).

Habermas's vindication of political modernity proceeded through the undoing of a series of false sublations that historically had characterized the philosophical discourse about rationality and modernity. "Ideology critique" in that sense meant the raising to consciousness of the false assumptions that philosophical theory harbored about its own labor. Not so much the concept of reason needed to be discarded as the discursive distortions to which it historically had been subjected, from Hegel to Marx and from Nietzsche to Adorno and Foucault. In essence, the legitimation of political modernity was to advance through the actualization of a positive and politically solvent conception of rationality: communicative reason anchored in intersubjectivity, which, as a new paradigm, was to supplant the worn-out model of "subject-centered reason" (PD 34, 294ff.). The potential of such another, nonreifying and nonalienating mode of reason needed to be reclaimed from its discursive misrepresentations in various philosophical language games. Most obviously, reason needed to be freed from the "trumped up" principle of subjectivity underlying Hegel's idealist philosophy of reflection, as well as salvaged from the violence of Nietzsche's "mythopoetic" discourse, which ended with the rejection of reason altogether (PD 22, 88ff.). But the concept of reason just as much needed to be rescued from those political theories that had sought to set an end to idealism in praxis philosophy: Marxism and the pessimistic phase of the old Critical Theory, represented by Adorno and Horkheimer's *Dialectic of Enlightenment* (1944/47) and Horkheimer's *Eclipse of Reason* (1947). By means of the one-sided, negative devaluation of rationality to the level of mere instrumental reason, these two first-generation Frankfurt School theorists had lent widespread currency to an insolvent social theory. Forced by the historical circumstances of Fascism and National Socialism, they eventually had lost the belief in the emancipatory, utopian, and unfinished potential of political modernity. Thus, rather than return to the unrealized reserve of hope that Enlightenment thinkers such as Condorcet or Kant had harbored about the Enlightenment, their Critical Theory appropriated the uprooting labor of Nietzsche's "critical history," cutting at the roots of a grounding rationalist tradition. In Habermas's overview of philosophy's discursive history, poststructuralist thought acquired the dubitable status of epigonic thinking. As the philosophical descendants of Nietzsche, poststructuralist thinkers were said to embrace an antidemocratic, anti-Enlightenment irrationalism that championed the "enthronement of taste" and revered the "other of reason" (PD 96). As aesthetic "anarchists," committed to a history of radical discontinuity – rather than to continuity with modernity – these so-called "Young Conservatives" abandoned the western "tradition of reason" (PD 4; MUP 53) in favor of a reductive theory that devalued all power to the level of force or violence. Ideology critique itself had made way for a "subversive" mode of critique that, again and again, unmasked reason as the deceptive manifestation of a deeper-lying "will to power" (*PD* 4). For all its political intent, post-structuralism in truth merely engaged in the aestheticization of politics (MUP 50). Whether it was a matter of post-Enlightenment, postmodernity, poststructuralism, or *posthistoire* (MUP 38), the temporal prefix "post" signaled a "false overcoming" of modernity and, by implication, a false consciousness of time, reminiscent of aesthetic modernity. Poststructuralist thought labored under the illusion of its own newness, which it posited at the expense of the cultural transmission of the past, the "semantic potential" of a past as yet unmined, as yet not fully realized. Behind claims to the overcoming of Enlightenment in post-Enlightenment went hiding the principles of counter-Enlightenment laid down by Nietzsche.

In proclaiming the deficit of rationality, post-Hegelian philosophical discourse simultaneously set at risk the viability of critique, ideology critique, and thus the Enlightenment (i.e. consciousness-raising) project of Critical Theory, as it was originally defined by the Frankfurt School thinkers. Thus, Horkheimer's programmatic 1937 essay, "Traditional and Critical Theory" had established Critical Theory in opposition to the epistemological value-free claims to legitimacy of traditional theory. Whether operative in the natural or social sciences, traditional theory was susceptible to being instrumentalized for the purpose of "societal conformism" and the "status quo." Connecting to Marx's "dialectical critique of political economy" (*CT* 206), Horkheimer instead proposed an immanent critical theory, which, in undermining the epistemological foundationalism and deontological claims to neutrality of traditional theory, took issue with the object–subject divide and, specifically, the bourgeois "illusory form of perfect freedom and autonomy" ascribed to the knowing subject. "Such an illusion about the thinking subject, under which idealism has lived since Descartes, is ideology in the strict sense" (*CT* 211). Warning against the contemporary "hostility to theory" (*CT* 232) among pragmatists, positivists, and empiricists, Horkheimer defined "true theory" as more "critical than affirmative," yet as a form of enlightenment, whose ultimate end was the "abolition of social injustice." As he added, "[T]his negative formulation, if we wish to express it abstractly, is the materialist condition of the idealist concept of reason" (*CT* 242). Thus, just like Marcuse's "orthodox" essay, "Philosophy and Critical Theory," Horkheimer and Adorno's early papers in the *Zeitschrift für Sozialforschung* attested to the "old Frankfurt Circle's" original commitment to "the rational potential of bourgeois society" and a "philosophico-historical concept of reason."[1] However, eventually they succumbed to a totalizing and inadequate "dialectic of Enlightenment," which merely chronicled how instrumental reason inadvertently equaled force/violence, or the subjugation and reification of both inner and outer nature. In their assessment of the aporias of cultural modernity, those of an incapacitated ideology critique surfaced, in which the force of a negative dialectic radically undercut the foundations of reason and therewith the logical conditions of ideology critique (*TCA* i, 366ff.). The strong criticism Habermas reserved for the old Frankfurt School thus also was meant to justify his own break with what he considered to be its negative burden, namely, the paradoxes and dilemmas that this "self-negating philosophy" presented to a scientifically based, fallibilistic, discursive, and normatively orientated critical social theory.[2]

Rejecting the early Frankfurt School's adherence to the "philosophy of history" and the "philosophy of consciousness," according to which modernity's rationalization manifested itself as the "reification of consciousness" (*TCA* ii, 1, 382), Habermas sought to ground his new theory of society in a communicative conception of rationality that was enriched by the formal pragmatic perspective of analytical philosophy (*TCA* i, 277). Arguing that the paradigms of consciousness and production had run their course, he sought to "rehabilitate" reason by espousing the paradigm of mutual understanding and communicative action (*PD* 296, 316; *TCA* i, 273ff.). By focusing on the reciprocal, intersubjective, and "performative attitude of participants in interaction," this paradigm renounced the old object–subject divide, according to which subjects were mainly defined by their "objectifying attitude . . . toward entities in the external world" (*PD* 296, 297). Drawing on linguistic pragmatism and speech act theory, the new critical social theory abandoned the vocabulary of objectification embodied in assertoric, propositional, or representational language for a perspective that could account for the universal structures of mutual understanding in the communicative interaction of subjects (*TCA* i, 285, *PD* 294ff., 311ff.). As such, the new theory understood the organic totality of the "lifeworld" to be communicative by nature. Anything but a defense of a new "substantive" reason, Habermas's procedurally defined Critical

Theory analyzed the formal discursive procedures that grounded and regulated the norms upon which members of culturally diverse and active speech communities agreed (*PD* 343–9). Insofar as such a procedurally regulated concept of rationality was context-bound and historically situated, the opposition "historicism vs. transcendentalism" became a moot point. Neither meant to be transcendental nor positivistic, Habermas's alternative paradigm remained aware of the historical genesis of its argumentative premises in communicative rationality. It also led him to reject what he believed to be the suprahistorical metanarrative of a radically decentered subjectivity overarching the discourse of poststructuralism.

For Habermas, the problem of securing a correct interpretation of political modernity thus at once raised the issue of modernity's communal self-understanding and therewith the necessary reflection on the tasks of critique and ideology critique as tools that monitored the claims to normative legitimacy of various language games. However, it is clear that the controversial political charges he leveled at poststructuralists in the course of what ostensibly was to be a philosophical debate made subsequent peaceable argument rather difficult – with the exception of rare occasions such as an encounter between Habermas and Foucault in Paris in 1983, which was to have resulted in a conference devoted to the Enlightenment. Habermas in turn stood accused of perpetuating a pernicious form of argumentative violence or terror already inherent in the very Enlightenment program he defended, with its claims to universality, its tacit adherence to a Kantian *sensus communis*, and its unfaltering belief in a utopian history of reason. Even before the publication of *The Philosophical Discourse of Modernity*, the French philosopher Jean-François Lyotard had criticized Habermas's *Legitimation Crisis* (1973) in his *The Postmodern Condition: A Report on Knowledge* (1979). Taking stock of the postmodern situation, Lyotard maintained that the discourse of legitimation only could be accounted for pragmatically as a "short-term bond" that was generated through performative repetition, thus invalidating the grand *récit* of universal and consensual justification based in dialogical argumentation. Opposed to Habermas's "aestheticizing" narrative of consensus formation, Lyotard preferred the agonistic principle of paralogy, or the multiplicity of dissenting *petits récits*, whose plural differences were expressive of the "*différend.*"[3] These reciprocal misunderstandings and mutual reproaches have often obscured the potential connections that might exist between Critical Theory and poststructuralism *beyond* the negative pattern of a Nietzschean aestheticism that Habermas traced from Adorno and Horkheimer to poststructuralist thought. As the 2001 recipient of the city of Frankfurt's prestigious Adorno prize, Jacques Derrida, for one, recently has called for a more reflective and sustained study of the possible dialogue between Critical Theory and deconstruction.[4]

Perhaps the charge of defending a Nietzschean anti-Enlightenment position has found the strongest riposte in the writings of Foucault, who, in objecting to the "blackmail" of so-called Enlightenment thinkers (presumably Habermas), took issue with the identification of "poststructuralism" (a term he did not much like) with post-Enlightenment. Although Foucault rejected *ideology critique* on the grounds that it sprung from an outmoded representational reflection philosophy, he promoted the term *critique* – not to be confounded, as I shall show, with the transcendental interpretation of critique – as the work of ourselves upon ourselves in recognition of our historical determination. While *The Philosophical Discourse of Modernity* appeared after his untimely death, Foucault's last writings already directly or indirectly addressed many of the points raised by Habermas. They charted a return to Kant's "What is Enlightenment?,"[5] to the Kantian conception of critique, and, not unimportantly, to the legacy of the first generation of Frankfurt School thinkers. Furthermore, in seeking to refine the concept of critique, Foucault also hoped to solder the rifts of modernity, including the rift between ethics and aesthetics codified at least since Kierkegaard's *Either/Or*. By arguing for an "aesthetics of existence," he sought to reconnect to spirituality – the *ēthos* lost to a post-Cartesian history of Truth beholden to cognition and epistemological questions, in which the subject of knowing was not subject to its own transformation. In his last writings, he sought to vindicate a conception of the aesthetic as "a way of life" that might undo the hegemony of Cartesian knowledge through the retrieval of a lost spirituality. This in turn implied the transformation of the self in the pursuit of Truth and the "care of the self" as the precondition to the care of others.

Does Foucault's turn to an *ethical aesthetics* amount to a mere aestheticization of life, or can it serve as a viable corrective to some of the pitfalls of modernity? For the purposes of answering this question, this chapter will focus chiefly on Habermas and Foucault, and more specifically on Foucault's analysis of critique as well as his attempt to forge a new critical *ethos* that might help actualize the inherent reserve of the Enlightenment.[6] However, before I can address Foucault's response, it is necessary to discuss Habermas's analysis of political and aesthetic modernity in more detail in order that a better understanding can be gained of what he might have meant by the "aestheticization of politics."

THE PHILOSOPHICAL DISCOURSE ABOUT RATIONALITY AND MODERNITY

Originally a lecture course held at the University of Frankfurt in 1983–4, Habermas's *The Philosophical Discourse of Modernity* offered a grand narrative about the salient philosophical attitudes the West has displayed towards the problem of modernity. Its trajectory along modernity's most prominent philosophical paradigms led from idealism's philosophy of the subject and reflection, the Marxist labor paradigm, and Nietzsche's aestheticism to first-generation Critical Theory and poststructuralism, concluding with Habermas's own universalist pragmatics. Anchored in the communicative ethics paradigm, Habermas's new version of Critical Theory vouched to overcome the shortcomings of the previous models by remaining faithful to the as yet to be completed project of political modernity. In communicative ethics, modernity was to find its normative self-legitimation without relapsing into the metaphysical or religiously grounded legitimizing narratives that preceded secularized modernity and without having to adopt a relativistic, even skeptical, attitude towards agonistically competing value pluralisms.

Indebted to Weber's analysis of cultural modernity, Habermas recapitulated the diagnosis set forth in *Theory of Communicative Action* of how the rational "disenchantment" of worldviews had led to the division of an original "substantive" reason into three value spheres: truth, morality/justice, and authenticity/beauty (*TCA* 1, 157ff.; *PD* 1, 18–19). Each domain had further ossified into separate expert cultures, which, determined by their own logic, existed at a far remove from the life-world, from the "current of tradition, which continues to flow on in a quasi-natural fashion in the hermeneutic medium of everyday life" (MUP 46). Yet, to Habermas this pervasive sundering of cognitive structures – from each other as well as from a practical life-world – was neither the logical outcome of a pernicious "dialectic of Enlightenment" nor a corroboration of Luhmann's systems theory, which had abandoned action theory for an analysis of society according to the operations of a self-regulating system. Rather, to Habermas the challenge now consisted in answering the question of how the original "intentions of the Enlightenment," espoused by Kant or Condorcet, were to be achieved: how to "further the understanding of self and world, the progress of morality, justice in social institutions, and even human happiness" (MUP 45). Interestingly, where Foucault in his reflections on the nature of critique and Critical Theory was to present Kant as the first philosopher of modernity, who initiated a "historical ontology of the present," Habermas, by contrast, identified Hegel as the first to have raised the philosophical problem of modernity to philosophical self-consciousness. Kant's transcendental philosophy merely "reflected" (in the sense of "mirrored") the diremption of substantive reason in the division of the three human faculties of his three *Critiques*, without "comprehending" modernity's need for a novel form of reconciliation (PD 19). In Hegel, modernity first understood itself as situated in the present of the "now," that is, in an actuality that came about through a decisive break with the normative exemplarity of past tradition, in the wake of the split between faith and knowledge (PD 30). Caught in a process of constant self-renewal, modernity now needed to generate its "normativity out of itself" (PD 7). Understanding modernity's need for "self-ascertainment" as a historical and philosophical problem, Hegel thus defined philosophy's task as the need to grasp itself and its own time – the time of modernity – in thought. The founding principle at the root of modernity was that of a self-relating subjectivity, which, endowed with freedom and reflectivity, had critically shaped the historical course of religious faith, right, state, and ethics, no less than science, art, or culture at large (PD 17–18). But together with the consciousness of modernity, so Habermas charged, appeared the aporetic flaws that would hamper almost all future discourse about it. For the first time in Hegel's thought a peculiar "dialectic of Enlightenment" emerged, whose figure Habermas was to detect in subsequent phases of the historical narrative of modernity. For, recognizing that the diremptions among the different spheres were the product of a subjectivity that was as much alienating as it was enabling, Hegel sought to overcome this state of division by proposing a flawed "philosophical solution for the self-grounding of modernity" (PD 31). Abandoning the seeds of intersubjectivity of his juvenile work, no less than the belief in the reconciling power of art of his Frankfurt phase (PD 31ff.), Hegel would eventually try to surmount the diremptions produced by subjectivity through the concepts of "absolute knowledge," "absolute spirit," and "absolute subject." That is, he would attempt to solve the problem of modernity immanently by deploying "the means of the philosophy of the subject for the purpose of overcoming a subject-centered reason" (PD 34). In seeking to mediate between the individual and the universal, his political philosophy would go so far as to sacrifice civil society to the purportedly higher rationality of the state (PD 37).

If Hegel had announced the end of art, which was superseded by philosophy in turn, then the Left Hegelians promised to set an end to philosophy altogether by means of political praxis. Marx replaced the reflective paradigm of a cognizing subject with the praxis of a producing subject to explain the release of productive forces (PD 63). Reflection philosophy was overhauled by praxis philosophy, reflexive self-consciousness by labor, which now was elevated to the status of determining principle of modernity. Yet, Marx, and the other Left Hegelians, remained true to Hegel's turn of thought: that the critique of modernity was to be developed out of the very stuff of modernity. To Habermas, this meant that Marx implicitly subscribed to the principle of the "dialectic of Enlightenment," insofar as the transformation of the contradictions of bourgeois society, or the release of its rational potential, was to be gained through the very same principle that produced those diremptions: subject-centered rationality (PD 63ff.). Despite appearances, Marx's early political theory proved obligated to a model of aesthetic productivity, reminiscent of the Romantics and Hegel's Frankfurt phase (PD 64), in which labor amounted to a collective form of expressive self-realization, while a normative model accounted for the difference between productive objectification and social alienation. Later, so Habermas maintained, Marx would complement this perspective with an economic value theory and a "natural-right model," adding a moral dimension to the productive-aesthetic perspective of his earlier work (PD 65). Yet, at the core of his thought he retained the objectifying relation of self to world of Hegel's philosophy. Lacking the communicative, intersubjective framework of his earliest thought, Marx's praxis philosophy was to show up the inherent contradictions of the idealist model it sought to reverse. Although no longer anchored in reflection, reason nonetheless was reduced to the purposive rationality of an acting subject, while technology and science were matters of progress rather than epiphenomena of the problematic domination of inner and outer nature (*PD* 63–8).

It bears pointing out that the allusions to the aesthetic in Habermas's discussion of Hegel's and Marx's thought referred to more than secondary features of the theories under analysis. Rather, the references to the aesthetic that run through Habermas's work constitute a crucial subtext, attesting to his attempt to uncover the fated "aestheticization of politics" that impeded modernity's course towards its political self-realization. Thus, emending his account of Hegelian philosophy, Habermas noted that the need for the self-grounding and self-legitimation of modernity had in fact first gained awareness in the realm of aesthetics, notably, in the early eighteenth-century French *querelle des anciens et des modernes* (*PD* 8; MUP 39). Contesting the time-honored imitation of classical art, the aesthetic moderns surrendered eternal beauty for a "relative or time-conditioned beauty" and, in doing so, they at once gave voice to "the self-understanding of the French Enlightenment as an epochal new beginning" (*PD* 8). In nineteenth-century culture the effects of this aesthetic turn would become particularly palpable. For the revolutionary understanding of aesthetic temporality as "actuality" would find its most eloquent spokesperson in the iconoclastic French poet and dandy, Charles Baudelaire. In the flux of actuality, or the now of the mundane everyday, the self-cultivating poet-dandy would glean "a moment in which the eternal comes into fleeting contact with the actual" (*PD* 9), a figure through which he sought to forge a union between transience and eternity.

However, the dangers posed to a modernity that vested the aesthetic paradigm with redemptive and reconciliatory value would become manifest in the bourgeois construct of "autonomous art," whose rise to prominence had found strong detractors in early Frankfurt School critics such as Marcuse, author of "The Affirmative Character of Culture."[7] Situating the rise to prominence of aestheticism within the context of Weber's rationalization paradigm,[8] Habermas detected in art's false aspiration to autonomy the signs of an "impoverished" life-world. Thus, despite the political reading Arendt was able to offer of Kant's third *Critique*, specifically the democratic potential of his "sensus communis," to Habermas the *Critique of Judgment*'s claim that autonomous art escaped the utilitarian instrumentality of purposive rationality was symptomatic of modernity's self-alienation. Granted, while this view paid tribute to the utopian side of art – art's *"promesse de bonheur,"* as Nietzsche was to call it, citing Stendhal – it at once exposed the very division among the value spheres that qualified modernity. Its fated logic would not just be acted out in the aestheticist agenda of the "art for art's sake" movement; it also surfaced in the early twentieth-century avant-garde, particularly Surrealism, whose false program of the transition of art into life was to proceed through art's desublimation and the disappearance of the mediating category of aesthetic "illusion" (*Schein*). Seeking to undo aesthetic autonomy, the Surrealists merely brokered a counterfeit "sublation" of rationalized, alienated, or reified culture, a "false *Aufhebung* of art into life."[9] Here counterculture, or so Habermas suggested, amounted to the "forcible" desublimation of art, devoid of any "emancipatory effects," whose primary aim seemed to consist in "the decentering and unbounding of subjectivity."[10] It was this very misguided revolutionary platform that the poststructuralists were to inherit from aesthetic modernism: the "revelation of a decentred subjectivity liberated from all the constraints of cognition and purposive action, from all the imperatives of labour and use value, and with this they break out of the modern world altogether" (MUP 53). Moreover, if the "aestheticization of politics," as defined here by Habermas, consisted in the "overextension" of the value sphere of art to the other value spheres (MUP 50), then the trick, henceforth, would be to accomplish the correct integration of artistic experiences into the life-world. A viable model was to be found in Schiller's *Letters on the Aesthetic Education of Man*, showing that the promise of an "aesthetic utopia" could only be fulfilled through a communal and communicative pedagogical project (PD 45–50).

If such was the fate of the aesthetic within the domain of art and modernism, then in the realm of philosophy the aestheticization of the political sphere properly set in with Nietzsche. In the climate of post-Hegelian historicism and value pluralism of the nineteenth century, Nietzsche's aestheticism emerged as a will to power, which, in filling the vacuum left by the erosion of legitimation narratives, set itself up as its self-justifying ground. Within the political arena, aestheticism ushered in the dangers of voluntarism and decisionism, in other words, the autocratic imposition of values on the basis of sheer power or force. The first philosopher to radically renounce the "dialectic of Enlightenment," Nietzsche dismissed subject-centered reason in favor of a decentered aesthetic subject (*PD* 86). In the thrall of reason's Other – archaic, premodern myth – he dedicated his thought to the coming of Dionysius and turned art into a medium endowed with the "suprahistorical" power to bring salvation to the moderns (*PD* 88–92). As such, he rekindled the idealistic and Romantic idea that poetry or myth might restore the unifying force formerly assumed by religion, while also drawing its problematic political consequences. For, in the absence of a legitimizing morality, the world could only be justified as "an aesthetic phenomenon" – an early thought prominent in *The Birth of Tragedy*, which was to find full expression in the later theory of power and the genealogy of morals, according to which moral codes equaled coercive force or violence (*PD* 94–5). Paradoxically, Nietzsche's "power-theoretical" concept of modernity, Habermas contended, proved to be dependent on an unmasking critique of reason that positioned itself outside of the terrain of reason (*PD* 96). For in trying to turn the "sting" of reason against itself (*PD* 86), Nietzsche ended up with a totalizing "self-enclosed critique of reason" and a "critique of ideology that attacks its own foundations" (*PD* 96). Lacking logical consistency, his aestheticized philosophy combined two equally fated and contradictory "strategies": on the one hand, a stinging skepticism that fueled his theory of power, for which norms were the sedimented layers of regimes of force in the service of normalization; on the other hand, a prophetic, quasimystical aura, which allowed him to assume the position of the Dionysian initiate (*PD* 97). Out of Nietzsche's work were to develop two perspectives that would define poststructuralism: (1) that of the "skeptical scholar," who exposed the "will to power, the revolt of reactionary forces, and the emergence of a subject-centered reason," a position formative for the anthropological, psychological, and historical perspectives of Bataille, Lacan, and Foucault; and (2) that of "the initiate-critic of metaphysics," who took on subject philosophy by initiating a return to pre-Socratic philosophy, a position represented by Heidegger and Derrida (ibid.).

While the latter strategy ran from Heidegger's postmetaphysical critique to deconstruction, Nietzschean skepticism pushed to the brink of nihilism surfaced in *Dialectic of Enlightenment*, whose somber appraisal of modernity threatened the very core of any future transformative social theory. Unwitting heirs to Nietzsche's counter-Enlightenment philosophy, more specifically to his "totalizing and self-referential critique of reason,"[11] Horkheimer and Adorno remained trapped in a performative contradiction: their skepticism hollowed out the very foundations of reason, while they still adhered to rational tools with which they implemented their critique of reason. Attesting to the Romantic "hyper-reflection" of Nietzsche's genealogical method, their work monotonously displayed the reduction of rationality to instrumental reason and the forcible use of power, thus leading them to a double risk: the elimination of reason and the end of all ideology critique. For, where ideology critique was to expose the defects of a theory by revealing its "inadmissible *mixture of power and* validity" (*PD* 116), the *Dialectic of Enlightenment* risked succumbing to a totalizing Nietzschean "critique of critique," in which *skepsis*, transmogrified into doubt, threatened the hard-won foundations of reason. Just as Nietzsche's *Genealogy of Morals* had abandoned the claim to truth to be left with the "rhetorical claim" that befits the aesthetic fragment (*PD* 120), so the *Dialectic of Enlightenment* could no longer safeguard its own political argument from the specter of political decisionism. By locating the starting point of their critique too deeply, at rationality's bedrock, Adorno and Horkheimer eventually forfeited Critical Theory's claim to normative legitimacy. To Habermas, the rationale of this false overcoming of reason was to emerge full-blown in the late work of Adorno, which ended with a final retreat into the esotericism of the avant-garde artwork and an aesthetic theory that *ex negativo* sought to capture the nondiscursive "logic" of *mimēsis*. The mimetic capacity escaped theoretical grasping to the point where Adorno's own thought, despite the caveats against philosophical mystification pronounced in his *The Jargon of Authenticity*, started to resemble the very esoteric rhetoric he had despised in Heidegger (*TCA* 1, 385).

Beholden to the aesthetizing model, Habermas was to detect the same malignant aestheticism in Foucault's historical project. Thus he surmised that the "passions of aesthetic modernity" hiding behind the "cool facade of radical historicism" were largely responsible for his iconoclastic success (*PD* 275). Focusing first of all on Foucault's early "archeological" and "genealogical" historiography of the human sciences, Habermas took issue with the antihumanism that sustained his pursuit of a transsubjective "will to knowledge" and "will to truth." To all appearances, Foucault's critique of humanism enacted the return of Nietzsche and Bataille's decentered subject, based on the false belief that this could effect the reversal of subject philosophy; yet, covertly, he still operated with a figure of subjectivity that retained objectifying connections to the world, whether expressed in cognitive or practical relations (*PD* 274). As far as Foucault's later transition from the history of the sciences to a theory of power was concerned, for Habermas this "genealogy of power" yielded a "presentist," "relativistic," and "crypto-normative" pseudoscience (*PD* 276ff.). Though seemingly committed to an antinormative history of contingent discursive practices, Foucault still relied upon a political platform dedicated to alleviating social injustice and hence required a minimum of normative basis. Perhaps most damningly, Habermas discerned the possible return of *Lebensphilosophie* in Foucault's materialistic historiography as it traced the coercive imposition of force at the level of the body – this despite the fact that Foucault's *History of Sexuality* proposed a strong critique of the rise to prominence of biopower. Measuring Foucault's so-called political theory against Carl Schmitt's political decisionism, Habermas implied that Foucault's agonistic historiography in fact resulted in a history of force, propelled by antagonistic battles among adversaries (*PD* 255, 285).

FOUCAULT'S CRITIQUE: THE ETHICS OF AESTHETICS

Much of the criticism that second-generation critical theorists, following Habermas, have leveled at Foucault's historiography relates to the fact that his work has been read as if it provided a comprehensive social theory. Such a reading supposedly was made possible through Foucault's turn to the genealogy of power, that is, through the shift away from the earlier archeology of the "will to knowledge" that informed his analysis of the epistemological presuppositions of disciplinary regimes, including the disciplines comprising the human sciences. From the perspective of such a comprehensive social theory it has become customary to require that Foucault also account for socialization processes by means of psychology or a theory of intersubjectivity, or that he submit a more diversified description of jurisprudence, beyond his analysis of the law as coercive force. Seen from the perspective of Foucault's work, however, it is not evident that his particular branch of historiography laid claim to such an all-inclusive application to diverse societies. Rather, Foucault chose to stress the seemingly irreducible points of departure of the respective theories under review. Charging that Habermas's position was fundamentally "transcendental" in nature, he claimed to be more of an empirical historicist,[12] interested in understanding the "points of resistance" to different types of power, from *pouvoir-savoir, pouvoir-guerre*, and biopower to the modern "individualization" strategies of the state. Like Habermas, as Foucault seemed to imply in "The Subject and Power," he relied on Weber's account of cultural modernity, but only in order to discover "another way of investigating the links between rationalization and power."[13] Cautious about all claims to universality, Foucault remained a staunch defender of the history of particulars and particularities. Rather than subscribe to Habermas's communication paradigm, he understood history as an agonistic force-field of multiple strategies, techniques, and discursive practices, which at any point allowed for the reversal of existing power relations through acts of insubordination or insurrection (*HS* 1, 92). This conception of a tactically organized history also motivated him strategically to appropriate portions of Nietzsche's philosophy for his own historiographic purposes without worrying about the nefarious conservative or potentially irrationalist subtext of some of Nietzsche's pronouncements, or even his appropriation by Nazi ideologues.[14] These differences between Foucault and Habermas, including their irreconcilable reception of Nietzsche, became obvious in conversations they conducted in March 1983, when Habermas presented the four opening lectures of *The Philosophical Discourse of Modernity* at the Collège de France (*PD* xix). At the same time, there emerged signs of proximity and approximation between the two thinkers, which eventually were to have resulted in a conference dedicated to the Enlightenment. Moreover, in his eulogy for Foucault, Habermas indicated that he might have misunderstood Foucault and he expressed surprise at the fact that the historian considered himself to be the heir of a philosophical current that ran from Kant through "Hegel, Nietzsche, and Max Weber to Horkheimer and Adorno."[15] Foucault in various interviews similarly sought to integrate aspects of Habermas's criticism or theory into his own evolving work. Indeed, beyond the reciprocal misreadings and misunderstandings that blocked the potential debate between both parties, it became clear that the redemption of the unfinished potential of the Enlightenment might provide common ground. At least in the case of Foucault, this required that he reconsider and make adjustments to the overwhelmingly negative representation of the Enlightenment (in the sense of *Les Lumières*) that marked earlier work such as *Discipline and Punish* (1975). Moreover, in this late period Foucault also seemed willing to admit that he had reduced the concept of power too monolithically to the exercise of force and violence, thus neglecting the conception of enabling power in Arendt's or Habermas's action theories.[16] Seemingly belying his earlier dedication to the death of the subject and author, he now took up one of the least understood questions of the western tradition, the relation of self to self, which he also called "the care of the self" or "the art of self-government." Rather than withdrawing into the confines of what Habermas had termed a subject-centered reason, however, Foucault historically situated the beginning of the ethical relation to self and other prior to the narrative of reason and knowledge that commenced with Descartes. Just as much as before, Foucault pursued the vicissitudes of the "history of Truth," except that now he sought to rekindle an earlier mode of truth as spirituality, which had been overlaid and obscured by the reductive discourse of truth as knowledge. By thus focusing on the question of self-government as a counterstrategy against "governmentalization," Foucault proved that he was not just the chronicler of a "transsubjective" will to knowledge (*pouvoir/savoir*), as his earlier *Order of Things* might have suggested, but that he was also concerned with the individual will, Kantian autonomy, and self-critique.

Having dedicated the greater portion of his research to the "Nietzschean hypothesis," around 1978 Foucault took on the heritage of the Enlightenment and Kant, a preoccupation that would remain prominent until his untimely death in 1984. Of central concern during this period were Kant's epochal essay "What is Enlightenment?," together with Foucault's own connections to the first-generation Frankfurt School. To no small degree, the proximity to Kant constituted a departure of sorts from the outspoken dedication to Nietzsche's "history of reason" and the "will to truth," which had helped him bid farewell to the dominant philosophical influence in pre- and post-war France: phenomenology and its transhistorical subject. In a similar vein, Foucault dismissed Marxist ideology critique, with its normative distinction between truth and falsehood, as an epiphenomenon of the will to knowledge. Influenced by Nietzsche's postmetaphysical method, *in casu*, his "radical reflection upon language" (*OrT* 305), Foucault devised his archeology as a "discourse about discourses" that was meant to decenter and disperse the prevailing occidental archives of knowledge (*AK* 205). Revolutionizing the history of the sciences, *The Order of Things* (1966) reflected an epistemological antifoundationalism that benefited from Nietzsche's analysis of the "rhetoric of truth" to chronicle the archeological mutations through which classical epistemic grids were supplanted by modern ordering codes. In this relatively early work, Kant's philosophy did not fare well, inasmuch as Foucault read it exclusively with an eye for the distortions its transcendental aspirations had wreaked on the history of modernity. To be sure, Kant's "critique of representation" was situated at the intersection of the classical and modern epistemes. Marking "the threshold of our modernity," Kant's transcendental philosophy had questioned the "rightful limits" of western regimes of representation (*OrT* 242). However, rather than pursuing the potentially revolutionary impact of this insight, Foucault noted how Kant, in disclosing the "metaphysical dimension" of the field of representation, had enabled the "withdrawal of knowledge and thought outside the space of representation" (ibid). Seeking to fill the ensuing vacuum, post-Kantian philosophy showed a marked bifurcation, in that it turned either to positivism or to the new metaphysics of vitalism (*OrT* 243).

That Foucault in his early period still conceived of "critique" along the anti-Kantian directives Nietzsche laid down in his *Genealogy of Morals* is apparent in the "Discourse on Language" (1970). Critique plainly was modeled on Nietzsche's historicist critique of all normative moral values, insofar as "the value of these values themselves" was to be put to doubt. To procure a new "counterknowledge" about the history of the West, the methods of critique and genealogy were to target the "will to knowledge" and the "will to truth." Thus, critique was to transpire through a figure of reversal, the unmasking of the legitimizing codes of truth discourses as falsehoods. To it was to be joined a second method, that of genealogy, which would look more specifically at the historical formation of discursive practices. Foucault's programmatic "Nietzsche, Genealogy, History" (1971) further refined the use of these terms, insofar as genealogy now was cast as the analysis of the historical sedimentation of force relations in moral norms, normalizations, and legitimation codes. Thus, Nietzsche's postmetaphysical philosophy of force spelled the end of all philosophies of the origin. On the one hand, it uncovered the history of hermeneutical interpretation to be a pernicious regime of violence;[17] on the other hand, it enabled the arrival of a new materialist historiography that would unmask power's violent inscriptions at the level of the body. Stripped of all claims to normativity, legitimacy, or utopian fulfillment, history now amounted to an agonistic playing field of contending forces, while the work of interpretation constituted the coercive imposition of stabilizing codes. In this force field, the transvaluation of historical values came about through "the reversal of a relationship of forces, the usurpation of power" (FR 88). Much like Deleuze, Foucault clearly subscribed to an agonistic conception of history, in which the "origin" was deconstructed as a differential dynamic of active and reactive forces. As counterhistory, genealogy was opposed to metahistory, traditional history, the metaphysics of the will to power; as a counterforce, the new history could at any moment intervene to reverse the status quo. Using the method of reversal and inversion as a counterstrategy that worked in history immanently, Foucault hoped to turn reason and knowledge against themselves.[18] Moreover, insofar as this new "effective history" remained indebted to Nietzsche's perspectivism, it rejected all value neutrality, aware as it was of its own entanglement in the object under study. Critique (from the Greek *krinein*, sundering, separating, or distinguishing) acquired the cutting edge of Nietzsche's forcible critical history; history was not the Platonic *anamnēsis* of eternal and universal truths but parody; it did not preach continuity but led to revolutionary dispersal. Equally ruthlessly it demanded the "sacrifice" of the knowing subject; only thus could counterhistory become the countermemory of the casualties that the history of Truth had produced.[19] These casualties were discernible not just at a theoretical level, through the exclusion of certain subjects from historiography, but also through the force that such disciplines had imposed on the fray of history. From the perspective of counterhistory, Enlightenment ideals, such as "perpetual peace" or the "universality of reason," were merely ascetic sublimations of drives. In *Discipline and Punish*, dedicated, among others, to the modern penitentiary's use of panopticism as a technique of bodily coercion, Foucault summed up these findings in his grim evaluation of modernity: "The 'Enlightenment' [*Les Lumières*], which discovered the liberties, also invented the disciplines" (*DP* 222). Not unlike Adorno and Horkheimer, who analyzed the noxious effects of instrumental reason, Foucault focused on disciplinary mechanisms, or what he called "systems of micro-power," which "constituted the other, dark side" of the "coded and formally egalitarian judicial framework" (ibid.).

As becomes evident from the later texts on Kant that have been published so far, Foucault would subject this presentation of reason and the despotic Enlightenment to major review. Still, he by no means dismissed his earlier genealogy of reason or the forceful effects of "rationalization," whether these manifested themselves in the asylum, the penitentiary, or the codes and regimes of sexual practices. Rather, while he now investigated reason's role in specific types of "governmentalization" or "excesses of power," he simultaneously strove to redeem its positive dimension by means of a quasi-Kantian redefinition of "critique." To forge this new conception of critique, Foucault collapsed the definition Kant offered of the Enlightenment with the antidogmatic slant of Kantian critique. This changed perspective became especially apparent in the Sorbonne lecture of 1978, "What is Critique?," which introduced the critical attitude (*ethos*) as a "virtue" that was not just vital to the study of the art of "governmentality" but also constituted the very essence of the will to self-government. By defining "critique" as the art of "voluntary inservitude" and "reflective indocility" in the games of Truth,[20] Foucault echoed the call to autonomy and maturity expressed in Kant's "What is Enlightenment?" Anything but a purely theoretical position, critique prepared and enabled any future *Aufklärung* by confronting the knowing subject with the limits of its own knowledge, encouraging it to discover its own autonomy. But the effects of *Aufklärung* could not as readily be felt in the French tradition of *critique*. Where the German *Aufklärung* gave rise to the questioning of reason in Left Hegelianism and Critical Theory, the French *Lumières* never really occasioned an interrogation of the relation between "rationalization and power" at the academic level.[21] In France, intellectuals had almost exclusively preoccupied themselves with the history of the sciences and epistemology, at the expense of a critique of power. Describing what he considered to be the uncoupling of critique from Enlightenment in the nineteenth century, Foucault hoped to set a different course. Following Weber's critique of a rationalized, bureaucratic, administered modernity, he devised the term *governmentalization* to render the rationalization of the art of governing. Above all, Foucault regretted the paucity of attention the Frankfurt School had received in France.[22] The virtually nonexisting reception of Critical Theory during the 1930s and 1940s but also in postwar France derived from the divergent paths French and German disciplines had followed in the post-Kantian era: the turn to the *epistēmē* in the history of the sciences and to phenomenology, on the one hand, versus the critique of power, which enabled the critical examination of phenomenology. What is more, the entire Sorbonne lecture seemed written as a corrective to Habermas's concept of a legitimation crisis, insofar as the obsolete question of how knowledge could be normatively justified was to be shunted for the constellation of power and "eventialization",[23] according to which "events" retained a mode of historical contingency and reversibility lacking in the ossified narrative of legitimation.

The lecture "Omnes et singulatum" of 1979 provided more seminal evidence for this analysis: if the original *Lumières* were interested in multiplying the political powers of reason, then in the nineteenth century it became a matter of inspecting and checking the dangers of reason and rationalization. Notable, however, was the decisive emendation Foucault presented to the first-generation Frankfurt School's "dialectic of reason," which he deemed to be just as totalizing as did Habermas, if on different grounds.[24] The rationalization of culture was not to be approached *toto caelo*, but in "micrological" fashion, through the investigation of the multiple rationalizing technologies of power in diverse fields and domains. It was not a globalized analysis of rationalization that was needed, but a culture-specific one; not rationalization needed to be studied, but the economies of specific rationalities.[25] Similarly, in an interview with Gérard Raulet, Foucault took issue with the return of "one" reason in Habermas's thought, including the so-called bifurcation between reason and nonreason that Habermas had mentioned in his positive appraisal of *The Order of Things*.[26] Further problematizing the totalizing sweep of "rationalization," Foucault was to argue for a more pronounced concern with the problem of individuality or individualizing power. As an interventionist strategy of reversal, critique was to be practiced individually and collectively; as a matter of attitude,[27] critique expressed the decisive will not to be governed "too much" – a freedom that needed to be exercised even at the level of historiography.

Dedicating himself to Kant in a course about the governing of self and others, Foucault recast ethics as self-government or the revolutionary will to insubordination. As he observed in "The Art of Telling the Truth" (1983) and in "What is Enlightenment?" (1983), Kant was the first to turn the present into a philosophical event in which the philosopher herself participated. In his revolutionizing "What is Enlightenment?," Kant had introduced a *historical* form of critique that was radically different from its transcendental conception. Thus, rather than seeking to end the Kantian tradition of critique, Foucault redefined its borders (*Grenzen*) by interpreting it as a "historical ontology" of the present. As the inaugural text of occidental modernity, Kant's Enlightenment essay bespoke a fundamentally historicist project, insofar as it displayed a historical consciousness of "now," and defined the historico-philosophical task that modernity could not afford to relinquish: how to procure a "historical ontology of ourselves."[28] Kant thus formulated a new philosophical *ēthos*, which consisted in the disclosure of the historicized understanding of the present. Like Habermas, Foucault committed himself to bringing the project of *Aufklärung*, together with Kant's call for our autonomy and maturity, to completion. Indeed, in covert reference to Habermas, Foucault announced that the *Aufklärung* was not just a historical period to be kept alive out of "piety,"[29] but that it also acquired the nature of a philosophical question – modern philosophy questioning itself about its own present. As such it invited and challenged present-day philosophers to pursue the genealogy of modernity as a question. By charging that such questioning was to include the interrogation of the "historicity of the thinking about the universal,"

Foucault provided the negative parallel to Habermas's ongoing analysis of modernity's discursive history (ibid.). Just as much as Habermas, therefore, Foucault thought through the unfinished potential of the Enlightenment, asserting that the critical attitude itself was to be subjected to productive repetition.

By defining critique as limit-attitude, Foucault's "What is Enlightenment?" offered a protracted reflection on the difficult Kantian concept of the limit.[30] In elaborating his critical philosophy, Kant explicitly distinguished the positive bounds (*Grenzen*) of human knowledge and action from their negative limits (*Schranken*). When understood negatively, therefore, Foucault's term "limit-attitude" signaled the border that could not be passed; when interpreted positively, it expressed the necessity of border-passing, an imperative or injunction to be ranked on a par with practical critique. Turning critique into critical border-crossing, Foucault again and again related critique to freedom, to an experimental attitude, the "essaying" of oneself through reinvention. Interested in dissident identity politics that opposed the preordained individualization tactics of statist political power,[31] he studied subversive collective techniques of identity formation, or "new forms of subjectivity" (*SaP* 216). In his late work, the term *pouvoir*, or power, no longer just meant force but also betokened "capacity," "ability," and "potentiality" in freedom.

By thus implicitly bracketing Kant's transcendental philosophy from the discussion, Foucault was able to devote himself to what he considered to be the neglected historicist dimension of Kantian critique. But, in the process, he also surrendered some of the "negativity" that adhered to Kant's Enlightenment project. For, if in the third *Critique* Kant had posited that self-enlightenment proceeded largely in negative fashion, then Foucault would replace this negative activity with an affirmative interpretation, which took the form of Baudelaire's self-styling aesthetic – one possible realization of alternative practices of identity formation.[32] To be sure, it would be easy to maintain that Foucault's turn towards the aesthetic merely confirmed that his late philosophy charted the same withdrawal into esoteric terrain for which Habermas had faulted Adorno's late philosophy; on this account, both Foucault and Adorno would have ended their intellectual careers in an aestheticization of politics. That matters are far more complex, in both cases, is obvious. In the case of Foucault, this becomes evident once one places his preoccupation with the aesthetic in the context of the various research topics upon which he was at work at the time. The division of labor he charted as part of his research platform clearly indicated that he never aimed to reduce the complexity of what Habermas termed the "life-world" to an all-consuming aestheticism; nor did he simply seek to liberate "subjectivity" from the "objectivity" of Marx's "collective consciousness," as Marcuse had tried to do in *The Aesthetic Dimension* (*AD* 4–5). Rather, the attempt to think ethics and aesthetics together, instead of seeing them as opposites, was related to Foucault's study of techniques of the subject and of Truth/knowing, whose interface he hoped to analyze as part of future research, presented in *The Use of Pleasure*, *The Care of the Self*, and the unfinished *Confessions of the Flesh*. Thus, when contemplated from one perspective, the genealogy of sexuality implied the study of a "hermeneutics of desire" (*HS* II, 5), by means of which the subject put itself on display. However, when seen from the other side, the historically changing practices of sexuality disclosed how subjects participated in the various vicissitudes that marked the history of Truth.

To "invent" a different code of ethics, Foucault revived the moralities of antiquity, and, more specifically, a former "ethics of existence," according to which subjects were to craft their own life as if it were a piece of art. The last two volumes of *History of Sexuality* explored so-called "practices of liberation," such as the "care of the self," which were ontologically different from the "practices of subjection"[33] examined in the history's first volume. The fact that Foucault termed these practices "techniques of the self" was in itself significant. For the expression evoked the etymology of the Greek word *technē* (practical know-how), meant to revitalize a noninstrumentalized mode of being. No longer – or not yet – the exponents of "technological" or "instrumental" reason, these techniques served the greater purpose of the self-realization of the self as an end in itself. Summed up in the Greek phrase *technē tou biou*, the aim of ethics was the art of living as mastery of oneself (*HS* III, 43ff.). *Bios*, or life, became the material for an existential piece of art and of self-styling, achieved through "etho-poetic" techniques (*HS* II, 13), such as meditation, the keeping of anamnestic manuals, dietary measures, and so on. Among the Greeks and the Roman Stoa, such an ethics, expressive of a profound "care of the self," did not end in the regimes of normalization that encumbered the moral codes of modernity. Aimed instead at the beautiful life, this "aesthetics of existence" (*HS* II, II) involved an activity of and upon the self, a way of working on the self, in the interest of "inventing" (not discovering) oneself through freedom and choice. Counteracting Nietzsche's skeptical "genealogy of morals," Foucault devised an affirmative "genealogy of ethics," premised on the retrieval of a primordial ethical sensibility or attitude to be salvaged from under sedimented moral codes. Having already rethought Nietzsche's circumscription of "critique," Foucault further reconsidered its scope, adding to its meaning the sense of self-critique as a "testing" or "essaying" of ourselves. Always willing to enact these techniques at the level of his own historiography, he offered *The Use of Pleasure* as one such philosophical "essay," that is, as an example of *askēsis*, "an exercise of oneself in the activity of thought" (*HS* II, 9).

The recently published 1981–2 lecture course, *The Hermeneutics of the Subject*, sheds further light on what one could call "the politics" of Foucault's aesthetic turn, to differentiate it from the aestheticization of politics. Taking on his potential critics well in advance, he conjectured two possible rejoinders to his late work: (1) that care of the self, as "moral dandyism," resembled Kierkegaard's negative aesthetic state, and hence presented an "ethical rupture"; or (2) that it reflected the deep-rooted "dislocation of a collective morality" (*HSuj* 14). Yet, at least since Socrates, so Foucault countered, the philosopher's self-occupation had carried positive value. Moreover, when seen within the history of Truth games, it appeared that these practices of the self, ever since the Cartesian era, had entered into competition with practices of "knowledge," yielding an instrumentalized "access" to the truth (*HSuj* 184ff.). The care of the self was replaced by knowledge of the self, which, in taking the "form of consciousness," at once ensured the indubitable existence of the subject and its privileged relationship to Truth (*HSuj* 16). To match the reduction of Truth to a propositional knowledge (*connaissance*), invested in objects, this tradition assumed a neutral subject in charge of amassing such knowledge. Its apparent stability and neutrality stood in marked contrast to the older subject of "spirituality" that would undergo far-reaching transformations in the act of spiritual knowing. Tracing the countercurrent to this reductive, rationalist tradition in modernity's philosophy and culture, Foucault saw the theme of the "care of the self" as first returning in Montaigne, but as being especially prominent in the nineteenth century, notably in Schopenhauer, Baudelaire, dandyism, and anarchism (*HSuj* 240–1). It is here, then, that the unique exegesis Foucault proposed of Baudelaire's aestheticism comes to the fore, especially when compared to Habermas's *Philosophical Discourse of Modernity*. Rather than inserting the act of reinvention into a narrative of aesthetic self-expression that had gone awry, Foucault sought to respiritualize it, seeing it as the materialist practice of spiritual reinvention. Linked back to Greek *askēsis*, the aesthetic activity became a practice of self-finalization, the constitution of the self as a subject of Truth. As such, this ethical practice raised the question of how a subject could become the subject of truth-saying (*parrhēsia*) through an *ēthos*, or *technē*, that was the radical opposite, historically speaking, of mere flattery and the rhetoric of persuasion (*HSuj* 362ff.). Not surprisingly, at the end of the course Foucault related his discussion of *technē* as practical "know-how" to the large-scale critique of technological reason that linked the original Frankfurt School to Heidegger, calling for an examination of Hegel's *Phenomenology of Spirit*. For the *Phenomenology*, Foucault submitted, was the fundamental text of modernity in which the two strands of the fateful course of Truth came together in absolute knowledge, showing how the world, having been objectified, at once functioned as the place of the "proof of the self" (*HSuj* 467).

Having thus retraced part of the trajectory of Foucault's philosophical historiography, we can now reconnect this reading to Habermas's *Philosophical Discourse of Modernity*, more particularly, to the seminal excursus dedicated to Walter Benjamin's redemption of "effective" history. To all appearances, Habermas's interpretation of Benjamin in the lecture course departed from the more condemning tone that seemed to permeate his 1972 essay, "Walter Benjamin: Consciousness-Raising or Rescuing Critique." Originally tendered in the context of the Benjamin revival that marked the German student movements of the 1970s, this essay decried Benjamin's early "esoteric" retreat into the *vita contemplativa*, which had gotten the better of his commitment to ideology critique or the analysis of structural violence.[34] Even his later "exoteric" theory of "experience," premised on human happiness and profane illumination, only entertained a "highly mediated position relative to political praxis."[35] In the final analysis, Benjamin's "semantic materialism"[36] had resigned itself to the Messianic "rescue" of the semantic shards of the cultural past, giving up on the "consciousness-raising" goal of practical politics. Yet, despite the somewhat misleading title of Habermas's essay, his appraisal did not necessarily intend to cast consciousness-raising and rescuing critique as mutually exclusive alternatives. Seeing them as collaborative practices, he hoped to demonstrate the relevance of Benjamin's philosophy of experience, or how it might be "enlisted" by an altered historical materialism, which would wed the alleviation of social repression to the salvaging of the cultural past. Indeed, in much the same spirit, Habermas's *Legitimation Crisis* was to ascribe a dual role to ideology critique: "To dissolve analytically, or in a critique of ideology, validity claims that cannot be discursively redeemed; but, at the same time, to release the semantic potentials of the tradition" (*LC* 70). Considered from this vantage point, then, it becomes possible to maintain that the theories of modernity and of historical remembrance, or *anamnēsis* (*Eingedenken*), tendered in *The Philosophical Discourse of Modernity*, in peculiar ways were dependent on Benjamin's "conservative-revolutionary hermeneutics."[37] Thus, in his theses on history and in *The Arcades Project*, Benjamin developed a theory of "now-time" (*Jetztzeit*) (*A* 462–3), laden with historical potential, through which the false continuum of history could be ruptured, while he replaced the "imitation of classical models" with the constellation of historical "correspondences" (*PD* 10, 11). What was at stake in Benjamin's rethinking of historical time was a contestation of the "theory of progress," which "shielded itself off" against the possible incursion of the future. Compared to Nietzsche or Heidegger, Benjamin's branch of "effective history" offered a "*drastic reversal* of horizon of expectation and space of experience" (*PD* 14), insofar as the past bore unrealized expectations to be brought to fruition by the future-orientated present. For, the ethical act of remembrance opened up the possibility of the "anamnestic redemption" of past injustices; past, present, and future might thus participate in "the communicative context of a universal historical solidarity" (*PD* 15). Only in this way, then, might the cultural historian and critic of ideology be able to retain the ethico-political task (*Aufgabe*) of the past for the future.

It is just this double impetus – of critique and semantic redemption – that motivated Habermas's double-edged movement in *The*

Philosophical Discourse of Modernity, as he sought to reclaim the unfulfilled potential of Enlightenment rationality. But, in much the same way, one might argue, Foucault's version of critical theory presented a secularized reply to Benjamin's effective history, as he hoped to release past possibilities that might help dissolve some of the dogmatic "truth-games" of modernity. What Foucault intended was to merge his quasi-Kantian critique aimed at rehabilitating the lost reserve of the Enlightenment with an aesthetic ethics of self-cultivation. While remaining at a distance from a universalist normative philosophy, he considered the "historicization" of western thought about universalism as part of the task of redeeming the Enlightenment's heritage. At work on a context- or situation-dependent ethics that seemed to rely on "practical judgment" (*phronēsis*),[38] Foucault did not advocate an individualistic or narcissistic form of ethics, but the cultivation of techniques or practices of reinvention; "aestheticism" henceforth then would mean the transformation of oneself in and through a nonobjectifying mode of knowing.[39] If this was the form the "rescuing" side of his critique took, then the consciousness-raising part was enacted in the far-reaching transformations to which he subjected the discipline of history and the study of identity struggles. It therefore not only seems necessary but also possible to move beyond the level of reciprocal reproaches and misunderstandings to which both Habermas and Foucault – second-generation Critical Theory and poststructuralism – have subjected each other. Necessary as the debates about the respective presuppositions of both schools of thought must remain, there also seems a need for a critical *ēthos* that allows for the coexistence of divergent methodological starting points, for differing fields of application for the respective theories, and for a multiplicity of critical practices, some of them redemptive, others consciousness-raising.

NOTES

Citations to writings of the Frankfurt School utilize the abbreviations standard to this volume. The following abbreviations refer to Foucault's writings.

AK   *The Archeology of Knowledge and the Discourse on Language* (New York: Pantheon Books, 1982)

DP   *Discipline and Punish*, trans. A. Sheridan (New York: Harper Vintage, 1977)

FR   *The Foucault Reader*, ed. P. Rabinow (New York: Pantheon, 1984)

HS I   *The History of Sexuality: Volume I: An Introduction* (New York: Random House, 1978)

HS II   *The Use of Pleasure: Volume 2 of The History of Sexuality* (New York: Random House, 1985)

HS III   *The Care of the Self: Volume 3 of The History of Sexuality* (New York: Random House, 1988)

HSuj   *L'herméneutique du sujet. Cours au Collège de France (1981– 1982)* (Paris: Gallimard/Seuil, 2001)

OrT   *The Order of Things: An Archeology of the Human Sciences* (New York: Random House,1994)

1. Jürgen Habermas, "The Dialectics of Rationalization," in Jürgen Habermas, *Autonomy and Solidarity: Interviews*, ed. P. Dews (New York: Verso, 1986), p. 97; see also Jürgen Habermas, "Psychic Thermidor and the Rebirth of Rebellious Subjectivity," in *Habermas and Modernity*, ed. R. J. Bernstein (Cambridge, Mass.: MIT Press, 1985), pp. 67–77.

2. Habermas, "Dialectics of Rationalization," pp. 98, 100.

3. See Jean-François Lyotard, *The Postmodern Condition: A Report on Knowledge* (Minneapolis: University of Minnesota Press, 1984), as well as its appendix, the 1982 essay "Answering the Question: What is Postmodernism?"

4. Jacques Derrida, *Fichus: Discours de Francfort* (Paris: Galilée, 2002).

5. Kant, "An Answer to the Question: 'What is Enlightenment?,'" in *Political Writings* (Cambridge: Cambridge University Press, 1991).

6. Given the formal confines of this chapter, it is not possible to address other aspects of the highly complex dialogue among second-generation Critical Theorists and poststructuralists without risking oversimplification and misrepresentation of the various positions. For a lengthier discussion of these debates and its main participants, as well as secondary sources, the reader is referred to my *Critique of Violence: Between Poststructuralism and Critical Theory* (London and New York: Routledge, 2000), notably, the chapters about Foucault's concept of critique and *Society Must be Defended*.

7. Jürgen Habermas, "Walter Benjamin: Consciousness-Raising or Rescuing Critique," in *On Walter Benjamin: Critical Essays and Recollections*, ed. G. Smith (Cambridge, Mass.: MIT Press, 1991), pp. 93ff.

8. Max Weber, "Religious Rejections of the World and their Directions," in *From Max Weber: Essays in Sociology*, ed. H. H Gerth and C. W. Mills (Oxford: Oxford University Press), pp. 340ff. See also TCA I, 143ff.; TCA II, 303–31.

9. Jürgen Habermas, "Questions and Counterquestions," in Bernstein (ed.), *Habermas and Modernity*, p. 202.

10. Ibid., p. 201.

11. Ibid., p. 196.

12. Michel Foucault, "Space, Knowledge and Power," in *Foucault Live: Collected Interviews, 1961–1984*, ed. S. Lotringer (New York: Semiotext(e), 1996), p. 343.

13. Afterword to Hubert Dreyfus and Paul Rabinow, *Michel Foucault: Beyond Structuralism and Hermeneutics* (Chicago: University of Chicago Press, 1983), p. 210.

14. "Politics and Ethics: An Interview," in *The Foucault Reader*, ed. P. Rabinow (New York: Pantheon, 1984), p. 374.

15. Jürgen Habermas, "Taking Aim at the Heart of the Present: On Foucault's Lecture on Kant's *What is Enlightenment?*," in *Critique and Power: Recasting the Foucault/Habermas Debate*, ed. M. Kelly (Cambridge, Mass.: MIT Press, 1994), p. 150; see also *PD* 417n.

16. See "Power/Force/War: On Foucault's *Society Must be Defended*," in Hanssen, *Critique of Violence*, pp. 149ff.

17. "Nietzsche, Genealogy, History," in Rabinow (ed.), *Foucault Reader*, p. 86.

18. Ibid., p. 92.

19. Ibid., pp. 93–7.

20. In *What is Enlightenment? Eighteenth-Century Answers and Twentieth-Century Questions*, ed. J. Schmidt (Berkeley: University of California Press, 1996), p. 384.

21. Ibid., p. 389.

22. "Critical Theory/Intellectual History," in Kelly (ed.), *Critique and Power*, pp. 116–17.

23. "What is Critique?," in *What is Enlightenment?*, p. 393.

24. *The Tanner Lectures on Human Values*, vol. II, ed. S. McMurrin (Salt Lake City: University of Utah Press, 1981), pp. 223ff.

25. "The Subject and Power," in Dreyfus and Rabinow, *Foucault: Beyond Structuralism*, pp. 210ff.

26. "Critical Theory/Intellectual History," pp. 117–18.

27. "What is Critique?," pp. 382ff.

28. "What is Enlightenment?," in Rabinow (ed.), *Foucault Reader*, p. 45.

29. "The Art of Telling the Truth," in Kelly (ed.), *Critique and Power*, p. 147.

30. "What is Enlightenment?," p. 45.

31. "The Subject and Power," pp. 213ff.

32. "What is Enlightenment?," pp. 39ff.

33. "An Aesthetics of Existence," in Lotringer (ed.), *Foucault Live*, p. 452.

34. In Smith (ed.), *On Walter Benjamin*, p. 120. In many ways, Habermas's later rejection of poststructuralism, above all his dismissal of Derrida's so-called mysticism, seem to echo this early account of Benjamin's esotericism.

35. Ibid., p. 118.

36. Ibid., p. 123.

37. Ibid., p. 124.

38. See my *Critique of Violence*, pp. 94ff.; see also Arnold Davidson, "Archeology, Genealogy, Ethics," in *Foucault: A Critical Reader*, ed. D. Hoy (Oxford: Blackwell, 1986), pp. 221–33; Richard Bernstein, "Foucault: Critique as a Philosophic Ethos," in Kelly (ed.), *Critique and Power*, pp. 211–42.

39. "An Ethics of Pleasure" in Lotringer (ed.), *Foucault Live*, p. 379.

12 The very idea of a critical social science: a pragmatist turn

When I initially embarked on this chapter, I mentioned it to a well-known scholar of the Frankfurt School of Critical Theory. His response was "That is indeed a risky venture." This attitude is probably fairly typical. The idea of a critical social science is, at best, unclear and, at worst, invested in a variety of outdated philosophical commitments of the early Frankfurt School.[1] As Axel Honneth says in his contribution to this volume, many of the original ideas of this school seem, at least at first glance, to be "antiquated, dusty, and irretrievably lost."[2]

I am going to argue, however, that some of the insights of the Frankfurt School can be retrieved. My approach will be to take up the claim of the early Critical Theorists that they provided a philosophical basis for a systematic orientation to social science. To use more recent terminology, they imagined that their work constituted a "research program" or "research tradition" of a distinctive, critical sort. My argument is that this tradition can, when appropriately revised, constitute a defensible, critical social science. The necessary revisions come from two sources, one internal and the other external. The first is Habermas's work after *Knowledge and Human Interests*, when he began developing the idea of communicative rationality as the ontological centerpiece of Critical Theory.[3] It will hardly come as news to anyone to say that this turn constituted a substantial revision of the Frankfurt tradition. But what has not been adequately teased out is how this clear ontological modification impacts the possibility of a critical social science. Despite Habermas's extensive elaboration of the notion of communicative rationality, he has nevertheless provided only rather sketchy remarks on this specific topic (see, e.g. *TCA* II, 374–403). In what follows, I hope to shed more

310

light on exactly how Habermas's work after about 1970 constitutes a progressive elaboration of the Frankfurt School's old ambition of articulating a systematically critical approach to social inquiry.

Mining this first, internal source will also better allow me to establish the plausibility of turning to a second, external source for the revision of Critical Theory: pragmatism. Now, in one sense, it is hardly novel to draw attention to affinities between Critical Theory and pragmatism.[4] Habermas has repeatedly made use of different pragmatist insights, including those of Charles Sanders Peirce, George Herbert Mead, and John Dewey (*KHI* 65–186; *TCA* 1.5; *FN* 171, 304, 316). But, in another sense, the connection between pragmatism and Critical Theory has not received a great deal of attention. By this I mean that relatively little has been done in regard to considering how that connection might be fruitfully developed with the specific intention of renovating the central claims of a critical social science.[5] If my efforts along these lines are successful, then it probably makes sense to speak of the resulting configuration as a *pragmatist critical theory*. In what follows, I want to work on both the enactment of this turn to pragmatism and its justification.

Regarding justification, it will be useful to start by providing some sense of the current state of at least one social science, namely, political science, so that one can better understand the contrast that Critical Theory offers. It is important that such a theory not stake its claims against the foil of an outdated account of social science. With this in mind, I begin by considering the controversies circulating around recent criticisms of what has been called the "hegemonic" understanding of science in the study of politics. Specifically, I argue that a pragmatically reconfigured Critical Theory offers the best way to pursue such criticisms in the current situation, where the "hegemons" seem to be migrating towards a postpredictivist and postuniversalist understanding of social science. Throughout the chapter, I will contrast the critical research tradition with what has been, over the last couple of decades, the most forceful champion of strong science claims, namely, the rational choice tradition.

Next, I take up some reasons why the reconfiguration of Critical Theory I recommend makes sense from within the perspective of the Frankfurt tradition. It is plausible and unforced in two senses. First, the opening is, in fact, already implicit in Habermas's notions of "communicative action" and "discourse." Second, the opening

312 STEPHEN K. WHITE

helps to resolve clearly a conceptual problem that has dogged Critical Theory from the start – namely, the difficulty of projecting "real interests" upon actors without either entailing some form of authoritarianism, or giving up entirely on an at least minimally universalist, normative viewpoint. Resolving this conceptual problem in the fashion I suggest will also enhance the empirical reach of Critical Theory.

Finally, I will try to clarify further some of the basic commitments of a pragmatist Critical Theory understood as a research tradition. Part of what will be at issue here is how the very idea of a research tradition may have to be modified as the anchors of predictivism and universalism are pulled up. In this context, I first briefly sketch what the critical model brings to the table as its specific contribution to explaining action. I then illustrate how, in the wake of a retreat from predictivism and universalism, all research traditions must confront more explicitly the normative implications of their ontological commitments. Once this is realized, the claims of Critical Theory gain a substantial comparative force *vis-à-vis* competing research traditions such as rational choice. As I indicated above, much of my focus will be on how the commitments of Critical Theory look versus those of rational choice.

SCIENCE AND PRAGMATISM IN POLITICAL SCIENCE

In American political science, the end of 2000 witnessed the full-scale outbreak of a methodological dispute that had been simmering for some time. What quickly came to be called the "Perestroika" movement mounted an attack on the "hegemonic" position within the discipline which aims to reduce the scope of legitimate inquiry to rational choice theory and large N quantitative studies. The grounds for this attack are varied, but one seems especially central. Political science, on the hegemonic model, is too concerned with developing its methodological purity and quantitative techniques, at the cost of engaging, more systematically, with significant political problems.[6]

From a historical perspective, two things are striking about the critique. On the one hand, it is almost identical to the ones that were lodged against the behavioralist social scientists of the 1960s and 1970s. On the other hand, the hegemonic position seems to be in the process of abandoning the earlier, emphatic ideals of a social science edging ever closer to the natural sciences. This shift was clearly apparent in the responses of prominent rational choice theorists to a much discussed critique of that research in the mid 1990s.[7] Although some proponents of rational choice still seem to be wedded to the grand ideal of a universalist, predictivist social science grounded in the assumption of instrumental rationality, it appears that the center of gravity in this tradition is moving away from such pretensions, towards notions that their models may be valid only in certain restricted domains of behavior, and that other domains may be better explained by different sorts of theories.[8] This growing epistemological modesty on the part of what is probably the most prominent and coherent research tradition in political science gives the current methodological ferment a peculiar character. For one thing, ambitions towards hegemony now seem to present themselves as more straightforwardly political – increasing the degree of one's power in departments and the discipline as a whole – and less connected with universalist ideals of science that presumably could provide some epistemological justification for hegemonic behavior. And yet prominent rational choice theorists seem, at precisely the same time, to want to project images of the discipline that are decidedly unpolitical. We are assured that the methodological strife can be calmly and rationally adjudicated by the "community of . . . scholars"; or that such adjudication will come through the implicit reason of a professional *laissez-faire* policy: let everyone "do their own thing" and the best commodity produced will win out in the free market of ideas.[9] The difficulty with such ideals is that they promise us adjudication without politics: a scientific community that has none of the struggle and power dimensions of imperfect democratic communities. This image of cleanly separate kinds of communities is a vast oversimplification, in the light of which proponents cannot even comprehend movements such as Perestroika as anything other than unscientific, confused, and ill-willed. I will be arguing below that we do better to probe continually the ways in which the characters of political and scientific communities resist such sharp analytical separation.

But if the new conjunction of more modest pretensions forces challenges upon the self-conceptions of rational choice theorists, it also forces comparable ones on Perestroikens. As long as hegemony was sought in the name of a universalist, predictive science, antihegemons had a clear, monolithic target against which a sort of negative solidarity was all that seemed necessary. But if the character of the target has changed, then that sort of negative solidarity – at least as it expresses itself theoretically – may begin to look a bit quixotic: the dragon may now be a windmill.

I want to suggest that it is in this context that the antihegemons might do well to turn more explicitly to pragmatist sources, as they face the task of sketching an affirmative account of social science. Although pragmatism has not played a central role in the methodological debates – either recently or in the 1960s and 1970s – it is certainly true to say that more interest in pragmatism has emerged in political science over the last few decades.[10] But this interest has been relatively uneven and diffuse. Part of the problem here probably results from the simple fact that it is notoriously hard to say what pragmatism amounts to. Even if one wants to turn to pragmatism, it is not easily determined what one should do to accomplish that. Moreover, the interpretation of pragmatism that has made the biggest splash in recent years – namely, Richard Rorty's – is not one that political scientists, whether hegemons or Perestroikens, have found to be very insightful.[11] The former have largely ignored him; the latter have found him to be far too uninterested in issues of power.

We are thus faced with a situation in which many critics of the hegemonic view of political science implicitly or explicitly make reference to pragmatist sources, but this appeal has remained relatively undeveloped. My suspicion is that in trying to make good on this appeal, there will be little success in efforts that look simply to what the classical pragmatists had to say. Pragmatism is probably best thought of as providing us with an *ēthos* for reconceptualizing social science; that is, with some minimal direction and sensibility.[12] But such a minimal orientation will probably have to be *joined with some existing research tradition* in order for any reconceptualization to have the necessary substance to stand as an adequate approach.

Even if one wishes to speak only of being inspired by a general "pragmatic ethos," there is still the question of which elements of such an ethos will be drawn upon most heavily. I want to focus on the following: the inescapability of a plurality of perspectives; the social character of the self and scientific inquiry; and the ultimate entanglement of a scientific public or community of inquirers with the broader public of society as a whole.[13] For those who are animated by such an *ēthos*, much of contemporary social science will appear to be, as Ian Shapiro and Donald Green have put it, too "theory-driven" or "method-driven," when it should be "problem-driven."[14]

The notion that social science should focus on society's important problems is rhetorically quite attractive. The Perestroikens' critique seems to urge us to take more seriously the real, concrete concerns of ordinary people, a call that resonates with good democratic values. But this rhetorical blade cuts in two directions. Although democratic values seem implied by pragmatism, it is also the case that this invocation has often been operationalized in ways that are decidedly *un*suspicious of structures of power.[15] On this interpretation, pragmatism is cashed out as the imperative of getting down to the real business of public problem-solving: crafting practical, institutional designs and incrementalist solutions.[16] Pragmatism, on this model, has often been relatively uninterested in power, whether arising from economic structures or the claims to expertise on the part of scientists and others.[17] This is not, however, a necessary fate. One can keep the issue of power in the foreground and do so in a way that is faithful to the pragmatic *ēthos*. But this means deploying conceptual resources that allow one to systematically assess the process of *problem constitution*. All this means is that the claim to want to deal with "significant social problems" has to be articulated in a way that does not imply that such problems fall, like Newton's apple, innocently into our line of sight.

If the foregoing sketch of the contemporary state of American political science is plausible, then perhaps it makes sense to think more systematically about what sort of research tradition pragmatism might fruitfully be joined with, keeping special focus on the difficult issues of power and problem constitution. It is here that an opening to Critical Theory is warranted. But to have any real conviction that this is a coherent move, it is necessary to consider how things look from the viewpoint of the Frankfurt tradition. Are there any general affinities with pragmatism that might make this marriage one that is congenial?

WHY A PRAGMATIST OPENING IS NOT FORCED

The communicative model of action and rationality

So far I have been referring to Critical Theory as a "research tradition," roughly following – at least to start with – the meaning given to that term by Larry Laudan, who, in turn, was building upon Imre Lakatos's notion of a "research program."[18] Such a tradition includes a set of theories linked by a common "ontology."[19] The latter refers to the kinds of basic entities, processes, and relationships that are assumed within the tradition, and upon which theories are constituted. Within social science, this ontology will involve certain minimal normative commitments.[20]

From its inception in the 1930s, the Frankfurt School envisioned itself in not too dissimilar terms, that is, as an approach that joined an interdisciplinary orientation to social inquiry with a normative commitment (*TCA* II, 378–9). But it also proffered understandings of normal science and of its own normativity that are indefensible today. A number of the claims it made about what it called "scientism" may have made some sense in the heyday of logical positivism, but they are not very telling as critiques of contemporary philosophy of science. Further, normative claims made by the early Critical Theorists were grounded in a philosophy of history that gave its promise of a "rational society" a special status (*CT* 188–252). Later, of course, this philosophy and its notion of the proletariat as the privileged agent of emancipation were progressively abandoned by the Frankfurt School. Into the late 1960s, however, Habermas still wanted to speak of an "anthropologically deep-seated" "emancipatory interest" and the goal of a "rational society." And he thought of Critical Theory as retaining its therapeutic role in helping agents to understand their real interests in throwing off structures of domination. Accordingly, in works such as *Knowledge and Human Interests* and *Towards a Rational Society* the relation of the social theorist to the addressee of the theory was sometimes likened to that of psychoanalyst and patient.

With his communicative turn in the 1970s, Habermas certainly did not abandon the idea of a critical social science, but he did begin quietly to leave behind many of the foregoing figures of thought. The normativity of Critical Theory was now to be tied to what is implicit in the linguistic claims agents raise in ongoing "communicative action." The redeeming of such claims, when challenged by others, is a process that can be evaluated by the idea of reaching an uncoerced agreement in "practical discourse" among all those involved in the contestation. And this guidance results ultimately – and foundationally – from the fact that "Reaching understanding is the inherent telos of human speech" (*TCA* I, 287; *PD* 311). Moreover, Habermas famously unpacked the idea of understanding as embodying the sketch of an "ideal speech situation" (*TCA* I, 42).

We have now had the better part of a quarter-century of critique of this turn to "communicative rationality." On the one hand, very few today find Habermas's foundationalist argument about language convincing. On the other hand, the idea of communicative rationality has proven quite fruitful in many venues. This is especially true in relation to discussions of justice, deliberative democracy, and civil society. But, as this influence on normative political theory expanded in the 1990s – helped along no doubt by the appearance in 1992 of Habermas's *Between Facts and Norms* – there was little in the way of concomitant effort to make sense of what a critical social science might amount to after the communicative turn.[21]

Before taking up this question, it will be useful to consider the broader issue of what exactly warrants any approach being labeled *critical* social inquiry. Two commitments seem minimally necessary. First, the approach must constitute what Paul Ricoeur famously called a "hermeneutics of suspicion." Second, this suspicion must be of the sort that casts into question social structures of inequality; in other words, it must cast them, at least initially, *in the role of* structures of power. On these criteria, a variety of approaches would qualify as "critical." This includes not only ones that would fit into the Marxian stream, but also much feminist and black political thought. All of these currents of thought have experienced a growing difficulty with their ability to specify the substantive, real interests of the oppressed category of actors. This was starkly apparent in the late 1980s when feminists of color, a well as those outside of the advanced, industrialized world, began to question how the real interests of women were being interpreted by predominantly white, middle-class feminists in the United States. A similar thing is occurring now in black political thought, where the argument is being made that one cannot legitimately posit a monolithic black identity that defines real interests.[22] What all this reflects, I would suggest, is simply the effect of an increasing awareness of how deeply the "fact of pluralism" extends in late modern life. Any social theory today that builds in from the start a specific substantive conception of the real interests of any large category of actors is simply going to be too restrictive in terms of both what those actors might constitute as problems and what they might choose as legitimate resolutions of those problems. A critical social science whose ontology is built around the notion of communicative rationality, on the other hand, produces a thinner, less contestable projection of real interests and yet still satisfies the two minimal criteria of a critical theory.

One might agree that Habermas's position implies a less contestable projection of real interests, but contend nevertheless that it is still too strong a projection. Such an assertion would draw support from Habermas's teleological commitment, according to which language, intrinsically, directs us towards social arrangements that embody the criteria of an ideal speech situation.

Is such suspicion of the communicative model warranted? Ultimately, I think the response can be no, but accepting this response requires one clear departure from Habermas. This involves dropping the strong ontological claim about the essence or *tēlos* of language. As I said above, very few scholars, even among those who admire Habermas's work, have ever accepted this claim; nevertheless, they continue to make productive use of the communicative framework without the foundationalist commitment. If one simply drops that baggage, then the only other problematic issue is the projection of the ideal speech situation as a possible form of future life. Even though this charge is still lodged in regard to the ideal speech situation, Habermas, in fact, made clear many years ago that this is not a valid interpretation of that idea.[23] The ideal speech situation is not a substantive ideal, but rather a procedural one that can at best serve to cast doubt on some practical deliberations and inspire tentative confidence in others.

When communicative rationality is understood as not harboring a strongly projective, substantive normativity, the strength of its claims about real interests is decidedly weakened. In fact, some would argue that they are too weak to still constitute an effective Critical Theory.[24] I will try to show in the next section that this charge does not stick. For the present, however, I want to try to draw out more clearly some of the ways in which communicative rationality has natural affinities with pragmatism.

Too much focus on the criteria of practical discourse, even when these are understood in a procedural, rather than a substantive, sense tends to divert attention from a crucial element in Habermas's account of the emergence of the discursive moment out of interaction. For Habermas, social life rests constitutively on the existence of cooperative interaction, a phenomenon he unpacks with his concept of ongoing "communicative action." Unimpaired communicative action implies an (at least tacit and reciprocal) acceptance by actors of three validity claims immanent in their speech acts: claims to truth, rightness, and sincerity (*TCA* I, 1–42). In a nutshell, ongoing communicative action is Habermas's account of unproblematic social interaction. For our present purposes, what is important is that the sense of discursive justification, both cognitive and normative, is constitutively related to this intersubjective bond's becoming problematic in some way. In other words, communicative rationality has to be understood finally as a practice of *coping with* the emergence of *problems within a context of intersubjectivity*.

When this deeply pragmatist quality of communicative reason is drawn to the foreground, it helps us think a little differently about the normative implications of taking up the discursive attitude. Often, consideration of these implications has gravitated towards the question of what determinate outcome might emerge when the criteria of practical discourse are applied to a given situation; that is, what *resolution* of the problem would count as right or just? Although there is nothing wrong per se with such a focus, it tends to deflect attention away from the fact that judgments about *problem resolution* are always entangled with the prior issue of *problem constitution*. It is crucial to attend carefully to this dimension of problem constitution, if one is to understand the value of the communicative model for a critical social science.

When one thinks of the breakdown of ongoing communicative action, in the sense of some validity claim becoming problematic, it is easy to imagine that phenomenon as clear-cut – sort of like an automobile breakdown due to a flat tire. But, as I suggested earlier, social and political problems are typically not like this. At issue normally are questions such as whether *x* is *really* a problem, and, if it is, *whose* problem is it; or what is the *proper characterization* of *x*. For example, is *x* a problem of local malcontents who are misinformed about the community's energy needs, or is it a problem of a power company trying to push through the construction of a power line with insufficient input from the public? If one thinks about the interruption of ongoing communicative action as bringing forward complex questions of problem constitution, then one begins to see a richer heuristic role for communicative rationality, on the basis of which inquirers frame questions to actors involved with a given problem that reflect upon how power relations in practices and institutions may be constraining the way that problem has emerged and developed.

Resolving the problem of real interests

I want now to return to consider more precisely the problem of real interests that I touched on earlier. This concept is crucial to anything calling itself a critical social science, and yet it has become deeply problematic. The resolution of such conceptual problems is an important sign of the health of a research tradition. Thus, it will be helpful to my case for a Habermasian, pragmatist interpretation of Critical Theory if I can show that it provides a plausible resolution of the issue of real interests. This issue is central to Critical Theory, because it is only against the background postulation of real interests of actors that one generates a suspicious hermeneutics. The notion of real interests always has recourse to some conception of human flourishing that the critical social scientist sees as possibly being constrained by relationships of power.

Traditionally, since Marx, Critical Theory has thought of actors having a real interest in the emancipation from structures of domination or oppression. But as the idea of what exactly constitutes emancipation has become more contested, and as the role of the Critical Theorist as therapist has looked more unsettling, the whole enterprise of Critical Theory has seemed to become uncertain. Where the traditional model has still seemed to get some traction is in cases of extreme domination, for example, the peasants in Brazil with whom Paolo Freire worked; poor coal miners in Appalachia; or women in Bangladesh.[25] In such cases, the structures of power and the enforced silence of the oppressed are so patently unjust that the idea of emancipation and the strong educative role of the Critical Theorist continue to make sense.

But even in such extreme situations, where the traditional model of Critical Theory seems to fit reasonably well, there have been some crucial progressive conceptual modifications. In his classic 1980 analysis of coal miners in Appalachia, John Gaventa severed the model from the troubled notion of false consciousness. The theorist, according to Gaventa, should never claim that the relevant actors' expressed interests represent false consciousness, but rather only that the surrounding social structures are of such a character that one is warranted in being suspicious that the quiescence reflects a "false consensus." In effect, he is arguing that the intersubjective field of problem constitution – what is taken to be a problem and what is not – is distorted enough by power relations that the actors' real interests, *whatever they may be*, are not being expressed.[26]

Gaventa's conceptual shift can be taken as a valuable initial step towards a rethinking of Critical Theory. This can be seen more clearly if we place this shift within the context of Habermas's subsequent work on communicative rationality. The progress achieved is both normative and empirical. Normatively, one now has a more modest, indeterminate conception of real interests, but not one that collapses immediately into the old behavioralist commitment that expressed interests simply equate with real interests. Under the new model of Critical Theory, real interests equate rather with a presumed interest in individual and political autonomy or self-rule.[27] What accords with those interests in any given social situation is always a matter of interpretation, both for the actor and for the theorist. Normatively, this modified approach has two upshots. First, the attention of Critical Theorists largely shifts away *from* pondering *consciousness* and *to* analyzing *intersubjective structures*, especially in regard to how they enhance or detract from the constitution of social problems in a fashion that is congruent with the expectations of autonomy. Second, although the theorist is warranted in having a robust suspicion initially, expressed in terms of a hypothesis about the oppressiveness of some practices or institutions in a given situation, the considered judgments of actors play a far more authoritative role in potentially chastening that hypothesis than was the case in older forms of Critical Theory. If, for example, a Critical Theorist were to systematically expose a variety of practices and institutional procedures that have biased the way a proposal to run a massive power line through a particular community is being comprehended, she must be open to the fact that this community may reject the "unmasking" efforts. Of course, the critical social scientist is still free to press her suspicion further; but, as she does, the burden of proof shifts increasingly away from the prevailing interpretation of the particular social problem and more towards the critical interpretation.

This modified model also has more empirical range. It can be applied plausibly in situations of less extreme, unproblematic injustice. This makes it more relevant for analyzing late modern, western societies that are highly complex and relatively well-off economically. In general pragmatist terms, the model does not force all problems into one substantive explanatory frame; namely, capitalism and its abolition. But it certainly does not preclude one from looking at patterns of suspicious problem constitution and at pressing questions about effects of the unfettered power of capital. Another way of saying this is that pragmatist Critical Theory retains the traditional concern with power, but allows for more indeterminacy in identifying it in specific cases. I mean this in two senses. Given the complex, pluralist nature of late modern, western societies, the question of who is responsible for the effects of power in a given situation is sometimes not easy to discern. Attributions of responsibility may identify multiple agents in the economy and in various levels of the state, none of whom seem to be as fully sovereign as the old capitalists of Marx's theory. In this regard, it is interesting to note that Habermas has referred positively to the effect Foucault has had on making us think in new and more decentered ways about power. But the decentering, the complexity, the context dependence, and the fallibility of reflections on how power constrains problem constitution do not relieve us of the need for a "generalizing theoretical background."[28] And that is provided by the frame of communicative rationality, with its expectation of autonomous voice.

The arguments I have made so far about the reformulation of the concept of real interests still face a substantial question that has become increasingly pressing, given how our understanding of political life has changed in recent years. This question concerns how Critical Theory will grapple with issues of recognition and identity. The difficulty – to state it somewhat simplistically – is that the notion of real interests has its roots in a materialist conception of what interests are all about. In classical Marxism (at least on one interpretation), real interests are not symbolic, only material.

What implications does this have for the prospects of Habermas's reframing efforts? The notions of communicative action and rationality do not, I would suggest, necessarily prejudice social science to take either material or symbolic factors as more fundamental. The communicative frame is simply indeterminate about this issue. If this means that the communicative model is not incompatible with taking issues of recognition and identity seriously, it must also be admitted that it does not do much to enlighten us about them. Axel Honneth's work on "the struggle for recognition" does, however, offer a further elaboration of Critical Theory that allows a better comprehension of such topics. It sketches an account of human flourishing that expands on Habermas and thus provides us with a broader reach for "suspicion" about the power dimension of intersubjective structures and for expectations about *when* actors might be motivated to voice dissatisfaction – or to feel so disempowered as to systematically shy away from a challenge.[29] With Honneth's augmentation, then, we can speak of a real interest in recognition as well as autonomy.

Even if one were to accept my claims so far in this section regarding the way in which Habermas's reformulation constitutes a progressive shift in handling the conceptual problem of real interests *within* the research tradition of Critical Theory, one might still object that the whole idea of real interests is just too weighed down with dangers to warrant it being acceptable as a central part of the conceptual armament of social inquiry. A full answer to such skepticism is not possible here. My position generally is that the only thing worse than a social science with the concept of real interests is one without it. Let me make one brief argument on behalf of this position that is specifically relevant to the issue of pragmatism.

Those looking for pragmatist sources for rethinking political theory and social inquiry have often turned to Dewey. He is especially fruitful for emphasizing the deliberative dimension of democracy. The core idea here, to put it crudely, is that the health of democracy is determined not just by whether electoral arrangements generally let majorities rule, but rather by the overall quality of deliberation in all sorts of public spaces. From Dewey, however, the only normative criterion we get is quantity in regard to deliberation. The critical point here is not that this is a bad criterion, but rather that it is insufficient, something critics of deliberative democracy have drawn attention to in a variety of ways. A critical social science of the sort I have been sketching can make good on this deficit, because it employs the connected notions of real interests and "systematically distorted communication." These concepts allow one to identify certain cases of conflict in which the processes or structures have helped to constitute the problem situation in such a way that the simple recommendation of "more deliberation" is not an adequate response; in fact, it may function so as to mask phenomena about which one should be rightly suspicious.

SOCIAL SCIENCE, ONTOLOGY, AND PROGRESS

Throughout this chapter I have been using the term *research tradition* to describe Critical Theory. Since at least some of the proponents of rational choice also describe themselves in such terms, it is my sense that invoking this notion will not be thought to prejudice my discussion in any significant way from the outset.[30] But if a general appeal to the notion of a research tradition is not immediately contentious, it is also no longer quite so clear what such an appeal implies exactly, given the recent backing away from universalism and predictivism in political science. If our sense of the character of social inquiry is drifting further away from that of inquiry in the natural sciences, then we need to do some rethinking as to how many of the traditional commitments of the standard notion of a research tradition we wish to retain. Lakatos and Laudan, in introducing their terminology, were of course thinking primarily about the natural sciences. And Lakatos, especially, was trying to put some teeth back in the idea of scientific progress, in the wake of Thomas Kuhn's apparent abandonment, in *The Structure of Scientific Revolutions*, of any clear criteria for measuring such progress. Clearly we would do well today to reflect carefully upon the ways in which the very idea of a *social* science research tradition may have to be reconceived.

The issues that emerge here are unwieldy and complex. In what follows all I want to do is indicate some sense of where a pragmatist Critical Theory might position us on this uncertain terrain and how that positioning looks *vis-à-vis* other research traditions. Towards this end, I first explore briefly the pursuit of precision in social scientific explanation. Then I turn to how, in a postuniversalist and postpredictivist world of social inquiry, issues related to the comparative assessment of the normative implications of ontological commitments push themselves forward in novel ways.

Explaining action critically

When the whole topic of explanation in the social sciences drifts away from the anchor of prediction, the question of what constitutes a good explanation obviously becomes more contested. These days, rational choice theorists typically delineate their superiority over all sorts of competitors – from those who merely seek correlations in large-N studies to Critical Theorists – with reference to the fact that their explanations are couched in terms of a causal mechanism: strategic calculations on the part of the actor. This, it is claimed, gives a kind of possible systematicity and precision to rational choice explanations that is not apparent in competitors.

In this context, James Johnson has made the useful suggestion that we can in fact understand Habermas's theory as positing its own distinctive causal mechanism, namely, communication; or, more specifically, a certain "forceless force" that is carried by cogent arguments.[31] The communicative version of Critical Theory asserts that the binding force of "institutionally unbound" speech acts can motivate action (*CES* 38–40, 60ff.). In matters of collective action, this amounts to the claim that actors may sometimes be able to cooperate when pure strategic reflection on their interests would not yield such an outcome. The communicative mechanism here operates through the susceptibility actors have to the universalizing claims of something like justice or fairness or rightness.

The Critical Theorist appeals to this mechanism to help explain what might be an otherwise inexplicable initiation of collective action and to provide the basis for its casting of a heuristic searchlight upon structures of power. From the standpoint of rational choice theory, of course, such a mechanism is going to appear pretty suspect, since the exactly "when" and exactly "how" questions regarding its operations have no precise answers. Perhaps some increase in precision can be expected in the future, but my guess is that it will be pretty limited. The number of variables related to the context and specific actors that influence how those actors will or will not come to problematize a situation in terms of the normative universalism of communicative rationality is rather daunting.

When this persistent impression is joined with the fact that the number of actors who can be motivated predominantly by such considerations is extremely small, it might seem that the communicative model falls immediately under a heavy indictment. For a social science on its way to universal laws and predictive power, this would no doubt be true; but in the kind of social science we have now – and seem likely to continue to have – perhaps this judgment is less warranted. This becomes especially true when we take into account what has been admitted by rational choice theorists; namely, that even though such morally motivated action is comparatively rare, it can be "crucial to sparking collective action."[32] In short, although the communicative frame may focus our attention on a motivation that operates imprecisely and appears in pure form relatively infrequently, the *disproportionate significance* of its power of initiation for important political events may make the continual investigation of such unruly phenomena look more justifiable.

Even if this is so, there remains another problem. So far, I have assumed that the only alternative to a strategic-rational explanation is a communicative-rational one. But, of course, this ignores explanations couched in terms of conformity to the expectations of norms or identities. As with strategic rationality, it will always be difficult empirically to disentangle communicative rationality from such norm-guided, expressive rationality. Conceptually, the differentiation between norm-expressive and communicative reason lies in the way the former imagines actors with only limited reflexivity in confronting novel claims and situations. Communicative reason imagines actors with a capacity to negotiate such novelty with more creative and inclusive normative responses. This is part of their "communicative competence" – to use Habermas's term – a universally available competence learned with natural languages, whose creativity and motivating force is called forth by "institutionally unbound" speech acts (*CES* 26–9).

Given the central role of this competence, it is important to indicate that my interpretation of it differs somewhat from Habermas's. Recall that earlier I rejected Habermas's strong thesis that the "understanding" – with all the universalist normative weight that Habermas gives it – is "the *tēlos* of language." For him, this thesis is what grounds the notion that communicative competence is universal. If we give up that thesis, we immediately cast into doubt the universality of communicative competence. What is left, I would suggest, is the notion of a competence – or maybe better, a culturally learned capacity – that is part of what we are as *modern* human beings. In effect, the ontology of Critical Theory should be rooted finally not in any strong foundational claim about language per se, but in assumptions about the embeddedness in us of certain deep interpretations of the modern world that cause actions to occur that are otherwise not explicable. This, ultimately, is the heart of the wager, normatively and empirically, of a defensible Critical Theory.

The foregoing reference to norm-expressive rationality raises a final issue with regard to explanation. So far, I have spoken of two causal mechanisms, strategic calculation and communication in the specific sense that Habermas thematizes. But any plausible social science has to include a third mechanism, something one might just call "meaning seeking," the propensity to seek coherence and sense in the norms and other symbolic structures (practices, institutions, identities, belief, cultures, etc.) through which one lives. Habermas has consistently claimed that communicative rationality is "more comprehensive" than either norm-expressive reason or strategic reason (*TCA* I, 10, 14). The point of this claim is that the former imagines a world with three mechanisms that cause action and with actors who have the reflective capacity to dispose over all three.

Rationality, progress, and society

There has been a long tradition in social science of deflecting criticism away from the fundamental assumptions a research program or tradition makes about human beings. From Milton Friedman to Lakatos, a key maxim has been to ignore questions focused on such basic, ontological assumptions and to attend only to the theories derived from those commitments and how well they predict.[33] Here again, in the contemporary context of doubt about universalism and predictivism, we are confronted with the need to rethink this maxim. More specifically, there seems to be no clear reason now why a variety of issues raised by the particular character of the ontological commitments of a given research tradition are not perfectly appropriate parts of the mix of considerations one takes into account in the overall evaluation of competing traditions.

In what follows I want to focus on one such issue: how we are pushed towards a comparative assessment of the normative implications of ontological commitments as a result of grappling with the question of progress in the social sciences. Here I draw upon John Dryzek's insightful effort to rethink progress in the social sciences in a fashion that is pragmatist and critical. Lakatos and Laudan understand a research program's or tradition's progressiveness to be a question of problem-solving capacity; what constitutes a problem is categorically a matter to be decided by the community of inquirers. Dryzek suggests that, while this may make sense in some of the natural sciences, in the social sciences the constitution of empirical problems is "socially mediated."[34] Progress in the social sciences thus cannot be divorced from what broader publics take to be problems. In short, our assessment of a given research tradition will always be somewhat dependent on its success in illuminating what society as a whole considers to be its problems.

Although this dependent relation might seem to eliminate any real sense to the idea of progress in social science, in fact it just requires us to rethink the meaning of progress. A discipline such as political science can progress, Dryzek says, to the

extent that its ability to cope with contingency in the character of its empirical problems (scarcity or plenty, stability or revolution, etc.) grows with time . . . This adaptive capacity is enhanced to the degree that a large number of potentially useful research traditions exist. Metaphorically, political science can be said to progress laterally rather than vertically.[35]

Once we understand progress in this pragmatist fashion, another question is necessarily pressed upon the social scientist. Now that the issue of problem constitution is no longer a matter strictly internal to the community of inquirers, the cognitive rationality of social science is entangled with questions of assessing the appropriateness of the procedures by which, and the conditions under which, society constitutes its problems. In short, the cognitive rationality of our judgments as to whether or not our science of politics is progressive is partially dependent upon judgments of "practical rationality," in the sense of how we evaluate the way a society allows its problems to be defined. As a consequence of this, Dryzek argues that the criterion of progress ultimately and necessarily constrains us to endorse the critical research tradition, with communicative rationality at the heart of its ontology: "[I]f social science is true to its (cognitively) rational foundations, it *must* criticize any distorting agents in society and polity"[36] (distortive, that is, of communicative rationality).

With this assertion, however, I think Dryzek has moved forward a bit too quickly from his valid insight about the entanglement of cognitive and practical rationality, to an unqualified endorsement of the critical research tradition. All that his insight necessarily implies, it seems to me, is that the notion of progress in the social sciences cannot be neatly divorced from *some* normative commitment regarding the conditions and procedures for social problem constitution; this insight, on its own, does not require us to affirm any *one* account of those commitments. Another way of making this point would be to say that Dryzek has indeed charted a key piece of terrain upon which we must comparatively assess the normative implications of a research tradition's ontology, but we do not thereby immediately know exactly where we should stand on that terrain.

Regarding this last question, I want to conclude by drawing a very brief contrast between rational choice and Critical Theory. Normatively, both recommend themselves to us as theories of modernity; more precisely, as deep interpretations of what became increasingly available to us in the modern world as resources for human reflection upon how a society should grapple with its problems. Seen in this light, the ontological commitments of rational choice imply an affirmation of the long-term benefits of having a society understand itself and its problems according to the standard of each individual's welfare, as measured by expressed self-interest. This understanding of the "normative core" of rational choice theory, as Russell Hardin puts it, is perhaps best understood as one way to flesh out that distinctively modern claim: each to count for one and no more than one.[37] The gist of the affirmation here is that a society with this self-understanding is more clear-sighted and fair than one where appeals to tradition, abstract principles, and identities have substantial force. And there is an implicit sense that the latter tends primarily to mask the ways in which it fails to attend adequately to the interests and welfare of all its members.

Along with this affirmation of each counting for one, there is the confidence that comes with having a metric in terms of which one can do the counting. But, within the tradition of rational choice, there is indifference as to which "one" does the counting. The appropriate calculations can be imagined with confidence by the social scientist and projected into schemes of coordinated action. The advantage of this approach is, of course, that it is continually drawing attention to possible, rational designs of practices and institutions. In my earlier discussion of causal mechanisms, I emphasized how Habermas's model allows us to think of communication as an additional facilitator of coordination. But too much focus on this dimension gives a one-sided impression, although this interpretive propensity has been invited to some degree by Habermas's talk of a *tēlos* of language. There is, however, another side of the communicative model. And while it is clearly present in Habermas's work, its significance has tended to be overshadowed by the image of speech-on-the-way-to-consensus.

We see this other side if we recall that the notion of communicative action is conceived around not just the idea of understanding or agreement, but also around the individual *utterance* and its capacity to *interrupt* ongoing, unproblematic frames of action coordination, whether they are strategically or normatively structured. The partial dependence of the reproduction of such frames on the validity claims carried by communicative interaction means that they are always potentially at risk from the individual's capacity to question them: to say "no" with a conviction of rightness that reaches beyond the existing frame in a more inclusive way (*TCA* I, 306). Utterances, in short, carry a rational force that disturbs, as well as lubricates, designs. The normative implication of this for the inquirer is that it warrants a greater sensitivity than is evident in rational choice theory to the potentially imperial quality of rational projections of coordination (whether from visible or invisible hands). In the broadest sense, this sensitivity plays itself out in Critical Theory as the propensity to be suspicious; to listen for, and even anticipate, voices of disturbance.

If my arguments are correct that our general assessment of research traditions must proceed somewhat differently than it has under the guidelines provided by Lakatos and Laudan, then perhaps the commitments of a Critical Theory in the Frankfurt tradition do not look quite as implausible as they did at the beginning of this chapter. In effect, all traditions must understand that they have an unavoidable critical dimension that needs to be affirmed and entered into the fray of comparative evaluation.[38] And if that is so, we might want to reconsider what was noted at the beginning of this chapter about embarking on a "risky venture." Nothing I have said makes this venture any less risky; but perhaps I have succeeded in showing that similar risks are going to be encountered by anyone today who seriously reflects on the character of social science.[39]

NOTES

1. For a classic critique of the claims of Critical Theory, see Raymond Geuss, *The Idea of a Critical Theory* (Cambridge: Cambridge University Press, 1981).
2. See Honneth, chapter 13 of this volume.
3. For an overview of this turn in Habermas's thought, see my introduction to *The Cambridge Companion to Habermas*, ed. S. White (Cambridge: Cambridge University Press, 1995).
4. The early Frankfurt School was pretty hostile to pragmatism; see, for example, Max Horkheimer, *ER*; see also Rush, chapter 1 of this volume. For the relation between pragmatism and Critical Theory more generally, see Richard Bernstein, "The Resurgence of Pragmatism," *Social Research* (Winter 1992): 835; John Patrick Diggins, *The Promise of Pragmatism: Modernism and the Crisis of Knowledge and Authority* (Chicago: University of Chicago Press, 1994), pp. 417–32, 443–50; Matthew Festenstein, *Pragmatism and Political Theory: From Dewey to Rorty* (Chicago: University of Chicago Press, 1997), chs. 6–7; and Baynes, chapter 8 of this volume.
5. Important exceptions to this generalization are John Dryzek, *Discursive Democracy: Politics, Policy, and Political Science* (Cambridge: Cambridge University Press, 1990) and "Critical Theory as a Research Program," in *Cambridge Companion to Habermas*, pp. 97–119; and James Bohman, "Democracy as Inquiry, Inquiry as Democratic; Pragmatism, Social Science, and the Cognitive Division of Labor," *American Journal of Political Science* 43 (1999): 590–607.
6. Rogers Smith, "Should we make Political Science more of a Science or more about Politics?," *PS: Political Science and Politics* 35 [2002]: 199–201.
7. Donald Green and Ian Shapiro, *Pathologies of Rational Choice* (New Haven: Yale University Press, 1994). The responses appeared in *Critical Review* 9 (1995).
8. For a restatement of the old dream of "a grand theory of human behavior," see the essay by Norman Schofield in *Critical Review* 9; for what appears to be the growing departure from that ideal, see also the essays by John Ferejohn and Debra Satz, Morris Fiorina, Kenneth Shepsle, Dennis Chong, and Michael Taylor, all in the same journal.

9. Morris Fiorina, "Rational Choice, Empirical Contribution, and the Scientific Enterprise," *Critical Review* 9; Russell Hardin, "Whither Political Science?," *PS: Political Science and Politics* 35 (2002): 185.

10. See Paul Diesing, *How Social Science Works* (Pittsburgh: University of Pittsburgh Press, 1991), ch. 4; Donald Green and Ian Shapiro, "Reflections on our Critics," *Critical Review* 9: 270; and the special section of articles on pragmatism in the *American Journal of Political Science* 43 (1999).

11. For a good critique of Rorty's views on pragmatism, see Keith Topper, "In Defense of Disunity: Pragmatism, Hermeneutics, and the Social Sciences," *Political Theory* 28 (August 2000) and *Sciences of Uncertainty: Perspectives on Naturalism, Politics and Power* (Cambridge, Mass.: Harvard University Press, 2004).

12. For the idea of a "pragmatic *ethos*," see Richard Bernstein, "Pragmatism, Pluralism, and the Healing of Wounds," in *Pragmatism: A Reader*, ed. L. Menand (New York: Vintage, 1994), pp. 383ff.

13. I am selecting from, and modifying somewhat, the list that Bernstein offers in ibid.

14. Green and Shapiro, *Pathologies of Rational Choice*; Ian Shapiro, "Problems, Methods, and Theories in the Study of Politics; or What's Wrong with Political Science and What to do about It," *Political Theory* 30 (2002): 589–90.

15. "The pragmatists never really developed an adequate discourse for dealing with the tangled issues of class, race, and gender." Richard Bernstein, "The Resurgence of Pragmatism," *Social Research* 59 (1992): 829–30.

16. David Braybrook and Charles Lindbloom, *A Strategy of Decision: Policy Evaluation as a Social Process* (New York: Free Press, 1963); see also James Farr's discussion of Braybrook and Lindbloom in "John Dewey and American Political Science," *American Journal of Political Science* 43 (1999): 521–41.

17. On the latter issue, see especially Bohman, "Democracy as Inquiry."

18. Larry Laudan, *Progress and its Problems: Towards a Theory of Scientific Growth* (Berkeley: University of California Press, 1977) and Imre Lakatos, "Falsification and the Methodology of Scientific Research Programs," in *Criticism and the Growth of Knowledge*, ed. I. Lakatos and A. Musgrave (Cambridge: Cambridge University Press, 1970).

19. Laudan, *Progress and its Problems*, p. 79. As I will indicate in a moment, I find Laudan's understanding of progress in social science to be still too wedded to a naturalistic model.

20. J. Donald Moon, "The Logic of Political Inquiry: A Synthesis of Opposed Perspectives," in *Handbook of Political Science*, vol. 1, ed. F. Greenstein and N. Polsby (Reading, Mass.: Addison-Wesley, 1975); Brian Fay and

J. Donald Moon, "What would an Adequate Philosophy of Social Science Look Like?," *Philosophy of the Social Sciences* 7 (1977): 209–27; Terence Ball, "Is there Progress in Political Science?," in *Idioms of Inquiry*, ed. T. Ball (New York: SUNY Press, 1987).

21. I noted some exceptions in note 5 above.

22. Tommie Shelby, "Foundations of Black Solidarity: Collective Identity or Common Oppression," *Ethics* 111 (2001): 14–15.

23. See my discussion in *The Recent Work of Jürgen Habermas* (Cambridge: Cambridge University Press, 1988), pp. 71, 75–6, 88–9.

24. Stephen Leonard, *Critical Theory in Political Practice* (Princeton: Princeton University Press, 1990), introduction and chapter 2.

25. See ibid., ch. 5; John Gaventa, *Power and Powerlessness: Quiescence and Rebellion in an Appalachian Valley* (Urbana: University of Illinois Press, 1980); Brooke Ackerly, *Political Theory and Feminist Social Criticism* (Cambridge: Cambridge University Press, 2000).

26. Gaventa, *Power and Powerlessness*, pp. 29–30.

27. Cf. Mark Warren's Habermasian-based account of democracy in *Democracy and Association* (Princeton: Princeton University Press, 2001).

28. Jürgen Habermas, "Nach Dreißig Jahren: Bemerkungen zu *Erkenntnis und Interesse*," in *Das Interesse der Vernunft*, ed. S. Müller-Doohm (Frankfurt am Main: Suhrkamp, 1999), p. 15.

29. Axel Honneth, *The Struggle for Recognition: The Moral Grammar of Social Conflicts*, trans. J. Anderson (Cambridge: Polity, 1995).

30. For defenders of rational choice who rely on Lakatos or Laudan, see, for example, the essays by Fiorina and Satz in *Critical Review* 9 and James Johnson, "How not to Criticize Rational Choice Theory," *Philosophy of the Social Sciences* 26 (1996): 77–91.

31. James Johnson, "Is Talk Really Cheap? Prompting Conversation between Critical Theory and Rational Choice," *American Political Science Review* 87 (1993): 80 ff.

32. Dennis Chong, *Rational Lives: Norms and Values in Politics and Society* (Chicago: University of Chicago Press, 2000), pp. 226–7. He is referring especially to his analysis of the civil rights movement in the United States.

33. Lakatos, "Falsification," pp. 132–4; Milton Friedman, "The Methodology of Positive Economics," in *Essays in Positive Economics* (Chicago: University of Chicago Press, 1953).

34. Dryzek, *Discursive Democracy*, p. 198.

35. Ibid., p. 206.

36. Ibid., p. 211.

37. Russell Hardin, "The Normative Core of Rational Choice Theory," in *The Economic World View*, ed. U. Maki (Cambridge: Cambridge

University Press, 2001). The notion of "each to count as one" is Jeremy Bentham's. A good sense of how the ontology of rational choice theory gives us an account of how society should constitute its problems can be gained from Chong's *Rational Lives*. At one level, this work is an effort to use rational choice to explain certain kinds of collective action. Chong falls into the group I mentioned at the beginning of this chapter that expresses an awareness that their strategic models are not capable of explaining all tradition- or identity-guided behavior. And yet he proposes that some of this behavior can be explained by putting it within the framework of rational choice. What appears to be pure, tradition-guided action may in fact, Chong argues, be rooted in an individual's economically explicable calculation of sunk investment and past gains that, in turn, motivate a continued orientation toward maintaining that tradition. For present purposes, I am less interested in Chong's explanatory claim than with the normative claim he associates with the redescription of such behavior. In political life at least, Chong urges us to redescribe our behavior and reimagine ourselves in such terms. He urges this because expressive action is often deeply tied to prejudice and rigid hostility toward those whose identity is different. Think of the racist. If we bring economic rationality more consciously to bear on our own reflections about political problems, we become more likely to dampen such negative dispositions. Likewise, our use of such a framework for comprehending the behavior of others may help humanize them in our eyes, as we try to see them as having reasons for their actions that are not so different from our own. Both of us respond to incentives and seek beneficial outcomes. In a general sense, then, the conception of human being at the center of rational choice's ontology can be seen as one that promotes "the development of greater tolerance for those who are different from ourselves" (pp. 230–2).

Thus, Chong is ultimately urging upon us the greater justness of a society that continually tries to draw its citizens and their practices of problem constitution away from tradition- and identity-guided dispositions and patterns, and toward more economically rational ones. This sort of plea for the humanizing effect of the spread of economic rationality in the modern world actually has a long heritage. Its eighteenth-century ancestor is the idea of "le doux commerce." See the discussion of this concept in Albert Hirschmann, *The Passions and the Interests: Political Arguments for Capitalism before its Triumph* (Princeton: Princeton University Press, 1977), pp. 56–63.

Chong's arguments strike me as perceptive and as just the kind of normative affirmation and argument that needs to become part of the accepted repertoire of this ongoing research tradition.

38. The recognition of such a minimal, critical dimension in all research traditions does not, of course, mean that they all become thereby critical theories in the specific, stronger sense that I have been trying to articulate.

39. I would like to thank those who read and commented extensively on this chapter: Jim Bohman, Bill Connolly, Axel Honneth, Jim Johnson, Don Moon, Ian Shapiro, Keith Topper, David Waldner, and audiences at Birmingham, Bristol, and Johns Hopkins universities.

13 A social pathology of reason: on the intellectual legacy of Critical Theory

With the turn of the new century, Critical Theory appears to have become an intellectual artifact. This superficial dividing point alone seems to increase the intellectual gap separating us from the theoretical beginnings of the Frankfurt School. Just as the names of authors who were for its founders vividly present suddenly sound from afar, so too the theoretical challenges from which the members of the school had won their insights threaten to fall into oblivion. Today a younger generation carries on the work of social criticism without having much more than a nostalgic memory of the heroic years of western Marxism. Indeed, already over thirty years have passed since the writings of Marcuse and Horkheimer were last read as contemporary works. There is an atmosphere of the outdated and antiquated, of the irretrievably lost, that surrounds the grand historical-philosophical ideas of Critical Theory, ideas for which there no longer seems to be any kind of resonance within the experience of the accelerating present. The deep chasm that separates us from our predecessors must be comparable to that which separated the first generation of the telephone and movie theatre from the last representatives of German idealism. The same vexed astonishment with which a Benjamin or a Kracauer may have observed a photo of the late Schelling must today come over a young student who, on her computer, stumbles across a photo of the young Horkheimer posing in a bourgeois Wilhelmian interior.

Critical Theory, whose intellectual horizon was decisively formed in the appropriation of European intellectual history from Hegel to Freud, still relies on the possibility of viewing history with reason as its *Leitfaden*. But there may be no other aspect of Critical Theory more foreign to today's generation, which has grown up conscious of cultural plurality and of the end of "Grand Narratives," than social criticism founded upon this sort of philosophy of history. The idea of a historically effective reason, which all the representatives of the Frankfurt School from Horkheimer to Habermas firmly endorsed, becomes incomprehensible if one can no longer recognize the unity of a single rationality in the diversity of established convictions. And the more far-reaching idea that the progress of reason is blocked or interrupted by the capitalist organization of society will only trigger astonishment, since capitalism can no longer be seen as a unified system of social rationality. Thirty-five years ago, starting from the idea of an "emancipatory interest," Habermas attempted to ground the idea of emancipation from domination and oppression in the history of the species, but today he concedes that "such a form of argumentation belongs 'unambiguously' to the past."[1]

The political changes of the last several decades have not been without their influence on the status of social criticism. The consciousness of a plurality of cultures and the experience of a variety of different social emancipation movements have significantly lowered expectations of what criticism ought to be, and be capable of. Generally speaking, there is prevalent today a liberal conception of justice that utilizes criteria for the normative identification of social injustice without the desire to explicate further the institutional framework for the injustice as embedding it within a particular type of society. Where such a procedure is felt to be insufficient, appeals are made to models of social criticism that are constructed in the spirit of Michel Foucault's genealogical method or in the style of Michael Walzer's critical hermeneutics.[2] In all of these cases, however, criticism is no longer understood as a reflective form of rationality that is supposed to be anchored in the historical process itself. Critical Theory on the other hand – and in a way that may be unique to it – insists on a mediation of theory and history in a concept of socially effective rationality. That is, the historical past should be understood from a practical point of view, as a process of development whose pathological deformation by capitalism may be overcome only by initiating a process of enlightenment among those involved. It is this working model of the intertwining of theory and history that grounds the unity of Critical Theory despite its variety of voices. Whether in its positive form with the early Horkheimer, Marcuse, or Habermas, or in its negative form with Adorno or Benjamin, one finds the same idea forming the background of each of the different projects – namely, that social relationships distort the historical process of development in a way that one can only practically remedy. Designating the legacy of Critical Theory for the new century would necessarily involve recovering from the idea of a social pathology of reason an explosive charge that can still be touched off today. Against the tendency to reduce social criticism to a project of normative, situational, or local opinion, one must clarify the context in which social criticism stands side by side with the demands of a historically evolved reason. In what follows I want to take a first step in that direction. First, I shall detail the ethical core contained in the idea in Critical Theory of a socially deficient rationality. Second, I shall outline how capitalism can be understood as a cause of such a deformation of social rationality. Third and last, I shall establish the connection to praxis seen in the goal of overcoming social suffering caused by deficient rationality. Each of these three stages involves finding a new language that can make clear in present terms what Critical Theory intended in the past. Still, I will often have to content myself merely with suggesting lines of thought that would have to be pursued to bring the arguments of earlier Critical Theory up to date.

I

Even though it is difficult to discover a systematic unity in the many forms of Critical Theory, taking its social-theoretical negativism as our point of departure will serve us well in establishing a first point of common interest.[3] Both the members of the inner circle, as well as those on the periphery, of the Institute for Social Research[4] perceive the societal situation upon which they want to have an effect as being in a state of social negativity. Moreover, there is widespread agreement that the concept of negativity should not be restricted in a narrow way to offences committed against principles of social justice, but rather should be extended more broadly to violations of the conditions for a good or successful life.[5] All the expressions the members of the circle use to characterize the given state of society arise from a social-theoretical vocabulary grounded in the basic distinction between "pathological" and "intact, non-pathological" relations. Horkheimer first speaks of the "irrational organization" of society (*CT* 188–243; *HGS* IV, 162–216), Adorno later of the "administered world" (*P* 17–34; *AGS* X.1: 11–30), Marcuse uses such concepts as "one-dimensional society" and "repressive tolerance" (*MS* VII: 136–66), and Habermas, finally, uses the formula of the "colonization of the social life-world" (*TCA* II, ch. 8). Such formulations always normatively presuppose an "intact" state of social relations in which all the members are provided with an opportunity for successful self-actualization. But what is specifically meant by this terminology is not sufficiently explained by merely contrasting it with the language of social injustice in moral philosophy. Rather, the distinctiveness of the expressions only becomes manifest when the obscure connection taken to exist between social pathology and defective rationality comes to light. All the authors mentioned above assume that the cause of the negative state of society is to be found in a deficit in social rationality. They maintain an internal connection between pathological relationships and the condition of social rationality, which explains their interest in the historical process of the actualization of reason. Any attempt to make the tradition of Critical Theory fruitful again for the present must thus begin with the task of bringing this conceptual connection up to date.

The thesis that social pathologies are to be understood as a result of deficient rationality is ultimately indebted to the political philosophy of Hegel. He begins his *Philosophy of Right* with the supposition that a vast number of tendencies towards a loss of meaning were manifesting themselves in his time, and that these tendencies could be explained only by the insufficient appropriation of an "objectively" already possible reason.[6] Behind Hegel's diagnosis of his time lies a comprehensive conception of reason in which he establishes a connection between historical progress and ethics. Reason unfolds in the historical process by recreating universal "ethical" institutions at every stage. And, by taking these institutions into account, individuals are able to design their lives according to socially acknowledged aims and thus to experience life as meaningful. Whoever does not let such objective ends of reason influence her life, on the other hand, will suffer from the consequences of "indeterminacy" and will develop symptoms of disorientation. If one transports this ethical insight into the framework of the social processes of an entire society, Hegel's diagnosis, which is basic to his *Philosophy of Right*, emerges in outline form. Hegel saw in his own society the outbreak of those dominant systems of thought and ideologies which, by preventing subjects from perceiving an ethical life that was already established, gave rise to widespread symptoms of a loss of meaning. He was convinced that social pathologies were to be understood as the result of the inability of society to properly express the rational potential already inherent in its institutions, practices, and everyday routines.

When this view of Hegel's is detached from the particular context in which it is embedded, it amounts to the general thesis that every successful form of society is possible only through the maintenance of its most highly developed standard of rationality, because it is only each instance of the rational universal that can provide the members of society with the orientation according to which they can meaningfully direct their lives. And this fundamental conviction must still be at work when, despite their different approaches, critical theorists all claim that it is a lack of social rationality which causes the pathology of capitalist society. Without this ethical assumption, already implicit in Hegel, one cannot justify establishing such a connection. The members of society must agree that leading a successful, undistorted life together is only possible if they all orient themselves according to principles or institutions that they can understand as rational ends for self-actualization. Any deviation from the ideal outlined here must lead to a social pathology insofar as subjects are recognizably suffering from a loss of universal, communal ends.

Nevertheless, this ethical core of the initial hypothesis, common to the various projects of Critical Theory, remains for the most part overlaid by anthropological premises. The rational universal that is supposed to vouchsafe an "intact" form of social life is understood as the potential for an invariant mode of human activity. Horkheimer's thought contains such an element in his conception of work, according to which human mastery over nature is directed "immanently" towards the goal of a social condition in which individual contributions transparently and mutually complement one another (*CT* 213ff.; *HGS* IV, 186ff.). One might say with Marx, then, that the emergence of social pathology depends upon the actual organization of society falling short of the standards of rationality that are already embodied in the forces of production. In the case of Marcuse, the authority of a rational universal shifts increasingly in his later writings to the sphere of an aesthetic praxis that appears as the medium of social integration in which subjects can satisfy their social needs in noncoerced cooperation (*L passim; EC* 20–49). Here, then, the social pathology sets in at that moment in which the organization of society begins to suppress the rational potential that is at home in the power of the imagination anchored in the life-world. Finally, Habermas secures the Hegelian idea of a rational universal by means of the concept of communicative agreement, whose idealizing presuppositions are supposed to meet the concern that the potential of discursive rationality regain universal acceptance at every stage of social development. We can speak therefore of a social pathology as soon as the symbolic reproduction of society is no longer subjected to those standards of rationality that are inherent in the most highly developed form of linguistic agreement (*Verständigung*) (*TCA* ii, ch. 6.1).[7] In all of these approaches to Critical Theory, the same Hegelian idea – namely, that a rational universal is always required for the possibility of fulfilled self-actualization within society – is continually incorporated, only in different characterizations of the original human praxis of action. Just as with Horkheimer's concept of human work or with Marcuse's idea of an aesthetic life, Habermas's concept of communicative agreement serves above all the aim of fixing the form of reason whose developed shape provides the medium for a rational and satisfying integration of society. It is with reference to such an authority of rational praxis that Critical Theorists can analyze society according to a theory of reason *qua* diagnosis of social pathologies. Deviations from the ideal that was to be achieved with the social actualization of the rational universal can be described as social pathologies, since they must accompany a regrettable loss of prospects for intersubjective self-actualization.

In the path of intellectual development from Horkheimer to Habermas, the idea of a rational universal changed of course, not only in regard to its content but also in regard to its methodological form. While Horkheimer combines with his concept of work the notion of a rational potential that is to serve subjects directly as a goal of cooperative self-actualization in a "community of free human beings" (*CT* 217; *HGS* iv, 191), Habermas understands the idea of communicative agreement no longer as a rational goal but rather only as a rational form of a successful mode of socialization. In Habermas, the idea that only a fully realized rationality guarantees a successful community of members of society is radically proceduralized, insofar as the rationality that gives rise to action oriented towards agreement is now supposed to ensure only the conditions for, and no longer the fulfillment of, autonomous self-actualization.[8] Yet this formulation cannot obscure the fact that an ethical idea is hiding beneath anthropological ways of speaking about an original mode of human action. The concept of communicative action, whose rationality imposes on human beings an invariant constraint, still contains indirectly the idea of a successful social life that one finds directly in Horkheimer's concept of work and in Marcuse's concept of aesthetic praxis. The representatives of Critical Theory hold, with Hegel, the conviction that the self-actualization of the individual is only successful when it is interwoven in its aims – by means of generally accepted principles or ends – with the self-actualization of all the other members of society. Indeed, one might even claim that the idea of a rational universal contains the concept of a common good upon which the members of society must have rationally agreed in order to be able to relate their individual freedoms to one another cooperatively. The different models of practice that Horkheimer, Marcuse, and Habermas offer are all representatives of that one thought, according to which the socialization of human beings can be successful only under conditions of cooperative freedom. However the particulars of the anthropological ideas may be sorted out, they ultimately stand for an ethical idea that places the utmost value on a form of common praxis in which subjects can achieve cooperative self-actualization.[9]

Even the work that appears to have been farthest from Critical Theory's fundamental ethical ideas reflects this basic first premise. In his *Minima Moralia* Adorno vehemently denies any possibility of a universal moral theory by arguing that the "damages" of social life have already led to such fragmentation of individual conduct that orientation in terms of comprehensive principles is generally no longer possible. Instead, his "reflections" are supposed to show only in aphoristic, isolated cases which ethical and intellectual virtues remain that might resist instrumental demands by stubborn insistence upon nonpurposive activity. But the standards by which Adorno measures the harm done to the form of societal interaction betray his retention of the ideal of a cooperative self-actualization in which the freedom of the individual makes possible that of others. In various places in the text he explains even the historical genesis of social damage by direct reference to the loss of a "good universal" (*MM* 31–2, 35–7; *AGS* IV, 33–4, 38–41). Moreover, Adorno takes as basic a concept of praxis that, following Hegel's example, ties ethical principles to the presupposition of rationality. The question of a successful form of socialization only arises where there are established common modes of action that individuals can accept as rational goals of self-actualization. The fact that Adorno at the same time has in mind, above all, the model of "nonpurposive" or "disinterested" communication – for which he takes unselfish, unalloyed giving or love as his paradigmatic examples (*MM* 31–2, 35, 42–3, 172; *AGS* IV, 33–4, 38, 46–7, 193–4)[10] – follows from the quasi-aesthetic premise he shares with Marcuse: the forms of mutual action that are best suited for self-actualization are those in which human nature achieves noncoerced expression by fulfilling sensuous needs through interplay with others.

The idea of the rational universal of cooperative self-actualization that all the members of the Frankfurt School fundamentally share is as critical of liberalism as it is of any intellectual tradition today that one might call "communitarian." While a certain approximation to liberal doctrines can be found in the recent work of Habermas because of the increasing weight he gives to the legal autonomy of individuals, he does not go so far as to say that there are no differences between the social-ontological premises of liberalism and those of Critical Theory. Instead, he continues to hold the conviction (as did Marcuse, Horkheimer, and Adorno) that the actualization of individual freedom is tied to the assumption of a common praxis that is more than just the result of a coordination of individual interests. All the concepts of a rational praxis that find application in Critical Theory are tailored according to their intended use to actions whose implementation requires a higher degree of intersubjective agreement than liberalism allows. In order to be able to cooperate on an equal basis, to interact aesthetically, or to reach agreements in a noncoerced manner, a shared conviction is required that each of these activities is of an importance which justifies, if necessary, the neglect of individual interests. To this extent, Critical Theory presupposes a normative ideal of society that is incompatible with the individualistic premises of the liberal tradition. Orientation in terms of the idea of cooperative self-actualization includes instead the notion that subjects are not able to achieve a successful social life as long as they have not recognized the common core of value judgments that lies behind their respective individual interests. The idea of a

"community of free human beings" that Horkheimer already formulates in his essay "Traditional and Critical Theory" (*CT* 217; *HGS* IV,
191) also forms the normative *leitmotif* of Critical Theory, where the
concept of community is strictly avoided because of its ideological
misuse.

Were one to press this line of thought further, one could easily get
the impression that the normative concern of Critical Theory coincides with that of "communitarianism."[11] But just as it differs from
liberalism in its orientation to a "universal" of self-actualization,
Critical Theory differs from communitarianism in terms of the link
between this universal and reason. No Critical Theorist has ever
abandoned the Hegelian idea that cooperative praxis, along with the
values attendant to it, must possess a rational character. Indeed,
it is precisely the point of Critical Theory to see individual self-
actualization as tied to the assumption that there is a common praxis,
one that can only be the result of an actualization of reason. Far from
understanding the tie to comprehensive values as an end in itself,
the Critical Theorist views the establishing of a cooperative context as fulfilling the function of increasing social rationality. Otherwise it would not be clear why the identified forms of praxis in
each case should always be the result of a social rationalization, or
why the negative state of the present must always be an expression of deficient rationality. In contrast to communitarianism, Critical Theory subjects universality – which should be both embodied by and realized through social cooperation – to the standards
of rational justification. While there may be various conceptions of
reason in Critical Theory from Horkheimer to Habermas, they all
ultimately come to the same idea, namely, that the turn to a liberating praxis of cooperation should not result from affective bonds or
from feelings of membership or agreement, but rather from rational
insight.

The tradition of Critical Theory thus differs from both liberalism and communitarianism by virtue of a particular kind of ethical perfectionism. To be sure, unlike the liberal tradition, Critical
Theory holds that the normative goal of society should consist
in making self-actualization mutually possible. But, at the same
time, it understands its recommendation of this goal to be the
well-grounded result of a certain analysis of the human process of
development. As is already the case with Hegel, it seems that the
boundaries between description, on the one hand, and prescription

and normative grounding, on the other, are blurred here as well. The explanation of the circumstances that have blocked or skewed the process of the actualization of reason should have in and of itself the rational force to convince subjects to create a social praxis of cooperation. The perfection of society that all the members of Critical Theory have in mind must be, according to their common view, the result of enlightenment through analysis. The explanatory interpretation that they offer to this end, however, is no longer written in the language of Hegel's philosophy of spirit. Rather, there is a general consensus that a definitive "sociologizing" of the categorial frame of reference is a precondition for such an analysis. The second defining feature of Critical Theory, then, consists in the attempt to explain sociologically the pathological deformation of reason. And this deserves as much of a place in the legacy of Critical Theory for today as is rightly accorded to the idea of cooperative self-actualization.

II

There is a growing tendency today for social criticism to be practiced in a form that is without a component of sociological explanation. This development arises from the fact that it is considered for the most part sufficient to expose certain injustices in society on the basis of well-founded values or norms. The question of why those affected do not themselves problematize or attack such moral evils is no longer seen as falling within the purview of social criticism as such. The division that has been established as a result is undermined, however, as soon as a causal connection is produced between the existence of social injustices and the absence of any public reaction. Social injustice would then be seen as possessing, among other things, the property of causing directly and on its own the silence or apathy that is expressed by the absence of public reaction.

A supposition of this kind serves as the basis for most of the approaches of Critical Theory. However strongly influenced by Marx they may be in their particulars, almost all of the approaches to Critical Theory share a central premise operative in his analysis of capitalism concerning this one point: the social circumstances that constitute the pathology of capitalist societies have the peculiar structural feature of disguising precisely those states of affairs that would otherwise provide particularly urgent grounds for public criticism. Just as one can find the assumption sketched above in Marx's account of "fetishism" or in his theory of "reification,"[12] it is present in Critical Theory in concepts such as "false consciousness," "one-dimensionality," or "positivism" (see generally *DE*, *O*, introduction to *PDGS* and *TRS* 81–121). Such concepts are means for characterizing a system of convictions and practices that has the paradoxical quality of distracting one's attention from the very social conditions that structurally produce that system. For the kind of social criticism that Critical Theory practices, this observation leads to a broadening of the tasks that must be carried out. In contrast to the approaches that have achieved dominance today, Critical Theory must couple the critique of social injustice with an explanation of the processes that obscure that injustice, for only when one can convince the addressees by means of such an explanatory analysis that they can be deceived about the real character of their social conditions, can the wrongfulness of those conditions be publicly demonstrated with some prospect of acceptance. Because a relationship of cause and effect is assumed to obtain between social injustice and the absence of any negative reaction to it, normative criticism in Critical Theory has to be complemented by an element of historical explanation. A historical process of the deformation of reason must causally explain the failure of a rational universal, a failure that constitutes the social pathology of the present. This explanation must at the same time make intelligible the dethematization of social injustices in public discussion.

Within Critical Theory, there has always been agreement that the historical process of a deformation of reason can be explained only within a sociological framework. Although the ethical intuition behind the whole undertaking ultimately sustains itself on the Hegelian idea of a rational universal, its proponents are at the same time so much the heirs of classical sociological thinkers that they are no longer able to draw upon the idealist concept of reason when explaining deviations from that universality. Instead, the processes of deformation that have contributed to a lack of social rationality – to the establishment of a "particular rationality" (*P* 24; *AGS* x.1, 17) – come to be analyzed within a categorial framework, which emerges from Horkheimer to Habermas, in which there is a theoretical synthesis of Marx and Max Weber. Marx had indeed already stood the Hegelian concept of reason "right side up again" when he tied the expansion of justified knowledge to the completion of a social praxis, in virtue of which subjects might step-by-step improve the conditions of their material reproduction. It would no longer be the internal compulsion of spirit but rather the external challenges of nature that would lead to a learning process consisting in a science of experience that justifies talk of the actualization of reason. But Marx's anthropological epistemology was insufficient for the Critical Theorists to give a truly sociological explanation of the historical process that Hegel had described in his philosophy as the self-unfolding of spirit. Only by taking up key concepts in Weber – whose early reception was often influenced by an unconventional Lukácsian reading[13] – is the picture first made complete, at least insofar as the connection between any praxis-bound learning process and social institutionalization is significantly clarified. In blending together Weber and Marx, the members of the Frankfurt School arrive at the shared conviction that the potential of human reason unfolds in a historical learning process in which rational solutions to problems are inextricably bound up with conflicts regarding the monopolization of knowledge. Subjects respond to the objective challenges that are posed at every stage – both by nature and by social organization – by constantly improving their knowledge of action; yet this knowledge is so deeply embedded in social conflicts over power and domination that it achieves a lasting form in institutions often only to the exclusion of certain other groups. For Critical Theory it thus remains beyond doubt that one must understand the Hegelian actualization of reason as conflictual – that is, as a multilayered learning process in which knowledge that can be generalized is only gradually won by improved solutions to problems and against the opposing groups in power.

Of course, this fundamental idea in the history of Critical Theory has also been subjected to constant revision. Initially, Horkheimer relates this conflictual learning process only to the working over of nature, making it difficult to imagine how rational improvements are also supposed to have taken place in the organization of social life (CT 188–243; HGS IV, 162–216).[14] Adorno widens the spectrum, in the wake of Weber's sociology of music, by recognizing a rationalization in the arrangement of artistic material, one that serves the goal of extending calculative sovereignty into aesthetic praxis (SF 1–14; AGS XVI, 9–23). In the work of Marcuse one can find indications that would seem to justify assuming a collective learning process, with corresponding setbacks resulting from formations of power, even in the acquisition of internal nature (EC 117–26). Habermas is the first to achieve a systematic breakdown of the various learning processes, an analysis he grounds on the variety of ways in which human beings relate to the world through linguistic praxis. He is convinced that we can expect human rational potential to develop along at least two paths: one directed towards an increase in knowledge of the objective world, the other towards a more just solution to interactive conflicts (TRS 81–121; TCA II, ch. 6). But the gain in differentiation comes at the cost of no longer being able to consider historical growth in rationality together with those social conflicts that, following Weber's sociology of domination, were more clearly present to early critical theorists. In Habermas's work we find a gulf between (a) the dimension that, for instance, Bourdieu investigates in the processes of the cultural formation of monopolies,[15] and (b) rational learning processes – a gulf whose presence is fundamentally inconsistent with the original concerns of the Critical tradition. Nevertheless, because Critical Theory requires a postidealist version of the thesis that Hegel outlined in his conception of the actualization of reason, it cannot forego the degree of differentiation that Habermas's conception of rationality exemplifies. In order to be able to see the ways in which socially institutionalized knowledge has rationalized itself – that is, how it has exhibited an increasing degree of reflexivity in the overcoming of social problems – one must distinguish just as many aspects of rationality as there are socially perceivable challenges involved in the reproduction of societies, which reproduction is dependent upon agreement. In contrast to Habermas's approach, which carries out such a differentiation on the basis of the structural particularities of human language, there may be a superior conception that ties the aspects of social rationalization (in an internal realist sense) more closely to the ability of socially established values to disclose problems. In that case invariant values of linguistic communication would not reveal the direction in which the rationalization of social knowledge is to proceed. Rather, the historically produced values present in social spheres of significance would play this role. Furthermore, the concept of reason with which Critical Theory attempts to grasp the increases in rationality in human history is subject to the pressure of incorporating foreign and new, and particularly non-European, points of view. For this reason it is not surprising that the concept of social rationality must also take on an ever wider and more differentiated meaning in order to be able to take into account the multifaceted nature of learning processes. In any case, it is a postidealist version of the Hegelian notion of the actualization of reason that now provides the necessary background for the idea that may well form the fundamental core of the entire Critical Theory tradition from Horkheimer to Habermas. According to that tradition, the process of social rationalization through the societal structure unique to capitalism has become interrupted or distorted in a way that makes pathologies that accompany the loss of a rational universal unavoidable.

One finds the key to this thesis, in which all the elements treated separately up until now are brought together, in a concept of capitalism energized by a theory of rationality. It is not difficult to see that Critical Theory has achieved such a concept less through a reception of Marx's works than through the impetus provided by the early theory of Lukács. With *History and Class Consciousness* it is first possible to glimpse in the institutional reality of modern capitalism an organizational form of society that is structurally tied to a certain, limited state of rationality. For Lukács, who was by his own admission significantly influenced by Weber and Georg Simmel, the characteristic feature of this form of rationality consists in the fact that its subjects are forced into a type of practice that makes them "spectators without influence,"[16] divorced from their needs and intentions. The mechanized production of parts and the exchange of goods demand a form of perception in which all other human beings appear to be thinglike, unfeeling entities, such that social interaction is bereft of any attention to those qualities that are valuable in themselves. If we were to describe the result of Lukács's analysis in a terminology closer to contemporary ideas, we might say that a certain form of praxis which is dominant in capitalism compels indifference towards those aspects of other human beings that are valuable. Instead of relating to one another with mutual recognition, subjects perceive themselves as objects that are identified only according to the interests of each.[17] In any case, it is this diagnosis of Lukács that provides Critical Theory with a categorial framework within which it is possible to speak of an interruption or distortion of the process of the actualization of reason. With the historical learning process taken as basic, the structural forces of society that Lukács reveals in modern capitalism present themselves as obstacles to a socially latent rationality that is on the threshold of the modern age. The organizational form of social relations in capitalism prevents the application to practical life of those rational principles which, as far as our cognitive potential is concerned, are already at hand.

Of course, we must again qualify this explanatory scheme according to the various presuppositions regarding the manner and course of the historical process of rationalization that are at work in each case of Critical Theory. In Horkheimer, for example, one finds the thesis that the capitalist organization of production brings with it an opposition of individual interests that hinders "application of the whole spiritual and physical means of dominating nature" (CT 213; HGS IV, 187). Horkheimer later broadens his reflections in concert with Adorno, via the somewhat implausible hypothesis that there is an emotional rationality inherent in the form of interaction between nineteenth-century bourgeois families whose potential could not be brought into play because of increasing tension introduced by competition and monopolization (CT 47–128; HGS III, 336–417).[18] The work of Adorno, in particular his *Minima Moralia*, is full of such speculations that inevitably take the form of a diagnosis of the growing impossibility of a type of love which, in the family, was able to reconcile individual and general interests without coercion. The social privileging of rationally purposive, utilitarian attitudes in capitalism prevents the development of a nonlegalistic form of a rational universal that is inherent in the structure of private relationships in the form of mutual affection and forgiveness (MM 30–2, 167–9, 172; AGS IV, 32–3, 188–90, 193–4). Marcuse, roughly taking Schiller's *Letters on the Aesthetic Education of Mankind* as his guide, describes the process of increasing aesthetic sensibility as ending with modern capitalism – a form of society that he, like Lukács (though also with an air of Heidegger), depicts as a complex of generalized knowledge at one's disposal (EC 117–26).[19] Finally, in Habermas we find the idea that one cannot separate the potential of communicative rationality from capitalist conditions because the imperative of economic exploitation penetrates even the sphere of the social. Even though the family and the political public have long since emancipated themselves from their traditional bases of legitimization, the principles of rational communication cannot gain acceptance in those settings because they are increasingly infiltrated by the mechanisms of systematic management (*TCA* II, ch. 8). However different these attempts at an explanation may be, the basic scheme of a critique of capitalism underlying each of them remains the same. Critical Theorists, not unlike Lukács (though in a more sophisticated manner and without the excessive historical emphasis on the proletariat), perceive capitalism as a social form of organization in which practices and ways of thinking prevail that prevent the social utilization of a rationality already made possible by history. And this historical obstruction presents at the same time a moral or ethical challenge because it precludes the possibility of orienting oneself in terms of a rational universal, the impetus to which could only come from a fully realized rationality. Whether the concept of capitalism, grounded in a theory of rationality and underlying the interpretation of history outlined here, can once again be recovered today is certainly an open question. The possibilities for organizing the activity of a capitalist economy seem too multifarious, as well as too mixed up in other nonrationally purposive patterns of social activity, to reduce the attitudes of the actors involved to a single pattern of instrumental rationality. Newer studies also suggest, however, that in capitalist societies those attitudes or orientations most rewarded with social success are those whose fixation on individual advantages demands merely strategic associations with oneself and other subjects.[20] As a result, we cannot exclude the possibility of still interpreting capitalism as the institutional result of a cultural lifestyle or of a product of social imagination[21] in which a certain type of restricted, "reifying" rationality is the dominant praxis.

But the commonalities within Critical Theory transcend this point. Its central representatives share not only the same formal scheme of diagnosing capitalism as a set of social relations of blocked or distorted rationality but also the same idea about the proper method of therapy. The forces that contribute to the overcoming of the social pathology are supposed to stem from precisely that reason whose actualization is impeded by the form of organization present in capitalist society. Just as was the case with the other elements of the theory, a classical figure of modern thought plays a formative role here too: Freud has the same significance for the central content of Critical Theory as do Hegel, Marx, Weber, and Lukács. It is from his psychoanalytic theory that Critical Theory takes the thought that social pathologies must always express themselves in a type of suffering that keeps alive the interest in the emancipatory power of reason.

III

Today, even the question of how one might practically overcome injustice no longer generally falls within the domain of social criticism. With the exception of approaches modeled upon Foucault that take transformation of the individual's relation to herself as a condition of criticism,[22] the question concerning the relationship between theory and praxis remains closed off from contemporary consideration. Explanation of the causes that may be responsible for obscuring social injustice are thought to belong just as little to the business of criticism as do perspectival characterizations of the conversion of knowledge into praxis. One such perspective calls for a social-psychological theory of the subject that will explain why individuals who themselves are conditioned by a particular way of thinking and praxis should be further responsive to the rational content of the theory. It must explain whence the subjective forces can come that – in spite of all the delusion, one-dimensionality, and fragmentation – would still offer a chance for conversion of knowledge into praxis. However heterogeneous the field of social criticism may be today, one feature of it is typical: there is scarcely any approach that understands such a characterization to be part of its proper task. The question concerning the motivational state of the subjects that must be the focus of attention here is instead largely passed over because one no longer expects reflection on the conditions of conversion into praxis to be a part of critique.

Nevertheless, Critical Theory from its beginnings has been so greatly indebted to the tradition of left Hegelianism that it considers the initiation of a critical praxis that can contribute to the overcoming of social pathology to be an essential part of its task (*PD* ch. 3).[23] Even where skepticism regarding the possibility of practical enlightenment prevails among its authors (see, e.g. *CM* 289–94; *AGS* x.2: 794–9), the drama surrounding the question of enlightenment arises merely out of the assumed necessity of an internal connection between theory and praxis. Critical Theory, however, no longer understands the determination of this mediation as a task that one might undertake by philosophical reflection alone. Instead of appealing to a speculative philosophy of history, which for a Marx or a Lukács was wholly self-evident, Critical Theory relies on the new instrument of empirical social research for information about the critical readiness of the public.[24] The result of this methodological reorientation, which constitutes a further distinctive feature of Critical Theory, is a sobering assessment of the state of consciousness of the proletariat. Contrary to what is assumed in the Marxist wing of left Hegelianism, the working class does not automatically develop a revolutionary readiness to convert the critical content of theory into society-changing praxis as a result of the consummation of the mechanized production of parts.[25] The idea that Critical Theory could provide the continuity between theory and praxis by merely appealing to a certain predetermined addressee is thus abandoned, and the considerations that take its place all come down to the expectation that the conversion into praxis will be effected by precisely that rationality which the social pathology has distorted but not wholly dispossessed. In place of the proletariat, whose social situation had previously been considered the guarantor of responsiveness to the critical content of the theory, a submerged rational capacity must resurface for which all subjects in principle have the same motivational aptitude.

Admittedly, this kind of change in perspective demands an additional line of thought, for, at first glance, it is not at all clear why the motivation of critical praxis should be expected from the same rationality that according to the theory is highly deformed. In other words, how can Critical Theorists trust that they will find a necessary degree of rational readiness for the conversion into praxis if the socially practiced rationality turns out indeed to be pathologically disrupted or distorted? The answer to this question falls within an area of Critical Theory that is established on a continuum between psychoanalysis and moral psychology. Its continual task is to uncover the motivational roots that sustain the readiness for moral cognition in individual subjects despite any rational impediment. Here it is helpful to distinguish between two steps of the argument, even if Critical Theorists have not always drawn a clear distinction between them. From the fact that a deficit in social rationality leads to symptoms of a social pathology, one first infers that subjects suffer from the state of society. No individual can avoid seeing herself as being impeded by the consequences of a deformation of reason (or being so described) because, with the loss of a rational universal, the chances of a successful self-actualization that depends on mutual cooperation are also diminished. Critical Theory undoubtedly takes Freudian psychoanalysis as its methodological model for the way in which it establishes a connection between defective rationality and individual suffering. Certainly a similar connection is already to be found in Hegel's critique of romanticism, which cannot have been without influence on the Frankfurt School; yet the impetus for bringing the category of "suffering" into connection with the very pathologies of social rationality probably finds its origin in the Freudian idea that each neurotic illness arises from an impeding of the rational ego and must lead to an individual case of stress from suffering. The methodological application of this fundamental idea of psychoanalysis to the field of social analysis is not just a theoretical move that Habermas has contributed to Critical Theory (*KHI* ch. 12). In his early essays, Horkheimer already describes social irrationality in concepts modeled on Freud's theory, insofar as they measure the degree of social pathology by the strength of the effect of the forces foreign to the ego (*BPSS* 111–28; *KT* 9–30). And everywhere Adorno speaks of individual or social suffering, one can hear overtones of the Freudian supposition that subjects must suffer under the neurotic restriction of their genuinely rational capacities. Thus one reads in *Negative Dialectics* that every suffering possesses an "inward-turning form of reflection": "the moment of the flesh proclaims the knowledge that suffering ought not be, that things should be different" (*ND* 203; *AGS* VI, 203). The deployment of this concept of suffering – which surfaces here as an instance of the experience of the interplay between spiritual and physical forces – has unfortunately remained up until now largely unexplored within the reception of Critical Theory.[26] A more precise analysis would probably show that, as with Freud, suffering expresses the feeling of not being able to endure the "loss of ego (capacities)" (*AGS* VIII, 437). From Horkheimer to Habermas, Critical Theory has been guided by the idea that the pathology of social rationality leads to cases of impedance that frequently manifest themselves in the painful experience of the loss of rational capacities. In the end, this idea comes down to the strong and frankly anthropological thesis that human subjects cannot be indifferent about the restriction of their rational capacities. Because their self-actualization is tied to the presupposition of a cooperative rational activity, they cannot avoid suffering psychologically under its deformation. This insight – that there must be an internal connection between psychological intactness and undistorted rationality – is perhaps the strongest impetus that Freud provides for Critical Theory; every investigation that is now conducted (though with improved methods) supports it.

But it is only by taking a second step, which Critical Theory does only rather implicitly, that one can extract from this thesis a means by which the severed relations to praxis can be intellectually restored. And it is once again Freud who provides the decisive suggestion: the stress from suffering presses towards a cure by means of exactly the same rational powers whose function the pathology impedes. An assumption about what in general is to count as a self-evident condition for admission into psychoanalytic treatment also accompanies this suggestion – namely, that the individual who subjectively suffers from a neurotic illness also wants to be free from that suffering. In Critical Theory, it is not always clear whether the stress from suffering that strives towards its cure pertains only to subjective experience or also to an "objective" event. While Adorno, who speaks of suffering as a "subjective impulse," seems to have the first alternative in mind, Horkheimer frequently uses formulations in which social suffering is treated as a magnitude of feeling that is objectively attributable. In the case of Habermas, there is sufficient evidence, particularly in his *Theory of Communicative Action*, to suggest the "subjective" alternative, and one can find both alternatives at work in Marcuse.[27]

In any case, Critical Theory presupposes that this subjectively experienced or objectively attributable suffering among members of society must lead to that same desire for healing and for liberation from social evils that the analyzer must impute to her patients. Moreover, in each case the interest in one's own recovery is supposed to be documented by the readiness to reactivate, against any resistance, those rational powers that the individual or social pathology has deformed. All the thinkers belonging to the inner circle of Critical Theory expect in their addressees a latent interest in rational explanation or interpretation, since only winning back an integral rationality can satisfy the desire for liberation from suffering. It is this risky assumption that permits a different connection of theory to praxis from the one that the Marxist tradition provides. The Critical Theorists share with their audience neither a space of common objectives nor one of political projects, but rather a space of potentially common reasons that holds the pathological present open to the possibility of transformation through rational insight. Here, as well, one must consider the differences of opinion that prevail between the individual members of the School. One can best assess them by seeing which social-psychological or anthropological assumptions substantiate the thesis that an individual responsiveness to rational arguments remains possible within any deformation of social life. Turning to Horkheimer on this point, we find the idea that the memory of emotional security from early childhood sustains the interest in overcoming that form of rationality committed to merely instrumental disposition. It remains unclear, however, how such a psychological drive is supposed to be directed at the same time towards attaining an "intact," nonreduced rational power. If we assemble Adorno's scattered reflections on the topic, there is something to be said for seeing in the "mimetic sense" (*mimetisches Gespür*) more than just an impulse to assimilate (to) the threatening object. We should also see in it the inexhaustible remnant of a desire to grasp the other intellectually in a way which leaves the other its singular existence.[28] We can find such characterizations in Marcuse, as is well known, in a theory that involves erotic impulses of a life-drive whose aesthetic actualization requires a "conscious effort of free rationality" (*EC* 204). It has been frequently asked of this project, however, whether it sufficiently guarantees an expanded concept of social rationality.[29] Finally, Habermas had originally assumed in his version of an anthropology of knowledge of the human species an "emancipatory interest" that focuses on the experience of a discourse praxis that is structurally present in a state of noncoercion and equality (*KHI* ch. 3). This early conception has since given way to a theory of discourse that no longer makes anthropological claims, yet retains an assumption that the praxis of argumentative discourse always allows the individual to be responsive to better reasons (*TJ* 277–92). All of these reflections present answers to the question of what the experiences, practices, or needs are that allow an interest in full rational realization to continue to exist in human beings despite the deformation or skewing of social rationality. Only so long as the theory can count upon such a rational impulse for its grounding will it be able to relate itself reflexively to a potential praxis in which the explanation it offers is implemented with a view to the liberation from suffering. Critical Theory will only be able to continue in the form in which it has developed from Horkheimer to Habermas if it does not forsake the proof of such interests. Without a realistic concept of "emancipatory interest" that puts at its center the idea of an indestructible core of rational responsiveness on the part of subjects, this Critical project will have no future.

With this last thought, the development of the motifs that constitute the core content of the legacy of Critical Theory has reached a matter-of-fact conclusion. The sequence of systematic ideas developed above forms a unity from which no individual component can be omitted without consequences. So long as we do not abandon the aim of understanding Critical Theory as a form of reflection belonging to an historically effective reason, it will not be easy to give up the normative motif of a rational universal, the idea of a social pathology of reason, and the concept of emancipatory interest. Yet it is also apparent that none of these three components of thought can still be maintained today in the theoretical form in which the members of the Frankfurt School originally developed it. All require conceptual reformulation and the mediation of the present state of our knowledge if they are still to fulfill the function that was once intended for them. That said, the field of tasks is outlined – tasks which are now left to the heirs of Critical Theory in the twenty-first century.

NOTES

This chapter was translated from the German by James Hebbeler.

1. Jürgen Habermas, "Nach Dreißig Jahren: Bemerkungen zu *Erkenntnis und Interesse*," in *Das Interesse der Vernunft*, ed. S. Müller-Doohm (Frankfurt am Main: Suhrkamp, 1999), p. 12.

2. For an exemplary work of social criticism in Foucault's sense, see James Tully, "Political Philosophy as Critical Activity," *Political Theory* 30 (2002): 533–55. On Michael Walzer, see his Tanner Lectures, published as *Interpretation and Social Criticism* (Cambridge, Mass.: Harvard University Press, 1987). I have attempted to develop a criticism of this model of social criticism in my "Idiosynkrasie als Erkenntnismittel.

Gesellschaftskritik im Zeitalter des normalisierten Intellektuellen," in *Der kritische Blick*, ed. U. J. Wenzel (Frankfurt am Main: Suhrkamp, 2002), pp. 61–79.

3. On the concept of "negativity," and above all on the distinction between content-centered and methodological negativism, see Michael Theunissen, *Das Selbst auf dem Grund der Verzweiflung: Kierkegaards negativistische Methode* (Berlin: Hain, 1999) and his "Negativität bei Adorno," in *Adorno-Konferenz 1983*, ed. L. von Friedeburg and J. Habermas (Frankfurt am Main: Suhrkamp, 1983), pp. 41–65.

4. On the distinction between the center and the periphery of Critical Theory, see my "Critical Theory," in *Social Theory Today*, ed. A. Giddens and J. Turner (Stanford: Stanford University Press, 1987), pp. 347–82.

5. On this distinction, see my "Pathologien des Sozialen. Tradition und Aktualität der Sozialphilosophie," in *Das Andere der Gerechtigkeit* (Frankfurt am Main: Suhrkamp, 2000), pp. 11–87.

6. See my *Leiden an Unbestimmtheit. Eine Reaktualisierung der Hegelschen Rechtsphilosophie* (Stuttgart: Reclam, 2001); Michael Theunissen, *Selbstverwirklichung und Allgemeinheit. Zur Kritik des gegenwärtigen Bewusstseins* (Berlin: de Gruyter, 1982).

7. See also Maeve Cook, *Language and Reason: A Study of Habermas's Pragmatics* (Cambridge, Mass.: MIT Press, 1994), especially ch. 5.

8. The aim of proceduralizing the Hegelian idea of a rational universal is especially clear in Habermas, "On Social Identity," *Telos* 19 (1974): 91–103.

9. It is this ethical perspective that I think presents a certain point of contact between Critical Theory and American pragmatism. As the reactions to pragmatism of the first generation essentially range from skepticism to outright disapproval, it is all the more astonishing that it is only with Habermas that a productive reception of pragmatism sets in. On the history of its reception, see Hans Joas, "An Underestimated Alternative: America and the Limits of 'Critical Theory,'" in *Pragmatism and Social Theory* (Chicago: University of Chicago Press, 1993), pp. 79–93.

10. On this motif, see Martin Steel, "Adornos kontemplative Ethik. Philosophie. Eine Kolumne," *Merkur* 638 (2002): 512ff.

11. On communitarianism, see generally *Kommunitarianismus. Eine Debatte über die moralischen Grundlagen moderner Gesellschaften*, ed. A. Honneth (Frankfurt am Main: Campus, 1993).

12. Marx, *Capital I*, in *The Marx-Engels Reader*, ed. R. Tucker (New York: Norton, 1978), pp. 319–29. For an excellent analysis, see Georg Lohmann, *Indifferenz und Gesellschaft. Eine kritische*

Auseinandersetzung mit Marx (Frankfurt am Main: Campus, 1991), especially ch. 5.

13. Georg Lukács, "Reification and the Consciousness of the Proletariat," in his *History and Class Consciousness* (Cambridge, Mass.: MIT Press, 1971), pp. 83–221. On the significance of the Lukácsian analysis of reification for early Critical Theory, see *TCA* i, ch. 6.

14. See my *The Critique of Power: Reflective Stages in a Critical Social Theory* (Cambridge, Mass.: MIT Press, 1991), ch. 1.

15. See Pierre Bourdieu and Jean-Claude Passeron, *La Reproduction: éléments d'une théorie du système d'enseignement* (Paris: Minuit, 1970).

16. Lukács, *History and Class Consciousness*, pp. 90–1.

17. See my "Invisibility: On the Epistemology of 'Recognition,'" *Proceedings of the Aristotelian Society*, supplement (2001): 111–26.

18. Horkheimer develops the same motif with unmistakable religious undertones in his "Die verwaltete Welt kennt keine Liebe, Gespräch mit Janko Muselin," in *HGS* vii, 358–67.

19. See also Johànn Arnason, *Von Marcuse zu Marx* (Neuwied and Berlin: Luchterhand, 1971), especially ch. 5.

20. See, for example, Anthony Giddens, *Modernity and Self-Identity: Self and Society in the Late Modern Age* (Stanford: Stanford University Press, 1991), pp. 196ff.

21. Of significance in this connection are Wilhelm Hennis, *Max Webers Fragestellung* (Tübingen: Mohr, 1987) and Cornelius Castoriadis, *Gesellschaft als imaginäre Institution* (Frankfurt am Main: Suhrkamp, 1984). For a more recent study, see Luc Boltanski and Eva Chiapello, *Le Nouvel esprit du capitalisme* (Paris: Gallimard, 1999).

22. Exemplary in this connection is Judith Butler, *The Psychic Life of Power: Theories in Subjection* (Stanford: Stanford University Press, 1997), chs. 2–4.

23. See also Karl Löwith, *From Hegel to Nietzsche: The Revolution in Nineteenth-Century Thought*, trans. D. Green (New York: Columbia University Press, 1964), pt. 1, ch. 2.

24. See Erich Fromm, *The Working Class in Weimar Germany: A Psychological and Sociological Study*, trans. B. Weinberger (Cambridge, Mass.: Harvard University Press, 1984).

25. See Helmut Dubiel, *Theory and Politics: Studies in the Development of Critical Theory*, trans. B. Gregg (Cambridge, Mass.: MIT Press, 1985), pt. A, ch. 5.

26. For an exception to this generalization, see Josef Früchtl, *Mimesis. Konstellation eines Zentralbegriffs bei Adorno* (Würzburg: Königshausen & Neumann, 1986), ch. 3.2.

27. See, for example, the reflections on Marx in Habermas, *TCA* II, ch. 8. Habermas wavers here, however, between a life-world use and a merely functional use of the idea of a social pathology.
28. See Früchtl, *Mimesis*, ch. 5.3.
29. See *Gespräche mit Herbert Marcuse*, ed. J. Habermas, S. Bovenschen, *et al.* (Frankfurt am Main: Suhrkamp, 1978).

SELECT BIBLIOGRAPHY

This bibliography is intended to provide the anglophone reader with references to the major works of individual members of the Frankfurt School, and also to be a source for important secondary literature. Select secondary materials in English have thus been emphasized, and only essential sources written in German have been included. For more in-depth bibliographies pertaining to single figures, readers might consult the volumes in the Companions to Philosophy series devoted to Adorno and Habermas. An excellent general bibliography may be found in Rolf Wiggershaus, *The Frankfurt School: Its History, Theories, and Political Significance*, trans. M. Robertson (Cambridge, Mass.: MIT Press, 1994). More exhaustive bibliographies can be found in the following:

Goertzen, René. *Jürgen Habermas: Eine Bibliographie seiner Schriften und der Sekundärliteratur 1952–81*. Frankfurt am Main: Suhrkamp, 1982.

"Theodor Adorno. Vorläufige Bibliographie seiner Schriften und der Sekundärliteratur." In *Adorno-Konfernz 1983*. Ed. Ludwig von Friedeburg and Jürgen Habermas. Frankfurt am Main: Suhrkamp, 1983, pp. 404–71.

Nordquist, Joan. *Herbert Marcuse (II): A Bibliography*. Social Theory: A Bibliographic Series, no. 58. Santa Cruz, Calif.: Reference and Research Services, 2000.

Tiedemann, Rolf. "Bibliographie der Erstdrucke von Benjamins Schriften." In *Zur Aktualität Walter Benjamins*. Ed. Siegfried Unself. Frankfurt am Main: Suhrkamp, 1972, pp. 227–97.

MAJOR WORKS OF CRITICAL THEORY IN GERMAN

Adorno

Gesammelte Schriften. Ed. Rolf Tiedemann. Frankfurt am Main: Suhrkamp, 1970–97.
Nachgelassene Schriften. Ed. C. Gödde, T. Schröder, R. Tiedemann, *et al.* Frankfurt am Main: Suhrkamp, 1993.

Benjamin

Gesammelte Schriften. Ed. Rolf Tiedemann and Herbert Schweppenhäuser. Frankfurt am Main: Suhrkamp, 1972–89.

Habermas

Der philosophische Diskurs der Moderne. Zwölf Vorlesungen. Frankfurt am Main: Suhrkamp, 1985.
Erkenntnis und Interesse. Frankfurt am Main: Suhrkamp, 1968.
Erläuterungen zur Diskursethik. Frankfurt am Main: Suhrkamp, 1991.
Faktizität und Geltung. Frankfurt am Main: Suhrkamp, 1992.
Kleine politische Schriften. Vols. I–IV. Frankfurt am Main: Suhrkamp, 1981.
Legitimationsprobleme im Spätkapitalismus. Frankfurt am Main: Suhrkamp, 1971.
Moralbewußtsein und kommunikatives Handeln. Frankfurt am Main: Suhrkamp, 1983.
Nachmetaphysisches Denken. Philosophische Aufsätze. Frankfurt am Main: Suhrkamp, 1988.
Philosophisch-politische Profile. Frankfurt am Main: Suhrkamp, 1971.
Strukturwandel der Öffentlichkeit. Frankfurt am Main: Suhrkamp, 1962.
Technik und Wissenschaft als "Ideologie." Frankfurt am Main: Suhrkamp, 1968.
Theorie der Gesellschaft oder Sozialtechnologie. Was leistet die Systemforschung? With Niklas Luhmann. Frankfurt am Main: Suhrkamp, 1971.
Theorie des kommunikativen Handelns. Vols. I–II. Frankfurt am Main: Suhrkamp, 1981.
Theorie und Praxis. Sozialphilosophische Studien. Frankfurt am Main: Suhrkamp, 1963.
Vorstudien und Ergänzungen zur Theorie des Kommunikativen Handelns. Frankfurt am Main: Suhrkamp, 1984.
Wahrheit und Rechtfertigung. Philosophische Aufsätze. Frankfurt am Main: Suhrkamp, 1999.

Zur Rekonstruktion des Historischen Materialismus. Frankfurt am Main: Suhrkamp, 1976.

Horkheimer

Gesammelte Schriften. Ed. G. Schmid-Noerr and A. Schmidt. Frankfurt am Main: Fischer, 1987–.
Kritische Theorie. 2 vols. Frankfurt am Main: Fischer, 1968.

Marcuse

Nachgelassene Schriften. Ed. P.-E. Jansen. Frankfurt am Main: Klampen, 1999–.
Schriften. Frankfurt am Main: Suhrkamp, 1978–89.

Neumann

Demokratischer und autoritärer Staat. Beiträge zur Soziologie der Politik. Amsterdam: European Press, 1971.

Pollock

Stadien des Kapitalismus. Ed. H. Dubiel. Munich: C. H. Beck, 1985.

MAJOR WORKS OF CRITICAL THEORY IN ENGLISH OR IN ENGLISH TRANSLATION

Anthologies of multiple authors

Adey, G. and Frisby, D. (trans.). *The Postivism Dispute in German Sociology.* London: Heinemann, 1969.
Arato, Andrew and Gebhardt, Eike (eds.). *The Essential Frankfurt School Reader.* New York: Continuum, 1978.
Bronner, S. E. and Kellner, D. (eds.). *Critical Theory and Society.* New York and London: Routledge, 1990.
Jameson, Fredric (ed.). *Aesthetics and Politics.* London: Verso, 1977.

Adorno

Aesthetic Theory. Trans. R. Hullot-Kentor. Minneapolis: University of Minnesota Press, 1998.
Against Epistemology: A Metacritique. Trans. W. Domingo. Cambridge, Mass.: MIT Press, 1983.

The Autoritarian Personality. With Else Frenkel-Brunswik, Daniel Levinson *et al.* New York: Norton, 1969.

Dialectic of Enlightenment. With Horkheimer. Trans. E. F. N. Jephcott. Stanford: Stanford University Press, 2002.

Essays on Music. Ed. R. Leppert and trans. S. Gillespie. Berkeley: University of California Press, 2002.

Hegel: Three Studies. Trans. S. W. Nicholson. Cambridge, Mass.: MIT Press, 1994.

In Search of Wagner. Trans. R. Livingstone. London: New Left Books, 1981.

Introduction to the Sociology of Music. Trans. E. B. Ashton. New York: Seabury, 1976.

The Jargon of Authenticity. Trans. K. Tarnowski and F. Will. Chicago: North-western University Press, 1973.

Kierkegaard: Construction of the Aesthetic. Trans. R. Hullot-Kentor. Minneapolis: University of Minnesota Press, 1989.

Mahler: A Musical Physiognomy. Trans. E. F. N. Jephcott. Chicago: University of Chicago Press, 1988.

Minima Moralia. Trans. E. F. N. Jephcott. New York and London: Verso, 1978.

Negative Dialectics. Trans. E. B. Ashton. London: Routledge, 1973.

Notes to Literature. Vol. I. Trans. S. W. Nicholson. New York: Columbia University Press, 1991.

Notes to Literature. Vol. II. Trans. S. W. Nicholson. New York: Columbia University Press, 1992.

The Philosophy of Modern Music. Trans. A. Mitchell and W. Blomster. New York: Seabury, 1973.

The Positivist Dispute in German Sociology. Trans. G. Adley and D. Frisby. London: Heinemann, 1976.

Prisms. Trans. Samuel Weber and Sherry Weber. Cambridge, Mass.: MIT Press, 1983.

Quasi una Fantasia. Trans. R. Livingstone. New York: Continuum, 1992.

Benjamin

The Arcades Project. Trans. H. Eiland and K. McLaughlin. Cambridge, Mass.: Harvard Belknap Press, 1999.

The Origin of German Tragic Drama. Trans. J. Osborne. New York and London: Verso, 1998.

Selected Writings 1913–1926. Ed. M. W. Jennings, M. Jenning, and M. P. Bullock. Cambridge, Mass.: Harvard Belknap Press, 1996.

Selected Writings 1927–1934. Ed. M. W. Jennings, H. Eiland, M. P. Bullock, *et al.* Cambridge, Mass.: Harvard Belknap Press, 1999.

Selected Writings: 1935–1938. Ed. M. W. Jennings, H. Eiland, M. P. Bullock, *et al.* Cambridge, Mass.: Harvard Belknap Press, 2002.

Fromm

Escape from Freedom. New York: Farrar & Rinehart, 1941.
Marx's Concept of Man. New York: Continuum, 1961.

Habermas

Between Facts and Norms. Trans. W. Rehg. Cambridge, Mass.: MIT Press, 1998.
Communication and the Evolution of Society. Trans. T. McCarthy. Boston: Beacon Press, 1979.
Knowledge and Human Interests. Trans. J. Shapiro. Boston: Beacon Press, 1971.
Legitimization Crisis. Trans. T. McCarthy. Boston: Beacon Press, 1975.
Moral Consciousness and Communicative Action. Trans. C. Lenhardt and S. W. Nicholson. Cambridge, Mass.: MIT Press, 1991.
On the Logic of the Social Sciences. Trans. S. W. Nicholson. Cambridge, Mass.: MIT Press, 1988.
The Philosophical Discourse of Modernity. Trans. F. Lawrence. Cambridge, Mass.: MIT Press, 1990.
Postmetaphysical Thinking. Trans. W. M. Hohengarten. Cambridge, Mass.: MIT Press, 1992.
The Structural Transformation of the Public Sphere. Trans. T. Burger and F. Lawrence. Cambridge, Mass.: MIT Press, 1991.
Theory and Praxis. Trans. J. Viertal. Boston: Beacon Press, 1973.
Theory of Communicative Action. Vol. I. Trans. T. McCarthy. Boston: Beacon Press, 1984.
Theory of Communicative Action. Vol. II. Trans. T. McCarthy. Boston: Beacon Press, 1987.
Towards a Rational Society. Trans. J. Shapiro. Boston: Beacon Press, 1971.

Horkheimer

Between Philosophy and Social Science. Trans. G. F. Hunter, M. Kramer, and J. Torpey. Cambridge, Mass.: MIT Press, 1995.
Critical Theory. Trans. M. O'Connell. New York: Continuum, 1975.
The Critique of Instrumental Reason: Lectures and Essays since the End of World War II. Trans. M. O'Connell. New York: Continuum, 1974.

Dialectic of Enlightenment. With Adorno. Trans. E.F.N. Jephcott. Stanford: Stanford University Press, 2002.

Eclipse of Reason. New York: Continuum, 1974.

Marcuse

The Aesthetic Dimension: Toward a Critique of Marxist Aesthetics. Boston: Beacon Press, 1978.

Counterrevolution and Revolt. Boston: Beacon Press, 1972.

Eros and Civilization: A Philosophical Inquiry into Freud. Boston: Beacon Press, 1955.

An Essay on Liberation. Boston: Beacon Press, 1969.

Five Lectures. Boston: Beacon Press, 1970.

Negations. Trans. J. Shapiro. Boston: Beacon Press, 1968.

One Dimensional Man. Boston: Beacon Press, 1964.

Reason and Revolution: Hegel and the Rise of Social Theory. Oxford: Oxford University Press, 1941.

Soviet Marxism. New York: Columbia University Press, 1985.

Technology, War and Fascism: Collected Papers I. Ed. D. Kellner. London: Routledge, 2001.

Towards a Critical Theory of Society: Collected Papers II. Ed. D. Kellner. London: Routledge, 2001.

Neumann

Behemoth. The Structure and Practice of National Socialism 1933–1944. Oxford: Oxford University Press, 1944.

WORKS OF CRITICAL THEORY AFTER HABERMAS

Brunkhorst, Hauke. *Der Intellektuelle im Land der Mandarine*. Frankfurt am Main: Suhrkamp, 1987.

Demokratie und Differenz: vom klassischen zum modernen Begriff des Politischen. Frankfurt am Main: Fischer, 1994.

Forst, Rainer. *Kontexte der Gerechtigkeit: Politische Philosophie jenseits von Liberalismus und Kommunitarismus*. Frankfurt am Main: Suhrkamp, 1994.

Honneth, Axel. *Das Andere der Gerechtigkeit. Aufsätze zur praktischen Philosophie*. Frankfurt am Main: Suhrkamp, 2000.

Desintegration. Bruchstücke einer soziologischen Zeitdiagnose. Frankfurt am Main: Fischer, 1994.

Kampf um Anerkennung. Frankfurt am Main: Suhrkamp, 1992.

Kritik der Macht. Frankfurt am Main: Suhrkamp, 1985.

Leiden an Unbestimmtheit. Eine Reaktualisierung der Hegelschen Rechtsphilosophie. Stuttgart: Reclam, 2001.

Umverteilung oder Anerkennung? Eine politisch-philosophische Kontroverse. With Nancy Fraser. Frankfurt am Main: Suhrkamp, 2003.

Unsichtbarkeit. Stationen einer Theorie der Intersubjektivität. Frankfurt am Main: Suhrkamp, 2003.

Die zerrissene Welt des Sozialen: Sozialphilosophische Ausätze. Frankfurt am Main: Suhrkamp, 1990.

Joas, Hans. *The Creativity of Action.* Trans. J. Gaines and P. Keast. Cambridge: Polity, 1996.

G. H. Mead: *A Contemporary Reexamination of his Thought.* Trans. Raymond Meyer. Cambridge, Mass.: MIT Press, 1997.

Pragmatism and Social Theory. Chicago: University of Chicago Press, 1993.

Menke, Christoph. *The Sovereignty of Art: Aesthetic Negativity in Adorno and Derrida.* Trans. Neil Solomon. Cambridge, Mass.: MIT Press, 1998.

Tragödie im Sittlichen: Gerechtigkeit und Freiheit nach Hegel. Frankfurt am Main: Suhrkamp, 1996.

Seel, Martin. *Die Kunst der Entzweiung: zum Begriff der ästhetischen Rationalität.* Frankfurt am Main: Suhrkamp, 1985.

SELECTED WORKS ON CRITICAL THEORY GENERALLY,
INCLUDING ITS HISTORY

Benhabib, Seyla. *Critique, Norm and Utopia: A Study of the Foundations of Critical Theory.* New York: Columbia University Press, 1986.

Bernstein, J. M. (ed.). *The Frankfurt School: Critical Assessments.* 6 vols. London: Routledge, 1994.

Bottomore, Tom. *The Frankfurt School.* London: Tavistock, 1984.

Bubner, Rüdiger. *Modern German Philosophy.* Trans. E. Matthews. Cambridge: Cambridge University Press, 1981.

Dahms, Hans-Joachim. *Positivismusstreit: Die Auseinandersetzung der Frankfurter Schule mit dem logischen Positivismus, dem amerikanishen Pragmatismus und dem kritischen Rationalismus.* Frankfurt am Main: Suhrkamp, 1994.

Dews, Peter. *Logics of Disintegration: Post-Structuralist Thought and the Claims of Critical Theory.* London and New York: Verso, 1987.

Dubiel, Helmut. *Theory and Politics: Studies in the Development of Critical Theory.* Trans. Benjamin Gregg. Cambridge, Mass.: MIT Press, 1985.

Geuss, Raymond. *The Idea of a Critical Theory: Habermas and the Frankfurt School.* Cambridge: Cambridge University Press, 1981.

Hanssen, Beatrice. *Critique of Violence: Between Poststructuralism and Critical Theory*. London: Routledge, 2000.

Held, David. *Introduction to Critical Theory: Horkheimer to Habermas*. Berkeley: University of California Press, 1980.

Jay, Martin. *The Dialectical Imagination: A History of the Frankfurt School and the Institute of Social Research, 1923–1950*. New York: Little, Brown, 1973.

Kelly, Michael (ed.). *Hermeneutics and Critical Theory in Ethics and Politics*. Cambridge, Mass.: MIT Press, 1990.

Kolakowski, Leszek. *Main Currents of Marxism*. Vol. III. Trans. P. S. Falla. Oxford: Oxford University Press, 1978.

Postone, Moishe. *Time, Labor, and Social Domination*. Cambridge: Cambridge University Press, 1993.

Rasmussen, David (ed.). *The Handbook to Critical Theory*. Oxford: Blackwell, 1996.

Rosen, Michael. *On Voluntary Servitude: False Consciousness and the Theory of Ideology*. Cambridge, Mass.: Harvard University Press, 1996.

Schmid Noerr, Gunzelin. *Das Eingedenken der Natur im Subjekt: Zur Dialektik von Vernunft und Natur in der kritischen Theorie Horkheimers, Adornos und Marcuses*. Darmstadt: Wissenschaftliche Buchgesellschaft, 1990.

Theunissen, Michael. *Gesellschaft und Geschichte: Zur Kritik der kritischen Theorie*. Berlin: de Gruyter, 1969.

Whitebook, Joel. *Perversion and Utopia: A Study in Psychoanalysis and Critical Theory*. Cambridge, Mass.: MIT Press, 1995.

Wiggershaus, Rolf. *The Frankfurt School: Its History, Theories, and Political Significance*. Trans. M. Robertson. Cambridge, Mass.: MIT Press, 1994.

MORE SPECIALIZED SECONDARY LITERATURE

Adorno

Bernstein, J. M. *Adorno: Disenchantment and Ethics*. Cambridge: Cambridge University Press, 2001.

  The Fate of Art: Aesthetic Alienation from Kant to Derrida and Adorno. University Park: Pennsylvania State University Press, 1992.

Buck-Morss, Susan. *The Origin of Negative Dialectics: Theodor W. Adorno, Walter Benjamin, and the Frankfurt Institute*. New York: Free Press, 1977.

Dalhaus, Carl. "Adornos Begriff des musikalishen Materials." In *Zur Termoinologie der Musik des 20. Jahrhunderts: Bericht über das zweite Kolloquium*. Ed. H. H. Eggebrecht. Stuttgart: Musikwissenschaftliche Verlags-Gesellschaft, 1974.

Honneth, Axel. "Foucault and Adorno: Two Forms of the Critique of Modernity." *Thesis Eleven* 15 (1985): 48–59.

Huhn, Tom and Zuidervaart, Lambert (eds.). *The Semblance of Subjectivity: Essays in Adorno's Aesthetics*. Cambridge, Mass.: MIT Press, 1997.

Jarvis, Simon. *Adorno: A Critical Introduction*. London: Routledge, 1998.

Jay, Martin. *Adorno*. London: Fontana, 1984.

Paddison, Max. *Adorno's Aesthetics of Music*. Cambridge: Cambridge University Press, 1993.

Rosen, Michael. *Hegel's Dialectic and its Criticism*. Cambridge: Cambridge University Press, 1982.

Von Friedeburg, Ludwig and Habermas, Jürgen (eds.). *Adorno-Konfernz 1983*. Frankfurt am Main: Suhrkamp, 1983,

Zuidervaart, Lambert. *Adorno's Aesthetic Theory: The Redemption of Illusion*. Cambridge, Mass.: MIT Press, 1991.

Benjamin

Adorno, Theodor. *Über Walter Benjamin*. Frankfurt am Main: Suhrkamp, 1970.

Buck-Morss, Susan. *The Dialectics of Seeing: Walter Benjamin and the Arcades Project*. Cambridge, Mass.: MIT Press, 1991.

Hanssen, Beatrice. *Walter Benjamin's Other History: Of Stones, Animals, Human Beings, and Angels*. Berkeley: University of California Press, 1998.

Hanssen, Beatrice (ed.). *Walter Benjamin and Romanticism*. New York: Continuum, 2003.

Menninghaus, Winfried. *Walter Benjamins Theorie der Sprachmagie*. Frankfurt am Main: Suhrkamp, 1980.

Pensky, Max. *Melancholy Dialectics: Walter Benjamin and the Play of Mourning*. Amherst: University of Massachussetts Press, 1993.

Roberts, Julian. *Walter Benjamin*. London: Macmillan, 1982.

Rosen, Charles. "The Ruins of Walter Benjamin." In *Romantic Poets, Critics, and Other Madmen*. Cambridge, Mass.: Harvard University Press, 1998.

Wolin, Richard. *Walter Benjamin: An Aesthetic of Redemption*. Berkeley: University of California Press, 1994.

Habermas

Baynes, Kenneth. *The Normative Grounds of Social Criticism: Kant, Rawls and Habermas*. Albany, N.Y.: SUNY Press, 1992.

Bernstein, J. M. *Recovering Ethical Life: Jürgen Habermas and the Future of Critical Theory*. London: Routledge, 1995.

Chambers, Simone. *Reasonable Democracy: Jürgen Habermas and the Politics of Discourse.* Ithaca: Cornell University Press, 1996.

Cooke, Maeve. *Language and Reason: A Study of Habermas' Pragmatics.* Cambridge, Mass.: MIT Press, 1994.

Dews, Peter (ed.). *Habermas: A Critical Reader.* Oxford: Blackwell, 1999.

Honneth, Axel, McCarthy, Thomas and Wellmer, Albrecht (eds.). *Cultural-Political Interventions in the Unfinished Project of the Enlightenment.* Cambridge, Mass.: MIT Press, 1992.

Ingram, David. *Habermas and the Dialectic of Reason.* New Haven: Yale University Press, 1987.

Kelly, Michael (ed.). *Critique and Power: Recasting the Foucault/Habermas Debate.* Cambridge, Mass.: MIT Press, 1994.

McCarthy, Thomas. *The Critical Theory of Jürgen Habermas.* Rev. edn. Cambridge, Mass.: MIT Press, 1982.

White, Stephen. *The Recent Work of Jürgen Habermas: Reason, Justice and Modernity.* Cambridge: Cambridge University Press, 1988.

Horkheimer

Benhabib, Seyla, Bonß, Wolfgang and McCole, John (eds.). *On Max Horkheimer: New Perspectives.* Cambridge, Mass.: MIT Press, 1993.

Schmidt, Alfred and Altwicker, Norbert (eds.). *Max Horkheimer heute: Werk und Wirkung.* Frankfurt am Main: Fischer, 1986.

Marcuse

Dubiel, Helmut (ed.). *Kritik und Utopie im Werk von Herbert Marcuse.* Frankfurt am Main.: Suhrkamp, 1992.

Kellner, Douglas. *Herbert Marcuse and the Crisis of Marxism.* Berkeley: University of California Press, 1984

MacIntyre, Alasdair. *Marcuse.* London: Fontana, 1970.

Pippin, Robert, Feenberg, Andrew and Webel, Charles (eds.). *Marcuse: Critical Theory and the Promise of Utopia.* Westport, Conn.: Greenwood, 1987.

INDEX